THE LORE OF THE CHINESE LUTE

by R. H. VAN GULIK

AN ESSAY IN THE
IDEOLOGY
OF THE
Ch'in

SOPHIA UNIVERSITY · TOKYO
IN COOPERATION WITH
THE CHARLES E. TUTTLE COMPANY
TOKYO, JAPAN & RUTLAND, VERMONT

REPRESENTATIVES
Continental Europe: BOXERBOOKS, INC., *Zurich*
British Isles: PRENTICE-HALL INTERNATIONAL, INC., *London*
Australasia: PAUL FLESCH & CO., PTY. LTD., *Melbourne*
Canada: M. G. HURTIG, LTD., *Edmonton*

Published by Sophia University
7 Kioi-chō, Chiyoda-ku, Tokyo
in cooperation with
Charles E. Tuttle Company, Inc.
of Rutland, Vermont & Tokyo, Japan
with editorial offices
at Suidō 1-chōme, 2-6, Bunkyō-ku, Tokyo

Copyright in Japan 1968, by *Monumenta Nipponica*, all rights reserved

Library of Congress Catalog Card No. 68-57056
First published, 1940
New edition, revised and reset, 1969

PRINTED IN JAPAN

PETER BROGREN, THE VOYAGERS' PRESS, TOKYO

This essay is respectfully dedicated
to the memory of
my first teacher of the lute
YEH SHIH-MENG

葉詩夢

[OBIIT 1937 AETATE 74]

a gifted musician

and

a great gentleman

PREFACE

琴聲雖可狀、
琴意誰可聽、

'Although the tones of the lute
 may be featured,
When listening to them
 who shall be able to fathom their significance?'[1]

THIS ESSAY *is an attempt to describe the cultural significance of a Chinese musical instrument, the seven-stringed lute. Commonly called* KU-CH'IN[2] *or 'the lute of antiquity', it was played more than two thousand years ago as it is still today. It is chiefly used as a solo instrument, producing a subdued and highly refined music.*

But rather than its imposing age or its charming tones, it was the unique place it holds in Chinese culture that prompted this study. For from a remote time the lute was set apart as the inseparable companion of the literatus, that engaging combination of official, poet, painter and philosopher, till gradually it became in itself a symbol of literary life, with all of its elegant and tasteful pleasures. The musical properties came to be accessory to the instrument as center of a special system of thought, an ideology fitly encompassing the eclectic tendencies characteristic of the old-fashioned Chinese scholar.

Although it is with this ideology—its origin, development and final formulation—that the present essay is concerned, there must be frequent references to the music itself. The author, merely a dabbler in musical science, had to take into consideration various aspects of it, withal aware that he encroached upon ground more properly reserved for musicologists. Among these, the author would

---

1 From the poem 'Chiang-shang-chang-ch'in' 江上張琴, 'Playing the Lute on the River', by the Sung scholar Ou-yang Hsiu (歐陽修, 外集, ch. 1).

2 古琴

be most gratified to find readers, although he addresses himself primarily to Orientalists, in the hope of drawing attention to one of the lesser known aspects of Chinese culture. Musicologists will discover here a veritable treasure house of ancient Chinese music in general, a rich source which might, with scientific analysis based on historical musicological principles, revolutionise the opinions on ancient Chinese music current now both east and west. This music of the lute may truly and proudly call itself T'AI-KU-I-YIN,[3] *'tones bequeathed from high antiquity'.*

It has seemed desirable to include a more or less exhaustive list and a critical discussion of the sources where these musicological materials are found, and it is hoped that they may serve musicologists in the further study of problems which could be but briefly treated here. Then, should one among them compile a complete handbook of lute music, the author would feel at least discharged of part of the large debt he owes it. Many were the joys the lute gave him. Old melodies enlivened weary summer evenings, and playing some light prelude often heartened him to attack again knotty passages in many a musty Chinese volume. During the writing of the following pages about the ideology of the lute, its music was an invariable inspiration.

Here a few remarks may be added on the use of the word 'lute' as a translation of the Chinese word 'CH'IN'. *In selecting for Oriental musical instruments equivalents in a Western language one must choose between those which would suggest the outer form, and others of closer cultural reference. In the former respect* 'cither'[4] *would seem most appropriate for the* CH'IN, *but because of the unique position it occupies in Chinese culture the author has preferred to follow the latter way, adopting the word which since olden times in the West has been associated with all that is artistic and refined, and sung by poets. Therefore* 'CH'IN' *is translated* 'lute', *and the word* 'cither' *is kept for such instruments as the* sê

---

[3] 太古遺音

[4] In English the word *cither* is rather loosely applied to various kinds of stringed instruments. I use it in the sense of the cither played in Tyrol and Austria: a flat, wooden sounding box, over which about thirty strings are strung. It is set upon a table, and played with both hands.

and chêng, *the construction of which, in any case, comes nearer that of the Western cither.*[5]

The body of this essay appeared in four successive issues of the semiannual periodical MONUMENTA NIPPONICA, *published at Tokyo. The author wishes to express his gratitude to the editor of that journal, through whose kindness it was made possible that this essay appears now in book form. Since part of it was printed from the moulds of the original type, it could not be made to answer to high typographical standards, and while a few misprints could be corrected, many page references had to be cancelled. The reader is requested to refer frequently to the index, to which much care has been given.* [*sic.*]

To the original two appendices, both bibliographical, there have been added two more. Appendix III, *'The Lute as an Antique', is the revision of an article 'On Three Antique Lutes', which appeared in the* TRANSACTIONS OF THE ASIATIC SOCIETY OF JAPAN, *second series, no.* XVII. *The author's thanks are due to the Society for kind permission to reprint the illustrations that accompanied the said article. Appendix* IV, *'The Chinese Lute in Japan', is based upon an article entitled 'Chinese Literary Music*

---

[5] *Ch'in* rendered as 'lute'. Dr. Curt Sachs wrote to me stating that, in his opinion, the rendering 'lute' is incorrect, since this term gives the Western reader a wrong impression of the shape and structure of the *ch'in;* he recommends the term *psaltery*. It is quite true that the shape of the psaltery resembles that of the Chinese *ch'in*, while our Western lute rather resembles the Chinese pear-shaped mandolin, the *p'i-p'a*. In my opinion, however, the shape of an Oriental musical instrument should not constitute the first consideration when selecting an English equivalent; the spirit of the music produced by an instrument and the place it occupies in the culture of its native country are as important factors as its shape and structure. This point holds true especially in the case of the Chinese *ch'in*, which occupies so unique a position in antique and modern Chinese life. In selecting 'lute' as translation of *ch'in*, my object was to convey to the general reader something of the cultural significance of this instrument and its music. Since the word 'lute' is associated by Westerners with poetry and refined enjoyment, it adequately suggests the atmosphere that surrounds the *ch'in*, while 'psaltery', on the other hand, suggests an instrument doomed to obsolescence since many centuries; moreover many readers would have been unfamiliar with this term. For these reasons I still prefer to render *ch'in* as 'lute', giving the inner meaning precedence over the physical form.

It should be noted that in Western literature considerable confusion reigns with regard to the translation and identification of Chinese and Japanese musical instruments. I am presently working with the Japanese historian and musicologist Kishibe Shigeo 岸邊成雄 on a list of Chinese and Japanese musical instruments—a list intended for reference use by Western students of Far Eastern music. Each item will consist of an illustration of the instrument, a brief description, and a proposed English rendering of its name. It is hoped that this list will assist the student in correctly identifying the instruments mentioned in various Western sources.

and its Introduction into Japan', which was contributed to the commemoration volume offered Prof. Chōzō Mutō, in 1937. Since the publication of these two studies a number of new materials have been found, necessitating a change in several of the statements made. Needless to say, the present essay supersedes all the author's earlier publications on the subject.

Finally, the writer has been induced by friends to add a Chinese preface wherein he has tried to summarise the significance of the lute. It is presented with diffidence, in the knowledge that a Westerner's excursions into Chinese composition must remain forever hazardous.

* * *

The author would have it understood that these pages are, most literally, an essay: an approach to the subject, an attempt to describe it, nothing more. The field being almost untouched, its materials had to be collected in originali and one by one, sometimes more than a year passing by before a rare item was at last found in the dim corner of some Chinese or Japanese bookstore. The argument which grew with the investigation of these texts led by frequent, unmarked cross-roads where the best direction may not always have been chosen. Moreover, official duties prevented sustained application; it is feared that along the way not a few errors or misstatements have escaped detection. In the end the author presumes to claim only the credit attendant on an honest effort: original sources are quoted in full, and each translation is accompanied by the Chinese text. The aim was to lay the full materials before the reader, at once enabling him to trace mistakes and supplying him with guideposts to further research.

* * *

Quite apart from scientific aspects, the description of beauty must always be an invidious undertaking, whether it be the beauty of form, thought, colour, or of tones. In endeavouring to write of things elusive as these one experiences perforce a feeling of frustration; one searches out words, only to realize their insufficiency to express the inexpressible.

Yet the exercise is restful to the mind, bringing as it does the happy thought that however inadequate and imperfect the description of it, beauty itself is perfect and shall last forever. As the Sung scholar Su Tung-p'o says in his celebrated poetical essay on the Red Wall: 'There remain only the clear breeze over the river, and the moon shining over the mountains. The ear catches the wind, and it is sound. The eye sees the moon, and it becomes colour. These things no one can forbid us to take in: they shall be forever with us, for they are part of the never exhausted fullness of the creation.'[6] It was such considerations that influenced the author to publish this study, feeble though be the effort it represents; for when his bones and these pages shall be mouldering, the wind will still rustle in the pines, and the rivulet murmur among moss-grown stones. And ultimately it may be said that perhaps the sole design of this essay was to show that lute music in its simplest essence is the echo of these undying voices of living nature.

* * *

In the forty-first year of the Wan-li period, A.D. 1613, *the Ming scholar Lin Yu-lin published a book on stones and rocks.[7] A year later[8] he wrote a treatise on the lute, in the introductory remarks to which he says: 'First I published a book on stones, in four chapters; it distracted my mind from the worries of daily life and made me dwell among mists and coloured hazes. Now I follow it up with this "Elegance of the Lute"... For there exists a close harmony between stones and the silk strings. Always when*

---

[6] 惟江上之淸風，與山間之明月，耳得之而爲聲，目遇之而成色，取之無禁，用之不竭，是造物者之無盡藏也.

[7] *Su-yüan-shih-pu* 素園石譜, by Lin Yu-lin 林有麟; the original Ming edition is now very scarce. In 1924 a reprint was published by the Zuhon-sōkankai 圖本叢刊會, at Tokyo.

[8] *Ch'ing-lien-fang-ch'in-ya* 青蓮舫琴雅, cf. Appendix II, no. 6.

I sit confronting the many-hued rocks and mountains, and play a tune on my antique lute while the moon shines through the spreading pines, I feel greatly elated and my thoughts are borne away to unearthly regions. Therefore, having published my book on stones, I felt it incumbent upon me also to write this treatise on the lute.'[9]

The present writer in 1938 published an essay on Chinese inkstones.[10] *When now in 1939 he ventures to send forth this other on the lute, he feels somewhat reassured, notwithstanding its many shortcomings; for he hopes that at least he adheres to the old approved principle of 'treading in the footsteps of the ancients'.*

Netherlands Legation 　　　　　　　　　　　*R. H. van Gulik*
Tokyo, 22 Dec. 1939

---

[9] 余先梓石譜四卷，烟霞一洗塵俗，琴雅繼出，蓋絲與石原自作合，每當山石璘玢，疏松月上，奏瑤琴一曲於其間，飄飄欲仙矣，故有石譜，似不可無琴雅.

[10] *Mi Fu on Inkstones*, pub. by The French Bookstore, Peking 1938.

後　序

夫此者內也、彼者外也、故老子曰、去彼取此、蟬蛻塵埃之中、優遊忽荒之表、亦取其適而已、樂由中出、故是此而非彼也、然衆樂琴爲之首、古之君子、無間隱顯、未嘗一日廢琴、所以尊生外物養其內也、茅齋蕭然、值清風拂幌、朗月臨軒、更深人靜、萬籟希聲、瀏覽黃卷、閑鼓綠綺、寫山水於寸心、斂宇宙於容黎、恬然忘百慮、豈必虞山目耕、雲林清閟、蔭長松、對白鶴、乃爲自適哉、藏琴非必佳、彈曲非必多、手應乎心、斯爲貴矣、丙子秋莫、於宛平得一琴、殆明清間物、無銘、撫之鏗鏘有餘韵、弗敢冒高士選雅名、銘之曰、無名、非欲以觀衆妙、冀有符於道德之旨云

　余既作琴道七卷、意有未盡、更申之如右、然於所欲言、未罄什一云

和蘭國笑忘高羅佩識於芝臺之中和琴室

EDITOR'S NOTE

For this revised edition, the parenthetic material which so cluttered the text in the first edition has been transferred to footnotes, so that the text now can be read more smoothly. Dates have been checked in H. A. Giles's *A Chinese Biographical Dictionary*, the *Nihon rekishi daijiten* 日本歴史大辞典 (20 vols., Kawade Shobō 1964), and the *Daijimmeijiten* 大人名事典 (10 vols., Heibonsha, 1962); a number of incorrect readings of Japanese proper names have been revised; page references in footnotes and index have all been checked and corrected when necessary. Since translation of the ancient measurements of 尺 and 寸 by *foot* and *inch* respectively, is not entirely satisfactory, the Chinese terms have been retained. Finally, the author's own corrections and additions found in *MN* VII (1951) have been incorporated fully.

CONTENTS

Preface   vii
Chinese Preface   xiii
Editor's Note on Revised ed.   xiv
List of Plates   xviii

CHAPTER ONE: General Introduction   *page* 1

Characteristics of lute music—twofold function of the lute: orchestral and solo instrument—the solo lute as the special instrument of the literary class—description of the lute, and of the way it is played—origin and development of the lute and SÊ—*place of the lute and lute music in Chinese cultural life—lute music in Japan*

CHAPTER TWO: Classical Conceptions of Music   23

Chinese classical conceptions of music according to the YÜEH-CHI—*twofold aspect of music, cosmological and political—music belongs to heaven, and corresponds to what is heavenly in man—it is a means for perfecting the government, and for improving the individual—music as a source for pleasure not recognized*

CHAPTER THREE: Study of the Lute   29

§1 SOURCES
(*from p. 29*)

More materials on the significance of the lute than on lute music—three groups of materials: scattered references to the lute, special treatises on the lute, and CH'IN-PU, *handbooks for the lute—reasons for the rarity of* CH'IN-PU—*their contents—recent Chinese books on the study of the lute*

§2 ORIGINS AND CHARACTERISTICS
(*from p. 35*)

The establishment and evolution of CH'IN *ideology due chiefly to three factors: Confucianist (social), Taoist (religious), and psychological—Buddhist influences: a Mantrayanic magic formula as lute tune, a Lamaist hymn adapted to the lute—a summary of the history of* CH'IN *ideology*

§3 DISPOSITION & DISCIPLINE OF THE LUTE PLAYER
(from p. 57)

*The lute should be played amidst charming scenery, or in the library, before flowers, during a moonlit night in autumn, while burning incense—rules defining the classes of people for whom the lute may be played, and for whom not—occasional sectarian views, excluding Buddhists—correct way of carrying the lute, lute pages—*CHʻIN-SHIN, *the lute chamber—*CHʻIN-SHÊ, *spiritual community of the lute*

§4 SELECTED TEXTS
(from p. 70)

CHAPTER FOUR: The Significance of the Tunes   85

The Ming repertoire taken as the basis for a study of the significance of the tunes—significance of the modes—Chinese TIAO-I, *and Japanese* netori—*the tunes divided into five groups—tunes describing a mystic journey (Taoistic)—tunes of a semihistorical character (Confucianist)—musical versions of literary productions—tunes descriptive of nature—tunes descriptive of literary life—summary*

CHAPTER FIVE: Symbolism   101

§1 SYMBOLISM OF TERMS AND NAMES
(from p. 101)

Symbolism of the technical names for various parts of the lute—preponderance of the dragon and phoenix elements—symbolism of special names given to lutes

§2 SYMBOLISM OF TONES
(from p. 106)

*Great importance of timbre in lute music—Chinese attempts to define the various sorts of timbre—*LÊNG CHʻIEN'S *sixteen definitions, in text and translation*

§3 SYMBOLISM OF THE FINGER TECHNIQUE
(from p. 117)

*Postures of the hands, and their explanations—set of special pictures illustrating the finger technique; their various editions—technical terminology used in the lute handbooks—the abbreviated signs (*CHIEN-TZÛ*)—list of elementary* CHIEN-TZÛ, *their meaning and symbolism—examples of how the notation is read*

CHAPTER SIX: Associations   141

  §1 LUTE AND CRANE
   (from p. 141)

  §2 LUTE AND PLUM TREE,
  LUTE AND PINE TREE
   (from p. 147)

  §3 LUTE AND SWORD
   (from p. 151)

  §4 SOME FAMOUS STORIES
  AND MUCH-QUOTED PASSAGES
  RELATING TO THE LUTE
   (from p. 153)

CHAPTER SEVEN: Conclusions   163

APPENDIX I: Occidental Literature on the Lute   171

APPENDIX II: Chinese Literature on the Lute   177

APPENDIX III: The Lute as an Antique   189

APPENDIX IV: The Chinese Lute in Japan   217

LIST OF ILLUSTRATIONS

FRONTISPIECE: Chinese scholar with attendant carrying his lute
COLOR: T'ang period lute from the
    Hōryūji Hōmotsukan in Ueno   *page* 192

*♯1a:	A lute dating from the end of the Ming period	4
*♯1b:	Bottom board of the same lute	4
*♯ 2:	A Sung lute, dated 1187	4
♯ 3:	Playing the lute: from the *Ch'in-hsüeh-ju-mên*	5
♯ 4:	The *sê*, ancient cither with 25 strings	7
♯ 5:	Old forms of the characters for *ch'in* and *sê*	10
♯ 6:	Carrying the lute, from the *Yang-ch'un-t'ang-ch'in-pu*	65
♯ 7:	Playing the lute in ideal surroundings	67
♯ 8:	Upper and bottom sides of a lute	102
♯ 9:	Page from a lute handbook	118
*♯10, 11:	Symbolic picture illustrating the finger technique	118
♯12:	Symbolic picture illustrating the finger technique	122
♯13:	Selected *chien-tzû*	124
♯14 & 15:	Two passages from the *Wu-chih-chai handbook*	125
♯16:	A scholar playing the lute before beautiful scenery	148
♯17:	Playing the lute in the shadow of pine trees	150
*♯18:	Rubbing of the lute *T'ien-lai*	190
*♯19:	Rubbing of an iron lute of the Chin period	190
♯20 & 21:	Upper board and bottom board	192
*♯22:	Impression of a seal engraved in the bottom board	196
*♯23:	Shōsōin lute: the upper board	196
*♯24:	Shōsōin lute: the bottom board	196
*♯25:	Shōsōin lute: the enclosure on the upper board	196
*♯26:	Shōsōin lute: side aspects	196
♯27:	Inscription on Shōsōin lute	208

♯28:	Characters from Wei inscriptions	208
*♯29:	Rubbing of the bottom board of the lute of Yeh Ho-fu	212
*♯30:	Tracing after the rubbing reproduced in ♯29	212
*♯31:	Lower part of the tracing	212
*♯32:	Bottom board of the lute made by the Prince of Hêng	212
*♯33:	Bottom board of a lute made by Prince of I, preserved in Japan	212
♯34:	Japanese picture representing the Chinese lute and accessories, with explanations in Japanese	219
*♯35:	A banquet at the house of a Chinese merchant in Nagasaki	224
*♯36:	A musical seance in the Chinese Factory at Nagasaki	224

A NOTE ON THE VIGNETTES

FACING PAGE 1: The lute master Hsü Shih-ch'i 徐時琪, putting on the strings. After the frontispiece of his lute handbook Lü-ch'i-hsin-shêng 綠綺新聲, pub. in the Wan-li period.

PAGE 22: Playing the lute in the intimacy of the library; from an illustrated Ming edition of the play Hsiu-ju-chi 繡襦記.

PAGE 27: The p'ai-hsiao 排簫, Pandean pipes used in the ceremonial orchestra; from the Chih-shêng-shih-tien-li-yüeh-chi 直省釋奠禮樂記, preface 1891.

PAGE 100: The hsüan 塤, ancient ocarina; from the Chih-shêng-shih-tien-li-yüeh-chi.

PAGE 105: Young nobleman playing the lute; from an illustrated Ming edition of the play Hsi-hsiang-chi 西廂記.

PAGE 139: Talking with the lute on one's knees; from the well-known handbook for painters, Chieh-tzŭ-yüan-hua-ch'uan.

PAGE 161: The lute as played in the ceremonial orchestra; same source as the preceding item.

PAGE 198: Lute inscription, reading i-ch'in-shuo-fa 以琴說法, 'promulgating the Dharma by means of the lute'; from the K'u-mu-ch'an-ch'in-pu (see p. 53).

CHAPTER ONE

General Introduction

Characteristics of lute music—twofold function of the lute: orchestral and solo instrument—the solo lute as the special instrument of the literary class—description of the lute, and of the way it is played—origin and development of the lute and sê—place of the lute and lute music in Chinese cultural life—lute music in Japan

THE MUSIC of the ancient lute as a solo instrument is widely different from all other sorts of Chinese music: it stands entirely alone, both in its character and in the important place it occupies in the life of the literary class.

It is easier to describe this music in negative than in positive terms. It may be stated at once that it is not like that of any of the better known stringed instruments to be found in present-day China, as, for instance, the two-stringed violin or *êrh-hu*, the four-stringed mandoline or *p'i-p'a*, or the moon guitar or *yüeh-ch'in*.[1] The music of these instruments being highly melodical, it can be appreciated by anyone who possesses some capacity for musical adaptation. At first hearing their music may seem a little strange, but the ear soon adjusts itself to the quaint chords and unusual movements, and this music is easily understood.

The lute, on the contrary, is not so easy to appreciate, chiefly because its music is not primarily melodical. Its beauty lies not so much in the succession of notes as in each separate note in itself. 'Painting with sounds' might be a way to describe its essential quality.

Each note is an entity in itself, calculated to evoke in the mind of the hearer a special reaction. The timbre being thus of the utmost importance, there are very great possibilities of modifying the colouring of one and the same tone. In order to understand and appreciate this music, the ear must learn to distinguish subtle nuances: the same note, produced on a different string, has a different colour;

---

[1] 二胡, 琵琶, 月琴

the same string, when pulled by the forefinger or the middle finger of the right hand, has a different timbre. The technique by which these variations in timbre are effected is extremely complicated: of the vibrato alone there exist no less than 26 varieties. The impression made by one note is followed by another, still another. There is thus a compelling, inevitable suggestion of a mood, an atmosphere, which impresses upon the hearer the sentiment that inspired the composer.

Playing the lute is therefore entirely a question of touch, necessitating complete mastery of the finger technique of both hands.[2] This is the reason why it takes a fairly long time before one can play the lute. Anyone with an ear for music may, in a month or so, become a tolerably efficient performer on the *êrh-hu*, or, in a few months, on the *p'i-p'a*. But studying the lute is like playing the violin or piano: it takes years of assiduous and regular practice. The results, however, reward the labour, as the best of China's past has found its expression in the music of the lute.

The origins of the lute and lute music lie hidden in the mist of China's remotest past.

According to literary tradition, from the most ancient times the lute had two essentially different functions. In the first place it was a part of the orchestra, played at ceremonies in the ancestral temple and on other solemn occasions, and further at banquets, for entertaining guests. On the other hand the lute in itself was used as a solo-instrument by the individual player, for his own enjoyment and whenever he liked.

It is in this twofold function that the lute occurs through all the dynasties, up to the present day.

The orchestral lute is essentially the same as the solo instrument, the only difference being in the way it is played. Whilst the music of the solo lute, as I pointed out above, is exceedingly complicated, the technique of the orchestral lute is very simple, the left hand being hardly used at all. In the orchestra for Confucian ceremonies six lutes are used, three on the left and three on the right. As its sounds are low, its music is drowned in the din of the percussion instruments, and playing the lute in the ceremonial orchestra is not a very gratifying task. However, according to a dissertation on music dating from the Sung period,[3] there existed during the Chou dynasty other or-

---

[2] Cf. *Wu-chih-chai-ch'in-pu* (Appendix II, 15), ch. 1, p. 63: 音韻之妙，全賴乎指，法之細微.

[3] *Yüeh-shu* 樂書 by Ch'ên Yang 陳暘, eleventh century, ch. 130.

chestras, where the lute played a more prominent part: thus the court music called *t'ang-shang-yüeh*[4] consisted chiefly of chant, accompanied by stringed instruments. In this orchestra there were 48 singers, accompanied by, inter alia, 12 lutes. Still, in Chinese books on music, and in literature generally, the orchestral lute is only occasionally mentioned, and is not distinguished especially among the other instruments of the orchestra.

The solo lute, however, has been fixed by tradition as the special instrument of the literary class, and as such since time immemorial has enjoyed a privileged position. The solo lute is called the 'Instrument of the Holy Kings', its music 'Tones bequeathed by High Antiquity'.[5]

Father Amiot, whose treatise on Chinese music was published in 1780, was much impressed by the deep significance which the Chinese literati attached to the lute. He says: 'In short, the Chinese say that the construction of the lute, its shape, everything about it, is doctrine, everything expresses a special meaning or symbolism. They add that the sounds it produces disperse the darkness of the mind, and calm the passions; but in order to obtain these precious benefits from it, one must be an advanced student of wisdom. Only sages should touch the lute: ordinary people must content themselves with contemplating it in deep silence and with the greatest respect.' And in a note he adds: 'Our Emperor [Ch'ien-lung, 1736–95] himself has several times consented to be painted in the attitude of a man profoundly absorbed in playing the instrument that in his Empire is considered as belonging by right to those whose studies are concentrated on literature and wisdom.'[6]

Around the solo lute has gathered a rich and varied lore, which has given rise to a special class of literature. It is this system of thought that surrounds the lute, this *ch'in* ideology, that forms the subject of these pages. Therefore the orchestral lute is mentioned only for the sake of comparison, and especially when discussing

---

4 堂上樂

5 聖王之器　太古遺音

6 Cf. *Mémoires concernant les Chinois*, vol. VI: *Mémoires sur la musique des Chinois tant anciens que modernes*, pp. 56–7: '[En] un mot, la construction du Kin, sa forme, disent les Chinois, tout en lui est doctrine, tout y est représentation ou symbole. Les sons qu'on en tire, ajoutent-ils, dissipent les ténèbres de l'entendement, et rendent le calme aux passions; mais pour en recueillir ces précieux fruits, il faut être avancé dans l'étude de la sagesse. Les seuls sages doivent toucher le Kin, les personnes ordinaires doivent se contenter de le regarder dans un profond silence et avec le plus grand respect.' Also, p. 58, footnote: 'Notre Empereur lui-même n'a pas dédaigné de se faire peindre plusieurs fois dans l'attitude d'un homme profondément occupé à tirer des sons d'un instrument, qui passe dans son Empire pour être dévolu de droit à ceux qui font leur principale étude de la littérature et de la sagesse.'

historical problems, where the orchestral and the solo lute must be considered together. Before touching these questions regarding the history of the lute I will first give here a short description of the instrument itself, and of the way in which it is played.

According to literary tradition the lute has undergone hardly any changes during the period of more than two thousand years when it was the favourite instrument of the literary class. The only fact that all sources agree upon is that the number of strings was originally five, representing the five tones of the Chinese pentatonic gamut. Later, two more strings giving two halftones were added, bringing the number of strings up to seven; this modification is said to have been introduced in the Chou period.

The body of the lute, which functions as sounding-box, consists of two boards of a special kind of wood, superimposed one upon the other (cf. fig. 1). The upper part, made of *t'ung* wood, is concave, while the lower part, made of *tzû* wood, is flat, with two openings for transmitting the sound.[7] Over this sounding box the seven silk strings are strung. They are all of different thicknesses: that farthest from the player and giving the lowest tone is the thickest, while that nearest the player and giving the highest tone is the thinnest of all. On the left the strings, in two groups of three and four, are fastened to two wooden knobs driven into the bottom board. On the right side each string ends in a peculiar knot. It passes through a loop of silk, which can be twisted by turning a tuning peg made of wood, ivory or jade. The knot prevents the string from slipping when it is tuned by twisting the loop. On the right side, where the loops pass through holes in the body of the sounding box, a bridge is set up, made of a special kind of hard wood (usually red sandalwood, *tzû-t'an*),[8] glued to the upper board. A little to the left of this bridge the fingers of the right hand, except the little finger, pull the strings. The four fingers of the left hand stop the strings at various places, the hand being guided by thirteen studs made of some precious metal or of mother-of-pearl, and embedded in the varnish along the front side of the sounding box. In playing, the performer lays the lute on a special table, so that the side where the tuning pegs are is at his right. He sits on a comparatively high seat, preferably without elbow rests, since these might interfere with the free movement of the arms (cf. fig. 3).

As to the method of playing, I have already pointed out above that the timbre of a note, and therefore the finger technique, is of the

[7] 桐, 梓   [8] 紫檀

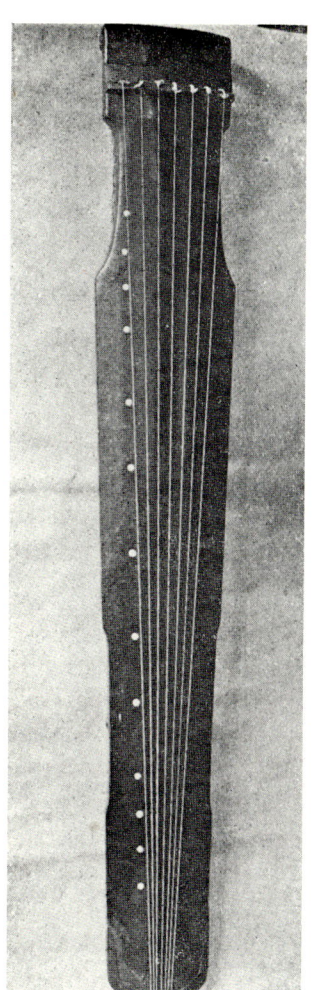  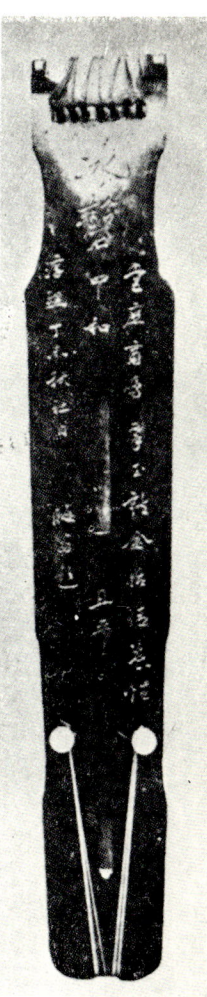

#1a: A lute dating from the end of the Ming period. Author's collection. Note the 13 studs inlaid along the left side, and the bridge on top, where the strings are fastened to the silk loops.

#1b: Bottom board of the same lute. Note the two apertures for transmitting the sound, and the silk loops hanging down, coming out of the tuning pegs. Name (covered by the silk loops) *Wu-ming* 無名; seal: *Chi-i-chai-chi* 集義齋記.

#2: A Sung lute, dated 1187. Collection of Mr. Cheng Ying-sun 鄭穎孫, at Peking. Bottom board, showing inscriptions, and the two jade knobs, to which the strings are fastened.

[I] GENERAL INTRODUCTION 5

#3: Playing the lute: from the *Ch'in-hsüeh-ju-mên*, cf. Appendix II no. 19.

highest importance. This appears clearly from the way in which lute music is noted down. The lute has a peculiar system of notation of its own, the most striking feature being that no notes are indicated, but only the way a string is played. Each note is thus represented indirectly by a complicated symbol, consisting of a combination of abbreviated Chinese characters, which indicate precisely: (a) the string to be played; (b) which finger of the right hand should pull the string, and whether inwards or outward; and (c) with regard to the left hand, which finger should touch the string, at what place and in what way. This system of notation, for which more than two hundred special signs are used, is called *chien-tzû*, 'abbreviated characters.'[9] Literary sources are vague as to the date of its invention, but it seems to go back at least to the first centuries A.D.

At first sight this notation seems complicated and confusing, but

---

[9] 減字. For a description of the *chien-tzû*, see below, Chapter v, section 3, *Symbolism of the Finger Technique*.

after a little practice it becomes quite easy to use it. Besides, since it is so explicit in its directions, after this system came into use lute music could during many centuries be transmitted with a fair amount of accuracy.

Literary tradition asserts that the original function of the lute was as a solo instrument; as such it was played by its inventor, one of the ancient Chinese mythical Emperors, said to have ruled in or about the third millennium B.C. Some sources say it was the Emperor Fu Hsi,[10] others Shên-nung,[11] others Shun.[12]

We may leave aside the question which claim for priority is justified; in any case literary tradition asserts that the lute in general is a very ancient Chinese instrument, existing already in the beginning of the Shang[13] period, for which the dates 1766–1122 B.C. are given.

But when we investigate reliable documents of this ancient period, such as inscriptions on fragments of oracle bones and tortoise shell, and on bronze sacrificial vessels, the truth of this tradition regarding the high age of the lute appears very questionable.

An investigation of these ancient documents seems to point to the fact that the earliest Chinese music consisted chiefly of percussion instruments, like drums, bells and sonorous stones.[14] The character for music, *yüeh*,[15] itself suggests a wooden standard with bells or drums attached to it.[16] The next stage seems to have been the addition of bamboo flutes. In the *Book of Odes, Shih-ching*,[17] there is preserved an interesting hymn, called *No*,[18] which describes music and is attributed to the Shang (Sung State, 7th or 6th century B.C.); various kinds of drums, sonorous stones and flutes are mentioned, but not a single stringed instrument. I have looked through several works on inscriptions on bone and tortoise shell, consulting also the convenient index *Chia-ku-wên-pien* published in 1934 by Sun Hai-po.[19] But I have not yet found any indication of the existence of a stringed instrument,

---

10 Cf. *Ch'in-tsao* (App. II, 1), opening line: 'Formerly Fu Hsi made the lute' 昔伏羲氏作琴.

11 *Fêng-su-t'ung-i*; see below, p. 70.

12 Cf. *Li-chi, Yüeh-chi*. See below, Chap. II.

13 商

14 The fact that the character *ku* 鼓, occurring frequently in inscriptions on oracle bones and representing a drum beaten by a stick, has the general meaning of producing music (出音曰鼓 cf. *Chou-li*, ch. 23, commentary), also points to the priority of percussion instruments. From ancient times to the present day this word *ku* is used for 'playing the lute' 鼓琴; expressions like *t'an-ch'in* 彈琴 and *chang-ch'in* 張琴 are of later date.

15 樂

16 Cf. fig. 5, no. 23, the character for *yüeh* as it appears on oracle bones, and no. 24, as it appears in the small-seal script.

17 詩經

18 那

19 甲骨文編, 孫海波

while there are numerous references to bells, drums and sonorous stones.

The old trustworthy references to the lute occur in other songs of the *Book of Odes*, e.g. *Lu-ming*,[20] which is ascribed to the Western Chou period (1122–770 B.C.). It is a 'festal ode, sung at entertainments to the king's ministers, and guests from the feudal states'.[21] The host says: 'I have elegant guests, the *sê* is played, the reed-organ is blown'; and in the third strophe: 'I have elegant guests, the *sê* is played, the lute is played.'[22] The ode *Kuan-chü* (the first ode of the *Shih-ching*) describes the music played at the homecoming of a bride: here *ch'in* and *sê* are mentioned, besides bells and drums.[23] Another ode, *Ch'ang-ti*, uses the harmony of lute and *sê* being played together as a symbol: 'Happy union with wife and children is like the music of *ch'in* and *sê*.'[24]

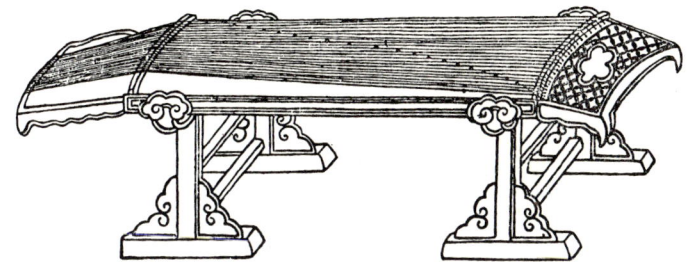

♯4: The *sê*, ancient cither with 25 strings.

Here the lute is mentioned together with the other ancient stringed instrument, the *sê*. In literature the lute is nearly always connected with the *sê*, *ch'in-sê* being in constant use.[25]

---

20 鹿鳴
21 This is the affirmation of Legge.
22 我有嘉賓, 鼓瑟吹笙; 鼓瑟鼓琴
23 關雎; 琴瑟友之, 鐘鼓樂之
24 常棣; 妻子好合, 如鼓瑟琴 (Legge, II, 1, Ode IV). By allusion to this line the harmony of the *ch'in* and *sê* is used in later literature as a fixed symbol for conjugal love. Cf. expressions like *ch'in-sê-chih-hsien* 琴瑟之絃 'husband and wife', *ch'in-sê-pu-hsieh* 琴瑟不叶 'conjugal discord', etc.
25 琴瑟. Purposely I have left out of consideration here the passage of the *Book of History* (*Shu-ching* 書經 ch. *I-chi* 益稷), where the lute and *sê* are mentioned. Here the music master K'uei (in some later texts exalted as the creator of all music) praises the power of the music directed by him: 'K'uei said:

"When the sounding stone is tapped or strongly struck; when the lutes [i.e. *ch'in* and *sê*] are swept or gently touched to accompany the singing: the [imperial] progenitors come to the service, etc."' 夔曰戛擊鳴球, 搏拊琴瑟, 以詠祖考來格 (Legge, *Book of History*, p. 87). The fortunes of the text of the *Shu-ching* are well known (cf. P. Pelliot, 'Le Chou-tching en caractères anciens et le Chang-chou-tche-wen', in: *Mémoires concernant l'Asie Orientale*, II, Paris 1816). Although the chapter *I-chi* belongs to the so-called 'text in modern writing', which was noted down by Fu Sheng shortly after the burning of the books in 213 B.C., the text shows evident signs of having been remodeled by later scholars. We must remember that inscriptions on oracle bones*

For the purpose of historical investigation it is impossible to consider the lute apart from the *sê*. I will therefore give here a brief description of this other stringed instrument of antiquity.

The *sê* is considerably bigger than the lute, but much simpler in construction. It has 25 strings, all of equal length and thickness. Each string runs over a separate, moveable bridge, the tuning being adjusted by pushing this bridge to the left or to the right. When all strings are tuned, the moveable bridges are seen to run in an oblique row over the surface of the instrument, a figure which is compared with a flight of wild geese.[26] The *sê* is played with both hands, touching the strings two at a time to the right of the bridges. As it is a heavy and rather unwieldy instrument, it is placed on a couple of low trestles (cf. fig. 4).

During the latter half of the Chou dynasty, besides their orchestral function, both *ch'in* and *sê* were played as solo instruments. This is shown by numerous passages in the older literature. Prince Hsiang had the lute taught to his favorite concubine.[27] Confucius also is said to have played the lute as well as the *sê*[28]. Two of his disciples, Tzû-lu and Tsêng Tien, are mentioned as *sê* players.[29] Further, the *Book of Rites*, *Li-chi*, refers repeatedly to the lute and *sê* as solo instruments: they may not be played by a man whose parents are ill; one should not step over a lute or *sê* belonging to one's master; an official should always have both instruments near at hand, etc.[30]

Already during the Chou dynasty the lute seems to have been preferred to the *sê* for serious music. Many references are made to famous masters of the lute,[31] whilst the *sê* is mentioned only occasionally. Beginning with the Han period the *sê* as solo instrument is hardly mentioned at all. It is said that the Han Emperor Kao-tsu[32] had two concubines, T'ang-shan fu-jên and Ch'i fu-jên, who were both experts on the *sê*, but other references are rare.

---

*show that the ancient ceremonial orchestra was much simpler than one would conclude from this passage. I suspect that it was mixed up somehow or other with the next one: 'K'uei said: "Oh! when I strike the stone or tap the stone, all kinds of animals lead on one another to gambol, etc."' 夔曰於予擊石拊石，百獸率舞. Perhaps the former longer passage is an elaboration of this shorter second one, which mentions only sonorous stones, and bears a more archaic character.

26 雁陣

27 a) 襄公 571–54 B.C. b) Cf. *Ch'un-ch'iu*, ed. Couvreur, Book IX, 14th year.

28 *Chuang-tzû* 莊子 ch. 31, Yu-fu 漁父; *Chia-yü* 家語 ch. 15, ch. 35. *Lun-yü* 論語 Book XVII, ch. XX, 1.

29 Tzû-lu: *Lun-yü*, Book XI, ch. XIV, 1; Tsêng Tien: *ibid*. Book XI, ch. XXV, 7.

30 a) 禮記. Ed. Couvreur, I, I, 4; I, I, 3; I, II, 1.

31 E.g. in *Chuang-tzû*: Chao Wên 昭文; in *Lieh-tzû*: Ku Pa 瓠巴, Master Wên 師文, Master Hsiang 師襄, Po Ya 伯牙.

32 高祖 206–195 B.C. 唐山夫人，戚夫人

That the *sê* as a solo instrument fell into disuse is probably due to the rise of a new instrument, the *chêng*,[33] in construction not unlike the *sê*, but smaller and much easier to handle. The *chêng* is said to have been invented by Mêng T'ien, who is also credited with the invention of the Chinese writing brush.[34]

Chinese sources assert that the tradition of the *sê* as a solo instrument was entirely forgotten from the Eastern Chin period[35] (317–420 A.D.). Later efforts at reviving the solo *sê* appear to have been more or less of an archaeological nature: the famous musician and poet of the 12th century, Chiang K'uei, studied the *sê*, and during the Yüan dynasty (1280–1368) the scholar Hsiung P'êng-lai composed a *sê-pu*.[36] Only in comparatively recent times have serious efforts been made to reconstruct the methods of playing the *sê* as a solo instrument or together with the lute.[37]

---

[33] 箏
[34] 蒙恬, died 210 B.C.
[35] E.g. the preface to the *Sê-pu* by Hsiung P'êng-lai. 東晉
[36] 姜夔, 熊朋來, 瑟譜
[37] At Canton there was published in 1870 a *Ch'in-sê-ho-pu* 琴瑟合譜, 'Handbook for Playing *ch'in* and *sê* Together', written by the scholar Ch'ing Jui (慶瑞, pen-name Hui-shan 輝山). Having studied the lute for several years, he became interested in the *sê*, but could find nobody to teach him this instrument. Then he set to work with the handbook of Hsiung P'êng-lai (see above), but came to the conclusion that Hsiung's method was not in accordance with the rules of ancient music. As his wife, a lady called Li Chih-hsien 李芝仙, was an able musician, he made her accompany on the *sê* his lute playing, and on the basis of these experiments he fixed a tuning for the *sê*, and composed the notation for eight old melodies, set to be played by the lute accompanied by the *sê*; these tunes are published in his handbook. I have tried out his system, using instead of the *sê* a so-called *fu-ch'in* 拊琴, a variant of the *chêng* 箏 which is used in Kiangsu province and is exactly the same as the small *sê* (小瑟, 15 strings), but easier to handle since it has tuning pegs. I find that he aims at a complete unison effect, each note of the *ch'in* being the same as the corresponding note on the *sê*. He introduces a vibrato for the *sê*, to be effected by pressing down a string left of the bridge, as is done while playing the Japanese *koto*. The results of his method are not very interesting. When unison is aimed at, it is much better to play a *ch'in* duo, as is often done by Chinese lute players. Moreover I doubt very much whether Ch'ing's method gives any idea of the way the *sê* was played in ancient days.

In 1838 Ch'iu Chih-lu (邱之陸; his biography is to be found in *Kuo-ch'ao-ch'i-hsien-lei-chêng* 國朝耆獻類徵 ch. 422) published a book called *Lü-yin-wei-k'ao* 律音彙考, in which he tries to fix the orchestral music for a great number of ancient ceremonial songs. He devotes a detailed discussion to the *sê*, which had an important function in the ceremonial music at district feasts and archery contests (cf. *I-li* 儀禮, ch. Hsiang-shê-li 鄉射禮). His observations are based on a careful investigation of the correct dimensions and tunings of instruments according to the standards of the Chou period.

In 1923 Yang Tsung-chi published a *Ch'in-sê-ho-pu* 琴瑟合譜 as a part of his *Ch'in-hsüeh-ts'ung-shu* (cf. App. II, 7); he examines various systems for playing and tuning the *sê*, and gives with annotations some tunes to be played by a duo of lute and *sê*. I regret that, having no *sê* in my collection, and my spare time in which to pursue these studies being limited, I have not yet had any chance to verify the theories set forth in the latter two books. It is not sufficient to work out the theories of the authors; one should make practical experiments. What looks perfectly all right on paper often proves to be quite wrong when applied in practice. As both books are the results of serious studies, I recommend them for a closer investigation.

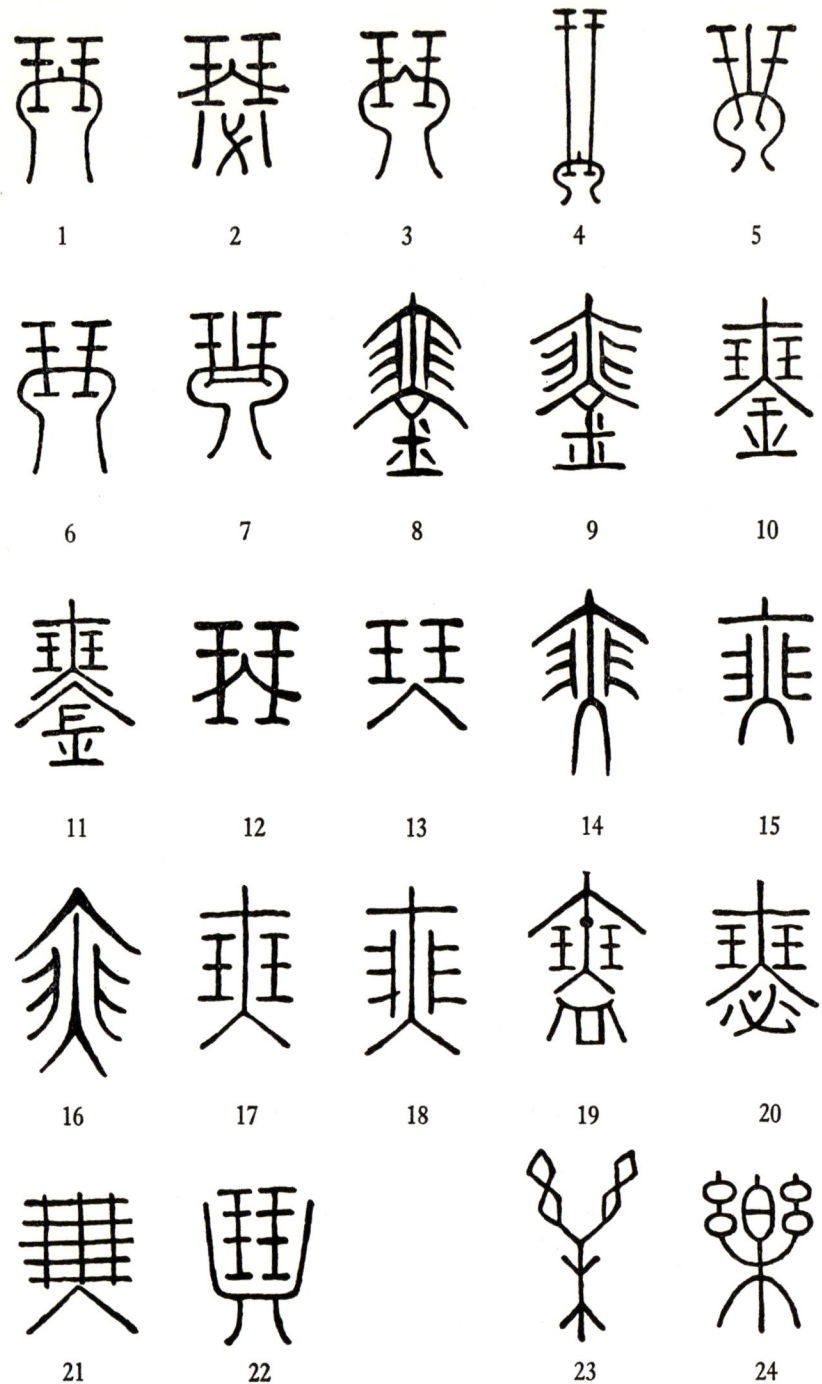

#5: Old forms of the characters for *ch'in* and *sê*.

Whilst the *sê* as a solo instrument fell into oblivion at an early date, the lute, on the contrary, has firmly maintained its position as a solo instrument during more than two thousand years—up to the present day.

Now we can return to the problem, touched upon above, of the origin of the lute. Although, as I pointed out, stringed instruments appear to have come into use later than instruments of percussion and flutes, still the origin of the lute dates from ancient times, let us say from the latter part of the Shang dynasty, about 1400 B.C. For investigating this question literary data are insufficient; besides, such data are misleading because they were artificially made to conform to the literary tradition of the Confucianist school of thought.

The only method for obtaining at least some vague idea about the oldest history of the lute, is, as far as I can see, to leave literary tradition aside, and to concentrate upon palaeographical data, comparing the various old forms of the two characters used to represent *ch'in* and *sê*, which in the modern script are 琴 and 瑟.[38]

In their modern form both characters are composed of an upper and a lower part. They both have the upper part in common; this element is explained as pictorial. The lower parts 今 and 必 are explained as phonetics.

These modern forms are derived from the shapes the characters show in the 'small' seal script (*hsiao-chuan*);[39] these forms I reproduce in fig. 5, no. 1: *ch'in*, no. 2: *sê*. The small seal was drawn up in 213 B.C. by Li Ssû, the minister of the First Emperor, Ch'in-shih-huang-ti, notorious for his burning of the books.[40] About A.D. 100 these characters were collected and recorded by the famous scholar Hsü Chên in his epoch-making dictionary *Shuo-wên*.[41] Although Li Ssû took as his basis the old characters which he found, he modified them to a considerable degree, so that this writing, as Karlgren observes, 'to a very large extent was an entirely new script'.[42] The *Shuo-wên* again is separated by more than 300 years

---

[38] Mention must be made of an archeological source, a *sê* of the Yin dynasty, found in a tomb in Ch'ang-sha, Hunan Province. This important archeological find has been described by Umehara Sueji 梅原末治 in the periodical *Tōyōshi kenkyū* 東洋史研究, VI, no. 2. The instrument is made of hardwood and measures about one foot by three feet. It seems to have had 23 strings (cf. Kishibe Shigeo, *Tōyō no gakki to sono rekishi* 東洋の樂器とその歴史, Tokyo 1948, p. 153).

[39] 小篆

[40] 李斯. An excellent critical summary of occidental discussions of the old forms of the Chinese script is to be found in O. Franke, *Geschichte des Chinesischen Reiches*, III, pp. 137–8; cf. also the publication by D. Bodde, *China's First Unifier* (Leyden 1938), the chapter on the unification of writing.

[41] 許慎, 說文

[42] B. Karlgren, *Analytic Dictionary of Chinese and Sino-Japanese*, p. 3.

from the time of Li Ssŭ, and during that interval several modifications were introduced, as is shown by the study of inscriptions on stone from the early Han period. During later dynasties the *Shuo-wên* was published in numerous editions, and lengthy commentaries were added, the standard one being the edition by Tuan Yü-tsai.[43]

The rudimentary text of Hsü Chên was faithfully reprinted, but with regard to the reproduction of the sealscript various editors introduced all sorts of modifications mostly motivated by calligraphic considerations.[44] We must not forget that the sealscript became a branch of calligraphy, and that consequently several styles for writing these characters exist. Thus there are hardly any two editions of the *Shuo-wên* which give exactly the same seal form of a character. For this reason I have reproduced five different forms of the character *ch'in* (fig. 5, nos. 3–7), taken from various editions. As will be seen from these, however, the essential parts of the character were in this case left unchanged.

In the *Shuo-wên* the character for *ch'in* is made into a separate heading, and also the character for *sê* is classified thereunder.

Chinese palaeographers have gone to much trouble to explain these *Shuo-wên* forms. Generally they are of the opinion that the character for *sê* (no. 2) is a derivation from that for *ch'in* (no. 1). As regards no. 1, the consensus of opinion is that it must be taken as a pictorial ideograph, representing the shape of the lute. A work of the Ming period, the *Liu-shu-ching-yün*,[45] preface dated 1567, says that this picture is made after the head of the lute, seen from the side, showing the tuning pegs and the two knobs for fastening the strings; it follows the heading *chio* 玨, two jade tablets, because the tuning pegs were made of jade. A work of the Ch'ing period, the *Shuo-wên-hsieh-tzŭ-chien* by Hsü Ching[46] gives the form shown in no. 4, and adds the remark that it is easy to see in this character a picture of the lute seen from above: one has only to pull it out lengthwise! These are but mild examples. The Ch'ing scholar Wang Chün in his *Shuo-wên-shih-li*,[47] pub. 1844, goes into more detail, and says that the picture was drawn after the bottom of the lute. The curved line rep-

---

43 段玉裁, style: Jo-ying 若膺, 1735–1815

44 Therefore for Chinese palaeographic studies it is advisable to consult as many different editions of the *Shuo-wên* as one can lay hands on. The labour involved is much reduced by the monumental work of Ting Fu-pao 丁福保, the *Shuo-wên-hsieh-tzŭ-ku-lin* 說文解字詁林, Shanghai, 1928; in it, under each character choice passages culled from 182 works on the *Shuo-wên* are reproduced in facsimile, permitting the reader to make comparisons and draw his own conclusions.

45 六書精蘊

46 說文解字箋, 徐灝

47 王均, 說文釋例

resents the shoulders of the lute, the two lowest strokes of *chio* stand for the two knobs, the two perpendicular strokes represent the strings fastened to the knobs, and the four upper horizontal strokes stand, *mirabile dictu*, for the bridge which is seen on the *upper* side of the lute. Other scholars think that *chio* must be taken as a significant, meaning something precious and indicating that the lute is a precious instrument. Still others think that *chio* must be taken in its literal sense of 'tablets of jade': the curved line is a cord on which they are suspended. They assume that the lute originally was a percussion instrument, something like the present-day *pa-ta-la*,[48] an instrument introduced from Burma. This interpretation is followed by Takata in his *Kochūhen*,[49] who therefore does not give the character a separate heading but classifies it under *yü*, 'jade'. Wieger, in his *Caractères chinois*, p. 216, gives the same explanation.

I have quoted the above opinions to show that such speculations, being based entirely on the small seal characters, are valueless. In order to be able to make more likely guesses we have to go farther back than the small seal, and refer to the older forms, known by the convenient Chinese term *ku-wên*,[50] 'ancient shapes'. *Ku-wên* stands for all the old forms of characters dating from before Li Ssû's reorganization of writing. They are taken from sacrificial vessels of the Chou period, inscriptions on bone, and various other archeological remains.

Nos. 8 and 9 reproduce two *ku-wên* forms of the character for *ch'in*; the style of the strokes of no. 8 points to its being taken from an inscription on bronze. The upper part of these two characters shows clearly that the element later written as 玨, has nothing at all to do with jade, but forms part of an independent pictorial element. The lower part *chin* 金 is the phonetic. These two forms given here are apparently the prototype of the two variants of the modern character for *ch'in*, given in current editions of *K'ang-hsi-tzû-tien*[51] (cf. nos. 10, 11). If we compare nos. 8 and 9 with no. 13, which is another old form, I think we may agree with many commentators on the *Shuo-wên*, who assert that this form no. 13 is a simplification (*shêng-wên*)[52] of the complete type reproduced in nos. 8 and 9: of the phonetic *chin* 金 only the upper part is taken over, which looks like *jên* 人. In the *li* script of the Han period this character was still further simplified

---

[48] 把打位; cf. *Ch'ing-hui-tien-t'u* 清會典圖.
[49] 高田, 古籀篇
[50] 古文
[51] 康熙字典
[52] 省文

by writing the element 人 not under, but over, the pictorial element; cf. no. 12, form taken from an inscription on the tombstone of the lute player Lu Chün (died A.D. 172).[53] This is the form we recognize in the small seal character from which we started, reproduced in no. 1. Some scribe felt it necessary to add again a complete phonetic element, and chose 今 as an abbreviation for 金, 今 being originally the phonetic element of the character 金; for this modification there are many parallels, e.g. 淦, later written 浛. This is the type shown in the modern character 琴.

When we turn now to the character for *sê*, we observe that in the small seal (cf. fig. 5, no. 2) the character for *sê* is derived directly from the character for *ch'in*, by adding to the pictorial element a phonetic that later scribes represented as 必; that this representation is very arbitrary is evident from phonetic reasons. How this phonetic element is constructed is difficult to say, as its seal form, which is taken over from the *ku-wên* script, cannot be identified with other phonetics. That it was a phonetic and not a pictorial element becomes evident when we turn to the *ku-wên* forms of the character for *sê*, reproduced in nos. 14, 15 and 16 (17 and 18 are the forms as printed in current editions of *K'ang-hsi-tzû-tien*): here the phonetic element is missing, and we see only a figure which can hardly be anything else than a pictorial representation. Now if we compare this *ku-wên* form for *sê*, nos. 14–16, with the *ku-wên* form for *ch'in*, nos. 8, 9, we find that the *ku-wên* for *sê* is exactly the same as the upper, pictorial part of the *ku-wên* character for *ch'in*.

Thus, while from the small seal forms of both characters we would assume that *sê* was a derivation from *ch'in* ('an instrument not unlike the *ch'in*, and called *sê*'), from the *ku-wên*, on the contrary, we would conclude that *ch'in* was derived from *sê* ('an instrument not unlike the *sê*, but called *ch'in*'). To make the problem still more complicated we also find *ku-wên* forms for *sê*, which show under the pictorial element the enigmatic phonetic which we find in the small seal (cf. nos. 19, 20). Chinese commentators go no further than to state that apparently in ancient times there existed a constant interchange between the two characters.

In my opinion we can go one step further: this interchange of the forms for *ch'in* and *sê* admits of but one conclusion, viz. *that originally there was but one character*, resembling the upper part of the *ku-wên* forms of *ch'in* (and occasionally of *sê*), which was neither *ch'in* nor *sê*,

[53] 隸書, 魯峻

but some archaic Chinese stringed musical instrument. This instrument was used together with the drums, bells, sonorous stones and flutes of the ritual orchestra, and also as a solo instrument. From a musical point of view these two functions are essentially different: whilst the orchestral instrument had only to produce music that was simple but of strong volume (not to be drowned by the loud sounds of the percussion instruments), the solo instrument on the contrary was meant to be played alone, or as an accompaniment for the human voice. Thus it was not necessary that the solo instrument should produce a great volume of sound, but on the other hand it had to answer much more complicated musical needs. The orchestral and the solo instrument thus followed different ways of evolution: while the orchestral instrument remained almost unchanged, the solo instrument was gradually more and more developed in a technical sense. After some lapse of time the difference between the orchestral and the solo varieties of this instrument became so great that the necessity was felt for a distinctive nomenclature. This having been established, the pictorial character was not sufficient for indicating which instrument was meant, so phonetics were added. That this was done so irregularly must be due to the scribes, who no longer knew that both characters were originally the same, and considered one a derivation of the other.

Finally there remains the question of how the pictorial character that represented the archaic instrument was constructed. On the basis of my experience with several lute-like oriental instruments I may remark that the most striking aspect of such an oblong stringed instrument in a picture is to draw some horizontal lines indicating the strings, and cross these by some vertical lines indicating some sort of bridges,[54] finally adding some element expressing the action of playing, or a stand to lay the instrument on. On the basis of this reasoning I drew the entirely hypothetical character reproduced in no. 21. This hypothetical character may be compared with an old form of the character *ch'in* (no. 22) recorded in the *Fu-ku-pien*,

[54] It seems probable that the thirteen *hui* are remnants of vertical lines, or possibly bridges. An old quotation, cited by Ch'ên Yang (陳暘, Sung period) in his *Ch'in-shêng-ching-wei* 琴聲經緯 seems to point in this direction: 'The Ancients said about the tones of the lute that they are divided into vertical and horizontal sounds' 古人之論琴聲有經有緯.

The seven strings pulled with the right hand only give the 'vertical' tones (緯 *wei*, literally *woof*), and the tones produced when the left hand presses a string down on the place indicated by one of the *hui* while the right hand pulls it, are called 'horizontal' (經 *ching*, literally *warp*). These terms could refer to the fact that the archaic lute offered an image resembling the texture of a woven*

by the scholar Chang Yu of the Sung dynasty.[55] One might explain by technical reasons the fact that the horizontal lines are cut up, and the vertical lines stressed, it being easier to engrave a long vertical line than a horizontal one, as anybody knows who has tried his hand at carving Chinese seals.

The above digression on the oldest history of *ch'in* and *sê* is not more than a hypothesis. The only advantage it has over other explanations is that it seems less far-fetched and a little more logical. Yet it has often appeared that historical truth runs counter to all logic, and explanations that seem far-fetched sometimes prove to be true ones. So I give this hypothesis here for what it is worth: only one of many possibilities.

There remains one remark to be added. In the above discussions I have relied exclusively on the pictorial element of the ancient script, leaving the phonetic side of the question untouched. Though agreeing with the opinion that the study of Chinese epigraphical problems in general must include also the phonetic aspect,[56] in this particular case I have refrained from doing so, since here it seems unlikely that it could shed some more light on the oldest history of lute and *sê*. For the sake of convenience I have used throughout my discussion the names of both these instruments as they are at present pronounced in Peking. But in ancient Chinese *ch'in* must have been pronounced something like *k'ièm*, and *sê* something like *shièt*.

* * *

Finally I have to add a few words on the place occupied by the lute in the daily life of the Chinese.

The lute has never been an instrument of the multitude, both theoretical and practical factors preventing it from ever becoming popular. The theoretical factor I have already referred to above in the quotation from Father Amiot: the lute was reserved for a small class, its study 'belonging by right to those whose studies are concentrated on literature and wisdom', i.e. the literati. And this does

---

*fabric, the seven strings being crossed vertically by thirteen lines or some sort of bridges. It might be worthwhile to investigate historically the terms for the thirteen studs, 徽 and 暉, together with this word 緯. Phonetically all three belong together.

55 復古編, 張有

56 Recently again stressed by P. Boodberg in his important article 'Remarks on the Evolution of Archaic Chinese', in *Harvard Journal of Asiatic Studies*, II, p. 329. With regard to *ch'in* and *sê* I would draw attention to the fact that since ancient times both words have been combined with an explanatory character, which at the same time roughly indicates their pronunciation, viz. *ch'in* is coupled with *chin* 禁 'restraining', and *sê* with *sê* 嗇, meaning 'sparing'. Old literature gives many of these couplets, like 音 and 飲, 笙 and 生, 德 and 得, 朔 and 蘇. It might be worthwhile to make a list of such couplets, and investigate them phonetically.

not apply only to the Ch'ien-lung period (1736–95), during which the learned Father was writing, but also to the two thousand years preceding. Among the practical factors I may mention the paucity of competent teachers, the difficulty of the technique, the high price and the rarity of good instruments. So the lute remained reserved for the small circle of the happy few, an exquisite treasure jealously guarded by the literati.

The lute is one of the indispensable paraphernalia of the library of the Chinese scholar. In a country like China, where literature is held in so high an esteem, and where until recent years (1905) the only way to an official position was through the gate of the literary examinations, the library has a deeper meaning than anywhere else. It was the sanctum where the literatus passed the greater part of his life, writing and reading, firmly convinced that the outer world could give nothing that was not to be found described and analyzed in choice language in the many volumes that were piled upon the shelves around him. The saying of the *Tao-tê-ching*, 'Without going outdoors I know the world, without looking out of the window I see the Way of Heaven',[57] might well be written as a motto over the door of each Chinese library.

In the course of time there was formed a fixed tradition regarding the library, which minutely described the things a literatus should always have near at hand. On his desk should lie the inkslab, a stick of ink on a special stand, a vase containing some thoughtfully chosen and well arranged flowers, an antique vessel to wash his writing brushes, a stand to lay the wet brush on, paper weights, seals, etc. On a small table there should be a chess board, and on another an incense burner. In all available corners bookstands should be arranged, while the remaining parts of the walls should be covered with scrolls showing graceful lines of characters or a famous painting. And in a dry corner, far from the window and not reached by the rays of the sun, there should be hanging one or more lutes.

The lute, symbol of literary life, enhances by its very presence the special atmosphere of the library, and at the same time is an elegant ornament. Its graceful, slender shape is pleasing to the eye, and the deep colour of its lacquer and its charming patina harmonizes with the antique appearance of its surroundings. Its venerable age suggests the wisdom of the sages of bygone times, and is it not said that

[57] *Op. cit.* ch. 47.

the scholar, though living in the present, should in his thoughts dwell with the Ancients?[58]

Like the old bronze sacrificial vessels often found in the abode of the scholar, the lute is an object for appreciative study by cultured connoisseurs. For the bottom board of antique lutes is covered with inscriptions and seals, engraved in its coat of lacquer.[59] For instance the valuable lute reproduced in fig. 2, shows an inscription engraved by the famous philosopher Chu Hsi.[60] Its special name is *Ping-ching*,[61] 'Icicle Sonorous Stone'; the inscription reads: 'The tone Kung corresponds to the tone Shang. The sonorous stones are tapped, the bells are struck. With calmed emotions nurturing one's nature, the music is harmonious and even. Written by Hui-wêng (literary name of Chu Hsi), in the ninth month, autumn 1187.'[62] After the lapse of some time the lacquer of old lutes shows tiny cracks (*tuan-wên*),[63] by the shape of which connoisseurs fix the age and genuineness of antique specimens.

But the lute is more than other antique objects, because it is at the same time a musical instrument. 'Of the most precious antiques none equals the lute. Bronze tripods of the Hsia dynasty, and sacrificial vessels of the Shang period, old autographs and famous paintings, all these are valuable. But tripods and sacrificial vessels can only be displayed as decoration, they cannot be used. They cannot be compared with the lute, which sings if its strings are touched, giving an impression of meeting the ancients in person, in the same room, and talking with them.'[64] These lines were written by a scholar who himself was an expert performer on the lute. But this is an exception: even among the literati consummate lute performers were always rare. The so-called requisites of the library became in large part mere conventions: the presence of a chess-board does not imply that the master of the library is a devotee of the Royal Game, nor does the presence of a lute necessarily mean that he can actually play it.

A knowledge of the special system of thought belonging to the lute is a part of the education of every literatus, but only a small number among them have mastered its music. Still it was considered

---

58 *Li-chi*, ed. Couvreur, ch. xxxviii, 11.
59 For more details, cf. App. iii, *The Lute as an Antique*.
60 朱熹, 1130–1200.
61 冰磬
62 宮應商鳴，擊玉戛金，怡情養性，中和且平，淳熙丁未秋社日晦翁題.

63 斷文
64 *Ch'in-hsüeh-ts'ung-shu*; cf. App. ii, no. 7, in the treatise *Ch'in-yü-man-lu* 琴餘漫錄: 古器中最可寶者，莫如琴，夏鼎商彝，古書名畫，非不貴也，然鼎彝祇能陳設，不適於用，非若琴按弦則鳴，如與古人晤談一室.

a sign of elegant taste to express some well-known principles of *ch'in* ideology in a new form, or to extoll in a poem the special merits of a lute one happened to possess—and could not play! A good example of a mass of literary productions centring round one famous lute is the collection *Hsieh-ch'in-shih-wên-ch'ao* published in 1815 by Wu Ching-ch'ao; one day he bought the favourite lute of the well-known loyal Sung scholar Hsieh Fang-tê.[65] Literary friends and acquaintances composed essays and poems in praise of this lute, and this collection, filling five volumes, was privately published by the happy owner of the instrument.

For his not playing a scholar might quote numerous elegant excuses. He might cite the old Taoist paradox that curiously resembles the famous line in Keats' *Ode on a Grecian Urn*: the unheard tones are the most beautiful. Or he might point to the great poet of the Chin period T'ao Ch'ien who, according to tradition, had a lute without strings or studs hanging on the wall, and who in one of his poems said: 'I have acquired the deeper significance of the lute; why should I strive after the sound of the strings?'[66] This attitude, though it may be well founded from a philosophical point of view, discouraged scholars from aspiring to become accomplished performers on the lute. Therefore this attitude was sharply criticised by real lute players. It is said in the *Ch'in-sê-ho-pu*:[67] 'In the houses of the wealthy there may sometimes be seen lutes hanging on the wall as a decoration, richly adorned with precious stones;[68] but they are only meant to dazzle people's eyes. If one asks (the owner) about music, he stands dumbfounded, and does not know about what one might be speaking. Then there are also those perverted and vainglorious people who do not attach strings and tuning pegs to their lutes, thus injustly using the Master of the Five Willows (fancy name of T'ao Ch'ien), and hoping thus to conceal their own worthlessness; those people are especially ridiculous!'[69]

Such protests by discerning connoisseurs of lute music are rare: the great majority of the literati, if they played the lute at all, contented themselves with being able to play only two or three of the simpler tunes or even but a few bars. The view stated by Ou-yang

---

65 謝琴詩文鈔; 吳景潮; 謝枋得, 1226–89.
66 陶潛, 365–427. 但得琴中趣, 何勞弦上聲.
67 See n. 37 above.
68 For a discussion of such richly decorated lutes refer to App. III, *The Lute as an Antique*.
69 富家整飾或有琴懸諸壁間裝璜點綴, 亦不過輝人目而已, 詢其音律懵然不識爲何物, 更有矯情干譽而絃軫不備, 謬借五柳先生爲掩醜計, 尤可笑也. (ch. 1, p. 8)

Hsiu,[70] the great scholar of the Sung dynasty, in his essay *The Three Lutes* (dated 1062), may be taken as representative of the general attitude of Chinese scholars to the lute. He says: 'From my youth I did not relish vulgar music, but loved the sounds of the lute. I particularly liked the tune *Flowing Streams*, in its simpler version. During my life I often was in distress, and I roved over the country from north to south. All the other tunes of the lute I entirely forgot, only this one tune *Flowing Streams* remained in my memory during dream and sleep. Now I am old, and I play it only occasionally. For the rest I only know some smaller tunes; yet this is sufficient for my own enjoyment. One need not know many tunes; in studying the lute the most important point is to learn to find satisfaction in playing.'[71]

Notwithstanding the fact that the music of the lute was transmitted only by a few masters scattered over the Empire, officially the instrument itself was held in universal respect. I have come across only very few books where the position of the lute as the unique representative of the music of the ancients is challenged.[72] Often, it is true, the lute was used to accompany vulgar music. Occasionally one will see on a painting a scholar playing the lute while a singing girl accompanies him on the four-stringed guitar or some other frivolous instrument. And, though playing the lute should restrain all passions, Chinese novels and theatre pieces more than once mention a young scholar who by playing the lute conquers the heart of his beloved.[73] But such misuse of the lute, though doubtless frequent, was never officially approved.

During the latter half of the Ch'ing dynasty it appears that the lute was played in only a few circles of musical scholars, some in

---

[70] 歐陽修, 1007–1072.

[71] 三琴記 (外集, ch. 14)：余自少不喜鄭衛, 獨愛琴聲, 尤愛小流水曲, 平生患難, 南北奔馳, 琴曲率皆廢忘, 獨流水一曲夢寐不忘, 今老矣, 猶時時能作之, 其他不過數小調, 弄足以自娛, 琴曲不必多, 學要于自適.

[72] For instance, a work on music in general, dating from the nineteenth century, called *Mien-ch'in-hsieh-hsüeh-yüeh-lu* 眠琴榭學樂錄, by Shên Wên-ying 沈文熒. In ch. 4 he says that it is wrong to call the lute the special instrument of the ancients, for it is not better than the *p'i-p'a*. Moreover the lute has no less than five defects; among others, its finger technique is so complicated that one cannot sing while playing, its tones are not pure, its rhythm is confused. Notwithstanding these statements, which must seem terrible heresy to the old-fashioned lute connoisseur, this book contains a mass of valuable information, especially because the author also discusses in detail the tuning, finger technique and notation of some popular instruments like the *yüeh-ch'in* 月琴. I possess only a very fine manuscript copy of this book; I do not know whether it was ever published.

Further I also refer to the *Hsüeh-chai-chan-pi* 學齋佔畢, by Shih Shêng-tsu (史繩祖, 13th century), where the second chapter starts with a discussion entitled 'The *sê* comes before the lute' 瑟先於琴; there the lute is called inferior to the *sê*, and also to the mouth-organ, *shêng*.

[73] See, for example, the *Hsi-hsiang-chi* 西廂記, part II, act IV.

Chekiang province, some in Fukien, others in Szuchuan: a negligible minority when compared with the vast number of scholars who devoted themselves to literary pursuits, and brought fame to Ch'ing letters. Lute music, a drooping flower, too much sheltered in the dimness of the library, was gradually withering away. It grew to resemble too much the *chih*[74] fungus, the agaric symbolizing longevity, dried specimens of which decorate the desk of the scholar; they are graceful to look at, but dry and lifeless.

Fortunately, since the establishment of the Chinese Republic interest in lute music has revived.[75] Unhampered by the old exclusionist tendencies, the study of the lute spread to broader circles. Younger Chinese scholars who have studied musicology abroad are investigating lute music on modern scientific principles.[76] Many pupils flock round the few old teachers, books and manuscripts on the lute are eagerly sought for, and in the near future we may confidently look forward to a renaissance of lute music in China.

Next to China the only other country where the lute was played and studied is Japan.

Japanese tradition mentions as the father of lute music in Japan a Chinese Ch'an priest, Shin'etsu.[77] Fleeing the troubles that marked the early years of the Ch'ing dynasty, he came to Japan (1677), and was invited to Mito by the feudal lord Mitsukuni,[78] a great patron of learning. Shin'etsu could play the lute, and soon a great number of devoted pupils gathered round him. According to Japanese sources this was the beginning of lute playing in Japan.[79]

Western scholars in several books on Chinese music in general have paid due attention to the lute.[80] In 1911 G. Soulié gave a general description of the lute, devoting some space to a description of the

---

[74] 芝

[75] How enthusiastically the lute is still studied appears from the book *Hui-ch'in-shih-chi* 會琴實紀, published in 1920 in one volume by the well-known lute player Yeh Chang-po (葉璋伯, called Hsi-ming 希明). This book is a collection of documents and pictures relating to a reunion of lute experts, organized in 1919 by Mr. Yeh. In this book one also finds a list of about fifty contemporary lute players, with their addresses. Further, I refer also to R. Taki, *Ongaku shiryō no chōsa*, in: *Tōhō gakuhō (Journal of Oriental Studies)*, Tokyo, July 1935, p. 254.

[76] For instance, Wang Kuang-ch'i 王光祈, who attempted to transcribe *ch'in* notation with European symbols; cf. his *Fan-i-ch'in-pu-chih-yen-chiu* 翻譯琴譜之研究, Shanghai 1931. Also Chang Yu-ho 張友鶴, who in the Peking periodical *Yin-yüeh-tsa-chih* 音樂雜誌 published a series of articles on the lute, entitled *Hsüeh-ch'in-ch'ien-shuo* 學琴淺說, in which several examples of lute tunes transcribed in European notes are given *(op. cit. 1)*.

[77] Chinese: Hsin-yüeh 心越, better known by his literary name Tōkō Zenji 東皋禪師, 1639–95.

[78] 光囧, 1628–1700.

[79] For a discussion of the study of the lute in Japan, I refer to App. IV of this essay, *The Chinese Lute in Japan*.

[80] For a more complete list of references to the lute in Western literature, see App. I.

way it is played.⁸¹ M. Courant discussed the instrument and its tuning *in extenso*,⁸² whilst L. Laloy dwelt more upon its significance.⁸³

The lute, however, has occupied since ancient times so unique a position in Chinese musical life, and its special literature is so extensive, that I think it well deserves to be treated separately. For the lute is the only instrument forming the center of a special system of thought; it is the only instrument the playing of which has been considered from ancient times as a means for reaching enlightenment.

In the following pages I propose to discuss the ideology of the lute, and its place in Chinese history, leaving aside as much as possible all questions directly relating to musical theory. I hope that some day a musicologist shall write a practical handbook for the lute player. For the time being these pages may suffice as a general introduction. According to the Chinese tradition on the study of the lute this is the correct order, for is it not said in the rules for the lute player that one may not touch the strings of the lute before its significance is clearly understood?

⁸¹ G. Soulié, *La Musique en Chine;* cf. App. I, no. 3.

⁸² M. Courant, *Essai historique sur la musique classique des chinois;* cf. App. I, no. 6.

⁸³ L. Laloy, *La Musique chinoise:* cf. App. I, no. 5.

CHAPTER TWO

Classical Conceptions of Music

Chinese classical conceptions of music according to the YÜEH-CHI—
*twofold aspect of music, cosmological and political—music
belongs to heaven, and corresponds to what is heavenly in
man—it is a means for perfecting the government, and for
improving the individual—music as a source for pleasure not
recognized*

THE ideology of the lute is a separate system of thought, which was gradually evolved in the course of the many centuries that the Way of the lute was cherished and cultivated by the literati. Various factors promoted the establishment of this ideology, and manifold influences determined its evolution. In the following chapters I shall endeavour to give a sketch of this development. As the rules of *ch'in* ideology were never assembled and canonized in one basic text, we shall have to collect our data from various literary sources, and with these materials on hand, try to form for ourselves a more complete picture of the system.

Before embarking upon this rather complicated task, we first must obtain an idea of Chinese conceptions of music in general. Fortunately there exists a special text, which gives a good survey of the classical conceptions. This is the *Yüeh-chi*, 'Annotations on Music', a part of the *Li-chi*,[1] usually called *Book of Rites*, one of the classics of the Confucianist school. The *Li-chi* was composed at a comparatively late date, viz. about the beginning of our era. The *Yüeh-chi* was drawn up by the scholar Ma Yung.[2] Yet a comparison with older data, such as passages relating to music scattered in the works of the various philosophers that flourished in the latter part of the Chou dynasty, shows clearly that although the formulation of the *Yüeh-chi* is late, the ideas which it contains are elaborations of considerably older conceptions. But the materials are cast in a Confucianist form, and as such this text is authoritative for literary musical ideals. As moreover

---

[1] 樂記, 禮記   [2] 馬融, style: Chi-ch'ang 季長, 79–166.

in Chinese literature it remained until quite recently the standard text on music, extensively quoted in nearly all later books on music or musical theory, I think we may well take this text as basis for our discussions of Chinese music in general.³

This treatise contains a great variety of information, not only on the significance of music, but also on the ceremonial orchestra, and the ritual dances that were executed to its music. Statements on the meaning of music in general are scattered throughout the work; I shall try to arrange the most important references of this kind more systematically and discuss them in order.

The significance of music appears to be twofold, depending on whether it is viewed in its universal, cosmological and superhuman aspect, or, on the other hand, in its specialized, political, human aspect.

In its universal aspect music is the harmony inherent in all nature, embracing heaven and earth. In its specialized aspect it is applied to man, both as an individual and as a member of the political unity, the State.

In the *Yüeh-chi* both the universal and the specialized aspects of music are discussed extensively. As this text belongs to the Confucianist school, however, it is only natural that the latter aspect is stressed.

Throughout this treatise music is considered as inseparable from rites (*li*):⁴ both are indispensable to the proper government of the State. In more than one passage, however, it is pointed out that music is superior to rites, mainly because music consists of heavenly harmony, rites of earthly harmony. 'Music is the harmony of heaven and earth, rites constitute the graduation of heaven and earth. Through harmony all things are brought forth, through graduation all things are properly classified. Music comes from heaven, rites are modelled after earthly designs.'⁵ 'Music aims at harmony, it belongs to the higher spiritual agencies, and it follows heaven. Rites aim at the distinction of differences, they belong to the lower spiritual

---

³ For musical materials of a more archaic character I may refer to a work of Taoist coloring dating from the third century B.C., the *Annals of Spring and Autumn of Lü Pu-wei* 呂氏春秋. In ch. v are embodied four sections on music, especially important because they quote ancient myths, indicating the role of music in archaic totemistic ceremonies. This book has been translated by R. Wilhelm: *Frühling und Herbst des Lü Bu-we*, Jena 1928. I may refer also to the works of the philosopher Huai-nan-tzû; cf. L. Laloy's discussion in *T'oung-pao*, May 1913, pp. 291–8.

⁴ 禮

⁵ *Yüeh-chi*, ch. I, paragraph 23: 樂者天地之和也，禮者天地之序也，和故百物皆化，序所群物皆別，樂由天作，禮以地制.

agencies, and follow earth. Therefore the Holy Sages composed music in order that it might correspond to Heaven, and they instituted rites so that they might correspond to Earth. When rites and music are manifest and perfect, Heaven and Earth will be regulated.'[6]

Music and man are closely connected, because music corresponds to what is Heavenly in man. 'When man is born he is serene: this is the nature of Heaven. Experiencing contact with outer things, he is moved, and in his nature desire is created... If man cannot regulate his likes and his dislikes, the outer things will lead him astray, he will grow incapable of introspection, and the Heavenly nature in him disappears.'[7] 'For this reason the Kings of olden times instituted rites and music in order to regulate human emotions.'[8] 'Music points to what all beings have in common; rites point to that in which all beings differ. What is common leads to mutual love, what is different leads to mutual respect.'[9] 'Music is based on the inner life of man, rites on outer appearances. Music comes from within, therefore it is serene; rites come from without, therefore they are elegant.'[10]

As music is a direct manifestation of Heaven, the wise ruler shall utilize it to assist him in governing the State properly. 'In Music the Holy Sages took delight, because music can improve the heart of the people. Music has a profound influence on man, it can improve customs and ameliorate morals. Therefore the kings of olden times promoted the teaching of music.'[11] 'Therefore, when music flourishes, human relations are clarified, eyes and ears are made more susceptive, body and mind are in balanced harmony, good customs prosper and morals are improved, and peace reigns everywhere under Heaven.'[12]

Thus music appears as one means for transferring the Heaven-inspired virtues of the Wise Ruler to his subjects.

'Music is formed in the heart. Tones are the shape in which music is expressed. Elegance and rhythm are the decoration of the tones. The Superior Man takes the feelings in his heart as basis, he gives

---

6 *Ibid.* ch. I, par. 29: 樂者敦和率神而從天, 禮者別宜居鬼而從地, 故聖人作樂以應天, 制禮以配地, 禮樂明備, 天地官矣.

7 *Ibid.* ch. I, par. 11: 人生而靜, 天之性也, 感於物而動, 性之欲也……好惡無節於內, 知誘於外, 不能反躬, 天理滅矣.

8 *Ibid.* ch. I, par. 13: 是故先王之制禮樂, 人為之節.

9 *Ibid.* ch. I, par. 15: 樂者為同, 禮者為異, 同則相親, 異則相敬.

10 *Ibid.* ch. I, par. 15: 樂由中出, 禮自外作, 樂由中出, 故靜, 禮自外作, 故文.

11 *Ibid.* ch. II, par. 7: 樂也者, 聖人之所樂, 而可以善民心, 其感人深, 其移風易俗, 故先王著其教焉.

12 *Ibid.* ch. II, par. 8: 故樂行而倫清, 耳目聰明, 血氣和平, 移風易俗, 天下皆寧.

them shape in music, and then he gives this music its final form.'[13] But, in performing, because of this deep meaning of music, stress should not be laid on superficial beauty of melody and specious notes; above all the spiritual, the transcendental significance of music must be made manifest. 'The greatness of music lies not in perfection of tone'[14] for: '(In rites and music) virtue is more than art.'[15]

This principle was already recognized by the Ancient Rulers: 'The kings of olden times instituted rites and music, not to satisfy the mouths and stomachs, the ears and eyes, but in order to teach the people to balance their likes and dislikes, and to bring them back to the Right Way.'[16]

Besides stating these lofty views on the general meaning of music —music in the universe and music in the State—the *Yüeh-chi* also devotes several lines to the meaning of music to the individual. 'A wise man has said: "Not for one single moment may one separate oneself from Rites and Music." When one perfects oneself in music with the aim of regulating the heart, then as a matter of course the heart shall be calm, straight, tender and pure.'[17] 'Therefore, during a musical performance in the Temple of the Ancestors, prince and statesman, high and low listen together, and an atmosphere of harmony and respect prevails. During a musical performance on the occasion of clan festivals or village festivals, old and young listen together, and an atmosphere of harmony and compliance prevails. During a musical performance in the household, parents and children, elder and younger brothers listen together, and an atmosphere of harmony and affection prevails.'[18]

And finally I may quote a passage describing the attitude towards music of the *Chün-tzǔ*, the ideal man of the Confucianist school: 'The Superior Man returns to his original heavenly nature, and thereto he conforms his thoughts. He distinguishes between good and bad, and in accordance therewith regulates his conduct. He does not perceive lewd sounds or indecent spectacles, he keeps his heart undefiled by lascivious music or unbecoming rites. His body is free

---

13 *Ibid.* ch. II, par. 23: 樂者心之動也，聲者，樂之象也，文采節奏聲之飾也，君子動其本，樂其象，然後治其飾．

14 *Ibid.* ch. I, par. 9: 是故樂之隆非極音也．

15 *Ibid.* ch. III, par. 5.: 是故德成而上，藝成而下．

16 *Ibid.* ch. I, par. 10: 是故先王之制禮樂也，非以極口腹耳目之欲也，將以教民平好惡而反人道之正也．

17 *Ibid.* ch. II, par 23: 君子曰，禮樂不可斯須去身，致樂以治心，則易直子諒之心油然生矣．

18 *Ibid.* ch. III, par. 28: 是故樂在宗廟之中，君臣上下同聽之，則莫不和敬，在族長鄉里之中，長幼同聽之，則莫不和順，在閨門之內，父子兄弟同聽之，則莫不和親．

from laziness and negligence, falsehood and depravity. He makes his ears and eyes, nose and mouth, all the functions of perception of his entire body conform to what is right, and so achieves righteous conduct. Then he expresses his sentiments in chant: he accompanies them on lute and *sê*, moves the shield and the axe, and uses as decoration the pheasant feathers and the ox tails, and finally he lets the flutes sound. The splendour of complete virtue makes the four seasons revolve in harmony, and establishes the right order of all things.'[19]

From the above quotations it will be clear that according to classical ideas there is but one sort of music deserving that name: that of the ceremonial orchestra. Its music and its dances are not meant for relaxation and for diversion, they are sacred institutions, established by the Holy Kings of old for the purpose of regulating the State and perfecting the individual. As for solo instruments, they are only recognized as music when they have also a function in the ceremonial orchestra, like the lute and *sê*.

In the well-governed Confucianist State music meant for pleasure does not exist. Occasionally, when the government is decaying, and the end of a state is approaching, there will arise tones not conforming with these high musical princi‑

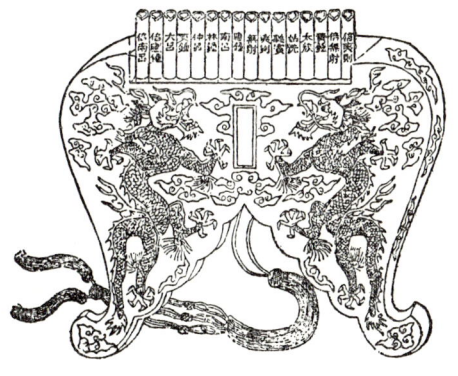

ples. But this music is usually not referred to as such, it is called 'lewd notes' or 'vulgar sounds'; these incite people to depravity, confuse the proper relations between men and women, ruler and subject, and sap the foundations of the State. They have nothing to do with what is called music.

---

[19] *Ibid.* ch. II, par. 15–16: 是故君子反情，以和其志，比類以成其行，姦聲亂色不留聰明，淫樂慝禮不接心術，惰慢邪僻之氣不設於身體，使耳目鼻口心知百體，皆由順正以行其義，然後發以聲音，而文以琴瑟，動以干戚，飾以羽旄，從以簫管，奮至德之光，動四氣之和，以著萬物之理.

CHAPTER THREE

Study of the Lute

§1 SOURCES

More materials on the significance of the lute than on lute music— three groups of materials: scattered references to the lute, special treatises on the lute, and CH'IN PU, *handbooks for the lute—reasons for the rarity of* CH'IN-PU—*their contents— recent Chinese books on the study of the lute*

It must be considered fortunate, at least for the subject of this essay, that materials for investigating the ideology of the lute are more extensive and reach much farther back in history than those for studying lute music itself.

To illustrate this I may mention the fact that whereas the oldest *ch'in* tune preserved in notation[1] dates from the T'ang period (618–907), references to the significance of the lute may already be found in the old Classical Books. And while the earliest printed handbooks for the lute date from the Ming dynasty (1368–1644), essays on the meaning of the lute date from the beginning of our era.

Thus for the study of *ch'in* ideology we have rich materials at our

---

[1] The tune preserved is the fifth chapter of a well-known old Chinese melody, called *Yu-lan* 幽蘭, 'The Orchid in the Profound Vale', and was found in Japan. This text is especially important because it gives, not the ordinary notation in abbreviated characters *chien-tzû* (see Chap. I, n. 9), but uses an apparently older system, where as a rule every movement is described in full. It was copied out by the famous Japanese Confucianist Ogyū Sorai (荻生徂徠, 1666–1728, also known as Mononobe Mokei 物部茂卿), after a T'ang manuscript, allegedly reproducing a text from the Sui period dated 590. When the Chinese scholar and bibliophile Yang Shou-ching (楊守敬 1835–1915) stayed in Japan in 1880–4 and searched everywhere for old Chinese books and manuscripts, he also purchased a copy of this manuscript. It was reprinted in the *Ku-i-ts'ung-shu* (古逸 叢書, cf. Pelliot, *Notes de bibliographie chinoise*, BEFEO, II, page 315); in 1911 it was again reprinted by Yang Tsung-chi (see below) in his *Ch'in-hsüeh-ts'ung-shu*, who endeavored to transcribe the tune in the usual *ch'in* notation. In the same *ts'ung-shu* Yang Tsung-chi reprinted an article on this tune by Li Chi 李濟. It would appear that the prolix method of notation used in this manuscript represents an early stage of the system. Still I hesitate to attach much value to this text for a study of the development of *ch'in* annotation. Ogyū Sorai's manuscript was copied out again and again. I recently purchased an old copy, with Japanese commentaries and explanatory illustrations. The question arises whether Ogyū Sorai faithfully followed the Chinese original, or whether he wrote out in full a manuscript originally in *chien-tzû*, for his own purposes.

disposal. For the sake of convenience I shall divide them into three groups.

In the first place there are materials of a more or less casual nature, to be found in all kinds of books on various subjects. The oldest references occur in the Classical Books, mentioned above. The writings of the philosophers of various schools that flourished about 300 B.C. also often contain valuable materials on the significance of the lute. I mention especially Huai-nan-tzû and Lü Pu-wei (see p. 24, n. 3).² The former so often uses musical conceptions to illustrate his ideas, that he might well be called the 'musical philosopher'. Further, in historical and encyclopaedic compilations stories about famous lute players are often related; such anecdotes indirectly shed much light on ancient Chinese conceptions of the lute.

Secondly there were also composed special treatises on the lute. The oldest that has been preserved seems to be the *Ch'in-ch'ing-ying* by the Confucianist philosopher Yang Hsiung.³ During the Han dynasty there were written several of such books on the lute: the bibliographical section of the History of the Han Dynasty mentions four,⁴ that of the Sui period seven items. Unfortunately these books are all lost, and were so already in the Sung dynasty.⁵ We still have, however, scores of books on the lute dating from the end of the Han to the beginning of the Ming period. And thereafter the literature on the lute increases rapidly: not only were there published a great number of special books on the lute, but also works on music in general devote entire chapters to the lute and its connotations. The mass of this literature is so vast that one can hardly hope to survey it all.

Thirdly there are the so-called *ch'in-pu*,⁶ handbooks for the lute player. Since because of their rarity these are the least known, I shall describe this category here more fully.

Although hundreds of *ch'in-pu* have been published since the beginning of the Ming dynasty, most of them are difficult to obtain. A collector of the 19th century observes: 'The so-called handbooks

---

2 淮南子；呂不韋

3 琴清英；揚雄, 53 B.C.–A.D. 18

4 *Han-shu-i-wên-chih* 漢書藝文志, by Pan Ku (班固 A.D. 32–92). Some of the items mentioned here may have contained some sort of notation. I mention: *Ya-ch'in-chao-shih-ch'i-p'ien* 雅琴趙氏七篇 'Compositions for the Solo Lute, by Mr Chao, 7 parts', with the remark added: 'Tunes that were played by Wei Hsiang, minister under the Emperor Hsuan' (73–49 B.C.) 宣帝時丞相魏相所奏. Another commentator adds that Chao and a few other authors of similar treatises were granted an audience by the Emperor, and played the lute in the august presence.

5 Cf. *Ch'in-shih* 琴史, the passage quoted on p. 56 below.

6 琴譜

of the lute are not very much sought after by bibliophiles: they content themselves with just collecting a few items, so as to have also this sort of book represented on their shelves. As bookshops cannot sell them at a high price, they do not value them much; as moreover these books were very rarely reprinted, they were easily lost. During eighteen years I was able to collect only 41 specimens, which were bought by me or presented to me by my friends.'[7] I may add to this that generally *ch'in-pu* were published in very limited editions, printed from badly cut wood blocks, and on inferior paper. The reason for this state of affairs is that they were usually published by lute teachers, for the use of their pupils. So the printing and editing were done as cheaply as possible, and only a small number of copies were made. An exception is formed by those *ch'in-pu* that were published by scholars of name and high official standing, who could afford to have a handbook published without regard to the cost.

For the present subject, the study of the ideology of the lute, the latter class is the more important, because the authors had a wide knowledge of the literature on the subject, and could easily express their thoughts in writing. It goes without saying, however, that from a purely musical point of view, the value of a *ch'in-pu* rests entirely in the quality of the tunes given in notation: this depends upon the musical gifts of the editor, and has nothing to do with his scholarship. Often the most enticing melodies will be found in the cheapest editions.

Of course melodies in notation form the main part of a *ch'in-pu*.[8] But apart from that they contain introductory chapters, and it is here that the principles of *ch'in* ideology are to be found.

The contents of a *ch'in-pu* are generally arranged according to one fixed model. As is usually the case with Chinese books, they open with one or more prefaces, by the author and his pupils or friends,

---

[7] See the *T'ien-wên-ko-ch'in-pu-chi-ch'êng* (Appendix II, 18), vol. 1: 琴譜參考. 琴譜一書, 藏書家不甚購求, 隨收數種以備一類, 書坊店無善價可售, 故亦不重之, 而此書又少翻刻, 故最易亡滅, 余至今十有八年, 所購及諸公所贈此此四十一種. At present nearly all early Ming handbooks are rare, and often known to exist only in two or three copies. If one is lucky enough to find one, it is usually either incomplete, or else fetches a prohibitive price. During the last four years I have combed the bookshops in China and Japan for *ch'in-pu*, and copied out some very rare specimens in libraries. But still I have not yet been able to obtain many Ming *ch'in-pu* mentioned in old catalogues, and I fear that some are irretrievably lost.

[8] The only exception is the *Yü-ku-chai-ch'in-pu* 與古齋琴譜; published in 1855 by Chu Fêng-chieh 祝鳳喈; in this *ch'in-pu* not a single tune is given, the whole book being filled with minute directions for building lutes, and with discussions on the theory of lute music.

and thereafter give the *fan-li*[9] or 'introductory notes'. The prefaces are important, because they not only furnish the reader with biographical details about the author and his circle of musical friends, but because they also often mention where he obtained the versions of the tunes given in his book. In the *fan-li* the author often states his views on the significance of the lute and its music.

Then follow chapters on the history of the lute; names of famous instruments are enumerated, sometimes accompanied by drawings showing their various shapes, and reproducing their inscriptions. Often there are also inserted some practical discussions as to how lutes should be built, how the strings should be made, etc. Then come rules defining what might be called the discipline of the lute player: where and to whom the lute may be played, in what costume etc.; I shall discuss these rules in detail in the third section of this chapter. Also explanations of the technical terminology are given, and suggestions as to how lutes should be stored away, how to repair them, and how to make the table on which the lute is laid. Lists of tunes, of famous lute players, and of lute builders of succeeding dynasties are also added.

Thereafter come lengthy dissertations on the musical theory of the lute. Sometimes they confine themselves to the practical aspects, as fixing the correct tuning and the various modes, at other times they lose themselves in abstruse speculations on the absolute pitch and the correct dimensions of the twelve sonorous tubes.[10] In these pages I do not quote from this part of the *ch'in-pu*, since it contains no information on the ideology peculiar to the lute.

Of greater importance to our present subject is the section on the significance of the tones: each tone has its special association, and should evoke a certain emotion. Below I devote a special chapter to this question.[11]

Finally there comes a special chapter on the finger technique, and the system of annotation used in describing this technique. This chapter is called *chih-fa*[12] and it forms, so to say, the key to the handbook, for without it the player would find in the notation of the tunes many obscure passages, since editors often use all kinds of variants

---

9 凡例

10 The *Ch'in-sê-ho-pu* very justly observes that the greatest musical theoreticians are usually not the best musicians: 'In ancient times the people who excelled in playing the lute did not bother themselves (cf. *Lun-yü* XIX, 4) with the laws of musical theory; those who did so were not good performers on the lute' 凡例, 12: 古之善鼓琴者不泥於律呂, 泥律呂者必不善於鼓琴.

11 Chapter v, § 2: 'Symbolism of Tones'.

12 指法

of the signs of the *chien-tzû* system. Unfortunately this chapter has often been torn out, to prevent the handbook from being used by unqualified people. The best edited *ch'in-pu* illustrate these directions regarding the finger technique with drawings of the correct positions of the hand, sometimes further explained by symbolical pictures.[13]

In addition to these introductory chapters the main body of a *ch'in-pu*—the tunes in notation—also contains materials for studying the ideology of the lute. The tunes are accompanied by prefaces, colophons and commentaries, which give the name of the composer and explain the meaning of the tune; sometimes they even go so far as to explain the special significance of each part of a tune, and of each bar.[14]

These handbooks of the lute differ considerably in quality. Not only does the make-up vary, as mentioned above, but also the quality of the contents. Generally speaking they may be divided into two groups which I propose to call *basic* and *secondary*. In the first group I would classify that small number of *ch'in-pu* that combine well-written and logically arranged introductory chapters, with original and carefully edited versions of the tunes. As one wrong stroke in the notation will cause a tremendous confusion, the verifying of the characters (of the cut blocks)[15] with regard to the *ch'in-pu* is even more important than with ordinary books, where a wrong character may usually at a glance be detected by referring to the context.

Already an author of the Ming dynasty complains of the many mistakes in the notation of the *ch'in-pu*. He says: 'Those who excelled among the lute masters transmitted [the doctrine of] the lute and the handbooks. Thus the compiling of the handbooks rested with the lute masters. Still there are mistaken ones; if one stroke is wrong, then the finger technique fails because of this false tradition. And if this false tradition continues for a long time, the mistakes cannot be corrected any longer, and the true spirit of the lute melodies is lost.'[16] Many *ch'in-pu* boast in their prefaces that not a single stroke or dot in the notations is wrong, but those that measure up to this standard are rare.

The majority of the *ch'in-pu* still extant belong to the secondary group; their introductory chapters are a medley of passages taken from the basic handbooks and various other sources, clumsily patched

---

[13] For a discussion of these, see Chapter v, § 3: 'Symbolism of the Finger Technique'.

[14] In Chapter iv, 'The Significance of the Tunes', I shall often have to refer to these remarks added to the tunes.

[15] In Chinese: *hsiao-tzû* 校字.

[16] 琴譜取正. 琴師之善者傳琴傳譜, 而書譜之法在琴師亦有訛者, 一畫之失指法即錯以訛傳, 訛久不可正, 琴調則失眞矣 (Appendix ii, 4, *Tsun-shêng-pa-chien*).

together. The tunes given in notation are copied after those of the basic handbooks, with but few alterations. But even the editors of these secondary *ch'in-pu* often added some new materials of their own: a new way of expressing rhythm, adding ordinary notes to the *chien-tzû*, etc. Cases of absolute plagiarism are rare; I have so far been able to discover only one.[17]

It is only since the establishment of the Chinese Republic in 1911 that Chinese scholars have tried to collect and critically investigate these various materials on the lute. I may mention here the work of two lute players, who devoted many years to these studies.

In the first place is Yang Tsung-chi, who died around 1929, having during a long time taught the lute in Peking.[18] He was an enthusiastic collector of rare *ch'in-pu* and antique lutes, and, although not an eminent scholar or brilliant stylist, he still had had a suitable literary education. The result of his studies on the lute and its literature are collected in his *Ch'in-hsüeh-ts'ung-shu*,[19] which contains not less than 32 original treatises. Unfortunately he did not work according to a fixed plan, but, *more sinico*, he jumps from one subject to another, giving the most heterogeneous items of information under one and the same heading. As no index or detailed list of contents has been added, one has to work through the entire work in order to locate a passage. But notwithstanding these shortcomings it is a valuable book, as yet the only one that tries to treat all aspects of the study of the lute.

His friend Chou Ch'ing-yün was a great collector of *ch'in-pu*, and he diligently studied their prefaces and colophons, comparing different editions of the same work. On the basis of what must have been a marvellous collection he compiled two books. In 1914 he published the *Ch'in-shu-ts'un-mu*,[20] a *catalogue raisonné* of all *ch'in-pu* he either possessed himself, or the titles of which he found in old and new catalogues. These items are all arranged chronologically, and in many cases he reprints their prefaces. It is to be deplored, however, that he did not add to each item a note as to whether he had actually seen the book or not. Therefore it is not always possible to know whether or not he relies on secondary information. The famous

---

[17] Namely, the *Chiao-an-ch'in-pu* 蕉庵琴譜, published in 1877 by Ch'in Wei-han 秦維翰, in which are given exactly the same versions as printed in the well-known *Wu-chih-chai-ch'in-pu* (Appendix II, 15). The editor has, however, made up for this to a certain extent by giving in the introductory chapters a particularly good survey of the various tunings.

[18] 楊宗稷, style: Shih-po 什百.

[19] Appendix II, 7.

[20] Appendix II, 8.

bibliophile Miao Ch'üan-sun[21] wrote a preface. In 1917 he supplied these bibliographical materials with biographical data, publishing a *Ch'in-shih*,[22] in which notes are given on the lives of famous editors of *ch'in-pu* and of lute players; Yang Tsung-chi added a preface to this book.

Notwithstanding their shortcomings these three books are indispensable works for the student of the lute. The materials which the authors used are hardly obtainable in the libraries of Europe or America, and even in China and Japan most of the rare items are found together only in some private collections.[23]

§2 ORIGINS AND CHARACTERISTICS

The establishment and evolution of CH'IN *ideology due chiefly to three factors: Confucianist (social), Taoist (religious), and psychological—Buddhist influences: a Mantrayanic magic formula as lute tune, a Lamaist hymn adapted to the lute— a summary of the history of* CH'IN *ideology*

CH'IN ideology may be called a separate system in so far as every time that one meets the lute in Chinese literature, it is found to be associated with a special system of thought.

In minor details this system is differently described by various authors, but its characteristic points remain the same. One would look, however, in vain for a special standard text, in which this system is clearly formulated, and its elements systematically arranged, so as to form a canon for the significance of the lute.

Since early times there is found the term *ch'in-tao*,[24] literally: the Way of the lute, meaning: the inner significance of the lute and how to apply this in order to find in the lute a means for reaching enlightenment. The literatus and lute player Huan T'an[25] wrote a treatise entitled *Ch'in-tao*; this title is registered in the *Yü-hai*,[25] but it has not been preserved. This book may have been an attempt to give a summary of the principles of *ch'in* ideology. This term *ch'in-tao* might be translated as 'the doctrine of the lute'; but as we

---

21 繆荃孫, 1844–1919.
22 Appendix II, 9.
23 For materials on the lute in Western books I may refer to Appendix I, while a description of the Chinese books on the lute and of the *ch'in-pu* quoted in these pages may be found in Appendix II.
24 琴道
25 桓譚 (he lived about the beginning of our era); 玉海

do not possess a special text where the principles of this doctrine are set forth, I think a vague term like 'ideology of the lute' is the more suitable translation.

In the long course of its development *ch'in* ideology benefited by its lack of delimitation; because of the absence of a fundamental text, *ch'in-tao* was able to absorb a great wealth of various conceptions. Below I shall try to sketch an outline of this ideology, at the same time making an attempt to analyze the factors that caused its establishment, and influenced its further evolution.

In Chapter II, I discussed the classical conceptions of music in general, as expounded in the *Yüeh-chi*. We are not justified, however, in taking that discussion as a final basis when embarking upon an investigation of historical problems, although till recent days the *Yüeh-chi* was looked upon by Chinese scholars as having unquestionable authority. In order to be able to make a discreet use of this text, we shall first have to consider it critically.

Chinese historical records are unique in so far that they cover an unbroken line, reaching from high antiquity to the present day. But we must always bear in mind that the cement of this imposing edifice is formed by the continuity of the written language. And this literary language, although extremely flexible and highly expressive, is yet too much a special product of a limited circle, a comparatively small group of writers, all belonging to the same class and having a similar trend of thought, not to strain a correct representation of the actual facts. History was, until recently, a section of the vast field of Chinese letters; it was, like most other Chinese sciences, kneaded and remoulded until it became literature. This fact becomes evident when one tries to study some subject in its historical frame; when comparing archaeological and ethnological data with their descriptions as transmitted in literary documents, we cannot fail to realize that these describe life and its phenomena from a particular and narrow angle: the point of view of the literary class. We are constantly confronted with what might be called a revolving process, something like the following. A certain phenomenon is observed and recorded. This record is written in the highly polished literary idiom, and by this mere process of recording, the actual facts are already modified to some extent. In this form it finds its way into some book or essay. Other literati quote the passage, but before doing so they test it by literary traditions, and make the necessary alterations to harmonize it with these. Moreover they will link it up with some appropriate classical quotation, and add that this was the phenomenon as it has appeared since ancient times. Now, when after the lapse of some centuries or so, another observer finds this same phenomenon in actual life, before writing about it he consults the records drawn up by former observers, and finds these to be rather different from what he actually sees. But as a rule his reaction is not to question the correctness of these records, but on the contrary he will accept them as the absolute truth, and in connection with the present condition of the phenomenon he will sadly point out the decadence of the times, deploring that a phenomenon that formerly was in such perfect accordance with literary ideals has come to be so vulgar. And this process repeats itself any number of times, till the discrepancy between the actual phenomenon and its description becomes so wide that a later writer treats them as two entirely different things.

It goes without saying that this theoretical example is far too simplistic and general, and that real cases are infinitely more complicated. Further, as a rule, such a development applies especially to subjects lying outside the direct domain of the literatus—which were many. Still I think it is as true as generalizations can be. It may serve as one explanation for the fact that there is inherent in Chinese literature what might be called a paradisaical complex: a tendency to reverse the natural course of the evolution of culture, to make it start with a summit of perfection, after which there is a steady decline. Of course there are numerous other and more potent factors underlying this tendency; factors based upon a trend of thought common to all human beings, and which explain the fact that this paradisaical complex occurs in many other civilizations. But in China the force of the literary tradition must certainly be counted as one of them.

When we consider the pronouncements of the *Yüeh-chi* in the light of the foregoing observations, it becomes evident that they are not to be taken as a faithful description of the opinion of the ancient Chinese on music in general. The views quoted are a production of literary tradition. For the literati ceremonial music was the apex of all music, and consequently they expected all other musical manifestations to be in accordance with these ideals. What deviated from this fixed canon had to be remoulded till it fitted in; then and then only could it be officially accepted. That this ceremonial music itself is in many respects an artificial production stands to reason. When the *Yüeh-chi* speaks of the music of the clan festivals, it depicts them as decorous celebrations, ignoring their origin. Comparative ethnology teaches us that the actual songs sung at clan festivals were far more archaic, though their meaning and portent was certainly not less deep or mystic than that of any classical text. The ancient terminology was maintained, but the interpretation was biased to the extent of giving a false representation of the real facts.

In some cases the materials that had to be remodeled by the literati set them some difficult problems. For instance, the songs of the *Book of Odes* so clearly showed their original character of folksongs, that the literati needed all their ingenuity to force them into the classical mould. Some of them, the odes of Chêng and Wei,[26] ancient lovesongs, they had to give up as being impossible to remould. Therefore the literati labelled them irrevocably with their *hic niger est*, and in Chinese literature they are, quite wrongly, always used to denote lewd and vulgar music. I need not discuss this question further here, since it has already been analyzed by M. Granet in his pioneer researches on the *Book of Odes*.

Thus the conceptions of music as expounded in the *Yüeh-chi* did not answer real conditions; neither the music at the court, nor the music of the people could pass the muster set by these literary standards. This is only natural, since music is a very human art that develops spontaneously, unhampered by moral or philosophical considerations.

Even though we can hardly see conditions of the pre-Han period except through the documents drawn up and refashioned by the literati, indirect information definitely points to the fact that popular music, theoretically designed as the 'lewd notes of Chêng',[27] was much in favour at the court and among the populace. Prince Wên of Wei[28] expressed his preference unequivocally when he said: 'When in full ceremonial dress I must listen to the Ancient Music, I think I shall fall asleep, but when I listen to the songs of Chêng and Wei, I never get tired.'[29] Thus in the period preceding the Han dynasty the Ceremonial Music was forced to the background by the ever-waxing influence of secular music. To use the words of the great historian Ssû-ma Ch'ien:[30] 'The right way of government decayed, and the music of Chêng prospered. The feudal lords and hereditary princes made their names famous in neighbouring states, and vied with each other in power. Since Confucius could not cope with the

---

26 鄭, 衛; *Shih-ching*, Books VIII and IX.
27 See *Lun-yü*, Book XV, ch. 10; Book XVII, ch. 18.
28 426–387 B.C.
29 See *Yüeh-chi*, ch. III, 6.
30 司馬遷, born in 145 B.C.

singing girls sent by Ch'i,[31] and had to give up his position in Lu, although retiring he rectified the music in order to lead people to the right path, he composed the Wu-chang music in order to criticise the trend of the times, but none heeded his counsels. The decay went on and in the period of the Six States the feudal lords indulged in dissipation and idleness. Then it was impossible for them to return to the right path, they lost their lives and their families were exterminated and all the states were unified under Ch'in.'[32]

Official recognition of popular music came under the reign of Emperor Hui[33] when a special bureau for this was established. This bureau was called *yüeh-fu*, and its task was to collect and record popular songs. Later these songs themselves were also called *yüeh-fu*.[34] When the Emperor Wu fixed the rites for the sacrifices to Heaven and Earth,[35] this bureau was reorganized, and considerably widened in scope. Well-known poets like Ssû-ma Hsiang-ju and Li Yen-nien[36] were ordered to investigate and correct the popular songs assembled, in order that charming melodies might be properly harmonized, and the accompanying texts polished, to make them more enjoyable for a cultivated and refined audience.

In later literature it is stated that the *yüeh-fu* was instituted in order to choose and put on record such folksongs as were considered to be of an edifying and elevated character, to ameliorate the morals of the people. But in my opinion this is clearly the distorted point of view of the Confucianist school of thought. The original function of the *yüeh-fu* was certainly not to restrain popular music, but on the contrary to encourage it, and to assemble as many gay songs fit for entertainment as possible. This is shown, e.g., by a passage from the *Account of Rites and Music of the Han History*,[37] where the endeavours of Emperor Ai[37] to curb the rampancy of popular music are described; a commentator adds: 'Although the Emperor Ai stopped

---

[31] This incident is referred to in *Lun-yü*, Bk. XVII, ch. 4. Legge adds the note: 'In the 9th year of the duke Ting, Confucius reached the highest point of his official service. He effected in a few months a wonderful renovation of the state, and the neighbouring countries began to fear that under his administration Lu would overtop and subdue them all. To prevent this, the duke of Ch'i sent a present to Lu of fine horse and of 80 highly accomplished beauties. The sage was forgotten, government neglected. Confucius, indignant and sorrowful, withdrew from office and, for a time, from the country too.'

[32] 史記, 樂書, 治道虧缺, 而鄭音興起, 封君世辟, 名顯鄰州, 爭以相高, 自仲尼不能與齊優, 遂容於魯, 雖退正樂以誘世, 作五章以刺時, 猶莫之化, 陵遲以至六國, 流沔沈伏, 遂往不返, 卒於喪身滅宗, 并國於秦.

[33] 惠帝, r. 194–188 B.C.

[34] 樂府

[35] 武帝, 140–87 B.C.; *chiao-ssû* 郊祀

[36] 司馬相如, 179–117 B.C.; 李延年, 2nd cent. B.C.

[37] 漢書禮樂志; 哀帝, r. 6–1 B.C.

the songs of Chêng and Wei, and restricted the number of officials of the *yüeh-fu*, he did not succeed in establishing elegant music on the basis of the Classics and the ancient rules.'[38] If the *yüeh-fu* was intended to control popular music, the Emperor would have enlarged, and not restricted, the number of officials.

Equally abortive were the efforts at a reform in favour of music conforming to literary standards made by Ho-chien Hsien-wang, the son of the Han Emperor Ching.[39] The growth of secular music was further encouraged when Central-Asiatic music, the so-called *hu-yüeh*,[40] became increasingly popular in China. The class of palace music called *huang-mên-ku-ch'ui-yüeh*[41] (music for entertaining the guests at Palace festivals and banquets) occupied a much more important place than Ceremonial Music, and its influence grew with every succeeding dynasty.

This light music reached its zenith during the Sui (590–618) and T'ang (618–907) periods.[42] In those times it did not, however, any longer derive its inspiration from Chinese popular music; the *yüeh-fu* genre had become a literary style, cultivated by scholars as an archaizing[43] sort of poetry cut off from its living root, the folk-song. Foreign modes and instruments prevailed, and an enormous amount of Indian and Central-Asiatic music was adopted.[44] And these foreign airs were not even in accordance with the twelve sonorous tubes, on which all Chinese musical theory has been based since times immemorial. We read in the *Account of Music of the Liao History*: 'The 28 foreign modes are not fixed by means of the Chinese sonorous tubes, but by the strings of the *p'i-p'a*.'[45] Even songs belonging to a semi-popular, but essentially Chinese class of music, were reset on Central-Asiatic modes.[46]

When the highest social circles set such an example, it can be easily understood that the music that was heard in the streets and at social

---

[38] 哀帝雖有放罷鄭衞之言，減樂府之員，然不能據經做古制爲雅樂.

[39] 河間獻王，景帝，r. 156–140 B.C.

[40] 胡樂

[41] 黃門鼓吹樂

[42] See the fundamental study by K. Hayashi: *Sui-t'ang-yen-yüeh-tiao-yen-chiu* 林謙三，隋唐燕樂調研究, Shanghai 1935 (appeared only in Chinese).

[43] *ni-ku* 擬古

[44] In the *Account of Music in the Dynastic History of the Sui Period* 隋書音樂志, we find the following amazing enumeration of seven musical departments instituted by the Emperor Yang (煬帝, r. 605–17): 國伎, 清商伎, 高麗伎, 天竺伎, 安國伎, 茲龜 (＝屈支) 伎, 文康伎.

[45] 二十八調, 不用黍律, 以琵琶絃協之. According to Chinese tradition the size of each of the twelve sonorous tubes (黍律 *shu-lü*) was determined by the number of grains of millet it could contain; the basic tube, *Huang-chung*, should contain exactly 1200 grains.

[46] Note the remarks of Hayashi (*op. cit.* p. 61) regarding *ch'ing-shang-yüeh* 清商樂.

gatherings was still further removed from the literary standards fixed by tradition. Still it formed a part of the daily life of the literati and of the common people. We have but to read through essays and poems of the T'ang period to see how immensely popular this so-called 'vulgar' music was with the gay and pleasure-loving people of that time. Yet, when one leafs through the scores of voluminous works on music referring to that period, one finds involved speculations on the absolute pitch of the ground-note, and other abstruse questions of musical theory, but not a word about popular, let alone about foreign, music. For this music was contrary to established literary principles, and there was no recognized precedent for it; so it was simply ignored. This is one of the many cases where the records drawn up by the literati give a biased representation of the actual conditions.

Returning now to the *Yüeh-chi* we can, after the above discussions, state that already about 400 B.C., when these conceptions were formulated, they were neither in accordance with the conditions prevailing at the time, nor did they give a good idea of the situation during past centuries. Still less could they be applied to the evolution of music during subsequent dynasties. Notwithstanding, the *Yüeh-chi* was, and remained, the only standard text on music recognized by the literati, and thus by official historians.

This digression into the history of music in general was necessary, because in my opinion the discrepancy between actual musical conditions and the standard set by literary tradition was one of the factors that caused the creation of the ideology of the lute, and strongly influenced its further evolution.

Although the literati ignored what they called 'vulgar' music in their learned musical dissertations, they were of course perfectly aware of its existence, and moreover liked it immensely. This is sufficiently shown by an inspection of the many old paintings which depict the life of the literary class: there one sees gatherings of literati, assembled on a beautiful spot in the open, and enlivened by a bevy of fair damsels, who play the three-stringed violin, the cither and a great variety of other instruments, all introduced from foreign countries. This popular music was in fact the only kind of music that the greater part of the literati could in reality hear. For the Ceremonial Music was only performed on special occasions, and for a limited audience. Yet, although known often only from books, the Ceremonial Music and literary musical standards had officially to be kept intact. For if popular music were allowed to invade also the sacred domain of literature, classical ideals might become endangered, and therewith the very foundations of the State.

It is here that the significance of the lute becomes apparent; it was the only instrument that, although properly belonging to the ceremonial orchestra and boasting of a venerable age, pure Chinese origin, and constant association with the most holy Sages of Confucianism, could still be played in private life as a solo instrument, and still demonstrate all the high musical ideals fixed by literary tradition.

Since ancient times notions that perfectly harmonize with classical ideals were associated with the lute. For instance, in the *Yüeh-chi* it is said that music belongs to Heaven, and as such may assist man to regain his original heavenly nature. Now, as the philosopher Huai-nan-tzû observes, the lute was created in mythical times to provide man with an instrument to regain his original serenity: 'to make man return to his divine origin, to restrain his low passions, and make him revert to his heavenly nature'.[47] In the *Ch'in-tsao*[48] this idea is formulated as follows: 'Fu Hsi made the lute, whereby to restrain falsehood, to guard the heart against low desires, that man might be cultivated and his nature regulated, to make man return to what is truly heavenly in him.'[48]

Further, the *Yüeh-chi* says that music was used by the Ancient Sages to regulate the Realm. Now in the *Book of History*, in *Huai-nan-tzû*, and several other philosophical texts of the period, the following line is quoted: 'When Shun was Emperor, he played the five-stringed lute, and sung the song *Nan-fêng*, and the Realm was regulated.'[49] Wise men of later times should also cultivate lute music, to illustrate the benevolent rule of the Ancient Sovereigns: 'to play the lute in order to sing the way of the Ancient Kings'.[50]

Already the Chinese word for lute in itself pointed to this high destiny. As is well known, a favourite Chinese way of explaining a word is to couple it with a homonym. So in the *Book of Rites*, *Li-chi*, the word for 'virtue', *tê* 德, is explained as *tê* 得, 'possessing (rectitude)'. In the same way the *Fêng-su-t'ung-i*[51] explains the word *ch'in* 琴 (lute), by coupling it with the homonym *chin* 禁, which means 'restraining'. The text reads: 'Lute means restraining. With this instrument licentiousness and falsehood are restrained, and the

---

[47] 以歸神杜淫，反其天心 (*op. cit.* 泰族訓).

[48] Appendix II, 1. 所以禦避僻，防心淫，以修身理性，反其天眞也.

[49] 舜爲天子，彈五絃之琴，謌南風之詩而天下治.

[50] 彈琴以詠先王之風 (韓氏外傳, Ch. 2).

[51] 風俗通義

human heart is rectified.' This phrase makes, according to Confucianist teachings, the lute an instrument for 'nourishing the heart': *yang-hsin*.⁵² The philosopher Mencius observes: 'To nourish the heart there is nothing better than to make the desires few. Here is a man whose desires are few—in some things he may not be able to keep his heart, but they will be few. Here is a man whose desires are many—in some things he may be able to keep his heart, but they will be few.'⁵³ Thus the lute, through its capacity for restraining human passions, was a suitable instrument for everyone desiring to become the ideal statesman and ruler of the Confucianist school of thought, the Superior Man, the *Chün-tzû*.⁵⁴

So the lute became one of the indispensable implements belonging to the outfit of the scholar; it became a symbol of literary life. As an old text says: 'The Superior Man does not suffer the lute to be separated from him during one single moment.'⁵⁵ Also, from a practical point of view it was suitable for solitary enjoyment. Scholars with musical inclinations could, when reciting the songs of the *Book of Odes, Shih-ching*, or some famous old essay, accompany this on the lute, as an elegant enjoyment sanctioned by tradition. Literati who, despite the trend of the times, clung to a strict observance of ancient principles also with regard to music, considered the lute as the stronghold of the music of the ancients, since here in one instrument were combined all the elevated conceptions expressed by the Ceremonial Music. Therefore they deepened its significance, in order to remove it farther from ordinary music and to consolidate its position as the treasure house of true music and the only officially recognized musical instrument of the literary class.

So we see that the very fact that music in general became the opposite of literary musical ideas, caused these conceptions to be ever more withdrawn into the narrow circle centring round the lute. The more that popular and foreign music advanced, the more the system of ideas connected with the lute was enlarged and elaborated on the basis of ancient classical passages. It was in the course of this process of emphasizing the difference between the lute and secular music that the ideology of the lute was established and developed till it became a separate system of thought.

This tendency to stress the isolated position of the lute as the one instrument of the true Confucianist scholar, appears constantly in

---

52 養心 53 See Legge, *Mencius*, Book VII, 35.
54 君子 55 *Fêng-su-t'ung-i*; see below, p. 72.

the tenets of *ch'in* ideology. Efforts are made to keep lute music for the use of the literary class only that it may not be tainted with vulgar or foreign influences. Already for purely practical reasons the lute lay outside the reach of the common people, since good instruments were expensive, the technique of playing extremely difficult, and teachers rare. The lower classes could afford to buy a guitar or a violin and play popular tunes on it, relying on the ear; but the lute had its own complicated system of notation, incomprehensible for those not specially educated in literature. In addition, artificial barriers were drawn up: explicit rules defined the classes of people to whom the lute may be played or taught. These lists are highly instructive. They mention, for example, that merchants and vulgar people are unqualified for occupying themselves with the lute, thus underlining the tendency to keep the lute reserved for the small circle of the elect.

Many of these rules can only be appreciated in their real significance by comparing them with the actual conditions of music which I described above. We find among the people who are forbidden to touch the lute, for instance, singing girls and actors. That this group was included is evidently in protest against the fact that at the more intimate parties at the court the lute was also played to execute *yüeh-fu* songs. This kind of music is even registered as a special class, the so-called *ch'in-ch'ü-ko'-tz'ŭ*.[56] That many handbooks for the lute also exclude Buddhist priests from lute music, and sharply denounce the music of foreign countries as 'barbarian', is doubtless to be interpreted as a reaction against the ascendency of the Indian and Central-Asiatic elements in secular music. In the next section of this chapter I shall discuss these rules in more detail. The examples given here may suffice to show that the break between real musical conditions and Confucian literary musical ideals was one of the factors that promoted the evolution of *ch'in* ideology.

Next to this social factor, which for convenience sake may be called Confucianistic, there was also a second, that might be called the Taoistic, lying in quite another domain of culture, viz. that of religion.

This second factor, which promoted the coming into being of *ch'in* ideology, is also slightly involved, and makes a detailed explanation necessary.

As mentioned above, the lute was considered as a means for regaining man's original purity by restraining low desires and banish-

---

[56] 琴曲歌詞. For a collection of poems sung to this music., see *Yüeh-fu-shih-chi* 樂府詩集, by Kuo Mao-ch'ien (郭茂倩, Sung period), chapter VIII.

ing evil thoughts. This belief in the original purity of human nature, doubtless one of the fundamentals of Chinese thought, is one of the most important links that connect Taoism and Confucianism. But the Taoist and Confucianist explanations and appreciation of this conception differ considerably.

In Taoism, however, speculations regarding the original purity of human nature rise far above the very earthly teachings of Confucianism; human nature is considered from a cosmic point of view. For the Taoist the universe is a manifestation, one peculiar aspect, of an all-pervading, supernatural agency, indicated by the term *tao*, which gave its name to the system. It is difficult to find for this term one entirely satisfactory equivalent; the Way seems most convenient. This *tao* is present in all things, in the most elevated as well as in the most base. The aim of Taoism is to learn to see one's own self as a part of this *tao*, so as to reach a complete reunion with it. Taoist writings constantly mention, as a condition for reaching this state of highest bliss and delivery from all earthly bonds, a regaining of the original purity. This original purity may be reached by returning to the utmost simplicity, both in mental and physical aspects. One must do away with all the superfluous things with which man has surrounded himself, thereby better to be able to concentrate upon the essence of *tao*, and by such introspection attain the primordial serenity. In the *Tao-tê-ching* this is called 'returning to the root, and so regaining serenity.'[57]

Taoist writers give several descriptions of this state of complete reunion with *tao*. Lieh-tzû describes this blissful condition as follows: 'After nine years [of meditation under the guidance of a master] I gave up speaking and thinking, I did not know the difference between benefit and damage, I did not know whether my master was really my master, nor yet that another was my friend. Outer and inner life had completely melted together. Thereafter the five senses also melted together, I could not determine whither sensations came. My mind was frozen, my body free, flesh and bones seemed to have become rarefied. I did not know on what my body rested, nor did I know what was under my feet. I was borne hither and thither, like a leaf that falls from a tree, or like dry chaff, without knowing whether the wind was riding on me, or I on the wind.'[58]

---

57 Ch. 16: 歸本曰靜.
58 *Ibid.* ch. 黃帝: 九年之後, 橫心之所念, 橫口之所言, 亦不知我之是非利害歟, 亦不知彼之是非利害歟, 亦不知夫子之爲我師, 若人之爲我友, 內外進矣, 而後眼如耳, 耳如鼻, 鼻如口, 無不同也, 心凝形釋骨肉都融, 不覺形之所依倚, 足之所履, 隨風東西, 猶木葉幹殼, 竟不知風乘我, 我乘風乎.

Another description of this state of detachment from earthly bonds is given in a passage in the works of the philosopher Chuang-tzû: 'Formerly I dreamt that I was a butterfly, freely fluttering about, just as it liked. I did not know that it was I. Suddenly I awoke, and realized that I was I. Now I wonder whether I dreamt that I was a butterfly, or whether I now am a butterfly, dreaming that it is I.'[59]

For the method of meditative self-culture, Chuang-tzû coined the term *yang-shêng*[60] 'nurturing (the spiritual life)'. In the chapter that has this title as its heading he says: 'If one takes *tao* as standard, then one may preserve one's body, complete one's life, and exhaust one's term of years.'[61] This *yang-shêng* is to be compared with *yang-hsin*, mentioned above with regard to Confucianist teachings: for *yang-shêng* also, a restraining of desires is obligatory.

These early Taoist conceptions are the foundation on which the most imposing monuments of Chinese thought are built. It seems, however, that these teachings were taken in their literal sense already at a fairly early date. Especially in the first century A.D., when Taoism was reorganized after the example of Buddhism, the accent fell more and more on the materialistic aspects of meditation. Meditation was no longer exclusively considered as a means for salvation, but chiefly as a means for obtaining occult powers, to perform all kinds of magical feats. So the passage of Lieh-tzû quoted above was interpreted as a description of a method of accomplishing levitation, while Chuang-tzû's definition of *yang-shêng* was taken to refer to the art of prolonging life. The lofty teachings of Taoism degenerated into alchemy, aiming at transmuting metals and finding the elixir of immortality.

Returning now to the lute, we see that the fundamentals of *ch'in* ideology described above fitted in exactly with Taoism, both with its philosophical and with its alchemistic aspect.

Playing the lute purifies one's nature by banishing low passions, therefore it is a sort of meditation, a means for communicating directly with *tao*. Its rarefied notes reproduce the 'sounds of emptiness', and so the music of the lute tunes the soul of the player in harmony with *tao*. Further, as we shall see below, the measurements and the construction of the lute all stand for cosmic elements, so its contemplation is conductive to a realization of eternal truths and cosmic harmony.

---

[59] Ch. II, last passage: 昔者莊周夢爲胡蝶, 栩々然胡蝶也, 自喻適志與, 不知周也, 俄然覺則蘧蘧然周也, 不知周之夢爲胡蝶, 胡蝶之夢爲周與.

[60] 養生

[61] 緣督以爲經, 可以保身, 可以全生 .... 可以盡年.

Therefore it is only natural that the passages of Lieh-tzû and Chuang-tzû quoted above were taken as subjects for lute compositions. During the Sung dynasty Mao Chung-wêng composed the tune '*Lieh-tzû-yü-fêng*'[62] (Lieh-tzû riding on the wind), and in the Yüan period Mao Min-chung composed the tune '*Chuang-tzû-mêng-tieh*'[62] (Chuang-tzû dreaming of the butterfly). The latter in particular is a very delicate composition, with striking passages entirely in harmonics, which suggest the detached state of mind indicated by the subject.

Seen from the more materialistic angle, playing the *ch'in* was a means for purifying the body, thus bestowing upon the performer freedom from sickness, and longevity. To obtain these blessings neo-Taoistic writers recommend, in addition to fasting, etc., exercises[63] for learning to regulate breathing, *lien-ch'i*.[64] Now playing the lute is said to harmonize the circulation of the blood, thereby regulating the breathing. In this way the vital Yang essence in the body is cultivated, and evil influences are driven away. As the philosopher Kuan-tzû observes: 'to regulate the blood and the breath, in order to obtain longevity'.[65]

Therefore the lute is allotted a very special place amongst the Treasures of the Library: playing the lute can not be mentioned in one and the same breath as playing chess, or other literary pursuits. In the *Questions and Answers on the Study of the Lute*,[66] we read: 'Question: Which is superior, the lute or chess?—Answer: The quadruplet lute-chess-calligraphy-painting has been used since the time of Hui-tsung of the Sung dynasty. But in reality the lute is an instrument that embodies *tao*, and as such it is entirely different from chess. The lute is near to Taoism, it teaches one how to subdue the scheming mind. To illustrate this the tune *Ou-lu-wang-chi*[67] was made. But

---

62 毛仲翁, 列子禦風; 毛敏仲, 莊子夢蝶

63 A most detailed description of all these exercises is given in the *Tsun-shêng-pa-chien* (Appendix II, 4), the section *Ch'ing-hsiu-miao-lun* 清修妙論. Also confer the excellent article by Henri Maspéro, 'Les procédés de "nourrir le principe vital" dans la religion taoiste ancienne' (*Journal Asiatique*, CCXXIX, 1937). A convenient summary of the materialistic side of Taoist teachings is given in O. S. Johnson, *A Study of Chinese Alchemy*, Shanghai 1928; see also M. Chikashige, *Alchemy and Other Chemical Achievements of the Ancient Orient*, Tokyo 1936, and A. Forke, *Geschichte der mittelalterlichen chinesischen Philosophie*, Hamburg 1939, pp. 131 ff.

64 鍊氣

65 管子, 導血氣以求長年

66 *Ch'in-hsüeh-ts'ung-shu*; see Appendix II, 7: 問, 琴與棋孰優. 答. 琴棋所畫四者並稱自宋徽宗時始, 實則琴爲載道之器, 與棋爲絕對反比例, 琴與道家爲最近, 宜戒機心, 是以有鷗鷺忘機之曲, 棋則專用機心, 精棋者常有嘔血傷生之事, 琴則以却病爲收效之初基, 此所以相反也.

67 A famous lute tune, composed during the Sung period by Liu Chih-fang 劉志方. Most *ch'in-pu* explain this song as follows: There was an old fisherman who used to take delight in long trips on the sea. The*

for playing chess one needs just such a scheming mind. Chess experts often suffer from hemophtysis and general decline in health. The lute, on the contrary, driving away sickness, is a first basis for attaining prosperity. Therefore it is quite the opposite of chess.'

In this connection I may also quote an anecdote about the Sung poet Lin Pu:[68] he excelled in playing the lute and in calligraphy, but he was not very good at playing chess. He used to say: 'All things of this world I can generally understand; only I cannot bear myself to be defiled by playing chess.'[69]

Lute amateurs indignantly protest against the designation of lute music as an art, for it is far more than that, it is a Way, a path of wisdom, *tao*.[70]

From the above it will be clear that next to the influence of Confucianist literary tradition, Taoist conceptions also contributed to the formation of *ch'in* ideology, and promoted its further development. As was also pointed out above, the lute was, however, played only by a comparatively small number of the literati. Therefore, to explain the wide divergence of *ch'in* ideology, to the above-mentioned factors a third one must be added, viz. the psychological one.

This psychological factor can be described in a few words. Few scholars were expert on the lute, but on various occasions in official and private life they enjoyed popular music. Now the lute supplied a means of self-justification for these scholars, both to other people and to themselves. In all sorts of mixed company the scholar could listen with delight to performances of popular music, and from time to time lustily chime in with some gay song; but when asked about his views on music, he could gravely point to the lutes hanging up in his library, and thereby definitely remove all doubts that might exist with regard to his elevated disposition. On the other hand, returning from a noisy banquet with some old friends, enlivened by the presence of some charming singing girls, the scholar could, in the silence of his library,

---

*flocks of gulls were so used to him that he could pat them. His wife knew of this, and one evening when he came home, she said to him: 'I like gulls. Why not bring one or two with you, so that I may enjoy looking at them?' At dawn the fisherman went out. But the flocks of the gulls flew high, and did not come down to him. 鷗鷺忘機, 有海翁者, 常遊海上, 羣鷗習而狎焉, 其妻知之, 抵暮還家, 謂翁曰, 鷗鳥可娛, 盍攜一二歸玩之, 至旦往, 則群鷗高飛而不下矣. This parable is an elaboration of a passage of *Lieh-tzŭ*, II, 11; its meaning is that as long as man is without desire, without a 'scheming mind', he shall live in complete harmony with nature.

68 林逋, better known by his posthumous name Ho-ching 和靖, 967–1028.

69 Lin Pu shows the typical mentality of the lute player: he did not care for worldly things, did not marry or adopt sons, but spent his days in a secluded abode, where he cultivated plum trees and reared cranes. People therefore used to say of him: 'The plum trees are his wife, the cranes his sons' 梅妻鶴子.

70 藝 as opposed to 道. See below, p. 82.

take the lute from its brocade cover, burn incense, and touch a few strings, thereby convincing himself that, although he might temporarily amuse himself with vulgar music in order to while away some moments of leisure, in reality he only appreciated the sacred music of the Ancients.

There could be mentioned also other reasons for the coming into being and further evolution of *ch'in* ideology, but in my opinion the three factors mentioned above must be considered as the decisive ones. I have discussed these three factors here separately, but it goes without saying that in the literature on the lute it is impossible to make such clear distinctions, and various views are found woven together.

Only in a few cases are the Confucianist and Taoist spheres of thought clearly differentiated as, for instance, in the two characteristics that should mark lute music, viz. *chin*, 'restraining', and *hsün*,[71] 'following', defined in this way: 'Restraining means driving away the false nature constituted by wantonness and low desire. Following means nurturing the Right Essence of balanced harmony.'[72]

Both views are also summarized in the two fixed epithets of the lute, viz. *ya*, 'accomplished, elegant' and *miao*, 'wonderful'.[73]

The question arises which of the two factors mentioned above had most influence on the development of *ch'in* ideology. As far as I can see, the answer must be that it was Taoistic ideas that predominated in the evolution of this system of thought. One might say that the formulation of the fundamental thoughts of *ch'in* ideology is Confucianistic, but that their contents are typically Taoistic. The literati, being as a rule of an eclectic disposition, accepted these Taoist teachings, since they did not clash with classical ideals, nor detracted from the special high position of the lute.

Herewith we must also take into consideration the fact that the Taoist considerations mentioned above corresponded directly with the most archaic, the pre-classical, Chinese notions. Taoism was the receptacle in which archaic Chinese thoughts were preserved. For instance, cultivating the Yang principle, the essence of light and vitality, is a very old conception; hence jade, cowry shells and other objects, credited with possessing a great amount of Yang power, were deposited in the tomb together with the deceased, to guard the

---

[71] 禁, 順
[72] 禁則去慾淫之絃心, 順則養中和之正氣 (Liu Yü, preface to Yang Piao-chêng's *ch'in-pu*; see App. II, 13).
[73] 雅, 妙

corpse, and thereby the earthly spirit *p'o*,⁷⁴ against decay. Thus the notion that playing the lute strengthens the Yang essence and thereby prolongs earthly life, fits in with the most archaic conceptions.

Through this preponderance of the Taoist element, *ch'in* ideology, notwithstanding the Confucianist tendency to keep the lute as purely Chinese as possible, still remained open for foreign influences, as long as these were not detrimental to the sacred character of the lute. These foreign elements are mainly Buddhist, and through Taoism some later schools of Mahayanic Buddhism, which might be comprised under the general name of Mantrayana, had some influence on the lute. The alchemist teachings of neo-Taoism show too many striking affinities with Mantrayanic magical practices for there not to have existed much interaction between them. Just as Taoist sorcery aims at prolonging life, levitation, subduing devils and other magical powers, so the Mantrayana teaches that the devoted practitioner may acquire the *aṣṭasiddhi*, the eight magical powers, i.e. levitation (*laghimā*), becoming invisible (*adṛçyā*), etc. To obtain these *siddhi*, Mantrayanic texts describe in detail complicated rituals, different according to the special deity worshipped and the aim desired. But the preliminaries remain the same: the practitioner must bathe, put on new clothes, then choose a clean place in a quiet abode, and burn incense. Only then may he go on to the drawing of the magic circle (*maṇḍala*), and in the center thereof imagine, or actually build, the altar. After these preparations he may start on the execution of the ritual.

Now when we read in the handbooks for the lute player the elaborate rules describing where and how the lute may be played, we cannot fail to notice their striking resemblance with Mantrayanic magical rites. To begin with, the table with the lute on it is constantly referred to as *ch'in-tan*,⁷⁵ 'lute altar'. This altar should be erected preferably on a beautiful spot in nature; it must be far from all worldly noise, pure, and surrounded by exquisite scenery. In the next section of this chapter I shall give more particulars. This short description may suffice to show the affinity with the rules given in, for instance, the *Mahāvairocana Sūtra* for *tsê-ti*,⁷⁶ 'choosing the place (for erecting the altar)'; there it is said that one should select a mountainous landscape, with trees and rivulets; borders of streams, frequented by wild geese and singing birds; a pure and secluded

⁷⁴ 魄   ⁷⁵ 琴壇   ⁷⁶ 擇地

abode.⁷⁷ The other rules also resemble the Mantrayanic ritual: before touching the lute the player must don ceremonial dress, wash his hands, rinse his mouth, and purify his thoughts. After having burned incense he may take the lute from its cover, and place it on the lute table. Then he should sit down before it in a reverent mood, and regulate his breath and concentrate his mind. His body should be kept steady and erect, 'unmoving and imposing like the T'ai shan'. Yet his mental attitude must be humble, 'as if he were standing before a superior'.

That thus playing the lute became a magical act, a ritual for communicating with mysterious powers, is, in my opinion, doubtless due to this indirect Mantrayanic influence.

Further, the lute underwent Buddhist influences directly. There were many lute players among famous monks, such as, during the T'ang period, Master Ying, and, during the Sung dynasty, I-hai and Liang-yü.⁷⁸ When some Indian priests came to China they also brought lute-like instruments with them, and Chinese scholars studied these foreign instruments in connection with the Chinese lute. We find, e.g., that Ou-yang Hsiu, famous poet and scholar of the Sung period, praised in a poem the performance of the monk Ho-pai on an Indian stringed instrument (probably the *vīṇā*).⁷⁹

A curious result of this direct Buddhist influence is the fact that among the better known *ch'in* tunes there is one entitled *Shih-t'an* 'Buddhist Words', which is nothing but a Mantrayanic magic formula, a *dhāraṇī*.⁸⁰ The music of this tune is decidedly Indian, vibratos and glissandos reproducing the frequent melismas used in Buddhist polyphonic chant in China and Japan up to this day. The words are also given, for the greater part in transcribed bastard Sanskrit, the usual language of *dhāraṇī*, and starting with the stereotyped opening formula 'Hail to the Buddha! Hail to the Law! Hail to the Community!'⁸¹

As far as I know, the first printed text of this tune was published by

---

⁷⁷ *Taishō-issaikyō* 大正一切經, No. 848, translated by Śubhākarasiṃha 施無畏, T'ang period. Cf. *Hōbōgirin, dictionnaire encyclopédique du Bouddhisme d'après les sources chinoises et japonaises*, 1937, s.v. *chakuji*. These Indian ideas fitted in with Chinese conceptions of the salutary effect of contemplating beautiful scenery; see below, section 3 of this chapter.

⁷⁸ See *Ch'in-shih* (Appendix II, 9), ch. 2. 穎師, 義海, 良玉.

⁷⁹ 歐陽修, 1007–1072; 和白. See the collected works of Ou-yang Hsiu, 外集 ch. 3, the poem *Sung-ch'in-sêng-ho-pai*.

⁸⁰ 釋談. Curiously enough this tune seems rather popular: it is included in the repertoire of the *p'i-p'a*, and in 1929 a version for the *san-hsien* was published (cf. *Yin-yüeh-tsa-chih* 'Music Magazine', vol. I, 5, Peking, 1929).

⁸¹ Namo buddhāya namo dharmāya namah samghāya 南無佛陀耶南無達摩耶南無僧伽耶.

Yang Lun in his *ch'in-pu*, *Po-ya-hsin-fa*.[82] The editor added a commentary, which is an interesting example of the scanty knowledge that the literati in general possessed of Buddhist texts. He says: 'I find that this tune is a magic formula by the Ch'an Master Pu-an, which later people set to music. Originally Sanskrit has the sounds *êrh-ho*, *san-ho* and *ssû-ho*,[83] each represented by a letter. In Chinese script only the notation for the lute has these letters. Therefore the Mirror of the Rhymes of the Seven Sounds[84] originated in India, answering to the seven strings of the lute. This is the origin of them [i.e. of the Seven Sounds]. Those tones which formerly were sung by the monks in the garden of Anāthapiṇḍada,[85] are now adapted to the lute. The music wherewith Gautama Buddha could subdue a mad elephant and cure the bites of venomous snakes, can now be used to make cranes dance and for taming pheasants. Although Confucianism and Buddhism fundamentally originate from different sources, their music mysteriously forms a true bond between them, although at first sight one would be inclined to dismiss this idea with a laugh.'[86]

The priest Pu-an lived from 1115–69, and was famous for his magical powers. He is said to have been able to heal maladies, command rain and drought, and to perform other magical feats. He left a book in three chapters, entitled *Pu-an-yin-su-ch'an-shih-yü-lu*.[87] It would seem that Yang Lun connects the seven kinds of sounds distinguished by Indian grammarians (guttural, palatal, etc.) with the seven notes of the Chinese scale (*kung, shang, chiao, chih, yü, pien-*

---

[82] Preface dated 1609; see Appendix II, 14.

[83] *Erh-ho, san-ho* and *ssû-ho* are technical terms used in Chinese transcriptions of Sanskrit texts, indicating that the two, three, or four characters preceding the sign should be contracted; e.g. 里波二合 is to be read *rva*, and not *riva*, 悉恒里三合 is to be read *stri*, and not *sitari*, etc. The author connects these signs with the same indications used in *ch'in* annotation, where they mean: make this note sound together with the preceding one (*êrh-ho*), or with the two preceding ones (*san-ho*); for instance one plucks the fourth string, while the sound of a vibrato produced on the second string has not yet died away. From this queer association one would conclude that Yang Lun misunderstood entirely the meaning of *êrh-ho* etc. in Sanskrit transcriptions. For a detailed discussion of the system the Chinese used for transcribing Sanskrit texts I may refer to my book *Hayagriva, the Mantrayanic Aspect of Horse Cult in China and Japan*, Leyden 1935, p. 48: 'The reading of the magic formulae'.

[84] *Ch'i-yin-yün-chien*: these four characters look like the title of a book, though I could not identify it as such.

[85] 給園, abbreviation of 給孤獨園, Sanskrit: *Anāthapiṇḍadā-syaramah*, the estate in which the Jetavana, the favorite abode of Buddha, was located. It was presented to the community by the rich merchant Anāthapiṇḍada, a fervent worshipper of the Enlightened One. Fa-hsien has given a description of this sacred place (see Beal's translation, p. 75).

[86] 按斯曲, 即普庵禪師之咒語, 後人以律調擬之也, 盖緣梵有二合三合四合之音, 亦有其字, 華書惟琴譜有之, 故七音韻鑑, 出自西域, 應琴七絃, 斯之所由出也, 昔作僧梵于給園, 今付徽音于百納, 瞿曇氏, 所爲調狂象, 制毒龍者, 玆可以舞鶴而馴雉矣, 雖儒釋固異源, 而音韻微有冥契, 聊寄一時之笑傲云耳.

[87] 普庵印肅禪師語錄

kung, pien-chih). With regard to this amazing statement I may draw attention here to the fact that Chinese scholars with Buddhist interests often were very well read in the Buddhist Canon, but seldom showed any knowledge of the real conditions depicted in those texts; further it is worth noticing that they were firmly convinced that Indian civilization was a kind of far-off and deteriorated Chinese culture.

Ch'in-pu of the Ch'ing period usually include this tune *Shih-t'an*, always adding the remark that the musical notation was drawn up by the poet and lute expert Han Chiang.[88] I have tried to find out where Han Chiang obtained this formula and its music, but without result; even for a lute player he was an extremely eccentric and cantankerous fellow, who never married but spent his days roaming up and down the vast Ch'ing Empire, always dragging along his lute and a couple of padlocked coffers with the manuscripts of his poetical works.[89] As the music of the tune *Shih-t'an* is doubtless of Indian origin, I am inclined to believe that he heard it somewhere in a Lamaist temple.

It was in this way that the other Indian tune among the lute tunes originated. In 1893 the Ch'an priest K'ung-ch'ên published a handbook for the lute, entitled *K'u-mu-ch'an-ch'in-pu*.[90] To the usual repertoire of lute tunes he adds some of his own composition, amongst others a lute version of a chant sung by Lamaist monks, called *Na-lo-fa-ch'ü*.[91] He added a colophon which says: 'In the autumn of the year 1888 I visited a friend in Peking. Wandering aimlessly about, I came to the Chan-t'an-ssû,[92] and there heard the lamas sing in chorus a Sanskrit chant, in clear and harmonious tones. I asked the people there what it was and learned that it was the old *Na-lo-fa-ch'ü*. The next day at noon I went there again, bringing my lute with me, and asked the lamas to sing the chant once more. Then I accompanied it on my lute. Having thus obtained the whole tune in notation, I

---

[88] 韓昌, style: Ching-chêng 經正, literary name Shih-kêng 石耕; he lived in the beginning of the Ch'ing period.

[89] See Han Chiang's detailed biography in the *Ta-ch'ing-chi-fu-hsien-chê-chuan* 大清畿輔先哲傳, ch. 27.

[90] 空塵禪師; 枯木禪琴譜

[91] 那羅法曲. *Na-lo* 那羅 may mean the deity Nārāyana 那羅延那, or it may stand for Nārada 那羅陀, or again for Naropa, 那羅巴祖師, the Indian Vajra-teacher, who in the eleventh century came to Tibet and there acquired great fame; the last alternative seems the most probable. *Fa-ch'ü* must mean here 'Buddhist (Dharma)-hymn', although Chinese dictionaries only give it as a Taoist chant, much in vogue at the court of the T'ang emperors (cf. *Tz'ŭ-yüan* 辭源, s.v.).

[92] 'Temple of the Sandalwood Buddha', destroyed by the Allied Forces in 1900 as it was one of the centers of the Boxers; it stood near the present National Library. Cf. Arlington and Lewisohn, *In Search of Old Peking*, 1935, pp. 134–5. As is shown above, K'ung-ch'ên visited this temple only twelve years before the Boxer troubles broke out.

gave it this title, that it may be put on record, at the same time following the example set by Shu Hsi in writing his *Pu-wang-shih*, requesting all high-minded connoisseurs to correct it.'[93]

I think it must have been in a similar way that Han Chiang obtained his version of the tune *Shih-t'an*.

Be this as it may, these two examples will perhaps suffice to show to what extent Buddhism influenced lute music, notwithstanding the Confucianist tendency to keep the lute as purely Chinese as possible.

* *

Summing up the remarks in Chapter I about the oldest history of the lute, and the above discussions about the various elements of *ch'in* ideology, we may state that the lute from the end of the Shang period appears as a part of the orchestra for sacred music. During the latter half of the Chou dynasty the lute appears also in the orchestra of more worldly music, and at the same time as a popular solo instrument of the cultured class. Some of its features made the lute particularly suited for retaining, more than any other instrument, certain ancient conceptions of a magical character, properly belonging not only to the lute, but to music in general. The lute being more widely used in daily life than the complete orchestra, the virtues ascribed to the orchestra and to music generally were gradually all transferred to the lute.

When the Confucianist school of thought was established, and actual musical conditions were found not to answer to the theoretical principles, the literati connected the archaic conceptions associated with the lute with their secondarily evolved dogmas of a paradisaical antiquity, and they praised the lute as the favourite musical instrument of the Holy Kings of olden times.

Especially during the Han period, which was marked by a tendency to return to the glorified images of mythical antiquity, the position of the lute as the unique symbol of all correct and accomplished music was further consolidated. Several special treatises on the lute and its significance appear: the *Ch'in-ch'ing-ying*, by Yang Hsiung, the *Ch'in-tao* by Huan T'an, and the *Ch'in-tsao* by the famous writer Ts'ai Yung.[94]

---

[93] 戊子秋訪友京都，間步旃檀寺，聽喇嘛齊歌梵唄，音聲清和，詢之左右，知其爲那羅法曲之遺音，翌午携琴復往，乞其反之而後撫絃和之，得譜成曲，卽題斯名以紀之，亦效束晳補亡之意，祈諸高明正之. Shu Hsi, style Kuang-wei 廣微, third century A.D. He wrote six poems in the style of the *Book of Odes* in order to complete their number, which according to tradition was 311. These poems he called *Pu-wang* 補亡, 'supplements of what has been lost'; they are to be found in the *Wên-hsüan* 文選, ch. 19.

[94] 琴清英, 揚雄, 53–18 B.C.; 琴道, and above, ch. 3, note 25; 琴操, and App. II, 1.

During the subsequent Chin and Wei periods, when Buddhism spread over China, and neo-Taoism flourished, the magical virtues of the lute as being conducive to meditation, and prolonging life, were again stressed. From this period dates the celebrated *Ch'in-fu*, 'Poetical Essay on the Lute', by Hsi K'ang.[95] Here the mysterious virtues of the lute are celebrated in exquisite language, and the materials suited for constructing lutes are described. This essay may be called the best-known literary production relating to the lute, and quotations from it will be found in nearly every treatise on this subject; it may be found in the *Wên-hsüan*.[96]

Protected alike by Confucianism and Taoism, and being also in accordance with Buddhist principles, the lute was firmly established in its privileged position. During the Sui and T'ang periods, when popular music was prospering, the lute was cultivated especially by the literati. It is at this time that we hear the names of famous lute makers; for instance, some members of the Lei[97] family.

During the Sung dynasty it seems that the lute was played in broad circles of literati; the literature of this period shows hundreds of poems and essays on the lute. It was at this time that the scholar Chu Ch'ang-wên composed his *Ch'in-shih*,[98] from which I shall quote below.

When, after the Yüan dynasty, China was again united under a pure Chinese dynasty, the Mings, there appeared a conservative tendency similar to that of the Han Period: a return to ancient Chinese standards. The Ming dynasty saw the heyday of lute and lute music; the standard handbooks for the lute were published, and endeavours were made to assemble the various elements of *ch'in* ideology and arrange them more systematically. In the refined social milieus of the period, where the tea ceremony, flower arrangement, genre painting and other arts were enthusiastically practised, the lute found congenial surroundings.

As pointed out above, during the Ch'ing period the interest in the lute waned gradually, to grow again in recent times.

I may end this chapter with translating a passage from the *Ch'in-shih* of Chu Ch'ang-wên, from which one may see how the development of the lute and lute ideology appeared to a scholar of the Sung period.

'The music of the lute prospered under the Emperors Yao and

---

[95] 琴賦; 嵇康 style: Shu-yeh 叔夜, 223–262.
[96] 文選 ch. 18.
[97] 雷
[98] 琴史 cf. App. II, 2.

Shun, and during the Three Dynasties [i.e. Hsia, Shang and Chou]. But since the beginning of the period of the Warring States, the accomplished tones decayed and lewd music arose: people liked meretricious and decadent notes and were averse to harmonious and serene music. Prince Wên of Wei[99] was a good ruler of those times, but he said: "When in full ceremonial dress I must listen to the Ancient Music, I think I shall fall asleep." [If a man of such an exalted position showed so little understanding,] how much worse then the ordinary people of those times must have been. Later the cither from Ch'in, the barbarian flute, the harp, the *p'i-p'a* and other similar instruments rose in succession and spread, while the lute fell into oblivion. When the Hans came to rule, they had no time for restoring the ancient customs, but Hsien-wang[100] devoted much time to a study of the accomplished music. During the reigns of the Emperors Hsiao and Hsüan, lute players like Mr Chih, Mr Lung, Mr Chao and Mr Shih for the first time used in their books on the lute the expression *ya-ch'in*, 'accomplished lute', to distinguish it from vulgar music. Moreover, Huan T'an and K'ung Yen[101] collected tunes of the lute, and great Confucianist scholars of that time, such as Ma Yung[101] and Ts'ai Yung, especially loved this art [of playing the lute]. Therefore all the people of those times held the lute in high esteem. Thereafter Yüan Chi[102] and Hsi K'ang promoted the lute. With the beginning of the Wei and Chin periods, famous literati and highminded scholars studied the lute in ever increasing numbers; I cannot set down here all their names which are recorded in history. Coming to the Sui and T'ang periods, there were many officials who cultivated this doctrine, but poets and artists who occupied themselves with the lute were rare. Still there were some virtuous and wise men who wrote about the lute, like Lü Wei, Li Liang-fu, Ch'ên Cho, Chao Wei-ch'ien, Li Yo, Chai Sung, Wang Ta-li, Chên K'ang-shih and others. They are all said to have written books on the lute, and their titles are registered in the bibliographical accounts of the histories of those periods, but I have not seen them, and neither have I heard whether they really understood the lute or not.'[103]

[99] 426–386 B.C.
[100] Son of Ching-ti, r. 156–140 B.C.
[101] Style: Shu-yüan 叔元, 268–320; style: Chi-ch'ang 季長, 79–166.
[102] 阮籍, famous poet and lute player, 210–263.
[103] *Ch'in-shih*, ch. 6: 琴之爲樂，行於堯舜三代之時，至戰國時，雅音廢而淫樂興，尙鏗鏘墜靡之聲，而厭和樂深靜之意，魏文侯當時之賢君，猶云吾端冕而聽古樂，則惟恐臥，況其下者乎，於是秦箏羌笛箜篌琵琶之類，迭興並進，而琴亡矣，漢興猶未暇復古，由河間漢王留神雅樂，孝宣時制氏，龍氏，趙氏，師氏之家，始於琴書謂之雅琴者，以別於俗樂也，又桓譚，孔衍，皆集琴操，乃馬融，蔡邕，以大儒名當時特好斯藝，時人翕然宗尙，阮嗣宗，嵇叔夜紹而倡*

§3 DISPOSITION AND DISCIPLINE OF THE LUTE PLAYER

*The lute should be played amidst charming scenery, or in the library, before flowers, during a moonlit night in autumn, while burning incense—rules defining the classes of people for whom the lute may be played, and for whom not—occasional sectarian views, excluding Buddhists—correct way of carrying the lute, lute pages—*CHʻIN-SHIH, *the lute chamber—*CHʻIN-SHÊ, *spiritual community of the lute*

Mountains and water (*shan-shui*)¹⁰⁴ is the name by which in artistic treatises the Chinese designate a landscape, thereby determining its two most essential elements; in mountains and streams, vast and imposing, the eternal *tao* shall reveal itself to the contemplative observer.

Under an old pine tree, sitting on a steep bank overhanging a flowing stream, absorbed in the contemplation of far mountain tops severed from the earth by floating mists, such is the scenery with which Chinese painters love to surround the lute player.

When, borne on the unworldly and serene tones of the lute, the mind of the player is purified and elevated to mystic heights, his soul may commune with the essence of the rugged rocks and vast stretches of water confronting him, and so he may experience a complete reunion with *tao*. This atmosphere of wide, open nature should always accompany the lute player; 'though his body be in a gallery or in a hall, his mind should dwell with forests and streams.'¹⁰⁵

It was not only aesthetical considerations, however, that caused this custom of preferably representing the lute player as confronted with an impressive mountain landscape. Doubtless here the function of the lute as an instrument to strengthen the vital essence of the player also was an important factor. Further, in painting, mysticism and magic

---

*之，自魏及晉，名儒高士，學者益多，而史冊之間，豈遑徧述，迨乎隨唐，搢紳多以是道爲務，而清言雅伎，罕嘗攻之，間有賢智有所論著，如呂渭，李良輔，陳拙，趙惟謙，李約，齋嵩，王大力，陳康士之徒，皆云有書，其名載於藝文志，然余所未覩，亦不聞其果精於琴與否.

104 山水

105 *Chʻin-sê-ho-pu, fan-li*, p. 8: 雖身列廊廟必意在林泉.

lie closely together. The contemplation of the beauty of streams and mountains may impart to the observer the vital forces that are inherent in nature, and thereby prolong his earthly life. 'The people of old say that landscape painters often live to an old age, because they feed upon mist and clouds. The entire scenery which they have before their eyes is one spring of life.'[106] This statement about the landscape painter may also be applied to the lute player, for the conception of the magical salutary influence of contemplating mountains and streams fits in exactly with some of the more materialistic aspects of *ch'in* ideology.[107]

The same double interpretation may be attached to the direct surroundings of the lute player when performing on the lute in the open: one should be near an old pine tree, admiring its gnarled, antique appearance. In the shade of the pines some cranes should be stalking, and the lute player should admire their graceful movements, modeling on them his finger technique. Since ancient times both pine tree and crane have been credited with possessing a special amount of vital essence, and therefore both are symbols of longevity.[108]

After some beautiful spot in the open, the abode of the scholar is the most suitable place for playing the lute. The ideal dwelling of the scholar should breathe an atmosphere of secludedness; it is surrounded by a garden, fenced off by pine trees or bamboos; narrow footpaths should meander among miniature rocks of interesting shapes and lotus ponds, leading to a small pavilion of rustic appearance, where the scholar may compose poetry or read his books. 'Where Ni Tsan dwelt there was the Ching-pi pavilion, breathing an atmosphere of profundity and remoteness from earthly things. There he had assembled several thousand books, all of which he had corrected with his own hand. On all sides there were arranged antique

---

[106] The Ch'ing painter Wang Yü 王昱, in his *Tung-chuang-lun-hua* 東莊論畫, 5th paragraph: 昔人謂山水家多壽，蓋煙雲供養，眼前無非生機.

[107] I may remark in passing that in other respects also we find the same notions connected with both painting and lute playing. In the same passage of the authoritative treatise on painting quoted above, it is said: 'Studying painting is a means for nurturing one's nature and emotional life —— it may elevate one to serenity' 學畫所以養性情 . . . . 迎靜氣.

Like the lute player when about to touch the strings of the lute, the painter too first has to make his mind pure and detached from all earthly desires: 'Before the painter takes up his brush, his mind must be aloof and his thoughts elated; when he starts painting, his spirit must be serene and his soul frozen' 未動筆前，須興高意遠，已動筆後，要氣靜神凝. (par. 8) This 'frozen' mental condition is a typical Taoist notion; see the passage of Lieh-tzu, quoted above on page 45. Finally it is said: 'Although painting is but one of the arts, it still is a manifestation of Tao' 畫雖一藝，其中有道. (para. 10)

[108] Below, in ch. VI, I shall discuss these associations in more detail.

sacrificial vessels and famous lutes, and the abode was surrounded by pine trees, cinnamon trees, orchids, bamboos, etc. It was fenced off by a high paling of poles and bamboo, suggesting aloofness and refined delicacy. Every time the rain had stopped and the wind had abated, Ni Tsan used to take his staff and wander about, just going where his steps led him. When his eye met with something which particularly struck him, he played his lute, thus finding aesthetic satisfaction. Those who saw him then knew that he was a man who dwelt outside this world.'[109]

Cultivating and arranging flowers, a favourite occupation of the retired scholar, also harmonizes with the lute player. 'One should play the lute for the cinnamon of the mountains, prune blossoms of the waterside, jasmine, gardenia, orchids from Fu-chien, mimosa, magnolia and similar flowers. Those with a pure fragrance but without loud colours are the best.'[110]

A moonlit night is dear to the lute player: 'In spring and autumn, when the weather is limpid and harmonious, even during the night people are often awake. Then the ten thousand sounds of emptiness are all silent, and moonlight fills the sky. When one lays the lute on his knees, and plays some small tunes, this also shall elate the feelings.'[111]

The moonlight makes the thirteen studs glitter, and so guides the hands of the player. Therefore these studs are often called *chin-hsing*, brilliant stars. 'But one should play after the first watch [after nine o'clock in the evening], and before the third watch [before 1 o'clock]; for before nine the noise of daily life has not yet become quiet, and after 1 o'clock one is too tired and sleepy.'[112]

Playing the lute on the knees is a favourite literary theme; it is more poetical to represent the musician sitting within the circle of his friends, or in a shaded valley, with the lute on his lap, than to have him seated behind the lute table. Still this position is not very suitable for executing the complicated finger technique. As a Ming scholar observes: 'When people play the lute on their knees, they can only

---

[109] Ni Tsan 倪瓚, style: Yün-lin, 1301–1374, famous painter and poet. This passage is taken from the *Ho-shih-yü-lin* 何氏語林, compiled by Ho Liang-chün 何良俊, sixteenth century. 倪雲林所居, 有清閟閣, 幽迥絕塵, 中有書數千卷. 皆手自校. 古鼎彝名琴陳列左右, 松桂蘭竹之屬敷舒繚繞, 其外則高木修篁蔚然深秀, 每雨止風收, 携杖履自隨逍遙容與, 遇會心處, 鼓琴自娛, 望之者識其爲世外人也.

[110] *K'ao-p'an-yü-shih* (App. II, 3): 對花, 宜共岩桂, 江梅, 茉莉, 簷葡, 建蘭, 夜合, 玉蘭等花, 清香而色不艶者爲雅. Orchids from Fu-chien are praised for their pale yellow and green colors.

[111] *Ibid.*: 對月, 春秋二候, 天氣澄和, 人亦中夜多醒, 萬籟咸寂, 月色當空, 橫琴膝上, 時作小調, 亦可暢懷.

[112] *Ch'ing-lien-fang-ch'in-ya* (App. II, 6) ch. III. 但須在一更後, 三更前, 蓋初更人聲未寂, 三更則人倦欲眠矣.

perform smaller tunes, such as they know very well. Otherwise it is impossible.'[113] From my own experience I would add that the only passages which can be executed correctly in this position are some preludes and codas, these being as a rule in the so-called 'floating sounds', that is to say the left hand does not press down the strings, but only touches them lightly, so as to produce harmonics.

When not rambling through the mountains to observe wild streams and gushing waterfalls, the scholar may still find by the quiet waterside in his own garden a congenial atmosphere for playing the lute. 'When a breeze floats through the pines, or when there is the rippling sound of a rivulet, then especially one should play the lute. For all these three things have natural tones, therefore they are in perfect harmony with each other. Or again by the pond near the library window where one smells the fragrance of the water lilies, or in the wood by the waterside, where the redolent waves wash the islets; when the light breeze is refreshing, and the swimming fish come to the surface to listen: what joy can exceed this?'[114]

As we saw in the foregoing chapter, when the lute is played incense must be burned. The handbooks for the lute recommend incense that gives a fine, crinkling smoke. Its subtle fragrance contributes to the exalted mood necessary for playing and appreciating lute music. For, 'The use of incense gives manifold benefits. When retired scholars, detached from the world, are sitting together discussing *tao* and its application, they burn incense to purify their hearts and rejoice their spirits. At the dead of night, when the morning moon is in the sky, artistic and sad poetical folk burn incense, and their hearts are elated and they whistle carelessly. By the bright window copying old famous scrolls, or leisurely humming, flywhisk in hand, or when reading at night under the lamp, incense is burned to drive away the demon of sleepiness. Therefore incense may be called the "Old Companion of the Moon."'[115]

The disposition of the lute player must be very much like that of a priest before sacrificing: he should be purified physically and mentally, freed from all earthly thoughts, and ready for communication with the deepest mysteries of life.

To attain to this, beside the more general rules to be found scat-

---

[113] *Tsun-shêng-pa-chien* (App. II, 4): 人膝上鼓琴, 惟純熟小操, 則可, 否, 亦不能.
[114] *K'ao-p'an-yü-shih* (App. II, 3): 臨水鼓琴偏宜於松風, 澗響之間, 三者皆自然之聲, 正合類聚, 或對軒窗池沼, 荷香撲人, 或水邊林下, 清漪芳沚, 微風洒然, 游魚出聽, 此樂何極.
[115] *Ibid.*: 香之爲用, 其利最溥, 物外高隱坐語道德焚之, 可以清心悅神, 四更殘月興味蕭騷焚之, 可以暢懷舒嘯, 晴窗搨帖, 揮塵閒吟, 篝燈夜讀, 焚以遠辟睡魔, 謂古伴月.

tered in the texts quoted in the foregoing chapter, the handbooks of the lute also prescribe a certain discipline. The rules of this discipline are summed up in various numerical categories. For instance, a handbook of the Ming period gives fourteen rules, decreeing when the lute may be played.

1. Meeting someone who understands music.
2. Meeting a suitable person.
3. For a Taoist recluse.
4. In a high hall.
5. Having ascended a storied pavilion.
6. In a Taoist cloister.
7. Sitting on a stone.
8. Having climbed a mountain.
9. Resting in a valley.
10. Roaming along the waterside.
11. In a boat.
12. Resting in the shadow of a forest.
13. When the two essences of nature are bright and clear.
14. In a cool breeze and when there is a bright moon.[116]

In nearly all other handbooks of the lute dating from the Ming and Ch'ing dynasties, these rules are given in about the same form. They are not very stringent, since by inserting the second rule the decision of for whom to play is practically left to the discretion of each individual performer. It should be noted that half of the items refer to playing the lute in the open air, and that two items especially mention Taoism.

The corresponding set of rules as to when the lute may not be played is much more precise and severe, and therefore the least observed. The same source gives these rules as follows:

1. When there is wind and thunder, and in rainy weather.
2. When there is a sun or moon eclipse.
3. In a court room.
4. In a market or shop.
5. For a barbarian.
6. For a vulgar person.
7. For a merchant.
8. For a courtesan.

---

[116] Yang Piao-chêng his in handbook of the lute (App. II, 13); 琴有十四宜彈. 遇知音, 逢可人, 對道士, 處高堂, 升樓閣, 在宮觀, 坐石上, 登山埠, 憩空谷, 遊水湄, 居舟中, 息林下, 值二氣清朗, 當清風明月.

9   After inebriation.
10 After having had sexual intercourse.
11 In dishevelled and strange clothes.
12 When flushed and covered with perspiration.
13 Not having washed one's hands and rinsed one's mouth.
14 In loud and noisy surroundings.[117]

For rule 3 other books give: 'Near a prison',[118] which seems more likely. With regard to rule 5, which forbids the playing of the lute for barbarians, the ch'in-pu urge especially strict observance of this. Another handbook of the Ming period explains this rule as follows: 'Outside China there are people who jabber barbarian tongues. As the sounds of their language are not correct, how can they ever harmonize with the correct words of the Holy Sages? Therefore one should not play the lute for them. The lute is fundamentally an instrument by the music of which the Sages and Superior Men of China nurture their nature and cultivate their persons. Such a thing is unknown in barbarian countries, therefore it is not allowed.'[119]

Rule 7, forbidding playing for a merchant, is amplified as follows: 'The lute is an instrument whereby the Holy Sages cultivate their persons and nurture their nature; [this includes] being contented in poverty, knowing moderation, and restricting luxury. But merchants have sharp appetites and strong desires. Therefore a tradesman's disposition runs counter to the Way of the Holy Man.'[120] This point is, however, subject to controversy. The merchant class is defended in these words: 'Bartering and trading are fundamentally not low and despicable things. The people of old often knew how to demonstrate holy truths by means of low things. Tzû-kung[121] accumulated great wealth; Fan Li[121] three times divided his wealth after having assembled it. When among the greatest of merchants are men like Tzû-kung and Fan Li, why then should they not be allowed to play the lute? It is far better to look only at the character.'[122]

---

[117] 琴有十四不宜彈．風雷陰雨，日月交蝕，在法司中，在市廛，對夷狄，對俗子，對商賈，對娼妓，酒醉後，夜事後，毀形異服，腋臊臭嗅，不盥手漱口，鼓動喧嚷．

[118] Yang Lun's *T'ai-ku-i-yin* (App. II, 14): 近囹圄．

[119] *Ch'in-ching* (App. II, 5) ch. 8: 非中土有鄉譚番語者，以其語音不正，安能合聖人之正音，故不宜也，琴本中國賢人君子養性修身之樂，非蠻貊之邦所有也，故不宜．

[120] *Ibid.* 琴本聖人修身養性，甘貧知止戒盈之樂，商賈乃利欲慳貪，市井之人反於聖人之道．

[121] The style of Tuan-mu Tzû 端木賜, famous disciple of Confucius who became a high official. Fan Li was a man from the Ch'un-ch'iu period, who three times accumulated great wealth and three times gave it away, as he preferred a life in retirement; cf. *Shih-chi* 史記, ch. 129, *Han-shu* 漢書 ch. 91.

[122] *Ch'in-ching*, ch. 8: 貿遷原非鄙賤事，古人每以鄙賤事而發神奇，子貢貨殖，范蠡三遷致富商賈之魁者以賜與蠡，撫琴豈有外之者哉，顧品格何如耶．

Rules 8 and 9 were taken least seriously. It is true that *courtesan* is a very elastic term, but considered in the light of the general principles there can be no doubt that it was meant to be interpreted very strictly. In practice, however, we find that this rule is made to apply only to the lowest kind of courtesan. Singing girls who brighten literary gatherings on old paintings are seen playing the lute, and novels cite lute playing as one of the accomplishments of the perfect courtesan. Other handbooks read for 8: 娼優, or 娼妓優伶, meaning: 'courtesans and actors'. As I have pointed out already, on p. 44 above, this exclusion of the actors was meant as a protest against the great numbers of actors from foreign countries who found employment at the Court.

Rule 9 also involved a delicate question, many of the most famous scholars being great wine-bibbers. The Ming scholar T'u Lung has found a mild and convenient explanation of this rule. He says: 'The disposition of people who play the lute is refined, they ought only to sip tea. Occasionally, however, they may use wine to stimulate their feelings, but only just sufficient to make them feel slightly exhilarated and no more. If one tries to play the lute when one is really dead drunk, then this is a great shame that cannot be tolerated.'[123]

The attitude which the *ch'in-pu* take regarding Buddhism is interesting. As I mentioned above, the lute was very popular with Buddhist monks, and several are cited in the lists of famous lute performers. Still, occasionally there appear in Taoist quarters sectarian views, and some handbooks of the early Ming period include an item 'Buddhist priests' in the list of people to whom it was not allowed to play or to teach the lute.[124] Naturally this rule met with much opposition, and as an extreme reaction some Buddhists tried to prove that the lute originated in India, since it is mentioned in the Buddhist sutras![125] Generally, however, lute amateurs were of too

---

[123] *K'ao-p'an-yü-shih* (App. II, 3): 飲酒. 彈琴之人風致清楚, 但宜啜茗, 間或用酒發興, 不過微有釀意而已, 若堆體酪羅葷膻蕩情狂, 飲致成醉者之狀, 以事琴此大醜最宜戒也.

[124] E.g., *Ch'in-ching*: 沙門子不宜鼓琴.

[125] The passage is taken from the 31st paragraph of the *Ssû-shih-êrh-chang-ching* (四十二章經, cf. *Taishō-issaikyō* 大正一切經 No. 784). The original obviously means some Indian stringed instrument, in Chinese translations of Buddhist texts always indicated by transcriptions of Sanskrit words. For more details I may refer to the useful essay by K. Hayashi: 'On Musical Terms in Chinese Buddhist Scriptures', in: *Tōyō ongaku kenkyū*, I, 1937 東洋音樂研究, 林謙三, 佛典に現れた樂器, 音樂, 舞踊.

That in the present case *ch'in* is used, is to be explained by the fact that this particular sutra was translated at a very early date (first century A.D.), when the correct renderings of Sanskrit technical terms had not yet been determined. The passage runs: 'Buddha asked a monk: "How do you occupy yourself when at home?" The monk answered: "I love to play the lute." Then Buddha asked: "What happens when the strings are strung too loose?"—"They give no sound."—"What happens when the strings are strung too tight?"—"Then they snap."—"What*

eclectic a disposition to be much impressed by either the extreme Taoist or Buddhist view, and they contented themselves with placidly quoting the two views together. A couple of extreme cases may here be cited: 'There was a monk called Chüeh (Enlightenment), who wished to study the lute under Master Pai-ho (White Crane). Master White Crane did not like the idea, and did not teach him. The monk was sad. Master White Crane said: "This is strange indeed! The study of a certain Śākyamuni originated from the doctrines of barbarians in western countries. But the lute represents the *tao* of the Holy Men of the Middle Kingdom, so it is not suitable for you. And he persisted in not teaching him." '[126]

'Master Huang-fu chose as literary name Tung-hsü-tzû (the Master of the Emptiness of the Cave). He explained the doctrines of Lao-tzû and Chuang-tzû by teaching lute Music, and his disciples were many. Among them there were also Buddhist monks. The Master said: How can bald pates and black robes fold in their arms the instrument of the Holy Men? And pointing with his flywhisk he told them to go away.'[127]

'To fold in the arms'[128] is the traditional term used for carrying the lute. Literature and art love to represent the ideal scholar roaming through the mountains or along the sides of streams, taking his lute with him, to play an appropriate melody when moved by a beautiful sight. Old paintings mostly show him accompanied by a boy servant, who carries the lute in its brocade cover in his arms. Also at home this boy was entrusted with the care for his master's lutes, and therefore such a boy is called *ch'in-tung*,[129] 'lute page'.

The handbooks give minute instructions as to how the lute is correctly carried. A Ming handbook[130] distinguishes two methods, the old and the new. Fig. 6, left, shows the old way: the ancients carried their lute with the upper board turned outwards and with the head in front and the tail, a little lower, behind. During the Ming dynasty

*happens when the strings are strung not too loose and not too tight?"—"Then all sounds come forth harmoniously."—Then the Buddha said: "The study of Truth is the same: if the heart is tuned correctly, one may obtain the Truth" ' 佛問一僧, 汝處家爲何業, 對曰愛彈琴, 佛問緩絃如何, 曰不鳴矣, 絃急如何, 曰聲絕矣, 緩急得中如何, 曰諸音普矣, 佛曰學道亦然, 心須調適, 道可得矣. This text, taken from the *Ch'in-ching*, differs slightly from that given in the Buddhist Canon.

126 *Ch'in-ching* (App. II, 5): 有僧名覺者, 學琴於道人白鶴子之門, 鶴子惡而不受, 僧不悅, 鶴子曰怪哉, 釋氏之學, 出於西方, 夷狄之教, 琴乃中國聖人之道, 非爾所宜也, 竟不傳.

127 *Ibid*.: 皇甫先生號洞虛子, 講老莊之學, 以傳琴鳴, 弟子甚眾, 而沙門雜然, 先生曰豈有禿髮緇衣而抱聖人之器乎, 悉麾去之.

128 抱

129 琴童

130 *Yang-ch'un-t'ang-ch'in-pu* 陽春堂琴譜, by the same authors who composed the *Ch'in-ching*.

people followed the new way (fig. 6, right) turning the bottom board outwards, a position which was said to ensure a firm hold.

Next to Buddhism, there is another question connected with the discipline of the lute player which has given rise to some controversy in the *ch'in-pu*, viz. whether one is allowed to accompany one's lute play with singing or not.

#6: Carrying the lute, from the *Yang-ch'un-t'ang-ch'in-pu*.

In the handbooks of the lute this question is discussed as *chan-wên*[131] (to cut out the words), *wên* standing here for both the text of the tunes and for prefaces and colophons added to them.

The Ming prince Tsai-yü says, in his standard work on music, *Yüeh-lü-ch'üan-shu*,[132] that music on stringed instruments in general is impossible without the accompaniment by the human voice. In the chapter *Tsao-man-ku-yüeh-pu* he devotes a special section to this question, entitled: 'Discussing how the ancients did not sing without accompanying the words on the strings, nor played a stringed instrument without singing to it.'[133] This he calls a 'fixed custom'[134] of the ancients; singing without accompaniment, or playing stringed instruments without singing he calls an 'exception'.[135] Then he ob-

131 刪文
132 朱載堉, 樂律全書
133 操縵古樂譜；論古人非弦不歌,非歌不弦

134 *chang-shih* 常事
135 變

serves: 'People today when reciting poetry cannot accompany these songs on the lute; that is because the tradition of the lute is lost.'[136]

Some among the composers of *ch'in-pu* are of the same opinion as Tsai-yü: in their notation of the tunes, they print the *chien-tzŭ*[137] and the corresponding words of the tune in parallel vertical columns. This method is followed by, e.g., Yang Piao-chêng.[138] Others add the text of the tune separately, before or after the notation. On the other hand there were also many lute players who maintained that to sing when playing the lute did not conform to the sacred character of this music.

The most sensible attitude seems to be that taken by Kuo Yü-chai in his *Tê-yin-t'ang-ch'in-pu*.[139] In his prefatory remarks he says: 'The lute stands for the original harmony of what is truly from Heaven in man; its tones rise from the serenity of the soul. Therefore I do not like to restrict this music with words. For then the tones become confused, and the melody and rhythm are impeded. Therefore as a rule I have kept to the music, and left out the words. Still there are also cases where, if the words are left out, it is impossible to get the tones right. Therefore, where the text should be cut out, I cut it out, and where it should not be left out, I preserved it to show the meaning of the melody to the player.'[140]

In this *ch'in-pu* all old melodies which have not from ancient times been connected with a special poem or essay, are given in notation only, whilst such as have always been associated with a definite text (as, e.g., some odes in the *Book of Odes*), are given together with the words. This system seems very commendable. When playing through the various tunes of the lute repertoire, one finds that they show a considerable difference in style: the music of some is evidently nothing but the accompaniment of a song, whilst others could hardly be accompanied by the human voice, and are apparently meant as instrumental music only. Two good examples may be found in the *Kao-shan-liu-shui* and *Lu-ming*.[141] The former is a highly expressive composition, impossible to accompany with the voice; the other, on the contrary, is simple and more melodical, and is doubtless a reproduction of one of the tunes to which this ancient ode was sung. In other cases it is more difficult to decide to which category a given tune

---

136 今人歌詩與琴不能相入，蓋失其傳耳.
137 減字
138 Appendix II, 13.
139 郭裕齋, 德音堂琴譜, published in 1691.
140 琴乃天眞元韻，音出自然，不喜以文拘之，拘之則音雜，滯其高下抑揚，故取音而棄文，然亦有舍文而不能成音者，故可刪者刪之，不可刪者存以備觀焉.
141 高山流水；鹿鳴

belongs: the decision must be left to the taste of each individual player.

In view of the present condition of lute music I hardly think it advisable to use the lute for the accompaniment of songs, since its music, for practical reasons, is not suited for this. Already during the Sung dynasty the finger technique had become so complicated that the lute could not be used for accompaniment. 'The lute players of the present age do not sing while playing, but try to obtain beauty by complicated sounds.'[142]

#7: Playing the lute in ideal surroundings. A painting by the famous Ming artist Shên Chou (沈周 1427–1509).

Often in the house of a lute amateur a special room or bower is set apart for playing; such a place is called *ch'in-shih*[143] (lute chamber). A Ming treatise[144] sets out the following conditions for such an abode: 'It should truly reproduce the tones, and not sound hollow. The best is a room in a storied building; there the boards of the ceiling ensure that the tones are not dispersed, and the empty space beneath makes the tones ring through. If one chooses a high hall or a spacious chamber, then the tones are dispersed and thin. And when one plays in a narrow room or in a small house the tones cannot ring

---

[142] 近世琴家所謂操弄者，皆無歌辭，而繁聲以爲美; *Ch'in-shih*, in App. II, 2.
[143] 琴室
[144] *K'ao-p'an-yü-shih* (App. II, 3): 琴室宜實，不宜虛，最宜重樓之下，蓋上有樓板則聲不散，其下空曠則聲透徹，若高堂大廈，則聲散漫，斗室小軒，則聲小達，如平屋中，則於地下埋一大缸，缸中縣一銅鐘，上用板鋪，亦可，幽人逸士或於喬松修竹，岩洞石室，清曠之處，地清境寂，更有泉石之勝，則琴聲愈清，與廣寒月殿何異哉.

through. If the building consists of only one floor, a big jar should be buried underneath. In this jar a bronze bell should be suspended, and then the jar should be covered by boards. Wise men living in retirement also take for their lute chamber tall pines and high bamboos, or a cavern in the rocks; in such a pure and airy abode in the serenity of nature and quiet surroundings, and especially when there is the impressive sight of a rivulet babbling over stones, the tones of the lute shall gain in clearness. Is not such a place like the Moon Palace of Wide Coolness?'[145] It seems difficult to justify the suggestion for burying a jar with a bell by the laws of acoustics, but it must have appealed to the imagination of the lovers of lute music. Other Ming authors[146] criticize this statement, which seems to be based on a story told about the Han poet Ssû-ma Hsiang-ju:[146] he used to play the lute on a special terrace called *ch'in-t'ai*. When later the state Wei attacked Shu, and soldiers camped on that place and dug trenches, they found more than twenty big jars, which had served to make the music resound.[147]

Finally we have to consider in greater detail the tendency to keep the study of the lute reserved to a small circle of the elect.

Above I quoted some rules which restrict the number of persons to whom the lute may be taught. With regard to this group of qualified persons the expression *ch'in-shê*[148] is often met with in the literature on the lute. This literally means: 'lute association'. When the term is used for a group of amateurs of the lute who happen to live in the same district, and who are in regular contact with each other, this translation suffices. But generally the word *shê* in this expression has a much wider meaning; as this special significance is not indicated in dictionaries, I will treat it here in some detail.

Especially since the latter half of the Ming dynasty, in circles of scholars of elegant interests and cultivated taste who were connoisseurs of raising chrysanthemums, of flower arrangement, of appreciating incense, of nursing orchids, etc., there came into existence a fixed tradition, canonizing the right methods for pursuing

---

[145] Refers to a story told in the *Lung-ch'êng-lu* 龍城錄 (ascribed to the T'ang poet Liu Tsung-yüan 柳宗元, 773–819): 'Once the Emperor Ming-huang together with one of his Taoist masters made a journey to the moon on a full-moon night, where he found a palace called "Abode of Wide Coolness and Pure Emptiness."' 廣寒清虛之府 This magic journey is the subject of a well-known lute melody. See below, pp. 89 ff.

[146] *Ch'ing-lien-fang-ch'in-ya* (cf. Appendix II, 6), ch. 3: 前輩理琴處，或埋甕于地下，此說恐妄傳 (2nd century A.D.):

[147] *Ch'ien-ch'üeh-chü-lei-shu*. 潛確居類書 (pub. 1630), ch. 79: 司馬相如好鼓琴，有琴臺在浣溪正路，金花寺北，魏伐蜀，于此下營，掘塹得大甕二十餘口，蓋以響琴也

[148] 琴社

these hobbies, and especially the right mental attitude to be adopted towards them. Some scholars noted down these traditions, which were called *yo* 約 (covenants, or rules). So the well-known essayist Chang Ch'ao wrote a *Wan-yüeh-yo*[149] (Rules for Enjoying the Moon), Chiang Chih-lan wrote a *Wên-fang-yo* (Covenant of the Library).[150] A *Ch'in-yo* (Covenant for the Lute) will be found below.[151] Such treatises on various subjects dear to the literatus bear a very personal character, and are mostly written in a chatty vein, contrary to those called *pu or shih*, which strive to be more scientific.

Now the term *shê* may be considered as being an expansion of *yo*; *shê* denotes the total of all people who know and faithfully observe the rules fixed by tradition for the pursuance of some elegant hobby. It does not imply any social or local unity; anyone who raises chrysanthemums in the correct way is a member of the *Chü-shê*[152] (Spiritual Association of Lovers of the Chrysanthemum), whether he lives in Peking or in Canton, or anywhere else. In such cases *shê* is perhaps best translated as 'Spiritual Community'. We find, e.g., a booklet entitled: *Chü-shê-yo*[153] (Covenant of the Spiritual Community of the Chrysanthemum Lovers) and another called *Ku-huan-shê-yo* (Covenant of the Spiritual Community of the Booklovers).[154] Books of this class form a special branch in Chinese literature, important because, next to the novels, they are sources of valuable data on the private life of the literary class.

As the lute was so highly valued by the literati, it goes without saying that in the handbooks for the lute the *ch'in-shê* is repeatedly referred to. In the *Ch'in-ching* the rules indicating to whom and where the lute may be played are prefaced by a short notice, entitled *ch'in-shê*, saying: 'In a modest dwelling[155] there should be a stand for laying the lute on, and a case for storing it away. There should be a flywhisk, a sonorous stone, brushes and ink to keep the lute company

---

149 張潮, style: Shan-lai 山來, 17th cent.; 玩月約

150 江之蘭, style: Shê-chêng 舍徵; 文房約. This and the *Wan-yüeh-yo* are to be found in the *T'an-chi-ts'ung-shu* 檀几叢書, a collection of the works of various minor authors of the Ch'ing period, published in 1695 by Wang Cho 王晫. All the books reprinted in it are important for the study of the domestic life and leisurely pastimes of the literati.

151 琴約. See pp. 82 ff.

152 菊社

153 菊社約

154 古歡社約. The *Chü-shê-yo* was written by Ti I 狄億, the *Ku-huan-shê-yo* by Ting Hsiung-fei 丁雄飛; both books are to be found in the *T'an-chi-ts'ung-shu*, mentioned above. The latter contains some very sane suggestions for bibliophiles: If a book is borrowed it may not be kept longer than a fortnight; one should not entrust a borrowed book to someone else to return it. 借書不得踰半月, 還書不得托人轉到.

155 *huan-tu*; cf. *Book of Rites, Li-chi*, Ch. XXXVIII, 10.

and there should be lustrous flowers and cranes to be its friends. All these things belong to the domain[156] of the lute. Those who are not in this class do not belong to the Spiritual Community of the lute.'[157]

The same book on the next page describes which people are qualified for being considered as members of the *ch'in-shê*; in conclusion I translate this passage.

'All who study the lute must be accomplished scholars, and they must be good at reciting poetry.

Their appearance should be pure and detached, suggesting antique originality; they may not be coarse and vulgar.

Their minds should be benign and tender, they should be virtuous and righteous, able to be content even in poverty, and always firmly clinging to their principles.

Their words should be true and reliable, they should not strive after superficial beauty or after obtaining a thin varnish of culture.'[158]

§4 SELECTED TEXTS

THE five texts relating to *ch'in* ideology translated below are purposely taken from sources that in both date and quality differ widely.

The first is the section on the lute taken from the chapter on music of the *Fêng-su-t'ung-i*,[159] a miscellaneous collection of encyclopedic character, compiled by Ying Shao.[160] This text furnishes us with a good example of the pure Confucianist view.

The second text is a small treatise by a well-known Confucianist scholar of the Yüan dynasty, Wu Ch'ên,[161] author of many learned books on the Classics. These two texts are both written in a polished literary style, as befits the high scholarly standing of their authors.

Their style contrasts sharply with that of the clumsily written third text, one of the introductory chapters of a handbook for the

---

[156] *t'ung-chi* 通籍, lit. a signboard hanging near the gate of the Palace, on which were written the name and full description of those people who were allowed to go in and out freely; *i-yang* 嶧陽, lit. 'on the southern slope of I Mountain', the place of origin of the lute—a mythical emperor was said to have found there the right sort of wood for making the first lute.

[157] 琴社. 環堵案簦以受桐，貌磬翰墨以侶桐，瓊葩僊禽桐之侑也，江風山月桐之供也，此皆通籍于嶧陽者也，非山族也不在社黨.

[158] 凡學琴必須要有文章能吟咏者，貌必要有清奇古怪不粗俗者，心必要有仁慈德義能，甘貧守志者，言必要有誠信無浮華薄飾者.

[159] 風俗通義, chapter VI.

[160] 應劭, style: Chung-yüan 仲遠, second century A.D.

[161] 吳澄, style: Yu-ch'ing 幼清, 1249–1331.

lute dating from the Ming dynasty.¹⁶² This book was compiled by Yang Piao-chêng, a professional lute expert of very low scholarly standing; evidently he has difficulty in expressing his thoughts freely in the literary medium, and often relapses into colloquial expressions. Still, as he was a clever musician, who knew how to recast the famous old tunes in a simpler but yet charming form (such as might be executed even by mediocre lute players), and because of the extraordinarily great number of copies in which his book was printed, it was one of the most popular handbooks of the Ming period. Even now copies can be easily purchased in Chinese and Japanese bookshops.

The chapter that I have chosen here for translation is interesting because it shows the quaint admixture of heterogeneous elements that *ch'in* ideology had come to be.

The same general remarks hold good for the fourth text, one of the introductory chapters of the *Wu-chih-chai-ch'in-pu*, a handbook which may be called the most popular guide for lute players during the Ch'ing dynasty. The editor of this book was also a mediocre scholar, but an excellent musician. The versions of the tunes given here are very attractive, and rich in subtle nuances. Moreover there have been added to the notation special marks, indicating the rhythm. It is still the handbook most widely used by lute players today, and may be obtained at very little cost in China and Japan.

The book of Yang Piao-chêng was an individual production; this handbook, however, is a typical example of a *ch'in-pu* that was composed by a group of students gathered round a famous master.¹⁶³ The editor was not a great stylist: he patched together several passages from other sources without being able to produce smoothly running prose. In his preface, printed in his own handwriting, he tries to cover the meagre contents by using all kinds of strange and antiquated characters, instead of the ordinary forms, a process which, when indulged in too much, is condemned as vulgar by Chinese literati.

The fifth text is *Covenant for Transmitting the Lute*, a treatise of the type discussed above, page 69. The author is Ch'êng Yün-chi, who is also the compiler of a *ch'in* handbook, the *Ch'êng-i-t'ang-ch'in-pu*.¹⁶⁴,¹⁶⁵

---

¹⁶² For characters and further particulars, see App. II, 13 and 15.

¹⁶³ For more details see App. II, 15.

¹⁶⁴ 程允基, style: Yü-shan 寓山, 18th century; 誠一堂琴譜, preface dated 1705.

¹⁶⁵ For other texts from various sources which illustrate the principles of *ch'in* ideology, the reader is referred to Chapter VI, § 4: 'Some Famous Stories and Much-quoted Passages Relating to the Lute'.

THE LUTE

BY YING SHAO, SECOND CENTURY A.D.

Reverently I read in the '*Shih-pên*:[166] 'Shên-nung made the lute.' In the *Book of History*: 'Shun played the five-stringed lute, and sang the song "Southern Wind", and the Realm was regulated.' In the *Book of Odes* it is said: 'I have elegant guests, the *sê* is played, the lute is played.'

The accomplished lute includes all music, it embraces all of the eight sorts of sounds.[167] Of those things the Superior Man always has around him, he loves the lute best, and he does not suffer it to be separated from him.

The lute need not necessarily be displayed in the Ancestral Hall or during the clan festivals, it is not like bells and drums that must needs be suspended on carved standards. Though [the lute be played] in a poor dwelling or a desolate street, deep in the mountains or in a profound valley, it will lose nothing [of its true meaning].

The lute is considered to hold the mean between great and small music, and its tones are harmonious. Its heavy sounds are not boisterous so as to be confusing, its light sounds are not too weak so as to be inaudible. It is suited for harmonizing the human mind, and may move man to the improvement of his heart. Therefore, the word 'lute' means 'restraining', and the word 'accomplished' means 'rectifying', indicating that the Superior Man keeps to the right by restraining himself. By right and accomplished sounds, right thoughts are instigated, therefore the good heart is victorious, and falsehood and wickedness are repressed. Therefore the Holy Sages and Superior Men of ancient times carefully watched over their emotions; and when falsehood arose they restrained it; when they met with something good they made it their own. When they had leisure they could act freely because they had perfected their thoughts. When there was something that oppressed them, when their Way was obstructed, so that they could not practise it, or again when they could not execute their teachings when serving the State, then [all these things] they expressed in the lute, in order to give vent to their thoughts, and proclaim them to posterity. The songs they composed when they

---

[166] A treatise by Liu Hsiang (劉向, 77-6 B.C.), lost since early times.

[167] That is, the sounds of the instruments made of stone, metal, silk, bamboo, wood, skin, gourd, and clay.

were able to practise their Way they called hymns, by this term expressing the beauty and elevatedness of the Way they practised. They did not grant themselves one moment rest, they were neither overbearing nor effusive, they loved rites, but they did not try to exalt their own thoughts. The songs they composed when oppressed and melancholic they called elegies, by this name indicating that even when meeting with disasters or falling into danger, when being oppressed and reduced to necessity, although steeped in sorrow and unable to reach their aims, they still kept to the rites and righteousness, without fear and without misgivings, rejoicing in the Way and not loosing their consistency.

When Po Tzû-ya[168] played the lute, Chung Tzû-ch'i listened. When Tzû-ya in his thoughts dwelt on high mountains, Tzû-ch'i said: 'How excellent! Impressing like the T'ai-shan!' When a moment later Tzû-ya in his thoughts dwelt by flowing streams, Tzû-ch'i again said: 'How excellent! Broad and flowing like rivers and streams!' When Tzû-ch'i died, Po [Tzû]-ya broke his lute and tore the strings, and all his life did not play any more, since he now deemed the world not enough to play for.

At present the length of the lute is four *ch'ih* five *ts'un* [c. 4½ feet, ed.], thus featuring the Four Seasons and the Five Elements. The seven strings symbolize the Seven Stars.[169]

TEN RULES FOR PLAYING THE LUTE

BY WU CH'ÊN, 1249-1331

1 When laying the lute on the table one should see that it sticks out on the right side a hand's breadth, so that one may easily turn the tuning pegs. If one seats oneself exactly opposite

---

[168] One of the most famous lute players of antiquity; for more details, see Chapter IV: 'The Significance of the Tunes', pp. 97-8.

[169] 琴. 謹按世本，神農作琴，尙書，舜彈五絃之琴，歌南風之詩，而天下治，詩云，我有嘉賓，鼓瑟鼓琴，雅琴者，樂之統也，與八音並行，然君子所常御者，琴最親密，不離於身，非必陳設於宗廟鄉黨，非若鐘鼓羅列於虡懸也，雖在窮閭陋巷，深山幽谷，猶不先琴，以爲琴之大小得中，而聲音和，大聲不譁人而流漫，小聲不湮滅而不聞，適足以和人意氣，感人善心，故琴之爲言禁也，雅之爲言正也，言君子守正以自禁也，夫以正雅之聲，動感正意，故善心勝，邪惡禁，是以古之聖人君子，愼所以自感，因邪禁之，適故近之，間居則爲從容以致思焉，如有所窮困，其道閉塞，不得施行，及有所通達而用事，則著之於琴，以舒其意，以示後人，其道行和樂而作者，命其曲曰暢，暢者，言其道之美暢，猶不敢自安，不驕不溢，好禮不以暢其意也，其遇閉塞憂愁而作者，命其曲曰操，操者，言遇菑遭害，困厄窮迫，雖怨恨失意，猶守禮義不懼不憾，樂道而不失其操者也，伯子牙鼓琴，鍾子期聽之，而意在高山，子期曰善哉乎，巍巍若泰山，頃之間而意在流水，鍾子又曰善哉乎，湯湯若江河，子期死，伯牙破琴也絃，終身不復鼓，以爲世無足爲音聲者，今琴長四尺五寸，法四時五行也，七絃者，法七星也．

the fifth stud, then one can freely execute all the movements of the left and right hand.

2 The right hand when attacking the strings should not go farther to the left than the fourth stud; when one attacks the strings near the bridge, the tones produced will be true. The finger technique should not be floating, nor should it be heavy and confused. The right hand should touch the strings lightly, but the left hand should press them down firmly.

3 When one plays the lute, regardless of whether there are other people present or not, one must always behave as if one were in the presence of a superior. The body should be erect and straight, the spirit should be clear, the mind at rest, the look concentrated, the thoughts serene. Then the touch of the fingers naturally is correct, and the strings emit no wrong sounds.

4 When producing sounds one should aim at simplicity, and also at naturalness. Its wonderfulness lies in the correct shifting over from the light touch to the heavy, and in applying correctly ritardando and accelerando. When the finger technique is applied clumsily and wrongly, the measure is not rigidly observed, and when one is striving after specious effects, the melody is spoilt and confused. These are all deficiencies, which should fundamentally be corrected.

5 The basis of the lute consists in simplicity and serenity. Therefore one should not try to add extra sounds, but rigidly observe the indications for the finger technique; then one shall get a solemn, controlled style of playing, worthy to be seen. If one does not take care in attacking the strings to discriminate between flesh sounds and nail sounds, if the various movements are not linked up correctly, and if, moreover, while executing the attack with the thumb, the chords, and the upward and downward harpeggio, the hand and arm are stiff and not correctly adjusted, then one has not yet achieved the wonderful finger technique.

6 The quality of the lute tends to loftiness. Therefore, if while playing one changes one's mien and allows the eyes to wander, or worse, if the body is stooping, the feet put one atop the other, the head shaking, and the shoulders moving up and down, then an atmosphere of unelegance is created. Knowing these deficiencies one should correct them. Moreover, when

the sentiments are not elated, all kinds of flaws and shortcomings arise, and one had better give up the lute altogether.

7 When the ancients composed tunes for the lute, they sometimes aimed at expressing leisurely and satisfied feelings, but sometimes they wished to express their melancholy. Therefore one must understand the meaning of a tune. If one just plays the music as it is written, one will not be able to express the sentiments of the composer. And how then shall the mood of the ancients be found in the wood and the silk?

8 In studying the lute, getting down to the essence is the most important. If one tries to learn too much [at one time], how then shall one be able to grasp the essence? Therefore, if one has succeeded in getting an eminent Master to teach some tunes, one should play these same tunes through again and again, lest one forget the significance inherent in them. Moreover, wonderful music arises from constant practice. This is what is meant by the saying that only by incessant application can one derive satisfaction from the strings. If not, then because one studies too many different tunes, the shortcomings shall be many, and it shall be as if thorns grew on one's fingers.

9 The saying 'Rigidly observe the rites by respecting the Way' means, when applied to lute playing, not to play when there is wind or rain, or in a common atmosphere. But if one meets someone who understands the deeper meaning of music, or having ascended a storied building, or a mountain, if one rests in a valley, sits on a rock, or tarries by a stream, or when the two original principles are in harmony, then all these conditions are to be called excellent and suited for the lute. On the contrary, the presence of a vulgar man, a courtesan, an actor, a drunken and noisy atmosphere, these all are bad conditions for playing the lute. Therefore one should be discreet in choosing the time and place to play the lute.

10 Playing the lute is meant for nurturing one's nature, therefore one should not aim at acquiring fame by it. If one meets a kindred spirit, then one should play; if not, then one had better put the lute in its cover, and reserve it for one's own enjoyment. If one plays the lute before people who do not

like it, or before disorderly and vulgar persons who boast of their qualities, how can one not be ashamed? In such a case one cannot but hastily conceal the fact that one plays the lute.[170]

MISCELLANEOUS REMARKS ON PLAYING THE LUTE

BY YANG PIAO-CHÊNG, SIXTEENTH CENTURY

THE meaning of the lute is restraining the false and bringing back to the right, in order to harmonize the heart of man. Therefore the Holy Sages made the lute for regulating their persons and for nurturing the harmony of their emotions. Restraining wanton extravagance, and rejecting excessive luxury, one should cherish the music of the Holy Sages, that thereby one may learn the mysterious wonder of their souls, and so rejoice in their thoughts.

Whosoever plays the lute must choose a pure dwelling or a spacious hall; or he must ascend a storied building; or he may tarry by trees and rocks, or climb a steep cliff; or again he may ramble along the verdant bank of a stream, or he may dwell in a monastic abode.

---

[170] 琴言十則．一．置琴案上輆前須容掌許，以便轉輆，身坐正對五徽，則左右手往來通便
一．彈絃不得過四徽，蓋近岳則聲實故也，下指不得浮漂，亦不得重濁，入絃欲淺，按絃欲實
一．鼓琴時無問有人無人，常如對長者在前，身須端直，且神解，意閒，視專，思靜，自然指不虛，下絃不錯鳴
一．取聲欲淡，又欲自然，其妙在於輕重切當緩急得宜，若布指拙惡節奏疏懶與艷巧多端聲調煩雜，皆琴之疵纇，不可不戒
一．琴資簡靜，無增容聲，然須理會手勢，則威儀可觀，若絃不問甲肉，前指不副後指，而且擧撮拂歷掌腕蹲探無法，是尚不得妙指，雖在彈，笑以爲哉
一．琴品欲高，若撫琴時，色變，視流，甚至僞身疊足，搖首，舞屑，氣象殊覺不雅，卽知而禁之，則又神情不暢瑕纇叢生，不如己之可也
一．古人製曲，或怡情自適，或憂憤傳心，須要識其意旨，若徒取聲，則情與製違，古人風調，何有於絲桐之閒
一．琴學貴精，多則便不能精，如從明師學得數曲，當時調弄，旣不失其遺意，而且妙音出於熟習，所謂密爾自娛於斯絃也，不然多學多廢，寧免手生荊棘何
一．日盡禮以尊其道，如風雨市塵不彈是也，至遇知音，升樓閣，登山，憩谷，坐石，遊泉，値二氣之清朗，皆際勝而宜於琴者，反是而對俗子，娼優，與夫酒穢塵囂，皆惡景也，自當善藏其用
一．彈琴養性，非取必於人知，故有好而邀者，宜爲一鼓，不則囊琴自適而已，若奏曲不好之前，與誇能流俗之士，亦幾無恥，亟須韜晦

'Wooden sounds' refers to the vibrato and other graces, produced by rubbing the string on the surface of the sound-box. *Yin* and *jou* are described below in Chapter v, § 3, nos. 41 and 42. Master Ch'i-yen was a lute player from Szuchuan Province (cf. *op. cit.* ch. XI, page 7 *verso*); Yeh-lü-ch'u-ts'ai in his later years adopted Ch'i-yen's classical style, and abandoned the technique taught by his earlier masters Mi-ta 彌大 and Wan-sung 萬松 (cf. *op. cit.* ch. XII, page 2).

I add in passing that Yeh-lü-ch'u-ts'ai was especially interested in the melody *Kuang-ling-san*. This melody I discuss in some detail in my book *Hsi K'ang and his Poetical Essay on the Lute* (Monumenta Nipponica Monographs, Tokyo 1941 (rev. ed., 1969) ch. 3[4]). There a reference should be added to the excellent article by Tai Ming-yang 戴明揚, entitled *Kuang-ling-san-k'ao* 廣陵散考, and published in the *Fu-jên-hsüeh-chih* 輔仁學志, Peking 1936, vol. v, nos. 1 and 2.

When the two essences of nature are balanced, lofty and clear, on a night when there is a cool breeze and a brilliant moon, he must burn incense in a quiet abode. He must steady his heart, introvert his thoughts, so that soul and body are in complete harmony. Then only shall his soul communicate with the spirit of Nature, and he shall be in harmony with the wonderful Way.

If there is not present a man who understands [the inner meaning of] music, one had better play to the cool breeze and to the brilliant moon, to the dark-green pines and quaintly-shaped stones, to an ape of the mountain tops or to an old crane. Then one naturally grasps the inner meaning of this music. When one knows its meaning, one understands its tendency; when one understands its tendency, then one may [truly] understand the music. Though the music be technically well executed, if its tendency is not understood, what benefit shall it give? It is nothing more than a big noise that avails nothing.

In the first place one's personality should be aloof [from all material things], and still elegant, and one's bearing must be pure. Further, the finger technique should be correct, the touch should be correct, the mouth should be bearded and the belly full of ink [i.e. one should be a mature literatus]. Only when these six qualities are all provided for may one take part in the Way of the lute.

If one wishes to play the lute, one should first see that one is dressed correctly: either a gown of crane-feathers, or a ceremonial robe. [For] only if one knows the appearance of the Holy Sages shall one be able to appreciate their instrument [i.e. the lute]. Next one should wash the hands, burn incense; then one should approach the table and lay the lute on its stand. One should be seated opposite the fifth stud, in such a way that this stud faces the heart of the player. Then both hands should be lifted. The heart is regulated, the body is steadied, it does not incline to right or left, or sway forward or backward. The feet should be planted on the earth like the stance of an archer.

One should take care that the right hand touches the correct string, and that the movements of the left hand are correct. The hands should be kept low and evenly balanced; they should not be raised unduly high. Left and right hand should touch the strings on the places indicated by the studs [in such a way that] the right hand is near the bridge; the nails of the hand should not be long, but just about the breadth of one grain. The strings should be touched half by the flesh and half by the nail; then the sound is not dry, but clear and rich. [The left hand] should press the board as if it would penetrate the wood. The outward and inward touch of the thumb, index and middle finger of the right hand, the vibrato, vibrato ritardando of the left hand, and the quick movements of the right hand over one or more strings, all these touches should be fully expressed, they should not be executed loosely and hastily, to give the impression of a light and flowing style. If one aims at specious dexterity and playing to the eye of the public, one had better leave the lute alone and take to acting; if one aims at producing ornate tones that captivate the ear, one had better drop the lute and take to the cither.[171]

The greatest emphasis must be laid on [distinguishing between] the light and heavy, the swift and slow touch, and between the decrescendo and crescendo.

When one's self is naturally aloof and earnest, then one shall correspond to the Mystery of the Way, and one's soul shall melt together with the Way. Therefore it is said that successfully executing music is not caused by the hands, but by the heart, that music is not produced by notes, but by the Way. When one does not strive to express music in tones, but lets it come naturally, then one may experience the Harmony of Heaven and Earth, then one may be in communication with the virtue of the Universal Spirit.

Also it is said: The vibrato, the vibrato ritardando, the ascending and the descending attack of the left hand, the light or the heavy, the swift or the slow touch of the right hand, all these things can hardly be explained in words. They can be understood only by a man of learning.[172]

---

[171] In connection with this plea for a simple style of lute playing I cite the following poem by the great statesman and scholar Yeh-lü-ch'u-ts'ai (耶律楚材, 1190–1244), who besides his many other accomplishments also was an expert lute player. This poem is found in his collected works, the *Chan-jan-chü-shih-wên-chih* 湛然居士文集 (*Szu-pu-ts'ung-k'an* edition, ch. xi, page 7 *recto*).

愛棲嚴彈琴聲法二絕
須信希聲是大音. 猱多則亂吟多淫.
世人不識棲嚴意. 祇愛時宜熱鬧琴.
多著吟揉熱客耳. 強生取與媚俗情.
純音簡易誰能識. 却道棲嚴無木聲.

Two poems on my loving the lute-technique of Master Ch'i-yen.

I

I firmly believe that rarefied tones constitute the real great music,

Frequent use of vibrato ritardando confuses the melody, frequent use of other vibrato leads to a lax style.
People of the present day do not understand the meaning of Master Ch'i-yen's music,
They only love the fashionable style, and play the lute so as to produce a rude noise.

II

Frequent application of vibrato grates upon the ears of the listener,
This style is aimed only at captivating the common fancy.
The pure tones are simple—but who can appreciate them?
People only say that Ch'i-yen does not use the wooden sounds.

[172] 彈琴雜說. 琴者禁邪歸正以和人心. 是故聖人之制將以治身育其情性和矣, 抑乎淫蕩,*

ON THE LUTE OF HIGH ANTIQUITY

FROM THE WU-CHIH-CHAI-CH'IN-PU, PUB. 1721

In olden times when Fu Hsi[173] ruled all under Heaven, he looked upwards and contemplated, he looked downwards and investigated. Through his supernatural influence he made the map rise from the Yung river [cf. *Shu-ching*, ch. 'Ku-ming', 19],[174] and accordingly he drew the Eight Triagrams. Then listening to the winds of the Eight Directions he made the sonorous tubes.[175] On I Mountain[176] he selected a lonely dryandra tree, and making the Yin principle complete the Yang principle, he created Elegant Music, calling it Lute.

Lute means 'restraining', that is to say restraining falsehood and guarding against wantonness. It further implies bringing to the fore benevolence and righteousness, and causing the return to the Way; it is a means for cultivating the person and regulating the mind; it makes man return to what is truly of Heaven in him;[177] it makes him forget his earthly shape and reunites him with Emptiness. The spirit becomes concentrated, and melts into the Great Harmony.[178]

The lute is made to measure three *ch'ih* six *ts'un* and five *fên*. This symbolizes the 365 degrees of the celestial sphere, and the 365 days of the year. Its breadth is six ts'un, symbolizing the six harmonies.[179] It has an upper and a lower part, which symbolize the

*去乎奢侈，以抱聖人之樂，所以微妙在得夫其人而樂其趣也，凡鼓琴必擇淨室高堂，或升層樓之上，或於林石之間，或登山嶺，或遊水湄，或觀宇中，值二氣高明之時，清風明月之夜，梵香靜室坐定心不外馳，氣血和平，方與神合靈，與道合妙，不遇知音，寧對清風明月，蒼松，怪石巔猿老鶴而鼓耳，是爲自得其樂也，如是鼓琴須要解意，知其意則知其趣，知其趣則知其樂，不知音趣，樂雖熟，何益，徒多無補，先要人物風韻標格清楚，又要指法好，取音好胸次好，口上要有髯，肚裏要有墨，六者兼備，方與添琴道，如要鼓琴，要先須衣冠整齊，或鶴氅，或深衣，要知古，之像表，方可稱聖人之器，然後盥水焚香，方纔就揖以琴，近案，坐以第伍徽之間，當對其心，則兩方擧指法，其心身要正，無得左右傾欹前後抑合其足履地若射步之，宜右視其手，左顧其絃，手腕宜低平，不宜高昂，左右要對徽，右手要近岳，指甲不宜長，只晉一米許，甲肉要相半，其聲不枯，清潤得宜，按令入木，劈托抹桃勾踢吟猱艦鎖歷之法，皆盡其力，不宜飛撫作勢輕薄之態，欲要手勢花巧以好看，莫若推琴而就擤，若要聲音艷麗而好聽，莫若棄琴而彈箏，此爲琴之大忌也，務要輕重疾徐卷舒，佀若體態骨重，方能與道妙

會神與道融，故曰德不在手，而在心，樂不在聲，而在道，興不在音，而自然，可以感天地之和，可以合神明之德，又曰左手吟猱綽注，右手輕重疾徐，更有一般難說，其人湏要讀書.

173 One of the mythical emperors, said to have lived in the third millennium B.C. The map is said to have shown the eight triagrams *pa-kua* (the base of the *Book of Changes*), and some other mystic drawings; it was drawn on the back of a dragon-horse which rose from the waves.

174 See *Shu-ching*, ch. *Ku-ming*, 19.

175 The twelve *lü* 律呂, bamboo tubes of various dimensions, which were said to produce the 12 chromatic semitones of the octave, and which since ancient times have formed the basis of Chinese musical theory.

176 A mountain in Shantung province.

177 Quoted from the opening lines of the *Ch'in-tsao* 琴操; see App. II, 1.

178 Quoted from Lieh-tzû; see above p. 45.

179 Heaven, earth, and the four cardinal points.

interchanging breath of Heaven and Earth. The upper part of the bottom is called pond, the lower part pool. Pond means water; water is even. Pool means to submit, [the two thus meaning] if the people on high are even [i.e. just] the people below will be obedient. The front is broad, the backpart is narrow, symbolizing the difference that exists between the venerable and the common. The upper board is concave, symbolizing Heaven, the lower board is flat, designating Earth.

The Dragon Pond[180] measures eight *ts'un*, to let pass the winds of the eight directions. The Phoenix Pool[181] measures four *ts'un*, to unite in it the four seasons. There are five strings, to correspond to the five tones, and to symbolize the five elements. The thick strings are the Prince; they are slow, harmonious, and unobtrusive. The thinner ones are the Statesmen; they are pure, unselfish, and obedient. The two strings that were added later are called *wên* and *wu*, and by their elegance they express the decorous feelings between Prince and Statesman; *kung* is the Prince, *shang* is the Statesman, *chiao* is the People, *chih* stands for affairs, and *yü* for things in general.[182] When these five tones together depict the Right, then the realm will be well regulated, and the numerous people will be peaceful.

Thus is the influence of the Accomplished Music on man: his nature is made to return to the Right, Prince and Statesmen shall be righteous, parents and children shall love each other, falsehood and low desires disappear, and man returns to his true heavenly nature.

The [licentious] music of Chêng brings doubt to man; in his nature, which is [originally] serene, false and wanton thoughts are born, the difference between man and woman is confused, and a propensity to licence is instigated.

Therefore, by contemplating the lute and by listening to its music [in a certain place or time] one may behold the disposition of the people and the condition of government [in that place or at that time], and one may know whether in the world the Way flourishes or is decaying.

Shun played the five-stringed lute, and sang the song *Nan-fêng*, and in order to give peace to the minds of all under heaven he composed the T'ai-p'ing music. It is said in the *Ch'in-shu*: The lute is an instrument that was created by Fu Hsi, and completed by Huang-ti. It symbolizes Heaven and Earth, and its use is to promulgate the wonderful Way. It contains the Spirit of Great Holiness, and produces

---

180 See below, p. 103.   181 See below, p. 103.   182 See *Yüeh-chi*, ch. I.

the ninety sorts of sounds. First it was made with five strings; later, during the reigns of King Wên and King Wu respectively, two more strings were added, to establish the chant of the Dragon and the Phoenix, and to penetrate the mystery of lower and higher spiritual agencies. Its tones are right, its essence harmonious; although its size is small, its significance is great.

When the inner meaning of the lute is understood, one may derive benefit from it. Through its influence people who are hasty shall become quiet, those who are quiet shall become harmonious. When the heart is harmonious and even, one is affected neither by sorrow nor by joy: one becomes in complete harmony with what is truly from heaven in one's nature. When this heavenly nature is clearly recognized, then the difference between human nature troubled by emotions, and original serenity, shall be made clear again, one shall not be confused any longer by life and death, nor shall one be affected by earthly laws.

The ancient Emperors and Enlightened Kings all understood profoundly [these mysterious qualities of the lute]. It has not yet been known for a man to hear the Right Music without being influenced by it. When formerly Master Hsiang[183] pulled the lute, the swimming fish rose from the water to listen, and [hearing the lute music of Po Ya][184] the six horses looked up from their fodder. Things that have a shape, and animals that have no speech, they all are influenced by the music of the lute; how much more then human beings! So it was until the Right Music was lost and [people] turned away from the Way of the lute.

The lute may establish fortitude and harmonize the primordial spirit. Only Yao understood this, therefore he composed the hymn *Shên-jên*. Further the lute may complete the Way, thereby establishing the minds of the weak and timorous. This is the meaning of the elegy *Ssû-ch'in*,[185] composed by Shun, of the elegy *Hsiang-ling*,[186] composed by Yü, and of the elegy *Hsün-tien*,[187] composed by T'ang.

---

[183] *Shih-hsiang* was a famous lute player of old, mentioned in *Lieh-tzû*, ch. *T'ang-wên* 湯問. This passage, however, gives the credit for making the fish come out of the water to another lute expert, Ku Pa: When Ku Pa played the lute, birds started to dance and fish jumped out of the water.

[184] I have inserted the reference to Po Ya, since the final words are a quotation from *Hsün-tzû* 荀子, ch. *Ch'üan-hsüeh* 勸學, where it is said: 'When Po Ya played the lute, the six horses looked up from their fodder' 伯牙鼓琴, 而六馬仰秣.

[185] The *Ch'in-tsao* (App. II, 1) says that the Emperor Shun composed this song to express his affection for his parents.

[186] According to the *Shu-ching*, Yü composed this song when he had completed the task of regulating the waters.

[187] Composed by Wu-wang of the Chou dynasty to train people in military arts. Cf. the Sung treatise *Ch'in-ch'ü-pu-lu* 琴曲譜錄: 習武事.

F

Since the Ancient Emperors and the Enlightened Rulers, the heart has been rectified and the person has been cultivated, the State has been regulated and peace has been brought to the realm[188] by the right sounds of the lute and by these alone. How then can one say that the wonderful Way of the lute is but a small craft? To consider the Way of the lute as one of the arts is a great mistake indeed.[189]

COVENANT FOR TRANSMITTING THE LUTE

BY CH'ÊNG YÜN-CHI, EIGHTEENTH CENTURY

1 The lute is the instrument of the Holy Sages: Superior Men therewith nurture the Essence of the Mean Harmony, cultivate their selves and regulate their nature. Playing the lute must therefore be called a Way to wisdom and not one of the arts. All who love the study of the lute should wait till they meet [a pupil who is] a scholar of cultured taste and correct conduct; only then may they teach him the lute. How could one speak about the lute to people of frivolous and ostentatious disposition?

2 As the various schools of lute players are not the same, so their traditions are different.[190] But the main point [which all

---

[188] See *Ta-hsüeh* 大學, ch. I.
[189] 上古琴論. 昔者伏羲之王天下也，仰觀俯察，感榮河出圖以畫八卦，聽八風以製音律，採嶧山孤桐，合陰備陽，造爲雅樂，名之曰琴，琴者禁也，禁邪僻而防淫佚，引仁義而歸正道，所以修身理性，返其天眞，忘形合虛，凝神太和，琴製長三尺六寸五分，象周天三百六十五度，年歲之三百六十五日也，廣六寸，象六合也，有上下，象天地之氣相呼吸也，其底上曰池，下曰沼，池者水也，水者平也，沼者伏也，上平則下伏，前廣而後狹，象尊卑有差也，上圓象天，下方象地，龍池長八寸，以通八風，鳳沼長四寸，以合四氣，其絃有五，以按五音，象五行也，大絃者君也，緩和而隱，小絃者臣也，清廉而不亂，迨至文武加二絃，所以雅合君臣之恩也，宮爲君，商爲臣，角爲民，徵爲事，羽爲物，五音畫正，天下和平，而兆民寧，雅樂之感人也，性返于正，君臣義，父子親，消降邪欲，返乎天眞，鄭聲之惑人也，正性邪，淫心生，亂男女之別，動聲色之偏，故視琴聽音，可以見志觀治，知世道之興衰，故舜彈五絃之琴，歌南風之詩，以平天下之心，爲太平之樂也，琴書曰琴之爲器，創自伏羲，成于黃帝，治象乎乾坤，用宣乎妙道，含大靈氣，運九十種聲，初製五絃，加於文武，建龍鳳之號，通鬼神之幽，其聲正，其氣和，其形小，其義大，如得其旨趣，則能感物，志躁者，感之以靜，志靜者，感之以和，和平其心憂樂不能入，任之以天眞，明其眞，而返照動寂，則生死不能累，方法豈能拘，古之明王君子，皆精通焉，未有聞正音而不感者也，昔者師襄鼓琴，則有遊魚出聽，六馬仰秣，有形之物，無語之獸，尚能感之，況於人乎，自正音失而琴道乖矣，琴能制剛，而調元氣，惟堯得之，故堯有神人暢，其次能全其道，則柔儒立志，舜有思親操，禹有襄陵操，湯有訓佃操者是也，自古帝明王，所以正心修身，齊家治國平天下者，咸賴琴之正音是賁焉，然則琴之妙道，豈小技也哉，而以藝視琴道者，則非矣。

[190] There can be no doubt that originally every single 'school' of lute playing goes back to one famous master; he initiated a certain style of playing the lute, and taught this to his disciples, thus founding a 'school'. His disciples transmitted his teachings to their own followers, and so the circle grew wider and wider. In the course of the centuries the names of the original founders of the 'schools' were lost, and the schools became a kind of local tradition, associated with a geographical location rather than with the name of a particular lute master. Many minor schools disappeared completely or were incorporated into broader geographical divisions.

At present there still exist the following*

'schools', named after the provinces where they were founded and where their tradition continued to flourish.

蜀派　　吳派　　浙派　　閩派
Shu-p'ai　Wu-p'ai　Che-p'ai　Min-p'ai
(Szuchuan)(Kiangsu)(Chekiang)(Fukien)

廣陵派　　　虞山派
Kuang-ling-p'ai　Yü-shan-p'ai

The Shu-p'ai or Szuchuan School retains many of the antique features of lute music, and seems to reproduce fairly accurately the style of lute playing popular during the T'ang period. This must be ascribed to the fact that Szuchuan Province, through its isolated position, has been less influenced by cultural developments in Central China. The Szuchuan style of playing the lute bears a robust character, and stresses those single notes and graces that constitute the melody of a tune; grace notes that do not affect the melodic pattern are either omitted or played in a casual way. On the other hand this school likes to use chords; in Szuchuan-notations of well-known tunes one often finds a chord where other lute handbooks only write a single note. This feature must probably be explained by the fact that during the T'ang dynasty the lute was often used together with other musical instruments of a greater sound volume, and also for accompanying the human voice; hence the tendency to emphasize the melody. It should be noted that even now in Szuchuan there exists a tradition of intoning ancient poetry, the singer accompanying himself on the lute.

The Chekiang School was greatly influenced by the popular music that flourished during the Yüan dynasty. The masters of this school often added verses in the fashionable style to older lute melodies, supplementing the original melodic pattern with many extra grace-notes. Hence this school is often criticized as being 'clever but common'. Probably Yeh-lü-ch'u-ts'ai's masters Mi-ta and Wan-sung (see n. 170) were members of this Chekiang School; this would explain his changing to the simpler style of the Szuchuanese master Ch'i-yen.

The Fukien School was established later than the others, probably during the thirteenth or fourteenth century. This school tried to adapt lute music to popular instruments such as the cither and the *p'i-p'a;* consequently it is not greatly esteemed by lute experts. Most musicians who, without ambition to become real lute players, still like to be able to play a few easy tunes, are followers of this school. They generally use the *Sung-fêng-ko-ch'in-pu* (see page 96), a handbook that gives a great number of simple, short melodies, all accompanied by words. Although I quite agree that the Fukien School does not stand for the highest expression of lute music, it is still worth a closer study, for many of its tunes contain charming melodic patterns.

The Kiangsu School is without doubt the greatest, both as regards the quality of its music and the number of its members. Its origin lies buried in the distant past, for it already flourished in the third century. About 1600 this school split into two branches, the Kuang-ling-p'ai and the Yü-shan-p'ai. The most prominent representative of the Kuang-ling-p'ai was Hsü Ch'ang-yü (徐常遇, style Êrh-hsün 二勳, literary name Wu-shan-lao-jên 五人老人), a lute player from Yang-chou who flourished during the early years of the Ch'ing period. In 1702 his son published his lute handbook, which was reprinted in 1718; in 1773 it appeared in its final form, under the title of *Ch'ên-chien-t'ang-ch'in-pu* 澄鑒堂琴譜. The Yü-shan-p'ai, also called Ch'ang-shu-p'ai 常熟派, has its center in Ch'ang-shu near Soochow, where the great master Yen Chêng (see page 182) revived the ancient tradition of lute playing.

Hsü Ch'ang-yü and Yen Chêng are commonly called the 'founders' of the two branches of the Kiangsu School. This appellation, however, derives mainly from the veneration with which members of the two schools regard these two great lute masters. What they actually did was to give final form to a tradition that had developed long before in Yang-chou and Ch'ang-shu.

These two schools aim at a faithful reproduction of the melodic patterns of the antique tunes, including both the melodic and non-melodic graces. They stress the significance of the lute as a solo instrument and pay close attention to the 'color' of each particular note, at the same time attaching great value to the proper application of forte and piano, and to the correct rhythm. The Kiangsu School represents the highest form of lute music. One need not wonder, therefore, that most of the eminent lute players of the present either belong to the Kuang-ling-p'ai or the Yü-shan-p'ai; the best exponent of the former is probably Mr Chang I-ch'ang (張益昌, style Tzu-ch'ien 子謙) of Shanghai, while the latter is headed by Mr Ch'a Chên-hu (查鎮湖, style Fu-hsi 阜西) at Soochow. The two schools resemble each other closely, the only difference I could discover being that the Yü-shan-p'ai stresses the rhythm, while the Kuang-ling-p'ai insists so much on a correct rendering of all the

schools have in common] lies in their strict observance of the rules of harmony, and in giving special care to the finger technique. Students of the lute should [first] hear the style which the masters of various schools follow while playing, [for once having chosen a master] it is necessary that one wholeheartedly like his style and follow his precepts sincerely; then teaching and learning shall be well regulated. If the student reaches a complete understanding of these teachings, what shall prevent him from becoming even more proficient than his master?[191] Further, if a student receives one method of playing, but at the same time hears all kinds of different teachings,[192] he cannot concentrate his mind; then one should not trouble to teach him.

3 When Confucius studied the lute under Master Hsiang, [after the first lesson] he did not show himself for ten days; when Po Ya studied the lute under Ch'êng-lien, during three years he did not make progress. Therefore, those who start studying the lute must have a constant mind and a firm resolution, and they must be resolved to succeed in the end; only such people should be taught the lute. But if there are such that come with great enthusiasm but give up when they are halfway,[193] they are not worthy that a teacher occupy himself with them.

4 The lute is the instrument with which the Ancients nurtured their nature; they did not use it with the idea of making their livelihood by it. Now I often see lute masters of the present time, when about to teach somebody, immediately start talking about the salary; this is disgusting indeed, and drawing elegance through the mud. All who have the same attitude as I, should guard themselves against this. Drawn up by Yü-shan.[194]

---

*grace-notes that the rhythm is sometimes broken.

It will be clear from the above observations that the four 'schools' differ only in the *interpretation* of the lute melodies. They did not add to, nor materially alter the melodies of the lute repertoire.

191 *Ch'ing-ch'u-yü-lan*, from *Hsün-tzû;* the opening line of ch. 1.

192 *Ch'i-ch'uan-ch'u-hsiu*, from *Mencius*, Book III, part II, 6.

193 *Pan-t'u-êrh-fei;* cf. *Chung-yung* 中庸, XI, 2.

194 傳琴約。一琴爲聖樂，君子涵養中和之氣，藉以修身理性，當以道言，非以藝言也，習琴之友，必期博雅端方之士，方可傳之，輕浮佻達者，豈可語此

一派旣不同，傳亦各異，首嚴音律兼重指法，習琴者須令聽過各家，務要心悅誠服，然後授受分明，苟會心明敏者，何妨靑出於藍，其或齊傳楚咻，志不專一，則亦不屑教誨之而已矣

一孔子學琴於師襄，十日不進，伯牙學琴於成連，三年未成，初學者須要心堅志決，必期有成，方可傳習，其或乘興而來，半途而廢，亦不足取也

一琴爲古人養性之具，非以資糊口計也，每見時師傳授，輒講酬儀，鄙穢難聞，風雅掃地矣，凡我同志，各宜戒之. 寓山識

CHAPTER FOUR

The Significance of the Tunes

The Ming repertoire taken as the basis for a study of the significance of the tunes—significance of the modes—Chinese TIAO-I, *and Japanese* NETORI—*the tunes divided into five groups—tunes describing a mystic journey (Taoistic)—tunes of a semihistorical character (Confucianist)—musical versions of literary productions—tunes descriptive of nature—tunes descriptive of literary life—summary*

THE lute as a means of communing with Tao, the lute as the favourite companion of the scholar, the lute as the holy instrument of the Ancient Sages—all these various functions of the lute, and the tenets of lute ideology corresponding to them, are reflected in the repertoire: they find their expression in the subjects of the tunes.

Now, the lute repertoire is different for every period; the various elements, both Chinese and foreign, that in the course of time influenced lute music, to a large extent also determined its repertoire. In the heyday of Central-Asiatic influence (the Sui and T'ang periods), more than half of the repertoire consisted of musical versions of songs of a very worldly character. But during the Sung dynasty, when under the influence of the philosopher Chu Hsi and his powerful school a more severe attitude reasserted itself, lute tunes of a more classical character came to the fore. For our present subject, a consideration of the extent to which the tenets of *ch'in* ideology may be found reflected in the tunes, we must take as the basis the repertoire of the Ming dynasty. For, as we have seen above, it was during the Ming dynasty that the outlines of this special system of thought were more or less fixed.

It was during the Ming period that there were printed on a large scale handbooks for the lute with tunes in notation, accompanied by explicit commentaries as to their history and significance; thus from a study of the Ming repertoire we may obtain an idea not only of the melodies of these tunes, but also of what they meant to the people of those times.

Before studying the significance of the separate tunes, however, a few words must be said about the various modes (*tiao*)[1] and their ideological value.

The handbooks of the lute mostly divide the repertoire into the five modes, called after the old Chinese pentatonic scale (*kuang-shang-chüeh-chih-yü*), *kung-tiao*, *shang-tiao*, etc.[2] Next to these there exist scores of what might be called 'minor modes', partly of foreign origin; these are called together *wai-tiao*.[3] For each mode the tuning of the strings is different.

Now in the lute handbooks of the Ming dynasty each group of tunes belonging to the same mode is preceded by a short musical composition that bears as title the name of the mode, with the word *i*[4] (meaning) added. So the collection of tunes belonging to the *kung* mode opens with a short composition entitled *kung-i* (or also *kung-tiao-i*)[5] 'Meaning of the *kung* Mode'. These *tiao-i* contain a fixed tonal pattern, characteristic of the mode they indicate, and constitute the essence of all tunes composed in this mode. Short as they are, these *tiao-i* comprise a great variety of tones, especially some chords and other harmonical combinations which are typical for the mode the *tiao-i* introduces. Usually a *tiao-i* ends with a simple melodic pattern, entirely in harmonics ('floating sounds' *fan-yin*: while the right hand pulls a string, the left just touches it lightly, without pressing it down on the board).[6]

These *tiao-i* provide the player with a convenient check upon the tuning of his instrument. Playing through the *tiao-i*, he notices at once whether the tuning is correct or not. At the same time the *tiao-i* is a kind of finger exercise: it contains all the main grips necessary for executing tunes set to this mode.

In *ch'in* ideology, however, the *tiao-i* mean much more than just melodic patterns; they are called *i* (meaning), because they convey to the player and the hearer the peculiar atmosphere, the emotional and philosophical value of each mode. A lute expert of the Ming dynasty, Yang Lun,[7] in his handbook *T'ai-ku-i-yin*[8] adds to each *tiao-i* an introductory note. There he combines each mode with one

---

1 調
2 宮商角徵羽, 宮調, 商調
3 外調
4 意
5 宮意, 宮調意
6 泛音. See above, page 60.
7 意
8 楊倫. See App. II, 14.

of the five elements (*wu-hsing*) and with one of the five virtues (*wu-ch'ang*).⁹ Then he connects each mode with a special manifestation of Tao, as they are explained in the *Book of Changes*, *Yih-ching*. So the whole scheme of the modes is placed in a cosmological frame. Playing the *tiao-i* may be called a preliminary ceremony: it prepares the player and the hearer for the real composition to come, it creates the correct atmosphere that belongs to the mode in which the composition is set.

The *tiao-i* are so intimately bound up with the tunes themselves, that in the Ming handbook *Shên-chi-pi-pu* most tunes end with the remark: 'Now add the harmonics of the *tiao-i* belonging to this mode.'¹⁰

During the Ch'ing dynasty the *tiao-i* seem to have been neglected; as a rule they are not printed in the handbooks of that period. But a survival is to be found in the codas (*shou-yin*, also called *wei*)¹¹ which in Ch'ing handbooks frequently are added to the tunes. These codas are entirely in harmonics, and for each mode closely resemble the passages in harmonics of the corresponding *tiao-i* of the Ming handbooks. The function of these codas is essentially the same as that of the *tiao-i*: while the *tiao-i* prepares the player and the hearer for the mode of the tune that is going to follow, the codas are retrospective, and, as it were, resume in one single passage the entire spirit of the mode to which the tune played belongs.

The *tiao-i* are doubtless very old. This may be concluded from the fact that although the tunes themselves as given in the early Ming handbooks differ greatly, the *tiao-i* are practically uniform. In Japan they are still used in the ceremonial Court music where they are called *netori* or also *torine*.¹² The *tiao-i* of the lute supply us with valuable materials for a study of ancient Chinese composition; in my opinion an investigation of the history of lute music should begin with a thorough analysis of the various *tiao-i* that are preserved.

For the study of the significance of the tunes themselves the handbooks of the lute supply ample materials. Usually to each tune given in notation there is added a preface, where the compiler of the handbook gives the name of the composer, and adds some remarks about the occasion that inspired him to compose the tune in question.

---

9 五行, 五常
10 入本調泛. See App. II, 11.
11 收音, 尾
12 音取, 取音. For more information about the *netori*, see H. Tanabe, 田邊尚雄, *Nihon ongaku kōwa* 日本音樂講話, Tokyo 1921, pp. 515 ff.

Special care is given to describing the mood the composer was in when he created his music, and what thought he wished to express in his composition. It is the highest aim of the player in his execution of the tune to reproduce faithfully the mood of the composer. Each tune has its special significance, which must be done full justice by the player.

To help the player to realize the significance, often the various parts of a tune (*tuan*)[13] are given special titles, suggesting the meaning of that particular part of the melody.

As a rule these subtitles are not especially made for the lute melodies; they are fixed phrases, borrowed from a separate section of the Chinese artistic vocabulary, i.e. that of the *t'i-mu*[14] (superscriptions). A *t'i-mu* is a short, highly pregnant phrase, a conventionalized expression that describes a subject considered fit for inspiring an artist. A *t'i-mu*, such as for instance 'a waterfall descending from pine-clad rocks',[15] may inspire alike poets, painters and musicians. Looking through a catalogue of paintings[16] one finds hundreds of these *t'i-mu*. Because of their pregnancy these phrases are by no means easy to translate; in the examples given below my translation often is but one of many possible renderings. Many handbooks add to these subtitles some remarks about the style: whether the touch must be slow, energetic, delicate, etc. Further there are many stylistic indications, which correspond to our piano, legato, forte and so on.

Sometimes even to every bar there are appended explanatory remarks. For instance, we find in a tune describing a beautiful mountain landscape, under a bar in the first part, the remark 'Here one thinks of high mountains,' and under another: 'Here one thinks of flowing streams.'

The better-known tunes of the Ming repertoire number well over a hundred. From a musicological point of view, every one of these tunes constitutes valuable material for research. But for the study of *ch'in* ideology we need only consider a few of them. For a comparative study of the tunes shows that according to their subjects they may be conveniently divided into five groups, each group comprising a number of tunes of the same ideological type. Thus for our present subject it suffices to select for each group some representative tunes.

---

13 段
14 題目
15 松岩飛瀑

16 For example, the *Li-tai-cho-lu-hua-mu* 歷代著錄畫目, published in 1933 by John C. Ferguson.

[IV] THE SIGNIFICANCE OF THE TUNES

The tunes here selected for discussion number about twenty. In some way or another all serve to illustrate the ideals of *ch'in* ideology. Some express Taoist principles, others celebrate antiquity, and all suggest the atmosphere that surrounds the lute and its music. Besides illustrating *ch'in* ideology, the tunes discussed below, as they form the nucleus of the *ch'in* repertoire, will at the same time give the reader a general idea about the subjects that inspired lute musicians. Most of the tunes mentioned here are often referred to in Chinese literature, and to this day are still the favourites of every Chinese lute amateur.

Above, in Chapter III, section 2, it was remarked already that in *ch'in* ideology the Taoist element predominates. A cursory inspection of the subjects of the tunes shows that there also the tunes with a Taoist colour top the list. Most prominent among these Taoist tunes are those of a type which I would call that of *The Mystic Journey*. The ethereal tones of the lute loosen the soul of the player from its earthly bonds, and enable him to travel to the mystic heights where the Immortals dwell, and to be initiated into the secrets of the Elixir of Life.

A good example is a tune called *Kuang-han-yu* (Traveling to the Palace of Wide Coolness) to be found in an early Ming handbook, the *Pu-hsü-t'ang-ch'in-pu*.[17] The various stages of the mystic journey described in this tune are indicated in the titles of its eight parts: the traveler ascends into the clouds, feasts with the Immortals, and finally again returns to earth.

1 Treading the cloud ladder.
2 Ascending into pure emptiness.
3 Feasting in the Pavilion of Wide (Coolness).
4 Cutting the cinnamon (used in preparing the elixir of immortality).
5 Dancing in rainbow garments.
6 Dancing with the Blue Phoenix. (In the middle of this part there occur some heavy chords, where the remark is added: 'The sound of the Jade Hare pounding the elixir of immortality.' According to Chinese popular belief, in the moon there lives a hare that prepares the elixir of life under a cassia tree.)
7 Asking about longevity.
8 Returning in the cloud chariot. (In the middle of this part

---

[17] 廣寒遊 (see p. 68, n. 145); 步虛堂琴譜 (App. II, 12).

there occur some high notes, with the explanatory remark: 'The sounds of laughing and talking of Chang-ngo, the Moon Goddess.')[18]

The tune *Lieh-tzû-yü-fêng* (Lieh-tzû Riding on the Wind) may serve as a second example; it refers to a passage in the old Taoist work connected with the name of this philosopher.[19] This tune is to be found in most *ch'in-pu*, and is generally ascribed to Mao Chung-wêng,[20] a composer of the Sung dynasty about whom little is known; only some of the more vulgar *ch'in-pu* ascribe it to the philosopher Lieh-tzû himself. The *Shên-chi-pi-pu*[21] gives the titles of its ten parts as follows.

1 Resting upon emptiness, riding on the wind.
2 Looking down on the earth.
3 The universe is spread out vast.
4 I do not know whether the wind is riding on me.
5 Or whether I am riding on the wind.
6 The mind dwells on mysterious plains.
7 The spirit roams in the great purity.
8 Whistling long in the vast azure.
9 Shaking one's clothes in the breeze.
10 Having attained the utmost ecstasy, turning back.[22]

Another well-known tune of this type, entitled *Ling-hsü-yin* (Song of Cool Emptiness) is also ascribed to Mao Chung-wêng.[23] This tune consists of three parts:

1 Ascending in the clouds with a crane as vehicle.
2 Riding on the wind up to the confines of heaven.
3 Treading the emptiness of the highest atmosphere.[24]

Besides the examples quoted here there exist scores of other tunes belonging to this same group. Under this group I would also classify another class of tunes that, though not exactly representing a mystic journey, still are closely related to it. These are the many tunes celebrating life in refined retirement.

Taoist lore often describes the abode of the Immortals and other paradisaical regions as being in a specified location, as, e.g. far in the

---

[18] 步雲梯, 登清虛, 宴廣亭, 折丹桂, 舞霓裳, 舞青鸞, 問長生, 回雲車
[19] 列子禦風; see above, translation on p. 45.
[20] 毛仲翁
[21] See App. II, 11.
[22] 凭虛馭風, 俯視寰壤, 渺焉六合, 不知風乘我, 不知我乘風, 志在冲溟, 神遊太清, 長嘯空碧, 振衣天風, 興盡而還
[23] 凌虛吟; see the Ming handbook of Yang Piao-chêng, App. II, 13 (other handbooks give it as anonymous).
[24] 蹈雲鶴駕, 乘風天表, 步虛太羅

[IV] THE SIGNIFICANCE OF THE TUNES

western mountains, or high up in the sky. But at the same time the unseen world pervades ordinary life: we are living constantly in close proximity to it, and we would clearly perceive it could we but see with the soul instead of with the eyes. This idea has inspired countless Chinese writers: best known is the delicate essay by T'ao Ch'ien entitled 'The Plum Blossom Fountain'.[25]

In this essay (really the introduction to one of his poems), T'ao Ch'ien relates how a fisherman happened upon a grove of peach trees; exploring this beautiful spot he found the hidden entrance to a cave. Having entered it he found that it led into a strange country: people there were living happily and peacefully, wearing the garb of several centuries ago. The fisherman was kindly treated by them, and resolved to return there. But once he had gone away he could never find his way back.

Tasting already during earthly life the joys of eternity is the privilege of the enlightened recluse, who, in his abode far from the loud world, returns to the simple life exalted by the Taoist writers. Thus the repairing of the sage to his mountain retreat, the scholar's rustic excursion which makes him realize the futility of worldly hopes, the ecstasy of the recluse who by contemplating the forces of nature beholds the eternal Tao; all these motifs may be classified under the group of the mystic journey.

In connection with this motif two persons, the Fuel Gatherer *ch'iao-jên* and the Old Fisherman *yü-fu* figure prominently.[26] They are the approved symbols of simple life in complete harmony with *tao*, as opposed to the cares and sorrows of the world. Above we saw that it was an old fisherman that discovered the Peach Blossom Fountain. Already the philosopher Chuang-tzû uses the Old Fisherman as a symbol of the sage who has realized truth; in the chapter entitled 'Yü-fu', the Old Fisherman appears: '... his beard and eyebrows were turning white, his hair was all uncombed, and his sleeves hung loosely down ...' He points out to Confucius the Right Way, and then: 'He shoved off his boat, and went away among the green reeds.'[27] Also in later literature the Old Fisherman and the Fuel Gatherer are preferably chosen for delivering wise words about the meaning of

---

[25] 陶潛, 365–427; 桃花源記, translated by Giles in: *Gems of Chinese Literature, Prose*, Shanghai 1923, p. 104. Notice that Giles' footnote, 'The whole story is allegorical, and signifies that the fisherman had been strangely permitted to go back once again into the peach blossom days of his youth', entirely misrepresents the purport of this essay and should be disregarded.

[26] 樵人, 漁父

[27] Legge.

life. The great Sung writer and artist Su Shih (Su Tung-p'o) wrote the *Yü-ch'iao-hsien-hua* (Leisurely Discourses of the Fuel Gatherer and the Fisherman), and the famous scholar Shao Yung of the same period chose this pair to deliver his philosophical principles.[28]

In the repertoire of the lute there occur many tunes that express this idea. As a first example I may mention the tune *Ch'iao-ko* (Song of the Fuel Gatherer), to be found in most handbooks and generally ascribed to Mao Min-chung, a composer of the end of the Sung period.[29] The *Shên-chi-pi-pu*[30] says that Mao Min-chung composed this tune when fleeing from the Mongol invasion of China. The eleven parts bear the following subtitles:

1. Flying from the world, without sorrow.
2. Proudly looking down on worldly affairs.
3. Settling down far on cloudy mountain tops.
4. Shouldering one's axe entering the wood.
5. Enjoying *tao* while reading one's books.
6. Shaking one's clothes on a steep cliff.
7. Whistling long in the echoing vale.
8. Singing the opportune wind.
9. Having obtained the true insight, whistling long.
10. Advanced in years like the long-lived pines.
11. In a drunken dance descending from the mountain.[31]

Secondly there is the *Yü-ko* (Song of the Fisherman),[32] the pendant of the tune mentioned above. This tune is ascribed to the great T'ang poet Liu Tsung-yüan.[33] In the handbook of Yang Piao-chêng this tune has not less than 18 parts, which bear the following subtitles:

1. Clouds over the rivers Hsiao and Hsiang (two rivers in Hunan province, famous for their beautiful scenery).
2. The autumn river glossy like silk.
3. Mist and rain over lake Tung-t'ing (the famous lake in the north of Hunan province).
4. The misty waves of the river Hsiang.
5. The brilliant moon in the broad heaven.
6. Antiphonal song of the fishermen.

---

[28] 漁樵閑話; 邵雍, 1011–1077 (cf. his *Yü-ch'iao-tui-wên* 漁樵對問 'Dialogue Between the Fisherman and the Fuel Gatherer').
[29] 樵歌, 毛敏仲
[30] Appendix II, 11.
[31] 遯世無悶, 傲睨物表, 遠棲雲嶠, 斧斤入林, 樂道以書, 振衣谷岡, 長嘯谷答, 詠鄭公風 (for the exact meaning of the expression *chêng-kung-fêng*, see *Hou-han-shu*, the biography of Chêng Hung 鄭宏), 豁然長嘯, 壽倚松齡, 醉舞下山
[32] 漁歌
[33] 柳宗元, 773–819.

[IV] THE SIGNIFICANCE OF THE TUNES 93

7 Cries of the wild geese.
8 At evening mooring near the western rock.
9 Evening song of the fishermen.
10 Lying drunk among the rushes.
11 Evening rain outside the weed-grown window.
12 The falling leaves of the *wu-t'ung* tree.
13 At dawn drawing water from the Hsiang river.
14 The fishing boats are rowed out.
15 Throwing the nets into the cool river.
16 The sun appears, the mists dissolve.
17 A splashing sound of the oars.
18 Highness of the mountains and eternity of the streams.[34]

All tunes belonging to this first group correspond to that part of *ch'in* ideology that I designated above as mainly Taoistic in character. Those tunes that belong to the next group, however, bear a more Confucianist character. They often treat of Confucius and other saints of antiquity, and celebrate the conduct of historical persons.

Tunes of a semi-historical character: under this group I classify all tunes that are connected with some famous person, or with a well-known historical theme. Among this category there must be mentioned in the first place the many compositions connected with Confucius. The Sage is said to have been a great lute player, and according to tradition he composed several lute melodies at critical moments of his eventful life. As a specimen I mention the famous old tune *I-lan*[35] (Alas, the Orchid!). This tune is already mentioned in a catalogue of *ch'in* tunes of the Han dynasty, the *Ch'in-tsao*,[36] the oldest list of *ch'in* tunes that exists. There it is said: 'The elegy *I-lan* was composed by Confucius. He had visited in succession all the Feudal Princes, but none of them could employ him. Returning from Wei to [his native state] Lu, he passed a hidden vale, and there observed a fragrant orchid flourishing alone. Heaving a sigh he said: "In truth, the orchid should be the perfume of kings, but now it is flourishing alone as a mate of common plants. It might be compared with the wise man, who finds that the times are not suited for practising his principles, and [consequently] associates with the common people." Having said this he halted his chariot, and drawing his lute near him, he

---

[34] 瀟湘水雲, 秋江如練, 洞庭烟雨, 楚湘烟波, 天濶月朗, 漁歌互答, 嗈嗈鳴雁, 夜傍西岩, 漁人晚唱, 醉臥蘆花, 蓬窓夜雨, 梧桐落葉, 曉汲湘水, 漁舟盪槳, 寒江撒網, 日出烟消, 欸乃一聲, 山高水長.
[35] 猗蘭
[36] Appendix II, 1.

composed a tune on the orchid.'³⁷ The handbooks generally ascribe the tune to Confucius himself; the *Shên-chi-pi-pu* remarks: 'Wise men of olden times, taking this occurrence as an example, composed this elegy.'³⁸ The tune as preserved in early Ming handbooks does not show the characteristics of old melodies.³⁹

Another tune of a semi-historical character that is found in nearly all handbooks is *Hu-chia*⁴⁰ (Barbarian Reed Pipe). This tune has 18 parts, and therefore is also often called *Hu-chia-shih-pa-p'o*⁴¹ (Eighteen Blasts of the Barbarian Reed Pipe). This tune was composed by the T'ang musician Tung T'ing-lan.⁴² The subject is the exile of Ts'ai Yen, daughter of the famous scholar and musician Ts'ai Yung,⁴³ round whom several lute stories center. The *Shên-chi-pi-pu* adds to this tune the following introduction: 'When the Han dynasty was in great confusion, Ts'ai Yen was abducted by Hu horsemen into the barbarian country, and there made the wife of their king. She stayed there twelve years, and bore the king two sons. The king held her in high esteem. Once in spring she ascended a barbarian chariot, and was moved by the sound of the reed pipes; she made a poem to express her feelings... Later the Emperor Wu, because of his friendship with her father Ts'ai Yung, despatched a general who redeemed her. She returned to China, but her two sons remained among the barbarians. Later, when the barbarians longingly remembered her, they rolled a reed into a pipe, and blew on it melancholy tunes. Thereafter Tung T'ing-lan of the T'ang dynasty, who excelled in the laws of music as expounded by Shên Yo and Chu Hsing-hsien,⁴⁴ transcribed this music of the barbarian reed pipe for the lute, and so made two tunes, called the Smaller and Greater Barbarian Reed Pipe.'⁴⁵ Evidently this story was made up to explain

---

37 猗蘭操者，孔子所作也，孔子歷聘諸侯，諸侯莫能任，自衞反魯，過隱谷之中，見薌蘭獨茂，喟然嘆曰，夫蘭當爲王者香，今乃獨茂，與衆草爲伍，譬猶賢者不逢時，與鄙夫爲倫也，乃止車，援琴鼓之.

38 古之哲人擬之而作是操.

39 See the transcription of parts 1 and 2 by Courant, *op. cit.* page 170.

40 胡笳

41 胡笳十八拍

42 董庭蘭, who flourished during the K'ai-yüan period, 713–41.

43 133–192; see p. 177.

44 *Shên-chia-shêng, chu-chia-shêng*: the meaning of these two terms is doubtful. Some sources give 汎 for 沈, and 柷 instead of 祝. It would seem that they refer to two schools (*chia* 家) of musical theory, each called after the name of its chief exponent. I wrote Shên Yo and Chu Hsiang-hsien, because the first (沈約, 441–513) was a famous musical theorist, and the second (祝象賢, Liang dynasty) a well-known lute expert of about the same period. This, however, is a mere guess, and it does not pretend to settle the question. Modern Chinese scholars have given up the problem as hopeless; cf. Yang Tsung-chi in his *Ch'in-hsüeh-ts'ung-shu* (App. II, 7), *Ch'in-hua* 琴話 ch. 2, page 11, and also the relevant items in the *Yin-yüeh-tz'ǔ-tien* 音樂辭典 by Liu Ch'êng-fu 劉誠甫, Shanghai 1935.

45 漢室大亂，琰爲胡騎所獲，入番爲后，十二年生二子，王甚重之，春月登胡車琰感笳之*

[IV] THE SIGNIFICANCE OF THE TUNES

a posteriori the presence in the *ch'in* repertoire of an obviously un-Chinese melody. The 16th part of this tune has been transcribed in western notation by Courant.[46] This tune is very popular in China, and is to be found also in the repertoire of the flute, *êrh-hu*, *p'i-p'a* and other instruments.

As a third example I may quote the highly attractive composition *Mei-hua-san-nung*[47] (Three Variations on the Peach Blossom). This melody was originally intended for the flute, and the famous flutist of the Chin period, the scholar Huan I, is mentioned as its composer.[48] Tradition asserts that he played this tune for Wang Hui-chih[49] when they happened to meet on the road. In the *Shên-chi-pi-pu* this tune has ten parts, which bear the following subtitles:

1 Evening moon over the mountains.
2 First variation: Calling the moon. The tones penetrate into the wide mist.
3 Second variation: Entering the clouds. The tones penetrate into the clouds.
4 The Blue Bird calls the soul.
5 Third variation: Trying to pass the Hêng river. The tones imitate a long-drawn sigh.
6 Tones of a jade flute.
7 Plaques of jade hit by a cool breeze.
8 Tones of an iron flute.
9 Peach blossoms dancing in the wind.
10 Infinite longing.[50]

The main melodic pattern of this tune is contained in parts 2, 3, and 5, which are transpositions of an extremely delicate and refined melody.

These three examples might be easily increased by scores of others. I mention only the *I-chiao-chin-li* regarding Chang Liang, the famous general of the end of the Ch'in period, the *Yen-kuo-hêng-yang*, said to have been made by the poet Su Wu during his captivity among the barbarians, and the *Ch'ü-yüan-wên-tu* ascribed to Ch'ü Yüan, the well-known poet of the 4th century B.C., etc.[51]

*音, 作詩言誌, 後武帝與邕有舊, 勅大將軍贖文姬歸漢, 二子留胡中, 後胡人思慕文姬, 乃捲蘆葉爲吹笳奏哀怨之音, 後唐董庭蘭善爲沈家聲祝家聲, 以琴寫胡笳聲爲大小胡笳是也.

46 *Op. cit.* p. 171.
47 梅花三弄
48 晉, 桓伊

49 王徽之 son of the great calligrapher Wang Hsi-chih, 321–79.
50 溪山夜月, 一弄叫月聲入太霞, 二弄穿雲聲入雲中, 青鳥啼魂, 三弄橫江隔江長歎聲, 玉簫聲, 凌風憂玉, 鐵笛聲, 風蕩梅花, 欲罷不能.
51 圯橋進履; 雁過衡陽, by 蘇武, died 60 B.C.; 屈原問渡

Musical versions of literary products: foremost among this group come musical versions of some odes of the *Shih-ching*.⁵² *Kuan-chü*, the opening ode of this classic, which celebrates the virtues of the bride of King Wên of Chou, is, of course, famous.⁵³ Then the *Lu-ming*,⁵⁴ a festive ode, where a banquet for high guests is described. It would seem that these two odes are inserted in the *ch'in* repertoire because both mention the lute.⁵⁵ These tunes are transmitted in greatly varying versions. Still they show some archaic features, and therefore deserve a special study; they may contain some old musical motifs.

The other tunes belonging to this category can be described in a few words; most of the better-known literary products which mention the lute and its music, or generally correspond to the tenets of *ch'in* ideology, have been made subjects for lute melodies. Most handbooks contain musical versions of the *Li-sao*, of *Kuei-ch'ü-lai-tz'û*, *T'êng-wang-ko*, *Nan-hsün-ko*, etc.⁵⁶ Many examples of poems and essays set to lute music may be found in the handbook *Sung-fêng-ko-ch'in-pu* compiled by Ch'êng Hsiung.⁵⁷ The reverse process is followed when new words are made to existing melodies; this is called *t'ien-tz'û*.⁵⁸ Examples of tunes with *t'ien-tz'û* may be found in the handbook *Shu-huai-tsao*,⁵⁹ the sister volume to the *Sung-fêng-ko-ch'in-pu*.

Tunes descriptive of nature: tunes of this type, together with those describing a mystic journey, occupy three-quarters of the entire *ch'in* repertoire. After the remarks made above (Chapter III, section *3*), this connection of the lute with scenic beauty needs no further commentary.

Ts'ai Yung is mentioned as the composer of *Ch'ang-ch'ing*,⁶⁰ a solemn melody that describes winter and the coming of spring. The *Shên-chi-pi-pu* remarks: 'This tune takes its inspiration from the snow, describes snow's purity and freedom from all earthly stains, and expresses contempt for the world and elevation to empty clearness.'⁶¹ The nine parts of this tune are entitled:

1 Heaven and earth breathe purity.
2 A clear, snowy morning.

---

52 詩經
53 關雎
54 鹿鳴
55 See above, p. 7.
56 離騷, 歸去來辭, 滕王閣, 南薰歌
57 松風閣琴譜; 程雄. His preface is dated 1677.
58 填詞
59 抒懷操
60 長清
61 取興於雪, 言其清潔而無塵滓之志, 厭世途超空明之趣也.

[IV] THE SIGNIFICANCE OF THE TUNES

3   Snow and sleet fall together.
4   Mountains and water merge in each other.
5   The brilliant sun in the sky.
6   The wind blows through the luxuriant forest.
7   River and mountain are like a picture.
8   The snow melts on cliffs and in vales.
9   Spring returns to the world.[62]

Further, Kuo Mien[63] composed a tune on the rivers Hsiao and Hsiang entitled *Hsiao-hsiang-shui-yün*[64] (Clouds Over the Rivers Hsiao and Hsiang). The ten parts bear the following subtitles:

1   Mist and rain over lake Tung-t'ing.
2   The rivers Chiang and Han are quiet and clear.
3   Shadows of the clouds cast down by the brilliant sky.
4   The water is one with the sky.
5   Rolling waves, flying clouds.
6   The rising wind stirs the waves.
7   Sky and water are of the same azure colour.
8   The cold river in the cool moonshine.
9   Limpid waves stretching for ten thousand miles.
10 The scenery contains all aspects of nature.[65]

And here of course must also be classified that most famous of all lute melodies, the tune called *Kao-shan-liu-shui*[66] (High Mountains and Flowing Streams). This composition is ascribed to Po Ya,[67] the paragon of all Chinese lute players. He is said to have been a man from Ch'u[68] who lived during the Ch'un-ch'iu period. The story about him and his friend Chung Ch'i[69] is related in *Lieh-tzû*, chapter 'T'ang-wên': 'Po Ya was a great lute player, and Chung Ch'i a great listener. Po Ya while playing the lute thought of ascending high mountains. Then Chung Ch'i said: "How excellent! Impressing like the T'ai-shan!" And when Po Ya thought of flowing streams, Chung Ch'i said: "How excellent! Broad and flowing like rivers and streams!" What Po Ya thought Chung Ch'i never failed to understand. Once Po Ya roamed on the northern flank of the T'ai-shan. Caught in a torrential rain, he took shelter under a cliff. Sad in his heart he drew his lute towards him, and pulled the strings. First he played the

---

62 乾坤清氣, 雪天清曉, 雪霰交飛, 山河一色, 日麗中天, 風鼓瓊林, 江山如畫, 雪消崖谷, 萬壑回春.
63 郭沔, Sung dynasty.
64 瀟湘水雲
65 洞庭煙雨, 江漢舒晴, 天光雲影, 水接天隅, 浪捲雲飛, 風起水湧, 水天一碧, 寒江月冷, 萬里澄波, 景涵萬象
66 高山流水
67 伯牙, also called Po Tzû-ya 伯子牙.
68 楚
69 鍾期, also called Chung Tzû-ch'i 鍾子期.

elegy of the falling rain, then he improvised upon the sounds of crumbling mountains. But as soon as he had played a tune, Chung Ch'i had already grasped its meaning. Then Po Ya pushed aside his lute, and said with a sigh: "Excellent, how excellent! Your hearing is such that you know immediately how to express what is in my mind. How could I ever escape you with my tones!'"[70] The *Lü-shih-ch'un-ch'iu* supplements this story as follows: 'When Chung Ch'i died, Po Ya broke his lute and tore the strings, and all his life did not play any more, as he deemed the world not worthy to be played to.'[71]

There is hardly any Chinese book or treatise on music that in some form or other does not quote this story; see for instance the quotation in Chapter III above, section 4, the last passage of Ying Shao's essay. In later times the story was elaborated further, and made into a novel.[72]

This story may be said to contain the essence of the system of *ch'in* ideology, stressing as it does the supreme importance of the *significance* of lute music: to express it while playing, and to understand it while listening. Although about Po Ya and Chung Ch'i nothing is reliably known, there can be no doubt that the motif itself is a very old one; perhaps it is en echo of the sacredness of music in ancient China.

The date of the composition which is transmitted under the name *Kao-shan-liu-shui*, however, must be placed comparatively late. It is not mentioned in the *Ch'in-tsao*, and appears only as late as the T'ang period. The author of *Shên-chi-pi-pu* divides the composition into two separate tunes, which he calls *Kao-shan* and *Liu-shui*. But in his preface to the former he says that originally they formed but one tune; during the T'ang period this tune was split up in two parts, each without further subdivision (*tuan*).[73] During the Sung dynasty the part *Kao-shan* was divided into 4 *tuan*, and the part *Liu-shui* into 8.[74] The Ch'ing handbook *Ch'un-ts'ao-t'ang-ch'in-pu*,[75] however, gives it as one tune, and asserts that it was during the Yüan dynasty that the tune was wrongly divided into two parts. Be this as it may, the tunes

---

[70] 伯牙善鼓琴，鍾子期善聽，伯牙鼓琴，志在登高山，鍾子期曰，善哉，峩峩兮若泰山，志在流水，鍾子期曰善哉，洋洋兮若江河，伯牙所念，鍾子期必得之，伯牙游於泰山之陰，卒逢暴雨，止於岩下，心悲，乃援琴而鼓之，初爲霖雨之操，更造崩山之音，曲每奏，鍾子期輒窮其趣，伯牙乃舍琴而嘆曰善哉善哉，子之聽，夫志想象猶吾心也，吾於何逃聲哉.

[71] 鍾子期死，伯牙破琴絕絃，終身不復鼓琴，以爲世無足復爲鼓琴者. 呂氏春秋卷十四，本味.

[72] 俞伯牙摔琴謝知音 n. 19 of the collection *Chin-ku-chi-kuan* 今古奇觀.

[73] 段

[74] 高山流水二曲本只一曲，至唐分爲兩曲，不分段數，至宋分高山爲四段，流水爲八段.

[75] Appendix II, 17.

[IV] THE SIGNIFICANCE OF THE TUNES 99

transmitted in the handbooks under this name do not seem to represent very old music. Very late is a special version of the part *Liu-shui*, a kind of 'show piece', composed by Chang K'ung-shan.[76] It was published in the *T'ien-wên-ko-ch'in-pu-chi-ch'êng*,[77] and reprinted and analyzed by Yang Tsung-chi in his *Ch'in-hsüeh-ts'ung-shu*.[78] This tune is technically so complicated that the composer had to invent a dozen new signs to be able to record this music in notation. Although interesting as a proof of the many possibilities of lute music, it has no value for the study of Chinese music. But the ideological motif which it bears in its name doubtless goes back to many centuries B.C.

Tunes descriptive of literary life: most of the tunes belonging to this type are of later date, as a rule from after the Sung dynasty. They sing the joys of the leisure hours of the scholar, passed with refined pleasures. As an example the following tune, ascribed to the literatus Liu Chi, may suffice.[79] It is entitled *K'o-ch'uang-yeh-hua*[80] (Literary Gathering in the Evening). The handbook of Yang Piao-chêng gives the names of its ten parts as follows:

1 Bridling emotions, indulging in meditation.
2 Celebrating antiquity, deploring the present.
3 Composing poetry and drinking wine.
4, 5 Discussing current topics.
6 A song with clapping of the hands.
6, 7 Elevated talk in the quiet night.
8 Thousand miles, one square.
9 Half of this evening equals ten years.
10 Kindred spirits, kindred traditions.[81]

About ninety-five per cent of the tunes that are contained in the lute repertoire may be classified under one of the above five groups. The remaining five per cent are purely musical compositions, and some Buddhist chants.

It goes without saying that the above classification is in many respects very arbitrary: the tunes have been selected from various Ming handbooks, and give but a very general idea of their contents. Still the above will suffice to show that nearly all the tunes of the Ming repertoire have some special meaning or portent: they are

---

76 張孔山
77 Appendix II, 18.
78 *Ch'in-pu* 琴譜, ch. 3.
79 劉基, 1311–75.
80 客窗夜話
81 覊情旅思, 慨古傷今, 題詩酌酒, 時世問答, 抵掌一嘯, 清談良夜, 千里一方, 半夜十年, 同志同傳.

what nowadays would be called 'programme music'. The music is not used independently, but chiefly as a means for expressing an idea, for conveying an impression. Music is made subservient to motif.

CHAPTER FIVE

Symbolism

§1 SYMBOLISM OF TERMS AND NAMES

Symbolism of the technical names for various parts of the lute— preponderance of the dragon and phoenix elements—symbolism of special names given to lutes

THE construction of the lute in general I have already discussed in Chapter I, at the same time quoting the technical names of some of its component parts. This technical terminology is very old; references in literature tend to show that it was already more or less fixed during the Han dynasty. As these terms illustrate some aspects of *ch'in* ideology, I shall here discuss them in greater detail.

Figure 8 shows the upper side (on the right) and the bottom (on the left) of a lute, with the technical names of each part added. Observing first the upper side, we see that the narrow, low bridge where the strings pass over the sounding box is called *lung-yin*[1] (dragon's gums); this part of the lute suggests the roof of a dragon's mouth. The higher bridge on the other end, where the strings are fastened to the silk loops, is called *yo-shan*.[2] 'Yo' is another name of the famous mountain, the T'ai-shan in Shantung province, a symbol of immovability and aloofness.

The narrow space seen beneath this bridge is called *fêng-ê*[3] (phoenix forehead); like *lung-yin* mentioned above, this term is apparently chosen because the slightly bent surface suggests also the forehead of the phoenix. The two terms for the small and the larger indentation, *hsien-jên-chien* (shoulders of the Immortal) and *yao* (waist),[4] are self-explanatory.

The left extremity of the lute is called *chiao-wei*[5] (scorched tail). This term refers to an anecdote told about the famous scholar and lute amateur Ts'ai Yung.[6] *Ch'in* handbooks usually give this story as fol-

---

[1] 龍齦
[2] 岳山
[3] 鳳額
[4] 仙人肩, 腰
[5] 焦尾
[6] 蔡邕, 133–92.

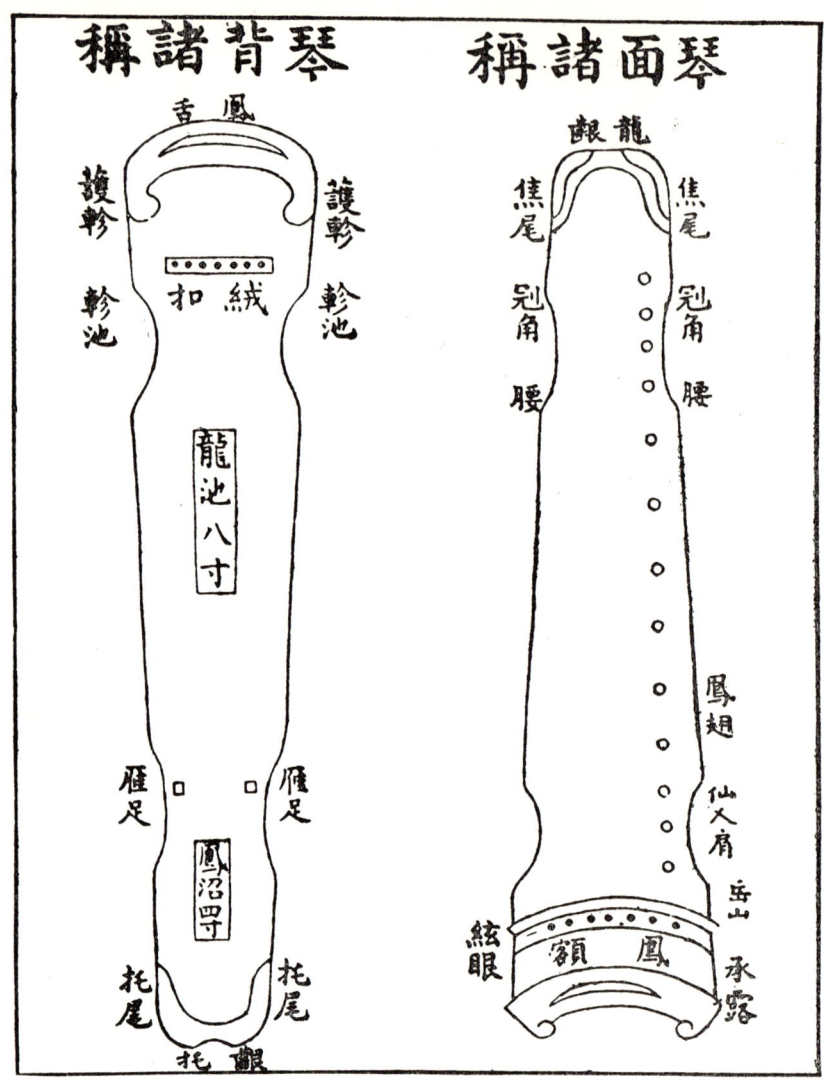

#8

lows: 'People from Wu were burning a log of *t'ung* wood for their cooking. Ts'ai Yung, when he heard its crackling sounds, said: "This will be the right material for making a lute!" He asked whether he might have the log, and made a lute from it. At one end, however, the marks of the burning still showed; therefore he called this lute Scorched Tail.'[7] In lists of lute names there occurs the appellation *I-hsin*[8] (left-over fuel); this name refers to the same anecdote.

The bulging part above the 'waist' is called *kuan-chüeh*[9] (cere-

[7] 吳人有燒桐以爨者，蔡邕聞其爆聲曰，此良材也，因請之，削以為琴，而燒不盡，因名之焦尾.

[8] 遺薪

[9] 冠角

monial cap), since it shows the same outline as this type of headgear. Both sides are called *fêng-ch'ih*[10] (phoenix wings), because they resemble the straight wing feathers with which this mythical bird is usually represented.

Turning now to the bottom board, we see in the first place the two sound holes, to which I have already referred above in Chap. I. Usually the largest one is called *lung-ch'ih* (dragon pond), and the smaller *fêng-chao* (phoenix pool).[11] But from the *Ch'in-tsao* it would appear that during the Han period the upper hole was called simply *ch'ih* (pond), and the lower one *pin* (shore).[12] A Korean source of the Ming dynasty (*Ak-hak-kwe-pôm*) calls the upper hole *lung-ch'üan* (dragon fountain), and the other *fêng-ch'ih* (phoenix pond).[13]

The two pegs for fastening the strings are called *yen-tsu*[14] (goose feet) doubtless because of their suggestive shape. The lower part of the *fêng-ê* is called *fêng-shê*[15] (phoenix tongue). The remaining terms have no special connection with the lore of the lute.

The terms mentioned above show the preponderance of the two elements phoenix and dragon. The lore connected with these two mythical animals pervades the ideology of the lute; as will be seen below, many special names of lutes refer to the phoenix or the dragon, and not a few tunes celebrate their eminent qualities.

It is not only in lute music that these two fabulous animals occupy a foremost position; they are closely associated with Chinese music in general. They figure prominently in the decoration of the instruments of the ceremonial orchestra, and some instruments even derive their names from them (e.g. *Lung-ti*, and *Fêng-huang-hsiao*,[16] both names of flutes).

Chinese sources explain the close connection of phoenix and music by the fact that according to tradition it was the notes sung by the male and female phoenix that in hoary antiquity inspired man to construct the twelve *lü*, the sonorous tubes that form the basis of Chinese musical theory.[17] And with regard to the dragon they say that the lofty and awe-inspiring qualities of this mythical animal, and its rolling growlings when it roams through the clouds, suggest the solemn tones of ceremonial music. But the secondary character of

---

10 鳳翅
11 龍池, 鳳沼
12 Appendix II, 1; 濱
13 樂學軌範, preface dated 1610; 龍泉, 鳳池
14 雁足
15 鳳舌
16 龍笛, 鳳凰簫
17 律; see *Han-shu* 漢書, *Lü-li-chih* 律曆志.

these explanations is evident: they represent endeavours to explain *a posteriori* an association, the real origin of which was no longer understood. The real origin must probably be sought in ancient Chinese beliefs, where the original forms of dragon and phoenix, i.e. *spirit of the waters* and *fire-bird*, played an important role, both being considered as granters of vitality and fertility. As such these animals figured prominently in the sacrifices and the ceremonial music connected therewith. This question, however, deserves a special investigation.

Next there are the special names borne by lutes. When a connoisseur obtains a lute the tones of which appeal to him, or which because of its colour, its shape or for some other reason captures his fancy, he will choose a special name for it. This name is carved in graceful characters in the bottom board (usually in the space above the Dragon Pond);[18] and henceforward the instrument is always referred to by this special name, which gives it something of a personal character and individual appeal.

Later connoisseurs may, and do, add laudatory inscriptions or other remarks, and so antique lutes are not infrequently covered with various inscriptions and seals, which make it a favourite object for the connoisseur's appreciation. For the carving of these inscriptions there exists a special technique, which I have discussed in Appendix III. For our present subject, however, it is only the names themselves that are of importance.

The happy owner of a beautiful instrument is free to choose any name for it that appeals to him. But usually it is selected from the existing lists of approved lute names. Such lists are to be found among the introductory chapters of most of the handbooks for the lute. A few were published separately. The best known is the *Ya-ch'in-ming-lu* compiled by Hsieh Chuang.[19] Just as in the titles of the tunes, also in these names of individual instruments various aspects of *ch'in* ideology are to be found reflected.

The greater part of the names describe the beautiful tones of the instrument. I mention, for instance, names like *Ling-lung-yü* (Tinkling Jade), *Hao-chung* (Singing Bell), *Yen-ying* (Echo of a Goose Cry), *Ch'un-lei* (Spring Thunder), *Ming-yü* (Singing Jade), *Lung-yin* (Dragon's Growling), *Lin-lang*, etc.[20]

---

18 See fig. 11, in Chapter 1 of this book.
19 雅琴名錄 (謝莊, style: Hsi-i 希逸, 421–66); this text is to be found in the *Hsün-chih* 順治 edition of the huge *ts'ung-shu*, *Shuo-fu* 說郛.
20 玲瓏玉, 號鐘, 雁應, 春雷, 鳴玉, 龍吟, 琳琅.

Others refer to the fact that the lute is the repository of the correct music of the Ancient Sages: to this category belong such titles as *Ts'un-ku* (Preserving Antiquity), *Yu-shêng* (Befriending the Ancient Sages), *Huai-ku* (Cherishing Antiquity), *T'ai-ku-i-yin* (Tones Bequeathed by High Antiquity), *Ta-ya* (Great Elegance).[21]

Others again suggest the atmosphere that surrounds the lute and its music. Here I would classify for instance: *Ku-t'ung* (Lonely Dryandra Tree), *Han-yü* (Cool Jade), *Sung-hsüeh* (Snow on the Pines), *Yang-shêng-chu* (Master of Nurturing Life), *Hsüeh-yeh-chung* (Bells on a Snowy Night), *Ho-yu* (Friend of the Crane), *Ching-yu* (Friend of Serenity), *Fou-ch'ing* (Floating Sonorous Stone), *Sung-hsien* (Immortal of the Pine Forest), etc.[22] Some names of four characters evoke a picturesque scenery, suggesting refined aesthetic enjoyment, so dear to the artist and the connoisseur: *Shih-shang-ch'ing-ch'üan* (A Clear Stream Flowing over Stones), *Hsüeh-yeh-chung-shêng* (The Sound of a Temple Bell on a Snowy Evening), *Pi-t'ien-fêng-ming* (A Phoenix Singing in the Azure Sky), *Ch'ing-hsiao-ho-lei* (A Crane Crying in the High Air).[23]

The above are only a few examples; the lover of the lute may choose any name that pleases him from the vast field of Chinese literary allusion.

[21] 存古, 友聖, 懷古, 太古遺音, 大雅
[22] 孤桐, 寒玉, 松雪, 養生主, 雪夜鐘, 鶴友, 靜友, 浮磬, 松仙
[23] 石上清泉, 雪夜鐘聲, 碧天鳳鳴, 青霄鶴淚.

§2 SYMBOLISM OF TONES

*Great importance of timbre in lute music—Chinese attempts to define the various sorts of timbre—*LÊNG CH'IEN'S *sixteen definitions, in text and translation*

Most handbooks for the lute player include among the introductory chapters a special section entitled *Ch'in-shêng*[24] (tones of the lute). There an attempt is made to express in words that extremely elusive element that constitutes one of the chief charms of lute music: the timbre, the colour of the tones.

Through the delicate structure of the lute, the strings respond to the most subtle nuances in the touch. The same note obtains a different colour when it is played with the thumb or with the forefinger of the right hand, and the timbre changes according to the force with which the string is pulled. This applies especially to the technique of the left hand: beneath the nimble and sensitive fingers of the expert player the strings show a wealth of unsuspected modulations. The high notes may either have a dry, almost wooden sound, or they may be sharp and metallic, and in another passage the same note may be clear and tinkling, like a silver bell. Low notes may be broad and mellow, or so abrupt as to be nearly rattling.

As the correct application of the various sorts of modulation is the basis of lute music, the Chinese have given much care to describe and define the various touches and the results they produce. In choosing the terminology they borrowed freely from the rich vocabulary of aesthetic appreciation, used by Chinese artists and connoisseurs.[25] Next to special musical terms like *ch'ing* (light), or *sung* (loose),[26] we also find old appreciative adjectives, which are not easy to translate. We find for instance words like *yu, ch'ing,* and *hsü*,[27] each of

---

24 琴聲

25 Both Chinese and Western dictionaries are sadly inadequate in their explanations of the hundreds of special terms that constitute this vocabulary. Yet an understanding of the scope of these terms, and of the subtle nuances in sentiment they imply, is absolutely necessary for a correct interpretation of the writings by Chinese art critics, whether their subject is fine art, belles-lettres, scenic beauty or music. It is to be hoped that some day a sinologue with artistic interest will undertake to compile a special dictionary of Chinese aesthetic terms, illustrated with appropriate quotations. A beginning on a small scale has been made by Lin Yu-t'ang in his *The Importance of Living*, New York 1937, Appendix B: 'A Chinese Critical Vocabulary'.

26 輕, 鬆

27 幽, 清, 虛

which suggests a definite atmosphere or mood. In most cases it is impossible to cover all the associations evoked by such a term with one single English word; their meaning must be understood through the context.

Not a few Chinese musicians have made endeavours to formulate such definitions for the various sorts of modulation. Well known, for instance, is a set of 24 articles, entitled *Ch'in-huang*, drawn up by the lute expert Hsü Hung and to be found in the *Ta-huan-ko-ch'in-pu*, a handbook for the lute connected with his name.[28] Universally approved, however, is the set of definitions formulated by Lêng-hsien, the 'Immortal Lêng', under the title of *Ch'in-shêng-shih-liu-fa* (Sixteen Rules for the Tones of the Lute).[29]

The 'Immortal Lêng' was a great musician of the beginning of the Ming dynasty; his real name was Lêng Ch'ien.[30] About 1370–1380 he occupied the position of Chief Musician in the *Yüeh-pu*,[31] the Board of Music. Besides music Lêng Ch'ien was deeply interested in Taoist magic; the *Imperial Catalogue* mentions a book by him entitled *Hsiu-ling-yao-chih* (Important Directions for Prolonging Life); apparently he lived to be a proof of the truth of his beliefs, for according to tradition he was over a hundred years old when he died.[32]

His *Ch'in-shêng-shih-liu-fa*, which I translate below, is reprinted in many of the later *ch'in-pu*, usually without quoting Lêng Ch'ien as the author. Therefore this essay is sometimes ascribed to other musicians. Besides the *ch'in-pu*, it is also to be found in the *Chiao-ch'uang-chiu-lu*[33] by Hsiang Yüan-pien and in the *T'an-chi-ts'ung-shu*.[33] For my translation I have used the text as published in the *Chiao-ch'uang-chiu-lu*.

This text presents various difficulties. The sentences are brief, and often ambiguous. It is often not clear whether descriptive adjectives apply to the finger technique or to the tones produced by it. In my translation I have taken all these adjectives to refer to the finger technique, in order not to confuse the reader.

The descriptive adjectives are not easy to render adequately:

---

28 琴況; 徐谼; 大還閣琴譜, first preface dated 1673. The second article has been translated by Laloy, on page 71 of his *La Musique chinoise*; see App. I, 5.

29 冷仙, 琴聲十六法

30 冷謙; style: Ch'i-ching 啓敬; literary name: Lung-yang-tzû 龍陽子. He died between 1403–24.

31 樂部.

32 In chap. 147, p. 10 *verso*; 修齡要指. For the tradition, see *I-nien-lu* 疑年錄, ch. 5.

33 蕉窓九錄, 項元汴, 1525–90; 檀几叢書.

they suggest rather than describe, they indicate but do not define. Many a sentence might in the translation have been spun out to a whole passage. I have aimed at brevity, leaving it to the reader to interpret the passages, and to elaborate their meaning. I do not pretend, however, that my translation is final; in many cases it is but one of a dozen different possibilities.

Often our text uses special terms referring to various parts of the finger technique; as those are discussed in the next section of this chapter, I have left them here without any special explanation.

SIXTEEN RULES FOR THE TONES OF THE LUTE

1 *Ch'ing*:[34] THE LIGHT TOUCH.

> Not light and not heavy are the tones of balanced harmony. When the melody starts,[35] one should aim at playing in these balanced tones. If, in applying the light and heavy touch, the rules of decrescendo and crescendo are adhered to, the sentiment of the tune appears of its own accord. The light touch is the most difficult of all. If not enough force is applied, then the tone is vague and not true, dim and not clear; though light, it is not elegant. The middle light tones are faultless, clear and true. [When applying the light touch] one should consider the string being as thin as one single silk thread of one ten-thousandth of an inch, the sound of which is spoilt when the finger as much as approaches it. Then these tones shall express a sentiment of infinite profundity. Sometimes one whole phrase or bar is played in the light touch, but there exist also the mixed, the higher and the lower light touches. Their tendencies vary, but, with regard to all, the main point lies in clearness and truth.[36]

2 *Sung*:[37] THE LOOSE TOUCH.

> The beauty of vibrato and vibrato ritardando lies in the loose touch. The left hand should move up and down over the string

---

[34] 輕

[35] 起周, in the handbooks often abbreviated to 己周; literally: 'beginning of the melody'. A tune usually opens with an introductory movement which has no melodic connections with the following parts. Then, mostly in the middle of the second movement, the chief melodic pattern of the tune appears for the first time. This passage is marked with the sign 己周.

[36] 一曰輕. 不輕不重者, 中和之音也, 起調當以中和爲主, 而輕重特 (read 持) 損益之則, 其趣自生, 蓋音之輕處最難, 力有未到則浮而不實, 晦而不明, 雖輕亦不嘉, 惟輕之中, 不爽清實, 而一絲一忽, 指到音綻, 幽趣無限, 酒有一節一句之輕, 有間雜高下之輕, 種種意趣, 皆貴於清實中得之.

[37] 鬆

in a rounded-off movement, light and freely, without any jerks or hitches. It should not be too hasty, nor too slow, but just right: this is what is called the loose touch. Heavy, thin, slow and quick vibrato and vibrato ritardando, all are based on the loose touch. Therefore, the wondrous music of the lute entirely depends upon touch. If the touch is rounded off, then the emotions are unified; if the loose touch is lively, then the thoughts are elated. The loose touch should evoke an impression as of water rising in waves, its substance should evoke an impression as of pearls rolling in a bowl; its sound should be like the resonance of intoning a text: this is what is called the loose touch.[38]

3 *Ts'ui*:[39] THE CRISP TOUCH.

The crisp touch is firm. Even for playing tunes of soft harmony and great elegance, both hands should attack the strings, firmly, so that the tones will not be turbid. For each hand this crisp touch is used, but it is hidden and does not come into sight, and it is not easy to express. When the right hand drags on the strings, then the tones will be turbid and dull. Therefore it is said: One should attack the strings with the tips of the fingers, touching them vertically from above. If one does not attack the strings smartly, then the tones will be sticky and irregular. Therefore it is said: The resonance should be like metal or stone, the movement of the fingers should be like the rising wind. For understanding the crisp touch, the swiftness of the fingers should first be known. The swiftness of the fingers is rooted in firmness. The firmness of the fingers is rooted in the arm. If the strength of the arm is applied, then the firm, crisp touch may be executed. Not until then can it be understood that the tendency to turbidity inherent in the strings does not annoy the true musician.[40, 41]

4 *Hua*:[42] THE GLIDING TOUCH.

Gliding means flowing: it is the opposite of halting. The tones

---

[38] 二曰鬆. 鬆卽吟猱妙處, 宛轉動蕩無滯無礙, 不促不慢, 以至恰好, 謂之鬆, 吟猱之巨細緩急, 俱有鬆, 故琴之妙在取音, 宛轉則情聯, 鬆活則意暢, 其趣如水之興瀾, 其體如珠之走盤, 其聲如哦咏之有韻, 方可名鬆.

[39] 脆

[40] The text reads: 在絃, 當為知音厭聲耳, which does not seem to make sense. I follow the text as reprinted in the *Wu-chih-chai-ch'in-pu* (App. II, 15).

[41] 三曰脆. 脆者健也, 於沖和大雅中, 健其兩手, 而音不至於滯, 兩手皆有脆處, 第藏之不見, 出之不易, 右指靠絃, 則音滯而木, 故曰, 指必甲尖, 絃必懸落, 在指不勁, 則音膠而格, 故曰, 響如金石, 動如風發, 要知脆處, 卽脂之靈處, 指之靈, 自出於健, 而指之健, 又出於腕, 腕中之力旣到, 則為堅脆, 然後識滯氣之在絃, 不為知音厭聽.

[42] 滑

tend to be halting, and the fingers tend to be gliding. By nature the tones tend to be drawn out, and to follow each other in slow succession, like the bubbling sound of a stream, that goes on gurgling endlessly. Therefore this is called halting. If the finger technique is impeded, then it is not swift. The fingers should move up and down like gusts of wind, therefore this touch is called gliding. The most important point in the movement of the fingers is of course gliding. But sometimes also stopping is important. This stopping should be considered as a pause in the gliding. So that when in a tune there is halting, there must also be gliding; and if there is gliding, there must also be halting. Then both obtain their real significance.[43]

5 *Kao*:[44] THE LOFTY TOUCH.

Although the lofty touch resembles the antique touch,[45] they are essentially different. The antique touch is expressed by resonance, the lofty touch is modelled after melody. If the finger technique is serene and clear, and if moreover one can apply the lofty modulation, only then shall the meaning of the tones reach the mysterious wonder. Therefore this touch is of the utmost tranquillity, like a deep well that can not be fathomed, like a high mountain whose top is lost to the eye. It flows on, like streams that are never exhausted, and it is soundless like the threefold sound[46] of emptiness.[47]

6 *Chieh*:[48] THE PURE TOUCH.

If one wishes to attain perfection in tone, one should first attain perfection in the finger technique. The way of perfecting the finger technique passes from being to not-being, through multiplicity to simplicity. Not discoloured by one speck of dust, not defiled by one flaw, the secret of the finger technique dwells in the stage of the highest purity. But generally people do not

---

[43] 四曰滑‧ 滑者溜也，又澁之反也，音嘗欲澁而指嘗欲滑，音本喜慢，而綏綏出之，若流泉之鳴咽，時滴滴不已，故曰澁，指取走絃而滯則不靈，乃往來之鼓動，如風發發，曰故滑，然指之運用，固貴其滑，而亦有時平貴留，所謂留者，即滑中之安頓處也，故有澁不可無滑，有滑不可無留，意各有在耳．

[44] 高

[45] See p. 113 below.

[46] In *Chuang-tzû* 莊子, chapter *Ch'i-wu-lun* 齊為論, are mentioned the sounds of Heavenly, of Earthly, and of Human Emptiness 天籟, 地籟, 人籟. *Lai* is the unheard harmony of the Universe, what the Greeks called the 'Harmony of the Spheres'.

[47] 五曰高‧ 高與古似，而古實與高異，古以韻發，高以調裁，指下既靜既清，而又能得高調，則音意始臻微妙，故其為甯謐也，若深淵之不可測，若喬嶽之不可望，其為流逝也，若江河之欲無盡，若三籟之欲無聲．

[48] 潔

realize this. If in the finger technique purity is perfected, then the tones become more and more rarefied.[49] The more rarefied the tones are, the more the spirit nears eternity. Therefore I say: if one wishes to perfect wondrous tones, one should first perfect the wondrous finger technique. In order to perfect the wondrous finger technique, one must necessarily start with cultivating purity in oneself.[50]

7 *Ch'ing:*[51] THE CLEAR TOUCH.

All tones are governed by clearness. If the place where the music is performed is secluded, clearness results; when the heart is serene, clearness results; when the spirit is solemn, clearness results; if the lute is true, clearness results; if the strings are clean, clearness results. Only when all these factors that affect clearness are assembled may one aim at clearness in the finger technique. Then left and right hand shall be like Male and Female Phoenix, chanting harmoniously together, and the tones shall not be stained with the slightest impurity. The movement of the fingers should be like striking bronze bells or sonorous stones. Slow or quick, no secondary sounds shall be produced, so that when hearing these tones one obtains an impression of purity—as of a pool in autumn; of brilliancy—as of the shining moon; of dim resonance—as of the babbling water in mountain gorges; of profundity—as of a resounding valley. These tones shall in truth freeze alike heart and bones,[52] and it shall be as if one were going to be bodily transformed into an Immortal.[53]

8 *Hsü:*[54] THE EMPTY TOUCH.

While playing the lute to express true tones, this is not very difficult. What is really difficult is to express emptiness. If asked 'The fingers move to produce tones; where does emp-

---

[49] *Hsi* 希, a typical Taoist adjective, difficult to translate. Together with the equally obscure terms *i* 夷 and *wei* 微, it is used in the 14th chapter of the *Tao-tê-ching* to describe Tao. There it is said: 'I listen to it but I cannot hear it, therefore I call it *hsi*' 聽之不聞，名曰希.

[50] 六曰潔. 欲修妙音者，必先修妙指，修指之道，從有而無，因多而寡，一塵不染，一垢弗緇，止於至潔之地，而人不知其解，指既修潔，則音愈希，則意趣愈永，吾故曰，欲修妙者，必先修妙指，欲修妙指者，又必先自修潔始.

[51] 清

[52] For this 'frozen' mental condition, see p. 58.

[53] 七曰清. 清者音之主宰，地僻則清，心靜則清，氣肅則清，琴實則清，琴潔則清，必使群清，咸集而後可求之指上，兩手如鸞鳳和鳴，不染纖毫濁氣，應指如擊金戞石，緩急絕無容聲，試一聽之則澄然秋潭，皎然月潔，劃然山濤，幽然谷應，眞令人心骨俱冷，體氣欲仙.

[54] 虛

tiness come in?' I would answer: It lies exactly in the producing of tones. If the tones are sharp, the player shows his precipitation; if the tones are coarse, then the player betrays his impurity; but if the tones are serene, then the player shows that he has achieved the expression of emptiness. This is the right way for appreciating music. The merit of the finger technique lies in two things; on the one hand in expressing the spirit of the melody, and on the other in refining its purity. When the spirit of the melody is expressed, then the heart will become serene as a matter of course, and when the purity is refined, the tones shall naturally be empty. Therefore though being quick they will not be disorderly, and though being many they will not be confused. The self-sufficiency of a deep well, an irradiating splendour, high mountains and flowing streams: with the spirit of these one's soul should harmonize.[55]

9 *Yu*:[56] THE PROFOUND TOUCH.

If tones are profound, then they come up to the standard of lute music. The quality of music depends upon the personality of the player; thus profundity comes from within. Therefore, when a high-minded and cultivated scholar executes a tune, then the resonance is profound. If one truly understands profundity as expressed by the fingers, the player can let himself go, whether the movement be slow or quick. The music will be broad and generous like the wind, and unstained by earthly dust. It will serve to show the elevated disposition of the player, and the fingers will depict the emotion that inspired each part of the composition. This is meant by the saying: Let the fingers express what the heart experiences.[57] When one hears his music one shall know the personality of the player. Such are the wonderful qualities of the profound touch.[58]

10 *Chi*:[59] THE RARE TOUCH.

The special quality of tone that is produced by the rare touch

---

[55] 八曰虛. 撫琴著實處, 亦何難, 獨難於得虛, 然指動而求聲, 烏乎虛, 余則曰, 政在聲中求耳, 聲厲則知躁, 聲粗則知濁, 聲靜則知虛, 此審音之道也, 蓋下指功夫, 一在調氣, 一在淘洗, 調氣則心自靜, 淘洗則聲自虛, 故雖急而不亂, 多而不繁, 深淵自居, 清光發外, 山高水流, 於此可以神會.

[56] 幽

[57] Quoted from *Lieh-tzû*, chapter *T'ang-wên*.

[58] 九曰幽. 音有幽度, 始稱琴品, 品係乎人, 幽由於內, 故高雅之士動操便有幽韻, 洵知幽之在指, 無論綏急, 悉能安閒自如, 風度盎溢, 些無塵染, 足覘瀟麗胸次, 指下自然寫出一段風情, 所謂得之心, 而應之手, 聽其音而得其人, 此幽之微妙也.

[59] 奇

appears in the vibrato and the glissando. If while playing it is applied in the right way, it should evoke an impression as if a thousand mountain peaks vied with each other in verdure, as if the ten thousand streams emulated each other's effervescence. It should impart to the hearer a sensation of flowing, of going on forever, an unbroken continuity. Where in a tune periods or bars are suddenly broken off, and at the end of a tune, care should be taken especially not to let the music end in a vague, careless way. For each part of a tune has its special sentiment that should be expressed by the performer. Moreover an expression should be given as if one were riding on horseback high in the mountains, amidst drifting clouds.[60] When every note is made to express the sentiment inherent in it, then only shall one know the wonder of the rare touch.[61]

11 *Ku*:[62] THE ANTIQUE TOUCH.

In studying the lute there are only two ways: either one follows the old methods, or one follows the methods that are in vogue at the time. Although the old music is obscured by its high antiquity, still if one tries to approach its meaning, its harmony and and simplicity may be reached as a matter of course. Therefore, when in playing one does not fall in with the tunes that are in vogue at the time, then the music breathes the spirit of the Emperor Fu Hsi. It should be grand, broad and simple, boldly moving over the strings, disdaining petty virtuosity. It should be unmoved like a profound mountain, like a cavernous vale, like an old tree or a cool stream, like the rustling wind, causing the hearer suddenly to realize the True Way. This is something that certainly is rarely seen or heard in this world; therefore it is called the antique touch.[63]

---

[60] Quotation from the poem entitled *Sung-yu-jên-ju-shu* 送友人入蜀 (Collected Works, ch. 15), a poem by the great T'ang poet Li T'ai-po (李太白, 701–62). Lin Yu-t'ang translates these lines thus: 'Above the man's face arise the hills; beside the horse's head emerge the clouds' (cf. *My Country and My People*, New York 1936, pp. 246–7, where the rich imagery of these lines is aptly explained).

[61] 十曰奇. 音有奇特處, 乃在吟逗間, 指下取之, 當如千巖競秀, 萬壑爭流, 令人流連不盡, 應接不暇, 至章句頓挫, 曲折之際, 尤不可輕意草草放過, 定有一段情緒, 又如山從人面起, 雲傍馬頭生, 字字摹神, 方知奇妙.

[62] 古

[63] 十一曰古. 琴學祇有二途, 非從古則從時, 玆雖古學久淹而彷彿其意則自和澹中來, 下指不落時調, 便有羲皇氣象, 寬大純朴, 落落絃中, 不事小巧, 宛然深山邃谷老木寒泉, 風聲籟籟, 頓令人起道心, 絕非世所見聞者, 是以名曰古音.

12 *T'an*:⁶⁴ THE SIMPLE TOUCH.

The lute masters of the present time aim at charming the ears; they insist upon producing captivating sounds, thereby greatly sinning against refined elegance. This is because they do not know that the basis of lute music is simplicity. I, on the contrary, tune my lute to simplicity, therefore the great mass does not understand my music. Where is it that simplicity dwells? I love its sentiment, which is not extravagant nor contending. I love its flavour, which is like snow or ice. I love its echo, which is like the wind blowing over pines, like rain on bamboo, like the bubbling of a mountain stream, or like lapping waves. It is only with great musicians that one can talk about simplicity.⁶⁵

13 *Chung*:⁶⁶ THE BALANCED TOUCH.

Balanced sounds occur in all music, but they are inherent⁶⁷ in the music of the lute. After the old music was lost, there were many that pulled the strings with ardent fervour, and carefully listened to the lute; but only the most excellent musicians⁶⁸ are able to transmit the echo of the empty vale. When, ignorantly, one rejoices in elaborating mellow and captivating tones, obliquity⁶⁹ results. When the finger technique is heavy and impure, obliquity results. When the resonance is strained and hasty, obliquity results. When the tones produced are coarse and sharp, obliquity results. When the strings are attacked hurriedly, obliquity results. When the personality of the player is unstable and casual, obliquity results. Rectifying this obliquity, returning to completeness, banishing the devious and aiming at the right, this is the way to obtain the tradition of the balanced touch.⁷⁰

---

64 淡

65 十二曰淡. 時師欲娛人耳，必作媚音，殊傷大雅，第不知琴音本淡，而吾復調之以淡，固衆人所不解，惟淡何居，吾愛此情，不靡不競，吾愛此味，如雪如冰，吾愛此響，松之風而竹之雨，澗之滴而波之濤也，故善知音者，始可與言淡.

66 中

67 See *Chuang-tzǔ*: 因其固然, 'following its natural course'.

68 *Ying-jên-kua-ho*, lit.: 'The people of Ying play [*ho* in the 4th tone] songs that few are able to perform'; quotation from the *Sung-yü-chi* 宋玉集. The meaning is as in the translation above.

69 *P'ien* is used as counterpart to *chung* 中, an allusion to the preface of the Doctrine of the Mean, *Chung-yung* 中庸, where it is said: 'Being without inclination to either side is called *chung*' (Legge) 不偏之謂中.

70 十三曰中. 樂有中聲，惟琴固然，自古音淹沒，攘臂絃索而捧耳於琴者比比矣，即有繼空谷之響，未免郢人寡和，不知喜工柔媚則偏，落指重濁則偏，性好炎鬧則偏，發響局促則偏，取音粗厲則偏，入絃倉卒則偏，氣質浮躁則偏，矯其偏，歸於全，袪其倚，習於正，斯得中之傳.

14 *Ho*:[71] THE HARMONIOUS TOUCH.

Harmony is the basis of all tones: it means neither overdoing nor falling short.[72] It is modulated on the strings, it is experienced in the fingers, it is diversified in the notes. The strings have their own nature: if they are compliant, then they will be in harmony with each other. If they are recalcitrant, then they are false. When the movement of the fingers moving up and down, from one string to the other, is smooth like varnish, then the strings harmonize with the fingers. The tones are regulated by the gamut: sometimes they are to be produced exactly on the spot indicated by one of the thirteen studs, sometimes they are not. The numerical indications fix the notes. The important point is to make the vibrato smooth, and to make the chords harmonize precisely, in order to express the sentiment of the tune. Then fingers and tones will be in harmony. Every tone has its own special singificance; the significance comes first, for the notes adjust themselves to the significance. So all the wonders of this music are completed. Therefore, heavy and not vain, light but not floating, swift but not hasty, slow but not slack; with regard to vibrato and vibrato ritardando: smooth but not vulgar; with regard to glissandos: correct and not inaccurate; when all the movements are linked up together smoothly; when the crescendos and decrescendos are crisp and yet connected... then tone and significance shall be in harmony. Then the soul shall be free and the spirit at rest, fingers and strings melt together, and the pure harmony that leaves no trace shall be produced. These are the signs by which I recognize the great Harmony.[73]

15 *Chi*:[74] THE QUICK TOUCH.

In the finger technique both the slow and the quick touch are used. The slow touch is the basis of the quick, the quick touch is the echo of the slow. In the tunes both touches are alternating

---

[71] 和

[72] Quoted from the *Lun-yü* 論語, Book XI, ch. 15. 3: 'The Master said: To go beyond is as wrong as to fall short.' (Legge)

[73] 十四曰和。和爲五音之本，無過不及之謂也，當調之在絃，審之在指，辨之在音，絃有性，順則協，逆則矯，往來鼓動有如膠漆，則絃與指和，音有律，或在徽，或不在徽，其有分數以位其音，要使婉婉成吟，絲絲叶韻，以得其曲之情，則指與音和，音有意，意動音隨，則衆妙歸，故重而不虛，輕而不浮，疾而不促，緩而不弛，若吟若猱，圓而不俗，以綽以注，正而不差，紆廻曲折，聯而無間，抑揚起伏，斷而復連，則音與意，因之神閒氣逸，指與絃化，自得渾合無迹，吾是以知其太和。

[74] 疾

continually. Sometimes in the middle of a bar the touch is quick, but near its end it slows down; and a bar that ends on the slow touch sometimes is followed up immediately by a movement in the swift touch. Moreover there are two ways for executing the quick touch. The first is called the little swift touch, which must be brisk. It must be firm, yet the movement of the fingers should not spoil the elegance inherent in the swift touch; it should suggest floating clouds and flowing water. The second is the great swift touch. Its most important point lies in its precipitation, but one should make special efforts not to cause confusion by playing too quickly. Then as a matter of course one expresses a mood of tranquillity, and the sounds will come forth bubbling, like rocks crumbling down or like a cascade falling from a high place. Therefore the quick touch is regulated by the meaning of the tones. It is the meaning that lends tones their divine qualities.[75]

16 *Hsü:*[76] THE SLOW TOUCH.

The ancients used the lute to nurture their nature and their emotions; therefore they called its tones rarefied. This quality is to be expressed by the very slow touch. Tones are produced by the fingers, broadly roaming over the strings, but observing the right measure. The finger technique should be in accordance with the right measure, so that the music produced is in harmony with the gamut. Sometimes one entire bar is played calmly and slowly, sometimes also in the same bar slow and quick alternate with each other. Sometimes a bar breaks off in the middle and then goes on again, sometimes also while going on smoothly it suddenly breaks off. When this technique is executed correctly as each case requires, then naturally one produces the rarefied tones of antiquity, and gradually one penetrates the deepest mystery of this music.[77,78]

---

75 十五曰疾，指法有徐，則有疾，然徐爲疾之綱，疾爲徐之應，嘗相間錯，或句中借速以落遲，或句宛遲者以速接，又有二法，小速微快，要以緊，遞指不傷疾中之雅度，而隨有行雲流水之趣，大速貴急，務使急而不亂，依然安間之氣象，而寫出崩崖飛瀑之聲，是故疾以意用，更以意神。

76 徐

77 The last lines of this paragraph seem badly transmitted. *Yang-ch'un* is a famous old tune, said to have been composed by Sung Yu (宋玉, third century B.C.). It is not clear, however, whether *Yüeh-man-hsi-lou* is also the name of a tune, or a sentence in itself. Because such Chinese musicians as I have consulted could not solve the problem without making drastic changes in the text, I leave these lines untranslated.

78 十六曰徐，古人以琴涵養性情，故名其聲曰希，嘗於徐徐得之，音生運指，優游絃上，節*

§3 SYMBOLISM OF THE FINGER TECHNIQUE

Postures of the hands, and their explanations—set of special pictures illustrating the finger technique; their various editions—technical terminology used in the lute handbooks—the abbreviated signs (CHIEN-TZÛ)—list of elementary CHIEN-TZÛ, their meaning and symbolism—examples of how the notation is read

WHEN the spirit of the various touches has been understood, then the lute player must devote his attention to their correct execution, and try to master the finger technique. Also with regard to this practical aspect of the technique of lute playing, the handbooks give explicit directions, illustrated by a rich symbolism. When the meaning of the abbreviated signs that constitute the lute notation has been understood, and when their spirit is recognized, then the student should be able to read and interpret correctly the tunes as they are recorded in the handbooks.

As has been stated above, lute music is written down not in notes, but in complicated symbols that indicate how a note is produced. These symbols are combinations of abbreviated characters, the so-called *chien-tzû*;[79] these shall presently be discussed in greater detail.

Among the introductory chapters of each lute handbook a special section, called *chih-fa*, or also *pu-tzû*,[80] is devoted to these *chien-tzû*. This section covers several pages; for as a rule in the handbooks no fewer than 150-200 special abbreviations are used, and each of these is carefully explained in this section. But the lute masters justly deem mere words inadequate for expressing all the subtleties of the technique described. When it is stated, for instance, that a certain sign means: 'Pull the third string inwards with the index of the right hand,' this explanation is not sufficient for the student who studies the lute without his master being present. For there are many ways to pull a string inwards with the index, but there is but one that is correct and that shall produce the desired timbre.

Therefore to the section *chih-fa* a second one is added, entitled

---

*其氣候,候至而下,以叶厥律,或章句舒徐,或綏急相間,或斷而復續,或續而復斷,因候制宜,自然調古聲希,漸入淵微,嚴道徹詩,幾回拈出陽春調月滿西樓,下指遲,其於徐意大有得也.

[79] 減字

[80] 指法, 譜字

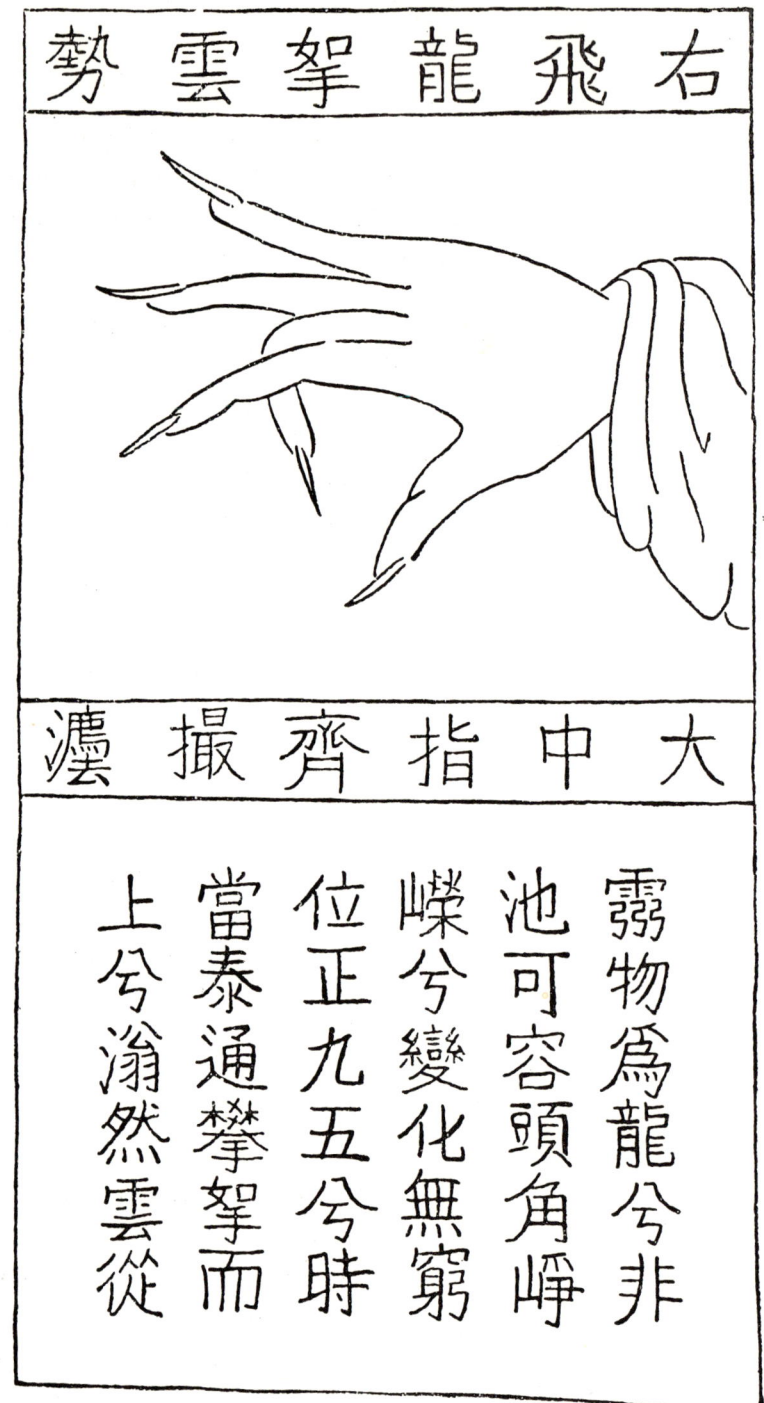

#9: Page from a lute handbook (Appendix II #18), showing a posture of the right hand, with explanatory notes.

#10: Symbolic picture illustrating the finger technique (from a Japanese manuscript copy of the *Yang-ch'un-t'ang-ch'in-pu*).

#11: Symbolic picture illustrating the finger technique (same source as figure 10).

shou-shih (postures of the hands).⁸¹ This section consists of a series of about forty drawings, showing in a schematic way the correct posture of right and left hand for each of the more frequently occurring touches. In some of the later handbooks these sketches are drawn so clumsily, that it is difficult to imagine how they could be of any use to the student of the finger technique. But the older handbooks often have more elaborate drawings, sketched with undeniable skill. To each drawing there is usually added a short sentence, which by means of comparison and symbol explains the spirit of each posture treated. Figure 9, for example, shows the correct posture of the right hand for executing a chord. This picture bears the legend: 'The right hand, suggesting a flying dragon grasping the clouds', and underneath is written: 'The way to produce a chord with thumb and middle finger.'⁸² Thus the master tries to suggest to the reader that the touch should be broad and firm, the hand having more or less a clawing posture. Often the meaning is still further elaborated in a short explanatory note, called *hsing* (mood),⁸³ of the posture in question. The *hsing* of figure 9 reads: 'The dragon is a holy animal, a pond can not contain it. Its head and horns show a noble shape, its transmutations are inexhaustible. Having ascended the Throne [allusion to the fact that 'Dragon' is a fixed epithet of the Emperor], the world is prosperous. It ascends in the air grasping with its claws, the floating clouds follow it.'⁸⁴ Finally, to make the meaning clearer still, some handbooks add a picture representing the dragon grasping its way through the clouds (see fig. 10).

Tradition has fixed such a special symbol (*hsiang-hsing*)⁸⁵ for each of the elementary postures occurring in the finger technique. Vibrato is illustrated by a cicada creeping up the branch of a tree, three strings pulled at the same time are represented by sailing clouds, the plucking of one string with two fingers at the same time, by a wild goose carrying a reed stalk in its bill (see figs. 11, 12), etc. A full list of these symbols will be found below, where the abbreviated signs are discussed.⁸⁶

---

81 手勢
82 右飛龍拏雲勢; 大中指齊撮法
83 興
84 靈物爲龍兮, 非池可容, 頭角崢嶸兮, 變化無窮, 位正九五兮, 時當泰通, 攀拏而上兮, 瀚然雲從.
85 像形
86 A brief note should be added to the discussion of the finger technique, concerning *artificial nails* (*tai-chia* 代甲 or *ch'in-chia* 琴甲), which lute players sometimes use on their right hands.

As a rule the lute is played without artificial fingernails. The Chinese, and more particularly the members of the literary class, permitted their finger nails to grow longer than is customary in the West; thus Chinese lute players have to cut down the nails of the*

These symbolic explanations of the various postures of the hands are very old; they may already be found in literary sources of the third and fourth centuries A.D. The set of pictures (about 40 in all) belonging to these explanations, however, is of a later date. I could not trace them back further than the Ming period. As this set of pictures is not without artistic value, I may describe their history in a few words.

I found them in three publications of the Ming period; two of these give the pictures in a rather crude form, the third presents them in a more elaborate and artistic way. The two more primitive versions are found:

1 in the lute handbook published by the great musician Hu Wên-huan, entitled *Wên-hui-tʻang-chʻin-pu*.[87a]

*right hand, while we have to let them grow a little. The correct way of pulling a string is to use simultaneously half of the finger tip and the rim of the nail. If artificial nails are used, then the sound volume of a note increases, but at the same time it will lack that muted quality that is one of the characteristics of lute music. Hence most lute players condemn the use of artificial nails.

The oldest reference to artificial nails seems to be a note entitled *chʻin-chia* 琴甲, in the *Tzŭ-hsia-lu* 資霞錄, by the Tʻang writer Li Kʻuang-i 李匡乂. 'At present,' he observes, 'lute players occasionally cut an artificial nail from bamboo, in order to strengthen the notes produced by the index pulling a string; this was first introduced by Chʻien-kung' 今彈琴或削竹爲甲，以助食指之聲者，亦因汧公也. 'Chʻien-kung' refers to the famous Tʻang statesman and lute player Li Mien (李勉 717–88), author of the *Chʻin-shuo* 琴說 (cf. the *Chʻin-shu-tsʻun-mu*, described below on p. 182, no. 8, note on the *Chʻin-shuo* ch. II, pp. 13 ff). A little farther, however, Li Kʻuang-i criticizes the use of artificial nails, which he condemns as 'rejecting the true for the false' 棄眞用假. According to Li, even when playing the harp or the cither no artificial nails should be used, 'for only if one is able to discard the false and return to the true, will their tones be of complete beauty 至如箜篌之與秦箏，若能去假還眞，其聲宛美矣. This aversion to the use of artificial nails is doubtless based on the ancient theory that the player should be in direct contact with his instrument, so that the vital essence may flow freely from the hands into the strings.

The *Wu-chih-chai* handbook (see p. 185, no. 15) gives in ch. I, in the section *Chʻin-chai-pa-tse* 琴齊八則 ('Eight Rules for the Lute Chamber'), a brief note on artificial nails. This book recommends to make them from deer horn, ivory, tortoise shell, or the shaft of a goose feather. He also tells what glue should be used for attaching them to the fingers so that they will stay there for two weeks or so, without becoming loosened even by washing the hands in hot water.

87 a) 胡文煥，文會堂琴譜. Hu Wên-huan, style: Tê-fu 德甫 (or also: Tê-wên 德文), literary name: Chʻüan-an 全菴 (or also Chin-an 金菴), and Pao-chʻin-chü-shih 抱琴居士. This interesting personality, a typical Ming literatus, would be well worth a special study. He was a man of elegant tastes, who combined an ardent love for old books and antique lutes with interest in the theatre and its fair inmates and in the lighter genres of poetry. His collection of books and rare manuscripts was well known, and he enjoyed great fame as a lute expert. In addition he wrote numerous plays, and was considered one of the greatest dramatists of the Ming period. Most of his plays, however, are practically unknown; they probably slumber in forgotten corners of Chinese libraries. Hu Wên-huan showed his bibliophilic zeal by publishing an extensive collection of rare works acquired by him; this collection bears the name of *Ko-chih-tsʻung-shu* 格致叢書. It contained 346 items divided over 37 categories; 47 items were published separately. A list of the contents of this *tsʻung-shu* is given in the *Tsʻung-shu-shu-mu-wei-pien* 叢書書目彙編, Shanghai 1929, page 337. Complete copies of this collection, however, do not seem to exist; at least I myself never came across one. Occasionally, however, I obtained separate*

2 in the picture-encyclopedia *San-ts'ai-t'u-hui*.[87b]

The more elaborate version is to be found in a famous Ming handbook for the lute, the *Yang-ch'un-t'ang-ch'in-pu*.[88] It is not without interest to try to establish the relation between these editions.

The *Wên-hui-t'ang* handbook is the oldest source; the preface is dated 1596, according to its last sentence.[89] A specimen page of this handbook is reproduced in figure 12. As to the date of the *San-ts'ai* encyclopedia, its latest preface is dated 1609. The *Yang-ch'un-t'ang* handbook bears no date at all; still it is possible to fix approximately when it was published. This handbook was compiled by Chang Ta-ming,[90] a well-known lute master of the Ming period, who lived in Fukien province. His first great work on the lute was the *Ch'in-ching*, a work on the lute in general, without tunes in notation; it was published in 1609.[91] Now, in his preface to the *Yang-ch'un-t'ang* handbook, Chang Ta-ming states that after having published a work of a more general nature like the *Ch'in-ching*, he felt it necessary to supplement this with a handbook containing tunes in notation: 'The lute needs a handbook with tunes in notation, just as a cart needs its two thills.'[92] From this we may conclude that the *Yang-ch'un-t'ang* handbook was published sometime after 1609, the date of the *Ch'in-ching*. Further, the famous scholar and calligrapher Tung Ch'i-ch'ang[93] added an undated preface to this handbook. In this preface he says that he met Chang Ta-ming in Fukien when traveling there on official business.[94] Now it appears from Tung Ch'i-ch'ang's biography that he visited South China in official capacity in the year 1622: 'He was ordered to proceed to the south to collect documents and other historical materials relating to the former dynasty.'[95] Therefore we shall not be very wrong when we

*items. These show that Hu Wên-huan's reprints were fine specimens of Ming block prints, carefully collated and printed in graceful characters, editions in no way inferior to the celebrated *Chi-ku-ko* 汲古閣 reprints published by Mao Chin 毛晉 (1599–1659). It is to be regretted that no attempt has been made to collect all the writings of Hu Wên-huan, and to publish them together. Data about his life, too, are scattered over various sources. One shall look in vain for his biography in the *Ming-shih* 明史. Only the *Ming-tz'ŭ-tsung* 明詞綜 gives, in ch. 10, a short biographical note.

b) 三才圖會. For a description of this interesting Ming encyclopedia, see S. Y. Teng & K. Biggerstaff, *An Annotated Bibliography of Selected Chinese Reference Works*, *Yenching Journal of Chinese Studies*, Monograph no. 12, Peking 1936, p. 124.

88 陽春堂琴譜
89 The last sentence of the preface running: 譜成於何時,時蓋萬曆丙申下元也.
90 張大命
91 琴經; see App. II, 5.
92 琴之必需夫譜猶車之不可廢兩轅也
93 董其昌, 1555–1636.
94 不佞客宦閩中興右衰張生有一日之知
95 *Ming-shih* 明史, ch. 288: 天啓二年命往南方採輯先朝章疏及遺事.

place the date of the *Yang-ch'un-t'ang-ch'in-pu* somewhere around 1625. Thus this publication is considerably later than the *Wên-hui-t'ang* handbook and the *San-ts'ai* encyclopedia. We may assume that Chang Ta-ming had the pictures of the *Wên-hui-t'ang* handbook redrawn by a skilled artist. The set of pictures as published by him offers a good example of the style of painting current during the

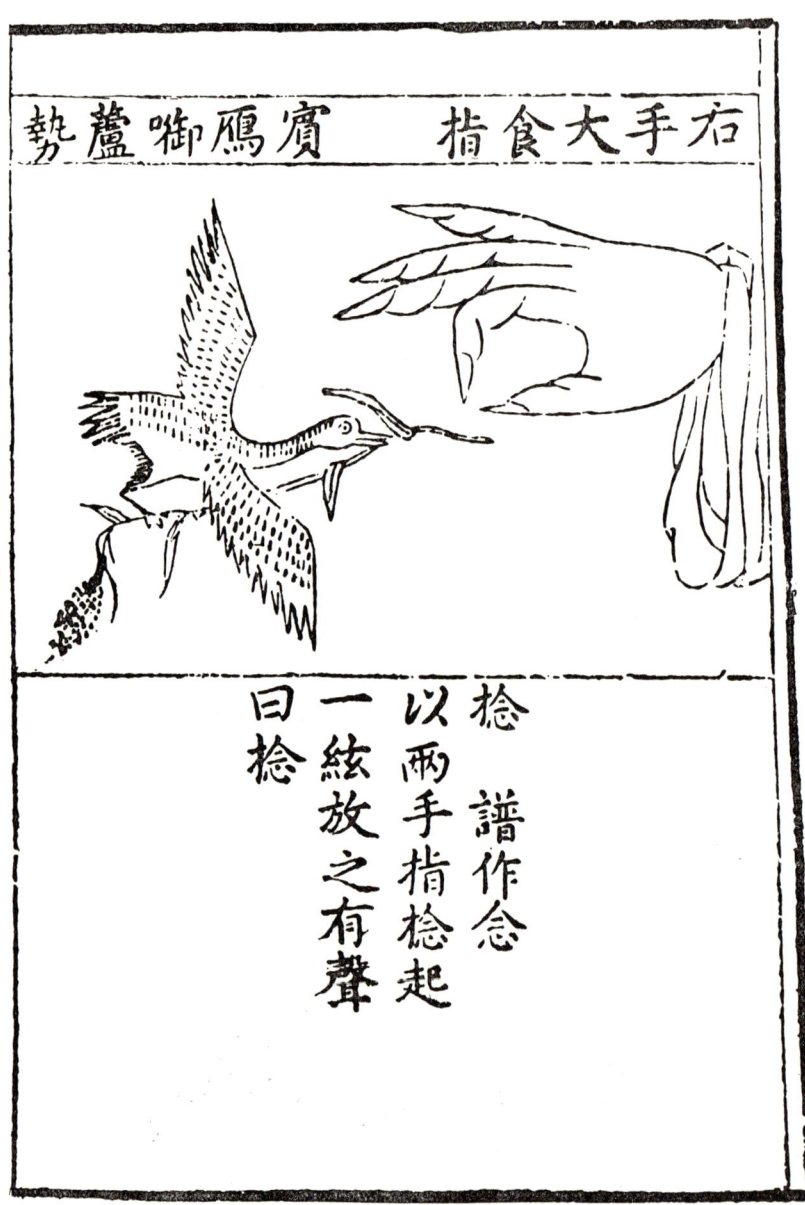

#12: Symbolic picture illustrating the finger technique, from *Wên-hui-t'ang-ch'in-pu*. The photostat was kindly sent me by the Library of Congress, Washington.

Ming period (see figures 10 and 11). The reader may compare the *Wên-hui-t'ang* picture reproduced in figure 12, and the *Yang-ch'un-t'ang* version of the same picture in figure 11.

During the Ch'ing period the pictures were mostly left out, and the publishers of lute handbooks contented themselves with reproducing the sketches of the right and left hands in various postures, together with their explanations. The series of pictures, however, found its way to Japan. In 1746 Satō Itchō published an introductory handbook for the Chinese lute, entitled *Kokin seigi*.[96] This book reproduces the set of pictures of the *Yang-ch'un-t'ang-ch'in-pu*, in a slightly revised form.

Before proceeding on to a more detailed discussion of the various movements that constitute the finger technique, and the abbreviated signs by which they are indicated, a few general remarks about the terminology used are necessary.

First it must be remembered that when the player has his lute lying before him on the table, ready to be played, the end with the tuning pegs is on his right (see figure 3 in the first chapter of this essay). Then the thirteen *hui*, studs inlaid in the varnish, appear along the side farthest from the player; this side is called *wai* (outside).[97] The space between the *hui* varies greatly; each of these intervening spaces is theoretically divided into ten equal parts, called *fên*.[98] These *fên* are not indicated on the instrument: the player must learn to find them by practice. The *hui* are numbered 1–13, counting from right to left, and the *fên* are numbered 1–10. The player should see in his mind the *hui* and *fên* lengthened to lines running transversally over the whole breadth of the lute. Thus when the handbook says: 'Press with the left thumb the fifth string down on 9/3,' the player knows that he must choose the spot where a perpendicular line, starting from 9/3 along the outer side of the body of the lute, crosses the fifth string. It is along the row of *hui* that the thickest string, emitting the lowest note, is strung. This string is indicated by the number 1, the others by the numbers 2–7. Thus the string nearest to the player, on the inner side (*nei*),[99] is the thinnest and produces the highest note, and is indicated by the number 7.

In the notation the numbers indicating the strings are written in large characters; they form, so to speak, the marrow of the notation, and easily strike the eye when one looks over a passage of lute music in notation (see figures 14 and 15). The numbers indicating *hui*

---

[96] 佐藤一張, 古琴精義   [97] 徽, 外   [98] 分   [99] 內

#13: Selected *chien-tzŭ*, abbreviated signs used in lute notation.

[V, §3] THE SYMBOLISM OF THE FINGER TECHNIQUE 125

#14 & 15: Two passages from the *Wu-chih-chai* handbook.

and *fên* are written in smaller characters, easily distinguishable by their size and location (right top corner of a combination of *chien-tzû*) from those numerals that indicate the strings.

Needless to say, just as in ordinary Chinese writing, so also the *chien-tzû* of the lute notation are written in vertical columns, to be read from right to left. And just as in an ordinary Chinese text the commentary and notes are added between the text, but in smaller characters and in two columns; in the same way the columns of *chien-tzû* of ordinary size (called *chêng-wên*), are interspersed with *chien-tzû* in smaller type (called *fu-wên*).[100] The *chêng-wên* indicate the notes, the *fu-wên* various 'graces' and general indications such as vibrato, piano, etc. For a specimen passage of lute notation, see figs. 14 and 15. The small circles which in an ordinary Chinese text

---

100 正文, 副文

stand for commas and full stops, here have the function of the bars in our musical scores.

It must always remain an invidious undertaking to describe a musical technique in words. This applies *a fortiori* to Oriental music. Oriental and Western music show so many fundamental differences, that it is a hazardous task to translate Oriental technical terms by our own. Such renderings can never be accepted without considerable reserve. While describing the finger technique of the lute, I therefore have tried to avoid as much as possible the use of Western technical musical terminology; this method has made my explanations perhaps rather verbose, but I hope that a greater degree of accuracy has thereby been obtained.

Below I list 54 of the elementary *chien-tzû*. The only Western book wherein some of these abbreviations are discussed is the work on Chinese music by G. Soulié.[101] As, however, Soulié's informant was apparently not a competent lute expert, there occur many mistakes in the explanations. These are corrected below.

On the accompanying plate (figure 13) I have written out 54 abbreviated signs; those selected are the *chien-tzû* that occur most frequently in the lute notation. Many of the *chien-tzû* that remain are but combinations of those discussed here. My explanations are based on those given in the standard handbooks, and they have been verified by some lute masters in Peking. Special attention has been given to the symbolic explanations of each movement.

 1 *San*:[102] this string should be played by the right hand only, the left hand not touching the string.

 2 *T'o*:[103] the thumb of the right hand pulls a string outwards. Explained as 'A crane dancing in a deserted garden'.[104] Also as 'A crane dancing in the wind'.[105] The meaning is that the touch should be firm, but at the same time loose.

 3 *Po* (sometimes read *p'i*):[106] the thumb of the right hand pulls a string inwards (with the nail). Explanation same as 2.

 4 *Mo* (Soulié wrongly reads *mei*):[107] the index pulls a string inward. 'A crane singing in the shadow';[108] from the accompanying picture it appears that the shadow of a bamboo

---

101 Appendix I, 3.
102 散
103 托
104 虛庭鶴舞
105 風前鶴舞
106 擘, 劈
107 抹
108 鶴鳴在陰

grove is meant. The touch of the index should be as firm as that of the thumb, but less jerky; a smooth movement should be aimed at.

5 *T'iao*:[109] the index pulls a string outward. Explanation same as 4.

6 *Kou*:[110] the middle finger pulls a string inward. 'A lonely duck looks back to the flock.'[111] The curve of the middle finger should be modelled on that of the neck of the wild duck: curved but not angular. If the middle finger is too much hooked, the touch will be jerky.

7 *T'i*:[112] the middle finger pulls a string outward. Explanation same as 6.

8 *Ta*:[113] the ring finger pulls a string inwards. 'The Shang-yang bird hopping about.'[114] The Shang-yang is a fabulous bird, said to have only one leg. The idea is that, in contradistinction to the smooth movements of the index and middle finger, the touch of the ring finger should be short and crisp.

9 *Chai*[115] (Soulié wrongly reads *ti*): the ring finger pulls a string outward. Explanation same as above.

10 *Ch'üan-fu*[116] (Soulié wrongly reads *ch'üan-mo*): index, middle finger and ring finger each pull at the same time a different string, making the three strings produce together one sound. 'Light clouds sailing in the wind.'[117] The touch should be light and delicate, so that the three notes melt together.

11 *Li* (also explained as *tu*):[118] the index lightly passes over two or three strings in succession, in outward direction (Soulié says inward, which is wrong). Explanation same as 10.

12 *Ts'o*:[119] a chord; two fingers pull two strings at the same time, making them sound together. The strings to be pulled are indicated by their numbers, written on either side of the perpendicular stroke in the center of the abbreviated sign. The normal chord is a combination *t'o-kau*;[120] the opposite

109 挑
110 勾
111 孤鶩顧群
112 剔
113 打
114 商羊鼓舞
115 摘
116 全扶
117 風送輕雲
118 歷, 度
119 撮
120 托勾

combination, *po-t'i*,[121] called *fan-ts'o*,[122] is indicated by adding the character *fan*[123] on top of the *chien-tzû* for *ts'o*.[124] 'A flying dragon grasping the clouds.'[125, 126]

13. *P'o-tz'û*:[127] index, middle and ring finger together pull two strings, once inward (*p'o*), and immediately after outward (*tz'u*). 'A swimming fish moving its tail.'[128] The illustration shows that a carp is intended. A measured, broadly sweeping touch should be aimed at.

14. *Ta-yüan*:[129] a movement consisting of seven sounds, played on two strings. First *t'iao*[129] on the string nearest to the body, and *kou*[129] on the string further away; a slight pause; then rapidly repeat the same movement twice; again a short pause, and end up with *t'iao* on the string one started with. This movement can be executed on any pair of strings, but usually it is found with regard to 1 and 4, 2 and 5, 3 and 6, 4 and 7. It is customary in the notation to write the first *t'iao* and *kou* in *chien-tzû*, and then to add underneath in a smaller character the *chien-tzû* for *ta-yüan*. 'A holy tortoise emerges from the water.'[130] The picture shows a tortoise climbing a small island in a pond. One should try to imitate the crawling movement of the legs of the tortoise: short, but determined touches, in absolutely the same rhythm.

15. *Pei-so*[131] (Soulié wrongly reads *pei-chao*): three sounds are produced on one and the same string, by a succession of *t'i-mo-t'iao*.[132] 'A wild fowl flapping its wings.'[133] Crisp touches in rapid succession.

16. *Tuan-so*,[134] one and the same string produces five sounds, first a slow *mo-kou*,[134] followed by *pei-so*. Explanation same as 15.

17. *Ch'ang-so*,[135] one and the same string produces seven sounds, first *mo-t'iao-mo-kou*,[136] then add *pei-so*. Explanation same as 15.

---

121 擘剔
122 反撮
123 反
124 撮
125 飛龍拏雲
126 Explained on p. 121 above. See also figure 10.
127 潑剌
128 游魚擺尾
129 打圓, 挑, 勾
130 神龜出水
131 背鎖
132 剔抹挑
133 鵾鷄翱翔
134 短鎖, 抹勾
135 長鎖
136 抹挑抹勾

18 *Lun*[137] 'a wheel': this is a rapid movement, executed on one string, viz. *chai-t'i-t'iao*[137] in quick succession. It should be executed very lightly and delicately, so as to cause the three sounds to melt together. This term in itself is very aptly chosen: it implies that the three fingers should imitate the spokes of a wheel. When a wheel turns round swiftly, each separate spoke is no longer visible. 'A purple crab walking sidewards'[138]—the same idea, differently expressed. One should think of the rapid movement of the legs of small crabs when they scurry over the sand. Among the movements of the right hand, this is the only one that might be compared with the 'graces' executed by the left hand (vibrato, etc.); often lute players introduce *lun* when it is not written in the notation; for the movement is so rapid that it does not affect the rhythm. Therefore a simple *t'iao* or *mo*[139] may be replaced by a *lun*. A discreet appliance of *lun* may give a tune additional charm, but one should guard against overdoing it: avoiding cheap effects is one of the most important rules for the lute player. *Lun* is very much used in *p'i-p'a* music where its technical appellation is *ta-i-ko-lun-tzû* (to beat a wheel).[140]

19 *Pan-lun*,[141] 'half a wheel': the same movement as the preceding, but with middle and ring finger only.

20 *Ju-i*,[142] 'as one': two strings sound together. 'Female and male phoenix singing in harmony.'[143]

21 *Shuang-tan*,[144] 'double pulling': one string produces two sounds in rapid succession; usually *mo-kou*.[145] 'Cold ravens pecking at the snow.'[146] The picture shows a flight of emaciated ravens on a barren tree in a winter landscape: they peck at the snow that covers the dry branches, hoping to discover something to eat. The movement should be executed with the very tips of the fingers, a short, crisp, pecking touch.

22 *So-ling*[147] (properly the name of a musical instrument, consisting of several bells hung on a cord; when the cord is

---

137 輪, 摘剔挑
138 紫蟹傍行
139 挑, 抹
140 打一個輪子
141 半輪
142 如一
143 鸞鳳和鳴
144 雙彈
145 抹勾
146 寒鴉啄雪
147 索鈴

pulled, the bells ring together): the left hand glides lightly over several strings in succession, while the right index moves over the same strings in a light manner *(t'iao)*[148] simultaneously with the movement of the left hand; the movements of both hands should be strictly parallel. 'Bells hung on a cord being shaken.'[149] The aim is a subtle, tinkling effect. Properly this movement belongs to the 'floating sounds'.[150]

23. *K'un*,[151] 'welling up' (I do not know how Soulié obtained his reading *liao*): *t'i*[152] over several strings in succession, from 7 to 2, or from 6 to 1. 'A heron bathing in a whirlpool.'[153] One should think of a heron taking a bath in the small eddies of a stream in the shallow places along its banks: the whirling movement of the water, together with the flapping of the wings should suggest the character of the movement. Mostly played on the free strings, with the right hand only; occasionally, however, one string must be pressed down with the left hand. When executed correctly, this movement, together with the next item (its opposite), constitutes a very attractive motif. A later, and technically extremely difficult version of the tune *Liu-shui* (Flowing Streams),[154] has one part consisting of practically nothing but variations on this *k'un*. When it is played by a virtuoso (ordinary players would hardly dare to touch this tune!), one hears the babbling of water all through the melody: now the melody dominates, then the sounds of water, a fascinating effect.[155] The lute master Chêng Ying-sun[156] is a well-known player of especially this tune.

24. *Fu*,[157] 'to brush': the opposite of the preceding item, played over strings 1–6 or 2–7.

25. *Tsai-tso*,[158] 'repeat the preceding movement'. This and the following ten items do not represent notes: they are indications of a general character.

26. *Ts'ung-kou-tsai-tso*,[159] 'repeat the preceding passage, from the

---

148 挑
149 振索鳴鈴
150 *fan-yin* 泛音
151 滾
152 剔
153 鷺浴盤渦
154 流水

155 However, see my remarks on this tune, on p. 99 above.
156 鄭穎孫
157 拂
158 再作
159 從ㄅ再作

[V, §3] THE SYMBOLISM OF THE FINGER TECHNIQUE 131

place indicated by the bracket'. Instead of *ts'ung-kou*[160] one may also find *ts'ung-t'ou*,[161] meaning *da capo*.

27 *Shao-hsi*,[162] a short pause.
28 *Ju-man*,[163] *ritardando*.
29 *Chin*,[164] '(up) to'; for instance: '*k'un* from the 6th to the 1st string.'[165]
30 *Lien*,[166] *legato*.
31 *Ch'ing*,[167] *piano*.
32 *Chung*,[168] *forte*.
33 *Huan*,[169] *lente*.
34 *Chi*,[170] *presto*.
35 *Ta-chih*,[171] the left thumb. This and the following items all regard the finger technique of the left hand.
36 *Shih-chih*,[172] the left index.
37 *Chung-chih*,[173] the left middle finger.
38 *Ming-chih*,[174] the left ring finger.
39 *Ch'o*:[175] a finger of the left hand, before pressing down a string on the spot indicated by *hui* and *fên*, starts about 5 mm. to the left of that place, and quickly glides to the right, till the place indicated is reached. The result is a rising, prolonged note. 'A wild pheasant ascending a tree.'[176] The sound produced should resemble the cry of the wild pheasant, who sings in the morning. Soulié's explanation of this and the following item is mistaken.
40 *Chu*,[177] the opposite of the preceding item: One starts about 5 mm. to the *right* of the spot indicated, and then glides down to the left, till the spot is reached. Explanation as in no. 39. Both *ch'o* and *chu* are produced *simultaneously* with the pulling of the string by the right hand. They should be distinguished from *shang* and *hsia*[178] (cf. below, no. 45), which are executed *after* the right hand has pulled the string.
41 *Yin*,[179] *vibrato*. A finger of the left hand quickly moves up

160 從勾
161 從頭 (abbreviated into 㠯).
162 少息
163 入慢
164 至
165 滾六至一
166 連
167 輕
168 重
169 緩
170 急
171 大指
172 食指
173 中指
174 名指
175 綽
176 野雉登木
177 注
178 上, 下
179 吟

and down over the spot indicated. 'A cold cicada bemoans the coming of autumn.'[180] The plaintive, rocking drone of the cicadas (well known to all foreigners living in China and Japan!) should be imitated. Of this *yin* there exist more than ten varieties. There is the *ch'ang-yin*,[181] a drawn-out vibrato, that should recall 'the cry of a dove announcing rain';[182] the *hsi-yin*,[183] a thin vibrato, that should make one think of 'confidential whispering';[184] the *yu-yin*,[185] swinging vibrato, that should evoke the image of 'fallen blossoms floating down with the stream',[186] etc. Remarkable is the *ting-yin*[187]—the vacillating movement of the finger should be so subtle as to be hardly noticeable. Some handbooks say that one should not move the finger at all, but let the timbre be influenced by the pulsation of the blood in the fingertip, pressing the string down on the board a little more fully and heavily than usual.

42 *Jou*,[188] *vibrato ritardando*. A vibrato somewhat broader and more accentuated than *yin*.[189] Properly the character should be pronounced *nao*, meaning 'monkey'; but lute players pronounce it *jou*. Doubtless the character *jou*[190] meaning 'to twist, to rub' is the proper one. It was replaced by that read *nao* because, for use as *chien-tzŭ*, the 94th radical is more distinct than the 64th one. And, further, the symbolic association may also have played a role: for the vibrato ritardando should suggest 'the cry of a *monkey* while climbing a tree'.[191]

43 *Chuang*,[192] 'to strike against': after the right hand has pulled a string, the left makes a quick, jerky movement, up and down to the right of the spot indicated.

44 *Chin-fu*,[193] 'advancing and returning': after the right hand has pulled the string, the left glides upwards to a certain point indicated, then glides down again till it reaches the point where it started, or another spot, as indicated in the notation.

---

180 寒蟬吟秋
181 長吟
182 鳴鳩喚雨
183 細吟
184 喁喁私語
185 遊吟
186 落花隨水
187 定吟
188 猱
189 *yin*
190 揉
191 號猿升木
192 撞
193 進復

[V, §3] THE SYMBOLISM OF THE FINGER TECHNIQUE 133

45 *Shang*[194] (ascending), and *hsia*[195] (descending): properly an elaborate form of the preceding item, but often interchangeable with it. *Shang* is gliding to the right, in stages. For instance, a string is pulled while the left hand presses it down on the spot indicated by the 9th *hui*. The notation adds the remark: 'glide upwards till 8/4, then till 7/8.'[196] *Hsia* is the same movement, but in opposite direction. Often *shang* and *hsia* count as many as three or four stages, and form part of the melody. Therefore movements like these properly should not be called 'graces': they do not 'grace' the original note, but are notes in themselves.[197]

46 *Fên-k'ai*,[198] 'divide and open': a peculiar movement, which makes one and the same string produce four sounds in succession. For instance, the right hand pulls a string while the left presses it down on the 9th *hui*; when the tone is still resounding, the left hand glides to the right in a resolute and bold movement till the next *hui* is reached, stays there for an infinitesimal moment, then glides back to the initial spot, and just when it arrives there, the right hand again pulls the string.

47 *Yen*,[199] 'to cover': the thumb, middle or ring finger of the left hand taps a string, producing a low, dull sound; the right hand does not touch the string. This touch is mostly executed with the left thumb; e.g., the ring finger presses a string down on the 9th *hui*, and the right hand pulls this string: thereafter one leaves the ring finger on the same spot, but taps the string with the left thumb, on the place indicated by the 8th *hui*. 'The woodpecker picking a tree.'[200] As many others, this symbol is remarkably well chosen from an acoustic point of view.

48 *Wang-lai*,[201] 'coming and going': a combination of *chin-fu* (no. 44) and *yin* (no. 41). A finger of the left hand, after the right has pulled the string, moves one *hui* to the right, produces 'vibrato', then returns to the original *hui*, and produces 'vibrato' there; and repeats this movement. After

---

[194] 上
[195] 下
[196] 上八四, 七八
[197] Cf. the very pertinent remarks about the 'graces' in Indian music, in A. H. Fox Strangeways, *The Music of Hindostân* (Oxford 1914), ch. VII.
[198] 分開
[199] 罨
[200] 幽禽啄木
[201] 往來

the first vibrato, the sound caused by the pulling of the string by the right hand will have died away: the difficulty is to revive the sound by moving to the right and to the left with a strong jerk. 'A phoenix, having alighted on a branch, combs its tail feathers with its bill.'[202] Anyone who has observed a bird combing its feathers will recognize how cleverly this image is chosen: one sees the broad movement with which the bird first arranges the feathers (*chin-fu*), occasionally interrupted by short, tugging movements for discarding the down (vibrato).

49 *T'ao-ch'i*,[203] 'pulling up and raising': a movement peculiar to the left hand only, executed with the thumb. When the ring finger is pressing a string down, for instance on the 9th *hui*, the left thumb pulls the string. The same note would be produced if the thumb of the right hand pulled the string, while the left ring finger pressed it down on the 9th *hui*; but the timbre is entirely different. The accompanying explanation, 'Two immortals transmitting the Way,'[204] seems enigmatical. It was explained to me as follows. An adept who really understands 'the Way' (*tao*), knows that words are of no use in explaining it; cf. the opening sentence of the *Tao-tê-ching*: 'The *tao* that can be explained is not the eternal Tao.'[205] Therefore, when two adepts discuss *tao*, they just utter a short abrupt sound, which is said to comprise the cosmic function of *tao*. This idea Taoism has borrowed from the Ch'an[206] school of Buddhism; in Ch'an technical terminology this sound is called *ho*.[207, 208] Zen Buddhism, in its turn, doubtless borrowed this idea of the all-embracing magical power of a single sound from Mantrayana teachings, where, for instance, the vowel *a*[209] is considered as the receptacle of all the deepest mysteries. The utterance of such a single magic syllable may move all the spiritual agencies of the entire universe.[210] But to return to our present subject: the sound produced should be abrupt and dry.

---

202 栖鳳梳翎
203 搯起
204 二仙傳道
205 道可道非常道
206 禪, Jap. Zen.
207 喝, Jap. *katsu*.
208 For a good description of the all-important role of this sound in Ch'an Buddhism, cf. D. T. Suzuki, *Essays in Zen Buddhism*, first series (London 1927), pp. 279–80.
209 阿
210 Cf. the article '*a*' in the *Hōbōgirin. Dictionnaire encyclopédique du Bouddhisme*, Tokyo 1929.

50 *Hu*,²¹¹ 'a sloping bank': the right hand has pulled a string, pressed down by the thumb of the left hand on the 10th *hui*; one waits a moment, then glides with the left thumb to the right, till the 9th *hui* is reached. This gliding movement is called *hu*. It should be slow and emphatic, like dragging something up the sloping bank of a river. After the pause, the sound produced has lost most of its volume; the aim is to utilize the last echo of the sound for the *hu*.

51 *Kuei*,²¹² 'to kneel': often it will prove inconvenient to press down a string with the tip of the left ring finger, especially when a *t'ao-ch'i* (no. 49) must be executed on the places indicated by the lower *hui*. In such cases the difficulty is solved by pressing down the string, not with the tip of the left ring finger, but with the back of its first joint. Thus that finger must assume a crooked posture. 'A panther grasping something.'²¹³ The idea is to suggest a firm, determined pressure. Soulié's explanation: *pao-chih*, 'little finger', is of course entirely erroneous, since the little finger of either hand is never used in lute music. For this reason in lute terminology the little finger is called *chin-chih*,²¹⁴ 'forbidden finger'.

52 *Fan-ch'i*,²¹⁵ 'here the floating sounds start': a sign warning the player that the succeeding notes are all in 'floating sounds', i.e., harmonics. As has been explained above, the harmonics are produced when the left hand, instead of pressing down a string on the board, just lightly touches it. The delicate touch of the fingers of the left hand is aptly described as 'white butterflies exploring flowers'.²¹⁶ Where the floating sounds should end, there occurs a sign read *fan-chih*;²¹⁷ the *chien-tzû* consists of the upper part of no. 52 added on top of the character *chih*.²¹⁸ Soulié's reading *fa* must rest on some mistake. It should be added that floating sounds are only possible on the places indicated by the *hui*, not on the intervening spots.

53 *Fang-ho*,²¹⁹ 'let go and unite': this touch especially applies to the ring finger of the left hand, and implies a kind of chord.

211 滸
212 跪
213 文豹抱物
214 禁指
215 泛起
216 粉蝶探花
217 泛止
218 止
219 放合

Suppose the right hand has pulled the 3rd string, while the ring finger of the left hand was pressing it down on the 9th *hui*. The next note is pulling the 4th string, free. Now, while the 4th string is being pulled, the left ring finger pulls the 3rd string, causing both strings to sound together. 'Echo in an empty vale.'[220] The accompanying picture shows two recluses standing in a vale, and clapping their hands.

54 *T'ui-ch'u*,[221] 'pushing outwards': a touch executed by the middle finger of the left hand. Suppose that the right hand has pulled the first string, while the left middle finger pressed it down on the 13th *hui*; while the next note is being played, the middle finger is left in its position on the *hui*. Then, when the next sound has been produced by the right hand, the left middle finger makes the 1st string sound by pushing it outward. 'A silver pheasant dancing.'[222]

In illustration of the above, I shall now explain two passages in lute notation, taken from the *Wu-chih-chai* handbook,[223] and reproduced in figures 14 and 15. To save space the strings are indicated by roman, the *hui* and *fên* by arabic numerals. Both passages are taken from the well-known lute melody *Mo-tzû-pei-ssû*[224] (the philosopher Mo-tzû sorrowing over the silk). The significance of this tune is understood by reading Mo-tzû, I, 3: *So-jan*,[225] the opening passage: 'Our Master Mo-tzû said with a sigh, when he saw silk being dyed: When silk is dyed with a dark colour, it becomes dark, when dyed with a yellow colour it becomes yellow: its colour changes according to the dye in which it is dipped, etc.'[226] The philosopher regrets the fact that man, originally pure, becomes soiled by contact with material life.[227]

Figure 14 shows the first part of this tune, an extremely attractive prelude, written entirely in harmonics. The gloss says: 'The harmonics of this first part must be played with sincerity, only then the meaning will be fully expressed.' The first line opens with the sign for 'start harmonics' (above, item no. 52); to the right an abbreviation for *huan-tso*,[228] 'slowly'.

---

220 空谷傳聲
221 推出
222 白鷴騰踏
223 Appendix II, 15.
224 墨子悲絲
225 所染

226 子墨子言見染絲者而歎曰，染於蒼則蒼，染於黃則黃，所入者變，其色亦變云云.
227 See A. Forke, *Mê Ti, des Sozialethikers und seiner Schüler philosophische Werke*, Berlin 1922, p. 166.
228 緩作

[V, §3] THE SYMBOLISM OF THE FINGER TECHNIQUE 137

The left middle finger touches I on 9, while the right middle finger pulls the string inwards.

The left thumb touches VI on 9, while the right thumb pulls it outward.

The left middle finger touches II on 9, the right middle finger pulls it inward.

The left thumb touches VII on 9, the right thumb pushes it outward.

The left index moves lightly over VII-II, the right middle finger simultaneously executes *k'un* (no. 23).

The left middle finger touches I on 9, the right middle finger pulls it inward.

The left thumb touches VI on 9, the right thumb pushes it outward. The following two signs being the same as the second bar, they need no explanation.

The left index touches VI on 9, the right middle finger pulls it inward.

The left ring finger touches VII on 10, the right index pushes it outward.

The right index glides lightly over VI and V, connecting them (*ch'ing lien*[229]), while the left ring finger touches them on 10. It should be noted that if no *hui* is indicated, and if the sign *san*,[230] 'free strings', is missing, the position of the left hand remains unchanged.

The right middle finger pulls IV inward, the left ring finger still touching it on 10.

The left thumb touches VI on 9, the right index pushes it outwards. Etc.

Near the end of this passage we find the direction, *miao*,[231] indicating that especially that note is important. The passage ends with the sign *fan-chih*,[232] 'here the harmonics end'.

Figure 15 shows the beginning of the sixth part of the same tune. As here no harmonics are employed, the notation is slightly more complicated. The note says: 'The earlier six bars show a rising and subsiding tendency. Every note of the last bar is full of passion, it should not end up in a sloppy way.'

The left thumb presses VI down on 6, with the introductory gliding *chu* (no. 40); the right middle finger pulls it inward. Then the left thumb executes a protracted vibrato on 6, subsequently gliding up to 5.

229 輕連   230 散   231 妙   232 泛止

The left thumb presses vii down on 5, the right index pushes it outwards, the left thumb adds the jerk *chuang* (no. 43).

The right middle finger pulls vi inward, thereafter vii, the left thumb pressing down these strings on 5. Then the left thumb vibrates on 5, and glides up to 4/4. The right middle finger pushes vii outwards, and immediately afterwards pushes outward the free sixth string, making vii and vi sound together (*ju-i*[233]). Then the left thumb lightly pulls the nail up from the board, producing a light sound (*chao-ch'i*,[234] not given in my list).

The right middle finger pulls the free vi inwards.

The left thumb presses down vii on 4/4, the right middle finger pulls it inwards. Add *shuang-tan* (no. 21).

The right middle finger pulls the free vi.

The left thumb presses down vii on 4/4, the right middle finger pulls it inwards. Then the left thumb glides up to 4, thereafter to 3/3.

The left thumb remains on 3/3, the right middle finger pushes it outwards, immediately afterwards pushing the vi free (*ju-i*); after a slight pause, vibrato (*lo-chih-yin*,[235] a sort of protracted vibrato, not given in my list), then the left thumb lightly pulls up this same vii.

The right middle finger pulls the free vi.

The left thumb presses down vii on 3/3, the right middle finger pulls it inwards. A thin vibrato (*hsi-yin*),[236] and the thumb glides up to 2/5 (*êrh-pan*).[237]

The left thumb presses vii on 2/5, the right index pushes it outwards. The *ch'i*[238] in the margin indicates that here again there is a 'rise' in the melodic pattern.

This system of noting down lute music may seem too complicated and cumbersome to be practical. Yet some regular practice will prove it to be as convenient as our Western musical score. Lute experts have no difficulty in playing a new tune at first sight; I actually saw a Chinese lute master hum a tune he had never seen before, while looking over the notation.

It will be observed that no real notes are indicated. As the various tunings of the lute are minutely fixed, and all instruments are built on the same pattern (even the number of single silk threads that form one string is fixed), this omission presents the player with no seri-

---

233 如一
234 爪起
235 落指吟
236 細吟
237 二半
238 起

ous difficulty. The pitch is left to individual taste; some like it high, others low. But the pitch proportion between the strings must of course be correct.

More serious is the lack of any sign indicating measure. This is partly made up for by the distribution of the small round circles functioning as bars, and further by such indications as 'slow down', 'accelerate', etc.

In later times lute experts have felt these two shortcomings of the *chien-tzû* system. In the 19th century we find some handbooks where the musical note is added to each *chien-tzû* combination in symbols of the *kung-ch'ih*[239] system. These handbooks indicate the measure by a line of dots, running parallel to the *chien-tzû* columns. The distribution of these dots suggests the measure: if the dots are dense, the measure is slow; if sparse, the measure should be accelerated. Yet these systems never won universal approval. Yang Tsung-chi evolved a most elaborate system of *chien-tzû*, with a running explanation alongside;[240] in his *Ch'in-hsüeh-ts'ung-shu* he published several of the better known tunes in this notation. For reading this system some special study is necessary, but it is so explicit (both notes and measure being recorded), that I can recommend his handbook to everyone who wishes to study lute music without a master.

In 1931 the musician Wang Kuang-ch'i[241] made an attempt at transcribing the *chien-tzû* in a semi-Western way. He used our stave and notes, but of course had to add a great number of special signs.[242] The result was a system far more complicated than the original *chien-tzû*, and his method was never adopted by other workers in the field. Where typically Chinese things are concerned, it will as a rule be very difficult to improve upon the methods the old Chinese devised for dealing with them.

---

239 工尺. Soulié, *op. cit.* p. 36, reproduces a page from such a handbook.
240 Appendix II, 7.
241 王光祈
242 See his publication, *Fan-i-ch'in-pu-chih-yen-chiu* 翻譯琴譜之研究, Shanghai 1931.

CHAPTER SIX

Associations

§1 LUTE AND CRANE

LITERARY tradition has surrounded the scholar with numerous attributes, which have come to be considered as the symbols of literary life. Among this group the lute occupies a prominent place. Of the others, those that are constantly mentioned in connection with the lute are the crane, the pine and the plum tree, and the sword.

The origin of these associations dates from far before the establishment of any literary tradition; what their exact beginnings were, we shall probably never know. Yet it is not impossible to make a fairly accurate surmise as to at least the direction in which the solution must be sought. Later literary tradition suggests that the reasons were of a purely aesthetic character. It says that the crane was dear to the scholar because of its graceful movements and dignified behaviour, that the plum blossoms delighted his eye with their exquisite colour, that the gnarled shape of the pine tree taught him antique beauty, and that the sword reminded him of the straightness and purity of the Superior Man. Now these explanations hold true for later times, but they do not bring us any nearer to an understanding of their origin. For in that remote past the literatus did not yet exist.

There did exist, however, the head of the family, who, during the sacrifices to the ancestors, officiated as priest, and whose duty it was to see that by a proper appliance of magical ceremonies evil influences were warded off, and that by a strengthening of the vital essences, the family line was continued and crops were plentiful. Now, as we shall see below, crane, plum tree, pine and sword are all, just like the lute, credited with a great amount of Yang power, and for that reason give protection against evil forces. It would seem probable that these objects, in later times praised as the faithful companions of the scholar, originally surrounded the head of the family, and played some part in magical ceremonies, whereby their vital forces were transferred to the officiant. Literary tradition tried to ignore these ancient magic beliefs; but they are firmly rooted in popular religion, and time and again evidence of their existence also appears in literary sources.

The crane is one of the traditional Chinese symbols of longevity. Just like the tortoise, it is said to live to more than a thousand years. *Ho-ling*, 'crane age', is a much-used metaphor for advanced years[1]. The idea of old age, when carried through logically, leads to that of immortality. Therefore the crane is associated with the *hsien-jên*,[2] the Immortals: the crane is their favourite mount, and many a holy recluse is said to have disappeared from human sight riding on a crane.[3] The *Ch'ing-lien-fang-ch'in-ya*[4] tells the following story about Chang Chih-ho.[5] 'Chang Chih-ho loved to drink wine, and when inebriated used to play his lute all night long without resting. One evening there suddenly appeared a grey crane, which danced round about him. Chang then took his lute, and riding on its back, disappeared in the sky.'[6] There are also many stories of Taoist recluses and priests who transformed themselves into cranes; the *Shên-i-ching*[7] relates that the Taoist recluse Hsü Tso-ching,[8] having taken the shape of a crane, was wounded by an arrow of the Emperor Ming Huang; the *Hsü-sou-shên-chi*[9] tells the story of a Ting Ling-wei[10] who long after his death revisited his native town in the shape of a crane; and the *Lieh-hsien-chuan* says that Su-hsien-kung[11] after his death visited the earth in the shape of a white crane. Because of its constant association with the Immortals the crane is called *hsien-ch'in*.[12] Then we find the crane as soul bird, the bird that conveys the soul of the deceased to the upper regions; cf. the Chinese custom of placing the figure of a crane with spread wings on the coffin in a funeral procession.

The *hsüan-ho*,[13] or dark crane, is especially credited with a fabulously long life. The *Ku-chin-chu*[14] says: 'When a crane has reached the age of one thousand years, it turns a dark blue colour; after another

---

[1] 鶴齡 (See the book entitled *Ho-ling-lu* 鶴齡錄 by the Ming author Li Ch'ing 李清: biographies of people who attained to old ages).

[2] 仙人

[3] See, for instance, the story about Hsün Huan 荀環 in the *Shu-i-chi* 述異記 (18th century).

[4] Appendix II, 6.

[5] 張志和, 8th century.

[6] 張志和好飲酒, 醉則鼓琴, 終夜不休, 一夕忽有雲鶴旋繞, 張遂攜琴跨鶴以昇.

[7] 神異經, 6-7th centuries.

[8] 徐佐鄉

[9] 續搜神記, ascribed to the Chin writer T'ao Ch'ien 陶潛, but evidently a much later production.

[10] 丁令威

[11] 列仙傳 (about the beginning of our era: see the remarks by P. Pelliot, *Journal Asiatique*, June-August 1912, p. 149).

[12] 仙禽

[13] 玄鶴

[14] 古今注 (by Ts'ui Piao 崔豹, Chin 晉 period).

thousand years it turns black, and then it is called dark crane.'[15] Since olden times especially this dark crane has been associated with music. The *Jui-ying-t'u-chi*[16] says: 'A dark crane shall appear at a time when there is a Ruler who understands music. When in olden times, Huang Ti executed music on the K'un-lun mountain for all the Spirits to dance, on his right side there flew 16 dark cranes.'[17]

Sixteen dark cranes also appear in a story related by the great historian Ssû-ma Ch'ien in his *Shih-chi*.[18] This story exists in more than one translation already;[19] because of its great importance for our subject, however, I may be allowed to quote it here once more. 'When Duke Ling of Wei[20] was travelling to Chin, he halted on the bank of the river Pu. In the middle of the night he heard the sounds of a lute being played. He asked the members of his suite, but all respectfully said that no one had heard the sounds. Then the Duke summoned Master Chüan, and said to him: "I have heard the sounds of a lute being played, but when I asked my suite no one had heard it. Thus it seems that it is caused by a spirit or a ghost. Write this tune down for me." Master Chüan assented and, seating himself in the correct position, having placed his lute before him, he listened and noted down the tune. The next morning he said: "I have obtained the tune now, but I have not yet learned it. I beg you for one more night to learn it thoroughly." The Duke agreed, and yet another night passed. On the following morning he reported that he had mastered the tune. Then they left that place, and proceeded to Chin. They were received by Duke P'ing of Chin[21] who gave a banquet for them on the Shih-hui Terrace. When all had come under the influence of the wine, Duke Ling said: "When on my way here I heard a new tune; permit me to let you hear it." When Duke P'ing agreed, Duke Ling made Master Chüan sit down by the side of Master K'uang, place his lute before him and play it. But before he was half through, Master K'uang put his hand on the strings [to deaden the sounds], and said: "That is the music of a doomed state; one must not listen to it." Duke P'ing asked: "What is the origin of this tune?" Master K'uang answered: "It was made by Master Yen, to please the tyrant Chou. When Wu-wang had defeated Chou, Master Yen fled to the east, and drowned himself in the river Pu. Therefore it must

---

[15] 鶴千載變蒼，又千載變黑，所謂玄鶴也。
[16] 瑞應圖記 (ascribed to Sun Jou-chih 孫柔之, of the Liang period).
[17] 玄鶴王者知音樂之節則至，昔黃帝習樂崑崙以舞眾神，有玄鶴二八翔其右。
[18] 史記, ch. 24.
[19] See Chavannes, *Mémoires historiques*, part III, p. 287: M. Courant, *op. cit.* pp. 4–5.
[20] 534–493 B.C.
[21] 557–532 B.C.

have been on the bank of that river that this tune was heard. Who first hears this tune, his state will be divided." Duke P'ing said: "I have a great love for music. I wish to hear this tune to the end." Then Master Chüan played the entire tune. Then Duke P'ing said: "Are there no tunes that are still more sinister than this one?" Master K'uang said: "There are." "Could you play them for me?" The Master answered: "My lord's virtue and righteousness are not great enough for that. I may not play them for you." But the Duke said again: "I have a great love for music; I wish to hear them." Then Master K'uang could not but draw his lute unto him, and play. When he had played once, there appeared sixteen dark cranes that alighted on the gate of the hall. When he played the second time, they stretched their necks and cried, they spread out their wings and started to dance. Duke P'ing was overcome with joy, and leaving his seat he drank the health of Master K'uang. Having returned to his seat, he asked: "Are there no other tunes that are still more sinister than this one?" Master K'uang said: "Yes, there are those by which in olden times Huang Ti effected a great reunion of ghosts and spirits. But my lord's virtue and righteousness are not great enough to allow you to hear this music. And if you hear it, you will perish." Duke P'ing said: "I am advanced in years, and I have a great love of music. I want to hear these tunes." Then Master K'uang could not but draw his lute unto him, and play. When he had played one, white clouds rose in the north-west. And when he played another, there was a storm wind, followed by a torrent, that made the tiles fly from the roof. All that were present fled, and Duke P'ing, in a great fright, threw himself down near the entrance of the hall.²² Thereafter Chin was beset by a drought that scorched the earth for three years in succession.' This story, which bears a most archaic character (note that in the text of the story above, instead of '16' we find 'twice

---

²² 衞靈公之時，將之晉，至於濮水之上舍，夜半時聞鼓琴聲，問左右皆對曰不聞，乃召師涓曰，吾聞鼓琴音，問左右皆不聞，其狀似鬼神，爲我聽而寫之，師涓曰諾，因端坐援琴聽而寫之，明日曰臣得之矣，然未習也，請宿習之，靈公曰可，因復宿，明日報曰，習矣，即去之晉，見晉平公，平公置酒於施惠之臺，酒酣靈公曰，今者來聞新聲，請奏之，平公曰可，即令師涓坐師曠旁，援琴鼓之，未終，師曠撫而止之，曰，此亡國之聲也，不可聽，平公曰，何道出，師曠曰，師延所作也，與紂爲靡靡之樂，武王伐紂，師延東走，自投濮水之中，故聞此聲必於濮水之上，先聞此聲者國削，平公曰，寡人所好者音也，願遂聞之，師涓鼓而終之，平公曰，音無此最悲乎，師曠曰，有，平公曰，可得聞乎，師曠曰，君德義薄，不可以聽之. 平公曰，寡人所好者音也，願聞之，師曠不得已，援琴而鼓之，一奏之有玄鶴二八集乎廊門，再奏之延頸而鳴，舒翼而舞，平公大喜，起而爲師曠壽，反坐問曰，音無此最悲乎，師曠曰，有昔者黃帝以大合鬼神，今君德義薄，不足以聽之，聽之將敗，平公曰，寡人老矣，所好者音也，願遂聞之，師曠不得已，援琴而鼓之，一奏之有白雲從西北起，再奏之大風至而雨隨之，飛廊瓦，左右皆奔走，平公恐懼伏於廊屋之間，晉國大旱，赤地三年。

8'), not only furnishes a good example of the relation of the dark crane to lute music, but also illustrates in a striking way the awe-inspiring qualities with which the ancient Chinese credited this music.[23] Something of the ominous atmosphere of this old tale has been preserved in a number of ghost stories connected with the lute of later date. For some specimens of these see below, the fourth section of this chapter.

It is only occasionally, however, that we find faint echos of the oldest magical character of the association between lute and crane. In later times literary tradition has entirely overgrown these old beliefs; they are replaced by considerations of a purely aesthetical character. When the scholar is playing the lute in his garden pavilion, a couple of cranes should be leisurely stalking about. Their graceful movements should inspire the rhythm of the finger technique, and their occasional cries direct the thoughts of the player to unearthly things. For even these cries of the crane have a special meaning. They are said to penetrate unto Heaven: 'The crane cries in the marshes, its sound is heard in the skies,'[24] and the female crane conceives when it hears the cry of the male.[25]

The crane is described as having a great love for lute music. The *Ch'ing-lien-fang-ch'in-ya*[26] says: 'Lin Pu[27] greatly enjoyed playing the lute; whenever he played, his two cranes would start dancing.'[28] And the same source says about Yeh Mêng-tê:[29] 'Yeh Mêng-tê loved the lute, and would play for a whole day without resting, the tones of the lute mingling with the sounds of a brook. Later Yeh returned to mount Lu and sang songs, accompanying himself on his lute. On one occasion there suddenly appeared a pair of cranes that gamboled about and danced in his garden. Yeh kept them, and they did not go away, but started to dance every time he played.'[30]

---

[23] I may remark in passing that this tale contains some interesting data regarding the history of lute music. It appears that as early as the fifth century B.C. there existed some system for noting down lute music; for our text says explicitly that Master Chüan 'wrote down' (*hsieh* 寫) the ghostly tune he heard. His method of recording the tune is not different from that used by present-day lute players: first the melody in general is noted down, but then several more hearings are necessary to record the exact timbre of the tones, and to add the various 'graces'. Then the tune should be played through many times (*hsi* 習), for only when the music has been memorized can the player in his performance do full justice to it. The terms *i-tsou* 一奏 and *tsai-tsou* 再奏 are not very clear; I follow Chavannes' translation.

[24] See *Shih-ching* 詩經, *Hsiao-ya* X: 鶴鳴于九皐, 聲聞于天.

[25] See the *Ch'in-ching* 禽經, authorship uncertain: 鶴以聲交而孕.

[26] Appendix II, 6.

[27] 967–1028.

[28] 林和靖喜琴, 每一鼓則二鶴起舞.

[29] 葉夢得, style: Shao-yün 少蘊, 1077–1148.

[30] 葉少蘊素好琴, 終日不倦, 泉聲與琴聲相亂, 後歸廬山, 倚琴而歌, 忽見二鶴翩躞飛舞庭中, 少蘊卽蓄之, 不去, 每一鼓未嘗不起舞.

Several lute tunes sing the excellent qualities of the crane. The *Pu-hsü-t'ang-ch'in-pu*[31] contains one tune that describes the crane in the scholar's garden; it bears the title 'Song of a pair of cranes listening to the babbling of a brook'.[32] Another tune celebrates the soaring flight of the crane: 'Cranes dancing in the sky'.[33] The *T'ien-wên-ko-ch'in-pu-chi-ch'êng*[34] has a tune entitled 'A pair of cranes bathing in a brook'.[35] The introductory note added to this tune is not without interest for our subject. 'Late in spring I visited a friend in Kuan-k'ou (Szuchuan Province). A pair of cranes were dancing in a clear rivulet. I observed their feathers white as snow, and the top of their heads red like vermilion. They fluttered up and down, and took their bath while dancing. Then they spread their wings and flew high up in the sky, and cried in harmony in the azure vault, making me doubt whether they were not Immortals. Then I drew my lute unto me, and composed[36] this tune.'[37] The Ming handbook *Shên-chi-pi-pu*[38] has a tune entitled 'Cranes crying in the marshes'.[39] The second half of the introductory remark says: 'The crane is a sacred bird. Its cries are most clear; they are heard at a distance of more than 8 miles. The meaning of this tune is to compare the tones of the lute with the cries of the crane. I kept two cranes in the bamboo grove surrounding my lute hall. Sometimes, in a shadowy place, they would dance together, other times they would fly up and cry in unison. But they would always wait for the appropriate time: they did not dance unless there was a cool breeze to shake their feathers, and they did not cry unless they could look up to the Milky Way as if they saw the gods. When the time was not propitious they would neither sing nor dance. Recognizing the spiritual qualities of these cranes, I composed this tune.'[40]

Various books give directions as to the proper way of rearing cranes and of recognizing birds of superior qualities. The qualities and outer marks of good cranes are described in the *Hsiang-ho-ching*;[41] this

---

31 步虛堂琴譜; see Appendix II, 12.
32 雙鶴聽泉吟.
33 鶴舞洞天
34 Appendix II, 18.
35 雙鶴沐泉
36 This statement does not conform to facts; when playing this tune, one soon discovers that it is nothing but a variation on the tune 'Song of a pair of cranes listening to the babbling of a brook' of the Ming handbook mentioned above.
37 暮春之初, 訪友灌口, 雙鶴沐於清泉, 則見白翰欺雪, 丹頂凝硃, 以頡以頏, 旋舞旋浴, 即而奮翮於霄漢之間, 和鳴於蒼冥之際, 意殆其仙歟, 因援琴而作是操.
38 神奇祕譜; see Appendix II, 11.
39 鶴鳴九皐; see the *Shih-ching* quotation cited above.
40 鶴爲仙靈之禽, 其鳴亮亮聞八九里, 此曲之義蓋以鶴鳴喻琴聲焉, 予嘗畜二鶴於琴院竹林之間, 或離影而對舞, 或雙飛而交鳴, 必有時焉, 其舞也感涼風則舞, 以振其羽, 仰見霄漢如有神物則鳴, 非時則不鳴, 非時則不舞, 故知其鶴之靈而有是操.
41 相鶴經

book, though of doubtful authenticity, seems fairly old, and is found in many *ts'ung-shu*. Ming treatises especially abound in discussions on the keeping and rearing of cranes, and on how to make them dance: one may train them to dance when one claps the hands.[42] Ch'ên Fu-yao[43] in an article on the rearing of cranes[44] says that from the thigh bone of a crane excellent flutes can be made: their sound is clear, and in harmony with the sonorous tubes.[45]

Finally I may quote a remark on the crane found in the *Tsun-shêng-pa-chien*: 'While staying in a country house in an empty wood, how could one do a single day without the company of this refined friend that makes one forget all worldly things?'[46]

§2 LUTE AND PLUM TREE, LUTE AND PINE TREE

CHINESE poets and painters have never tired of the delicate beauty of the plum blossom, and the robuster grace of the gnarled pine tree. Poets celebrate the subtle colour and subdued fragrance of the plum blossom, and they admire the intriguing contrast of the tender flowers and the crooked and rough branches of the tree. And for more than a thousand years painters have chosen as their subject an old pine tree, standing lonely among steep rocks. The ideal of the lute player is to possess a little cottage somewhere in the mountains, surrounded by a grove of prunes. When there is a light breeze, the falling plum blossoms shall suggest to him the spirit of the more delicate touches of the finger technique. But if he can not afford that, when the right season has arrived he will take a flowering branch of the plum tree, and place it in a vase on his desk (see fig. 16). If one can have a house where some hoary pines guard the gate, they will lend dignity and style to one's mansion. And contemplating their antique appearance, the scholar shall

---

[42] Consult the *Tsun-shêng-pa-chien* (Appendix II, 4), ch. 15, pp. 80 ff., and the *K'ao-pan-yü-shih* (Appendix II, 3), ch. 3.

[43] The real name of Ch'ên Fu-yao 陳扶搖 is Ch'ên Hao-tzu 陳淏子; he was born in 1612, a native of Hangchow. Cf. B. Laufer, *T'oung-pao*, 1917, no. 4; Merrill and Walker, *Bibliography of East Asiatic Botany*, p. 552; A. Wylie, *Notes on Chinese Literature*, p. 150; L. Carrington Goodrich, *Monumenta Serica*, II, p. 407.

[44] Ch. 6 of the *Hua-ching* 花鏡, a charming small book on the cultivation of trees and flowers, published in 1688. The *Hua-ching* was in 1773 reprinted in Kyoto, in 6 vols. The Chinese original has been provided throughout with Japanese reading marks, and the pictures have been reproduced with much care. The Japanese editor of the text was a certain Hiraga 平賀.

[45] 又鶴腿骨爲笛，聲甚清越，音律更準.

[46] 空林別墅，何可一日無此忘機清友.

recognize once more the antique atmosphere that hovers about the lute and its lore. But the appreciation of the stern beauty of the pine tree is not only a privilege of the rich: the poor recluse may derive enjoyment from growing a dwarf pine tree in a flat basin.

A study of the origin and subsequent evolution of the Chinese love for plum tree and pine (together with the bamboo) would fill a bulky volume. Below only a few of the most striking features are outlined.

When one observes the place occupied by the plum tree in Chinese

♯16: A scholar playing the lute before beautiful scenery.
Note the vase with plum blossoms, and the incense burner on the lute table.
From a rare illustrated Ming print, the *T'ang-shih-hua-pu* 唐詩畫譜.

culture, it will be clear that here, just as with the crane, magical conceptions play an important role. The plum tree is closely associated with creative power and fertility. Because of the fact that the black and seemingly lifeless branches of an old plum tree still produce tender blossoms, the Chinese ascribe to this tree an unusual amount of Yang power, of vital energy, and have made it a symbol of longevity. Blossoming when winter has barely ended, it is a symbol of the New Year, and the revival of nature. Because of this and other associations, the plum tree and plum blossom are often used in metaphors relating to women and female beauty. A slender waist is compared to the twig of a plum tree, a beautiful woman is called a plum blossom, a rose-and-white face is called a plum-blossom complexion. In Chinese literature one often reads stories of plum blossoms that took the shape of beautiful girls. Well known is the charming story told in the *Lung-ch'êng-lu*.[47] During the K'ai-huang period (581–603) a certain Chao Shih-hsiung fell asleep when resting in a grove. He saw a beautiful girl in simple white attire, but surrounded by a subtle fragrance. Her attendant was a little boy clad in green. Chao talked and laughed with this girl till dawn. When he awoke, he discovered that he had been sleeping under a plum tree. It was in full bloom, and small green birds were twittering on its branches. As in many other countries, in China also the plum has sexual associations. *Mei-tu*[48] (plum poison) in both China and Japan is a usual word for venereal disease, *lo-mei*[49] (falling of the plum blossoms) may be used as a metaphor for defloration, and the word *mei* itself frequently occurs, both in China and Japan, in the names of houses of ill repute. Next to its beauty, it is also this connection with the generative forces of nature, that assured the plum tree its established place among the constant companions of the scholar.

Just like the crane, the plum blossom is said to be sensitive to the beauty of lute music. The *Ch'ing-lien-fang-ch'in-ya*[50] tells the following story. 'Wang Tzû-liang obtained a lute of very antique appearance. Every time he played it, there would suddenly blow a gentle breeze that made the plum blossoms in his garden come down in a dancing movement. Tzû-liang said with a sigh: "These blossoms not only understand words, they also understand music." '[51]

---

[47] 龍城錄, ascribed to the T'ang poet Liu Tsung-yüan, 773–819, 7th heading.
[48] 梅毒 (Jap. *baidoku*).
[49] 落梅
[50] Appendix II, 6.
[51] 王子良得一琴, 質色甚古, 每一鼓清風忽發, 庭中梅花飛動, 子良嘆曰, 此花不獨解語, 更能知音.

Therefore playing the lute before plum blossoms is especially recommended; as an old poem says: 'Take your lute with you and play before an old plum tree.'[52] In prose and poetry the plum tree and its blossoms are repeatedly mentioned in connection with the lute, and in the technical terminology of the lute the plum blossom often appears: a certain touch of the finger technique is compared to

♯17: Playing the lute in the shadow of pine trees.
The man on the left is tuning a four-stringed guitar. Same source as ♯16.

52 携琴合向古梅彈.

plum blossoms floating on the waves, and a type of crack in the varnish of antique lutes is called 'plum-blossom crack' (*Mei-hua-tuan-wên*).[53]

As to the pine tree as an old symbol of longevity, its associations are so well known that after the remarks made above,[54] there is no need to add much more. Also the pine tree is credited with a great amount of vital energy; it remains green through winter, and old, gnarled pines suggest a vigorous advanced age. That nearly all its parts figure largely in the Chinese *materia medica*, must chiefly be explained by sympathetic magic. In the foregoing pages we have seen that the pine tree is constantly mentioned in connection with the lute; if the lute player is not represented as sitting in a plum grove, he will be seated on a moss-covered stone under a couple of spreading pines.

§3 LUTE AND SWORD

THE sword, symbol of military valour, was not much in favour with the literati, who, as a rule, considered all warlike pursuits as unbecoming to their dignity. Beginning with about the early years of the Ming period, literary sources have not much to say in praise of this weapon. Yet a sword belongs to the outfit of a scholar, and it will be seen in his library, hanging on the wall side by side with the lute. This seeming contradiction is explained when the older associations of the sword are taken into consideration.

Despite its warlike character, the sword maintained its place among the attributes of the scholar because of magical considerations: the sword is a powerful defense against the forces of darkness. The belief that cutting instruments scare away ghosts and demons, is, of course, spread over the whole world. In China we find that in olden times the sword belonged to the outfit of the Taoist devil-banner. Already in the writings of the Taoist writer T'ao Hung-ching[55] we find the statement: 'All who wish to study Taoist magic must possess a good sword, which should never leave their sides.'[56] Old treatises on the sword, such as the *Tao-chien-lu*[57] and the *Chien-chi*,[58] abound in stories about the magical properties of the sword: swords change into dragons, hidden swords betray their presence by super-

---

53 梅花斷文
54 p. 58.
55 陶弘景, 452–536.
56 凡學道術者皆須有好劍隨身.

57 刀劍錄, by T'ao Hung-ching, mentioned above.
58 劍記, by Kuo Tzû-chang 郭子章, 16th century.

natural phenomena, old swords may foretell the future, etc. Popular religion shows many traces of these beliefs in the magic power of the sword. Two swords buried under the threshold shall keep away robbers;[59] swords made of cash strung together will keep evil forces away, etc. An interesting survival is the Chinese custom of placing a big knife on the dead body in a coffin.[60] Nowadays it is explained as a means of preventing the ghost of the deceased from haunting the house. But it seems probable that this custom originated in the old rite of burying swords with the dead. For the sword also is considered as a container of Yang power, and as such the sword as burial gift must have had the same significance as the jade had as burial gift, i.e. to preserve the corpse from decay.

The traditional attitude of the later scholar to the sword as belonging to the library of the literatus is shown in the following passage from the *Tsun-shêng-pa-chien*.[61] It is the second half of a section entitled *Ch'in-chien*[62] (Sword and Lute). 'Since olden times the methods for making all sorts of things have been transmitted; only the art of casting swords is not recorded in literary sources. That is why nowadays there are no more knights-errant, and few famous swords exist; this is because the tradition of swordsmanship has been broken off. Moreover it is easier to handle a dagger than a sword, therefore though people now know how to carry daggers, they do not know how to carry a sword. As for me, although I do not use the sword for guarding against the violent and opposing the strong, I yet employ it for fortifying my mind and strengthening my spirit. If one can not obtain an old sword, then a good modern sword, like those manufactured in Yünnan, will do for being hung in the library.'[63] The author winds up by praising in a wealth of literary allusions the brilliant lustre of the sword, which outshines the stars.

The cultured scholar will prefer for his library a beautiful, antique sword, with a finely decorated scabbard, and covered with old inscriptions. But often an ordinary sword or dagger is used.

Of the copious references in literature to lute and sword together, I quote only one, the first couplet of the introductory poem to the famous 'roman de moeurs', *Chin-p'ing-mei*,[64] which says: 'Opulence

---

59 See H. Doré, *Manuel des superstitions chinoises*, Shanghai 1926, p. 91.
60 *Ibid.*, p. 51.
61 Appendix II, 4.
62 琴劍
63 自古各物之製莫不有法傳流，獨鑄劍之術，不載典籍，故今無劍客，而世少名劍，以劍術無傳，且刀便於劍，所以人知佩刀而不知佩劍也，吾輩設此，總不能用以禦暴敵强，亦可壯懷志勇，不得古劍，即今之寶劍如雲南製者，懸之高齋。
64 金瓶梅

and glamour have gone, and the guests have stopped coming. Flutes and cither are silent. Song and chant are no more heard. The heroic sword has lost its grimness, its beautiful shine has become dull. The precious lute has fallen asunder, and its brilliant studs are lost.'[65]

§4 SOME FAMOUS STORIES AND MUCH-QUOTED PASSAGES RELATING TO THE LUTE

THE 22 stories and passages translated below are all taken from the *Ch'ing-lien-fang-ch'in-ya*[66] and the *T'ien-wên-ko-ch'in-pu-chi-ch'êng*.[67] In many cases it would have been possible to trace the story to its original source, where often the text is more complete. But for our purpose it seemed better to give them in the form in which they occur in books on the lute, for then it will appear which particular points especially appealed to the lute masters. The stories need no commentary; they speak for themselves. And each of them may serve, in its own way, as illustration of some of the aspects of *ch'in* ideology discussed in the foregoing chapters.

1 Ou-yang Hsiu [the famous Sung literatus][68] used to say: 'I have assembled one thousand rolls with old records; of books I have collected ten thousand volumes; further I possess one lute, one set of chess, and usually thereto is added one pot of wine. Amidst these things I grow old, being as it were one of a company of six.' On account of this he chose as his literary name: the Retired Scholar One-of-six.

He also said: 'I used to suffer from fits of melancholy, and a leisurely life could not cure them. Then I studied the lute under the guidance of my friend Sun Tao-tzû, who taught me a couple of tunes in the Kung mode. I found enjoyment in these during a long time, and did not know that I harboured such a thing as melancholy.'[69]

2 Ch'ao Pi [T'ang period] used to play a five-stringed lute. When people asked the reason for this, he replied: 'First

---

[65] 豪華去後行人絕，簫箏不響歌喉咽，雄劍無威光彩沉，寶琴零落金星滅，Chin-hsing is a literary expression for *hui* 徽; neither F. Kuhn nor O. Kibat in their translations of the novel has realized this, and they both render *chin-hsing* wrongly as 'Brilliant star'.

[66] Appendix II, 6.

[67] Appendix II, 18.

[68] 1007–72.

[69] 歐陽修言，吾集古錄一千卷，藏書一萬卷，有琴一張，棋一局，而嘗置酒一壺，吾老於其間，是為六一，遂號六一居士.

又曰，吾嘗有幽憂之疾，而間居不能治也，既而學琴於友人孫道滋，受宮聲數引，久而樂之，不知疾之在其體也.

I strove to understand the meaning of these five strings with my mind; the second stage was that my soul sensed their significance. Finally I played them quite naturally, not knowing whether the five strings were I, or I the five strings.'[70]

3 Chang Hung-ching had an old lute. The shine of its varnish was entirely gone, and its colour was jet black. He had given it the name of 'Falling Flowers and Flowing Water'. One night he heard a rat make a loud noise. Fearing that it might gnaw his lute or his books, he ordered a maid servant to put on a light. Then he saw that one string of his lute had broken [and was hanging down], having strangled a rat. Chang Hung-ching was amazed at this, and changed the name of his lute to: 'Terror of the Rats'.[71]

4 Chang Chi, style Chung-ching, a man from Nan-yang, was skilled in healing illness. One day he entered a cedar wood, looking for medicinal herbs. There he met a sick man, who asked for a consultation. [Having examined him,] Chang Chi said: 'How is it that you have the pulse of an animal?' Then the man told him the truth, that in reality he was an old monkey living in a cave on Mount I. Chang Chi took from his bag some pills, and gave him one. Having taken this, the monkey was cured immediately. The next day this monkey came again in his human form, bearing on his shoulder an enormous log. He said: 'This is a cedar ten thousand years old. I offer it as a slight requital.' From this beam Chang Chi made two lutes. One he called Old Monkey, the other Ten Thousand Years.[72]

5 Silk worms are very clever; when they spin themselves into cocoons, they often take the shape of the things they come in contact with.

Once there was a young widow. Spending the night alone, resting on her pillow, she could not sleep. In the wall near her there was a hole, and through this she looked at the silk-

---

[70] 趙璧彈五絃琴，人問其故，曰，吾之五絃也，始則心驅之，中則神遇之，終則天隨之，不知五絃之爲璧，璧之爲五絃也.

[71] 張弘靜有古琴，漆光盡退，色如墨石，銘曰，落花流水，一夕聞鼠聲甚急，懼嚙琴書，命婢以火燭之，見有斷絃，繫得一鼠，弘靜異之，改名曰鼠畏.

[72] 張機，字仲景，南陽人，精於治療，一日入桐栢，覓藥草，遇一病人求診，仲景曰，子之腕有獸脈，何也，其人以實告，乃嶧山穴中老猿也，仲景出囊中丸藥界之一，服輒愈，明日其人肩一巨木至，曰，此萬年桐也，聊以相報，仲景斷爲二琴，一曰古猿，一曰萬年.

worms of her neighbour; they were just leaving their frames. Next day the cocoons all showed a resemblance with her face. Although one could not clearly distinguish eyebrows and eyes, still when seen from some distance they closely resembled the face of a sad girl. Ts'ai Yung, the famous scholar, saw these cocoons, and bought them for a high price. He reeled off the silk threads, and from it made strings for his lute. When he played, however, their sound appeared to be sad and melancholy. When he asked his daughter Yen about it, she said: 'This is widow's silk. When listening to its sounds one cannot but weep.'[73]

6 During the Chou dynasty Master Ching served in the State of Wei. He excelled in playing the lute. Prince Wên[74] was enthusiastic about it, and began to dance. Ching became angry, and struck the Prince with his lute. Then the Prince got angry, and ordered Ching to be dragged out of the Palace and killed. Ching said: 'I beg leave to say one thing before I die.' The Prince said: 'What is it?' Ching said: 'I have struck a prince like the tyrants Chieh and Chou, and not a wise ruler like Yao and Shun.' Prince Wên said 'I have been wrong,' and let him go free. But the lute he suspended on the wall, as a reminder.[75]

7 Wei Yeh, style: Chung-hsien[76] [well-known poet of the Sung period],[77] naturally loved songs and chants and did not strive after worldly fame. He lived in the eastern suburb of the town, where with his own hands he planted bamboos and trees. His abode was surrounded by a flowing water, and breathed an atmosphere of great profundity. There he dug out a cave of one fathom square, and called it 'Cave where harmony with Heaven is enjoyed'. In front of this he made a hut of grass, and there played his lute. When people visited him there, irrespective of whether they were of high or low standing, he would receive them in white clothes and a cap of black gauze. He took the literary name of 'Retired Scholar

---

73 蠶最巧，作繭往往遇物成形，有寡女獨宿，倚枕不寐，私傍壁孔中，視鄰蠶離箔，明日繭都類之，雖眉目不甚悉，而望去隱然似愁女，蔡邕見之，厚價市歸，繰絲製琴絃，彈之有憂愁哀慟之聲，問女琰，琰曰，此寡女絲也，聞者莫不墮淚．

74 426–387 B.C.

75 周師經仕魏，善鼓琴，文侯耽之，起舞，經怒，以琴撞文侯，文侯怒，使人曳下殿，將殺之，經曰，乞申一言而死，文侯曰，何，經曰，臣撞桀紂之君，不撞堯舜之主，文侯曰，寡人過矣，乃捨之，懸琴於壁以為戒．

76 960–1019.

77 His collected works, the Ts'ao-t'ang-chi 草堂集, are still preserved.

of the Grass Hut'. He played the lute and composed poetry, and therein found full satisfaction. When the Emperor T'ai-tsung of the Sung dynasty sacrificed at Fên-yin, he summoned Wei Yeh, but Wei Yeh did not go, giving illness as an excuse. One day, when he was busy teaching cranes to dance, he was informed that Imperial messengers had arrived. Then he took his lute in his arms, leapt over the fence and fled.[78]

8 In the time of the Emperor Hsiao-wên[79] there was found a musician of Prince Wên of Wei,[80] called Pao-kung, who was 180 years old. He used to say about himself that at the age of 12 he became blind, and that his parents then taught him the lute. He excelled in playing accomplished music, and did not lose his great skill, in spite of his great age. Thus Pao-kung since his youth played the lute for more than 160 years, and during all that time he never once knew what a lute looked like.[81]

9 Sun Fêng had a lute, which was called 'Turkey-cock'. When played, its tones were not very beautiful. Only when someone sang would the strings of their own accord then accompany it. So Sun changed its name to 'Singing by Itself'. On its bottom board there was a hole the shape of which resembled that of a moth. One day there came along a Taoist monk, begging for food. On seeing this lute, he said: 'Inside there is a moth. If it is not driven away, the lute will soon be worm-eaten.' Thereupon he took from his sleeve a small bamboo tube, and from it poured out a black medicine near the hole. No sooner had he done so than a green insect came running out. On its back it had a pattern of fine golden threads. The Taoist monk caught it and put it in the bamboo tube, then went his way. Thereafter, when a song was sung, the lute did not respond to it any more. Sun Fêng was amazed at this. When he told a sage of wide knowledge of this occurrence, the wise man said with a sigh: 'This [insect] was a rare treasure, called Chü-t'ung. When

---

78 魏野字仲先,性嗜吟咏,不求聞達,居州之東郊,手植竹木,流泉環繞,境趣幽絕,鑿土袤丈,曰,樂天洞,前爲草堂,彈琴其中,人訪之者,無貴賤皆白衣紗帽見之,號草堂居士,彈琴賦詩以自適,宋太宗祀汾陰,召之,辭疾不至,一日方教鶴舞,報中使至,抱琴踰垣而走.

79 250 B.C.
80 426–387 B.C.
81 孝文時,得魏文侯樂工寶公,年一百八十矣.自言十三歲失明.父母敎之琴,能爲雅聲,能老不廢忘,然則寶公自少,鼓琴一百六十餘年,而平生未嘗識琴之形也.

it is put next to the ear of a deaf man, he will be immediately cured. It likes to eat cedar wood, but it likes especially old ink.' Only then did Sun Fêng realize that the black medicine which the monk kept in the bamboo tube was nothing but dregs of old ink.[82]

10 Ch'ên Chih loved the lute, and would play on it day and night without stopping. When he had done so for twenty-eight years, suddenly a purple flower blossomed forth from the lute. He ate it, and disappeared as an Immortal.[83]

11 Wang Ching-po was a man from Kuei-chi. His lute was called 'Influencing Ghosts'. Once he passed the night in a pavilion, on an islet near his town. That night there was a brilliant moon, and a light dew was settling down. By playing his lute he compelled the ghost of the dead daughter of Liu Hui-ming to come to him. She looked just as if she were alive, and two maids accompanied her.[84]

12 Hsi K'ang [famous lute player],[85] one evening was playing his lute, when suddenly a ghost appeared, wearing chains and sighing deeply. Lifting up his hands in supplication, the ghost said: 'Let me play a tune for you.' Hsi K'ang then gave him his lute, and he played; the tones were clear but uncanny. When questioned, the ghost did not answer. Hsi K'ang thought it might have been the ghost of Ts'ai Yung [the famous musician and statesman],[86] for he had died in fetters.[87]

13 Another evening when Hsi K'ang was playing the lute, there suddenly appeared a man more than ten feet tall, clad in black cloth and leather belt. When Hsi K'ang had given him a good look, he extinguished his lamp, saying: 'I would not venture to emulate the light of a goblin.'[88]

14 In the beginning of the Shao-hsing period [1131–62] Shêng

---

[82] 孫鳳有一琴，名吐綬．彈之不甚佳，獨有人唱曲，則琴絃自相屬和，因改名曰自鳴．但琴背有一孔若蛙者，一日有一道人乞食，因見曰，此中有蛙，不除之，則將速朽，袖中出一小竹筒，倒黑藥少許孔側，即有綠色蟲走出，背上隱隱有金線文，道人納蟲竹筒中，竟去，自後唱曲，絃不復鳴矣，鳳怪之，有博物君子說及此事，歎曰，此異寶也，謂之鞠通，有耳聾人置耳邊少時，即愈．喜食梧桐，尤愛古墨，鳳始悟道人竹筒中藥，蓋古墨屑也．

[83] 陳植好鼓琴，晝夜不輟，凡二十八年，忽見琴生紫花，食之即仙去．

[84] 王敬伯會稽之人，琴曰，感靈，一日洲渚中昇亭而宿，是夜月華露輕，敬伯鼓琴，感劉惠明亡女之靈告敬伯，就體如平生，從婢二人．

[85] 223–62.

[86] 133–92.

[87] 嵇中散夜彈琴，忽見一鬼，械而長嘆，舉其手袂曰，為君一調，中散與琴彈之，聲清泠遙，問不對，疑是蔡邕，邕死之日，身著桎梏．

[88] 嵇康燈下鼓琴，忽有一人長丈餘，着黑單衣革帶，康熟視之，乃滅燈曰，恥與魑魅爭光．

Hsün was prefect of Hsiang-yang. He made himself a pavilion built over a stream, and there daily played his lute. One day a stormwind arose, and rain poured down. His lute changed into a huge red carp, and riding on it Shêng Hsün disappeared into the sky.[89]

15 Ch'ên Ch'iu-yang fell ill and died. His father thought much of him, and placed his son's lute before his soul-tablet. Always after that in the middle of the night the tones of this lute would be heard; they could be heard even outside the house.[90]

16 Chuang An-hsiang was once playing the lute when it was dark. At once close by the fingers of her right hand there appeared a golden flower, which filled the whole room with its shine. In remembrance of this occurrence, she composed the tune called 'Golden Flower'.[91]

17 In the beginning of the T'ien-pao period [550–9] Li Chia-yin was a great lover of the lute; he would never stop playing, whether it was summer or winter. By the side of his seat there grew up five-coloured agarics [symbol of longevity], all showing the shapes of Immortals.[92]

18 Tai K'uei [literatus of the Chin period],[93] in his youth already excelled in all arts, and was good at playing the lute. His lute was called 'Black Crane'. The Prime Minister, Prince Hsi of Wu-ling, despatched some people to invite him to come to his court. Tai K'uei then broke his lute to pieces before the eyes of the messengers, saying: 'Tai K'uei can not become a payed comedian at a prince's court.'[94]

(The same story is quoted in the *Ku-ch'in-shu*;[95] there the behaviour of Tai K'uei is contrasted with that of another famous lute player of the same period, Yüan Chan:[96] 'Yüan Chan was an expert on the lute. People heard of his fame, and came in great numbers, asking him to play for them. He played for all, noble and low, young and old. I

---

[89] 紹興初盛勛知襄陽, 自造水閣, 日鼓琴于此, 一日風雨大作, 琴化爲巨赤鯉, 勛跨之騰空而去.

[90] 陳秋陽以病卒, 其父思之, 以琴置靈几, 每夜半必聞琴聲, 且達戶外.

[91] 莊暗香暗中彈琴, 右手指有金花, 照爛九案, 因自作金花之曲.

[92] 天保初, 李嘉胤素好鼓琴, 冬夏不輟, 所居座中生五色芝草, 皆狀如神仙.

[93] Died 396; besides being a famous lute player, he was also known as a fine calligraphist and painter.

[94] 戴逵少有文藝, 善鼓琴, 琴名黑鶴, 太宰武陵王睎使人召焉, 逵對使者前打破琴曰, 戴安道不能爲王門伶人.

[95] 古琴疏, ascribed to Yü Ju-ming 虞汝明; see the *Shuo-fu* 說郛.

[96] 阮瞻, style Ch'ien-li 千里.

consider the understanding shown by Yüan Chan superior to the persistency of Tai K'uei.')[97]

19 During the Chên-yüan period [785–804] Ts'ui Hui, having lost his way, fell into a dry well. At the bottom he found a cave. Having penetrated into this cave for several miles, he struck a stone door, and having entered it he found a room measuring more than a hundred feet. The walls were beset with jewels, the glamour of which illuminated the whole room. A lute was lying on a table. Ts'ui Hui observed all this, without understanding where he was. After some delay he started playing on the lute. Then suddenly a door in the back wall opened, and in came two girls, saying: 'How is it that Master Ts'ui makes bold to enter the palace of the Emperor?' Ts'ui Hui asked: 'Where is the Emperor?' They answered: 'He has gone to the banquet of Chu Yung [a personage of the mythical age, later revered as Fire God; the implication is that Ts'ui Hui had entered the palace of one of the mythical Emperors]. Thereupon the girls told him to be seated before the table, and play on the lute for them. Ts'ui Hui played the tune *Hu-chia* [see above, page 94: 'The significance of the tunes', under heading 2, where the origin of the tune is differently explained]. The girls asked: 'What tune is this?' He answered: 'It is called *Hu-chia*.' They asked further: 'Why is it called *Hu-chia*?' He said: 'The daughter of Ts'ai Yung of the Han dynasty was carried off by the barbarians as a prisoner. While in their midst she was moved, remembering her former life, and taking her lute she composed this tune, representing the mournful sounds of the barbarians blowing their reed pipe.' The girls were overjoyed, and exclaimed: 'What a beautiful new tune this is!' Thereupon they made him drink toasts with them.[98]

20 On a moonlit night Su Shih [the famous Sung literatus][99] heard outside his window a song. It ran: 'Tones, tones . . .

---

[97] 阮千里善彈琴, 人聞其名往來求聽, 不問貴賤長幼, 皆爲彈之, 余以爲安道之介, 不如千里之達.

[98] 貞元中, 崔煒因迷道失足, 墜一枯井中, 井中空洞, 傍行數里, 觸一石門, 入門一室, 可百餘步, 壁綴明珠, 光亮一室, 几上設琴, 煒細視莫測, 良久取琴試彈, 室後一戶, 忽啓有二女, 出曰, 何崔生擅入皇帝玄宮耶, 煒問, 皇帝何在, 曰, 暫赴祝融晏耳, 因命煒就榻鼓琴, 煒彈胡笳, 二女曰, 何曲也, 曰, 胡笳也, 曰, 何以爲胡笳, 煒曰, 漢蔡邕女, 被虜入胡中, 及歸感胡中故事, 因撫琴而成斯弄, 象胡中吹笳哀咽之聲, 女皆恬然, 曰, 大是新曲, 遂命酌傳觴.

[99] 1036–1101.

You are ungrateful, truly you are ungrateful! You have treated me badly, up to this day. I remember that formerly I used to sing softly, softly, drinking small cups. One tune of mine was then deemed worth a thousand pieces of gold. Now I am thrown away at the base of an old wall ... The autumnal breeze blows over the dry grass, the white clouds are high ... The bridge is broken, the water flows on, and my lover is nowhere to be seen. Sadness, sadness, melancholy ... ' Opening the window to trace this sound, Su Shih saw a slender young woman, who vanished under the wall. The next day he dug there, and found an old lute.[100, 101]

21 Wang Yen-po was playing his lute in a houseboat that was lying ashore for the night. Then he saw a girl, who drew aside the door curtain, and entered. She took the lute and started to tune it; the tones were very sad. When Wang asked her what tune she was going to play, she answered: 'It is called *Ch'u-ming-kuang*; only Hsi K'ang[102] can play it.' Wang asked her to teach it to him, but she said: 'This is not a tune that may be played at a lover's meeting. It is intended only for the enjoyment of recluses living on high rocks or in hidden vales.' Then she played the lute and sang thereto. She shared his couch with him, and disappeared at daybreak.[103]

22 Yüan Hsien [disciple of Confucius] lived in a little hut, his doorposts were mulberry trees, his clothes were made of coarse wool. The hut was leaking from above and damp underneath, but he sat there correctly, and played on an old lute. [In the meantime] Tzû-kung [another disciple of Confucius] had become a minister in the state of Wei, and he came to visit Yüan with a four-in-hand team and a suite of cavalry. When he saw Yüan Hsien he said: 'Alas! In what distress you are!' Yüan Hsien answered: 'I have heard that a

---

100 蘇東坡於月夜聞窗外歌曰,音音音,你負心,眞負心,辜負我,到於今,記得當時低低唱,淺淺斟,一曲值千金,如今拋我古墙陰,秋風荒草白雲深,斷橋流水無故人,淒淒切切,冷冷清清,推窗卽之,見一女子冉冉沒於墻下,明日掘之,得古琴一張.

101 To the words of the girl's song, there was made a minor lute tune, entitled *Ku-ch'in-yin* 古琴吟 'Lament of the old lute'; G. Soulié (Appendix I, 3), has given on p. 116 a transcription of this tune in Western notation. His translation of the words on p. 115 is full of mistakes, and should be disregarded.

102 See p. 55.

103 王彥伯維舟理琴,見一女子披帷而進,取琴調之,聲甚哀,彥伯問何曲,答曰,此楚明光也,唯嵇叔夜能之,彥伯請受,女曰,此非豔俗所宜,唯岩棲谷隱者可以娛耳,鼓琴且歌,止於東榻,遲明辭去.

man who has no riches is said to be poor, and a man who has studied the Way but can not practise it, is said to be in distress. Now I for one am poor, but I am not in distress. In truth, doing things always looking for approval from the bystanders, being partial in choosing friends, loving a display of benevolence and righteousness, and showing off chariots and horses, these are things which I could not bear to do.' Tzû-kung hastily went away, and looked sour for the rest of his life.[104]

[104] 原憲居環堵之室，桑以爲樞，褐以爲裳，上漏下溼，匡坐而彈古琴，子貢相衞，結駟連騎而來，見憲曰，嘻，先生何病也，憲應之曰，憲聞之無財謂之貧，學道而不能行，謂之病，若憲貧也，非病也，夫希而行，比周而友，仁義之慝，車馬之飾，憲不忍爲也，子貢逡巡而退，終身猶有慚色. (Taken from the K'ung-tzû-chia-yü 孔子家語; the same story is to be found in a slightly different version in Chuang-tzû, book Jang-wang 讓王.

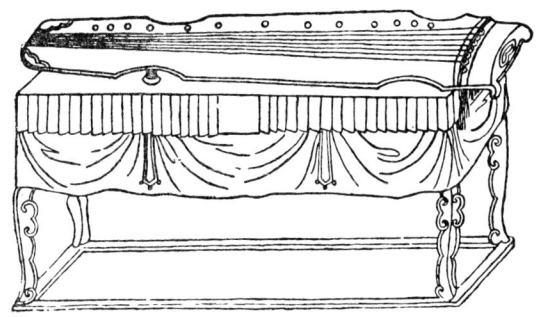

CHAPTER SEVEN

Conclusions

THE lute, the cither (*sê*), the reed-organ (*shêng*), and the quaint ocarina (*hsüan*), these are the instruments by which the ancient music of China can be studied. These instruments preserve tones that accompanied solemn sacrifices, notes that delighted the ears of ancient princes, more than three thousand years ago.

To revive this music, however, is no easy task. For the succeeding centuries have dimmed the tradition regarding the music of *sê*, *shêng* and *hsüan*: age has sealed their secrets. At present we find only some faint echos in their score for the ceremonial orchestra, stray fragments of what once must have been impressive solo music. It is only the lute that has an unbroken tradition. It was on the lute that many generations of scholars concentrated their musical efforts, inspired by reverent love for this instrument of the ancient sages. And so it was the lute that became a symbol of literary life and elegant refinement. At the same time it has retained its character of musical instrument, while *shêng*, *sê* and *hsüan* are more and more regarded as mere curiosities.

In the foregoing pages I have tried to describe one aspect of this unique Chinese musical instrument; I have tried to give the reader some idea of the place occupied by the lute in Chinese culture. I have tried to show how various, often originally conflicting elements, melted together and came to form a more or less unified ideology, the lore of the Chinese lute. And at the same time I have endeavoured to outline some historical perspectives. On rereading the above, my historical observations especially appear to me rather haphazard, and too much scattered over different chapters. As the material treated is almost entirely new, these defects were often unavoidable. Too often I was obliged to abandon the course of an argument, and branch off on some side track, in order to substantiate my theories. For the reader's convenience I here sum up in a concise form the conclusions that may be drawn from the foregoing chapters.

The origin of the lute lies hidden in China's past. There is evidence, however, that at some remote time, lute and cither were one and the same instrument: a stringed instrument, about the form and sound of which we can only make conjectures. This primordial lute must have borne an exclusively sacral character.

During the later part of the Chou dynasty, and until roughly the beginning of our era, we find lute and cither as separate, though still cognate, instruments, both used in the ceremonial orchestra. At the same time both were also used as solo instruments, for executing music of lighter genre. Yet it appears that it was especially to the lute that clung faint echoes of those ancient magical beliefs that were connected with old ceremonial music. This appears clearly from the story related in the *Shih-chi*, and given in section 1 of the preceding chapter: the lute is played at a banquet to amuse the guests, but unexpectedly it becomes the instrument through which hidden powers, originating in magic ceremonies of the dim past, manifest themselves in sinister omens. Thus gradually the lute is set more or less apart as a kind of sacred instrument. And when during the later Han dynasty the Confucianist literati are established as a mighty official caste, they declare the lute their special instrument. Here the ways of lute and cither part. The ancient magical notions that formerly were connected with music in general, are henceforth applied to one instrument in particular, the lute. Many of these notions are cast in Taoist formulae, these being by nature more suitable for that purpose than Confucianist terminology. Buddhism also makes its influence felt, and thus we find in the fourth and fifth centuries A.D. that something like a special *ch'in* ideology has been founded. The ceremonial orchestra, too, under literary influence, has become an expression of politico-philosophical conceptions. But it is in the lute ideology that the ancient magic conceptions survive: playing the lute is described as a means for prolonging life, and as an aid to meditation.

During the Sui and T'ang periods an intense artistic impulse inspired Chinese culture. Mainly through Central-Asiatic influence, the Chinese were obsessed by a hunger for bright and gorgeous colours, for highly melodious, light and entrancing music. New instruments were imported from foreign countries, and old Chinese instruments were put to a new use. The lute, with its rich acoustic possibilities, is tuned to less severe melodies, and is incorporated in the orchestra for entertainment music, to enliven literary gatherings and festive banquets. But on the other hand, as a reaction, some

[VII] CONCLUSIONS

conservative scholars now start to define more sharply the principles of the special ideology of the lute, to guard their beloved instrument against the vulgarity of the crowd.

The Sung dynasty then shows both the profane and the sacred aspects of the lute, and between these two aspects its music is almost evenly balanced. It is a period of gestation, a slow preparation for the great climax. This process of maturation goes on for some time, until, at length, during the Ming period lute and lute music reach full fruition. The great importance of this period for the lute justifies a slightly more detailed treatment.

It is much to be regretted that it has become a habit of Western writers, when describing the history of China, to pass over the Ming dynasty in a few words, or at best, with a few pages. They dwell on the political decay that set in with the predominance of the eunuchs in Palace circles and, speaking of the cultural aspect of the period, they say that no new artistic impulses of importance are noticeable, that in all branches of art and literature nothing was accomplished beyond copying old models. And with regard to scientific pursuits, they repeat the judgement given by the scholars of the Ch'ing dynasty, pronouncing Ming scholarship shallow and uncritical.

Now, that Ch'ing scholars did little to show the glory of the Ming dynasty is quite understandable. The hand of the Manchu conqueror rested heavily on the Chinese intellect, and to grow enthusiastic over the merits of the former dynasty was courting disaster. Less excusable is the negligent attitude of Western scholars. For they have free access to the vast mass of original Ming materials that is preserved. That they did not use this opportunity, shows that until very recently there existed among Western sinologues a strong tendency to study only the approved sections of Chinese literature, books that were found in the Ch'ing catalogues. But in order to see the culture of the Ming period as it really was, we must entirely ignore Ch'ing materials; they can only blur our view. We must turn to the original Ming materials, which, fortunately, still exist in abundance. Ming editions of the works of almost every Ming literatus of any importance have been preserved.[1] Ming porcelain still tells its own tale, and genuine Ming paintings are by no means rare.

---

[1] During the Ch'ing dynasty the censor often took entire chapters out of these Ming prints; it is in Japan that one must look for unmutilated copies. For a great number of Ming editions were brought over to Japan shortly after their publication, and were carefully preserved. Such Ming editions are especially found in the collections of old feudal families. These books are called in the Japanese book trade *kowatari* 古渡り, and are*

Surveying these materials I come to the conclusion that from a cultural point of view, the Ming period was one of the most glorious epochs in Chinese history. It was the period that saw a culmination of pure Chinese culture, the period that shows the most complete expression of Chinese ideals. The foreign influences that entered China during the T'ang and subsequent dynasties had been digested; in the Ming period a complete amalgamation is effected. During this period the Chinese spirit blossomed most luxuriantly; it was during the Ch'ing dynasty that the withering set in. When a tree is in full blossom, its gorgeous beauty amazes the observer; little does he care what the branches and the trunk look like. With the coming of autumn, the blossoms fall down, then the leaves, and the observer sees the tree in a more realistic way; he sees that here branches are broken, there a stem ends in an abrupt gnarl. The observer will know more, but enjoy less. This image may give an idea of the fundamental differences between the general spirit of Ming and Ch'ing cultures. Ming scholars wrote enthusiastic eulogies on a passage in the Classics that struck them as eminently wise; Ch'ing scholars pointed out that the punctuation of one sentence was erroneous. Ming literati reprinted the poetry of the T'ang and preceding periods in magnificent editions, with graceful characters on large-sized paper. Ch'ing scholars reprinted this same poetry in cheap-looking editions, with small, angular characters, but with the text really improved.

During the Ming period the daily life of the scholar-official neared something like perfection. The literati of that time, mostly of an eclectic turn of mind, understood the secret of life, which consists of judiciously mixing beauty with comfort, and high ideals with purely practical views. This way of living is mirrored in the literature of the period. Numerous books are written on the refined pleasures of the cultured scholar. They describe in minute detail the art of tea drinking, the art of flower arrangement, of laying out gardens, of building rockeries, of playing chess and complicated wine games, of practising arrow throwing, ball games, and a multitude of other subjects that later were neglected, or fell entirely into oblivion.

---

*greatly valued. Japan generally furnishes important materials for our knowledge of Ming culture. In the turbulent years that marked the end of the Ming dynasty, Chinese priests, scholars and artists fled to Japan in great numbers, and were patronized by Japanese nobles and scholars. So great was their influence, that for obtaining a right understanding of, say Tokugawa culture, a study of the Ming dynasty is imperative; and, conversely, when studying the Ming period one cannot afford to disregard the mass of Ming material preserved in Japan.

[VII] CONCLUSIONS

It is only natural, therefore, that it was during the Ming period, too, that the lute and lute music displayed their full and most sublime unfolding. In cultural centers all over the country great lute masters arose, and numerous handbooks were published. Their composers did not aim at retracing the old music. Although they loved to dwell on the beauty of bygone days, this was a sentiment, a mood, but little conducive to intensive study. They composed very original and most attractive new tunes, to which they assigned the old approved titles. This music is new, but how rich in tone, what subtle effects, what fullness of musical expression! Granted that the Ming lute players were mediocre students of musical history (with some brilliant exceptions like the Prince Tsai-yü), it cannot be denied that they were gifted musicians.

In the circles of the literati, cultivating leisurely enjoyment and abstract contemplation, the various conceptions connected with the lute were more or less systematized and pressed into formulae. Since many of the literati engaged in Taoist disciplines for prolonging life, and interested themselves in the search for the elixir of life and similar pursuits, the magical character of the lute was stressed more and more. Now the system of *ch'in* ideology reaches its full development, and the significance of the lute is definitely fixed.

During the Ch'ing dynasty the life of the literati loses much of its glamour. Especially in the earlier part of the Ch'ing period, literary pursuits are postponed to military prowess: the most skilful brush is powerless when confronted with the swords and bows of the Manchu bannermen. Later, it is true, literary ideals reasserted themselves; but the vigour and *élan* of the Ming period were never regained. South China was less affected. Up to the present it is still in South China that remnants of Ming culture must be looked for. Also it was the southern provinces that produced most of the great lute masters of the Ch'ing period.

When the Manchu supremacy had become more firmly established, the rulers could devote more attention to literary matters. Then Ch'ing scholarship develops, and acquires its many distinguishing features: a sharp critical spirit, extensive antiquarian research, the compiling of enormous works of literary reference, etc. Now serious attempts are made to reconstruct the old music. Old musical scores are collected, various systems of notation investigated, and musical theory is re-examined.

Many useful books about the lute and its music are written, but important additions to the repertoire are few. For the most part, lute masters confine themselves to publishing the tunes of the Ming and preceding dynasties in revised forms. The system of *ch'in* ideology is not worked out further, often even completely disregarded. At best, the statements scattered over the various Ming handbooks are reprinted. In most handbooks the teachings on the significance of the lute are left out, and replaced by lengthy discussions on musical theory. A good example of such a dry handbook is the *Tzŭ-yüan-t'ang* handbook (cf. Appendix II, no. 16). During the Ch'ing period, also, the social standard of the lute experts dropped considerably. While during the Ming and preceding periods famous lute performers were as a rule great literati or high officials, in the Ch'ing period they were mostly more or less professional musicians, who taught the lute for a living. One shall look in vain in biographical works of the period for the names of the publishers of the best handbooks.

The twentieth century brings the establishment of the Republic, and a revaluation of all values. Here we must break off our discussion of the history of *ch'in* ideology. Instead I may end with some remarks about the present state of lute music, and its future.

In the turbulent first decennia of this century the lute very nearly suffered the same fate as so many other Chinese old musical instruments, namely, to see its tradition broken off and its music forgotten. Fortunately a few old masters, scattered over the country, faithfully preserved their cherished art, and transmitted its secrets to a few pupils. They acted as guardians of the lute and its music, while the ranks of scholars who understood it grew thinner every day, and while younger Chinese musicians were entirely absorbed in studies of Western music.

Now, in recent years, the persistency of those few elder masters is bearing fruit. For gradually in China there has come into existence a class of younger musicians, who combine a sound Western musicological training with a deep interest in their own national music. Many of these have taken up the study of the lute; first they patiently learn the art from the few elderly masters that are left, then they investigate the materials thus obtained in the light of modern musicological science. From these researches we may expect important results.[2]

---

[2] How necessary the work of these scholars is, is all too apparent; for the ignorance of many present-day Chinese with regard to their own music is appalling. In 1937 I read in a Chinese-managed periodical, which as a rule maintains a high literary and scientific standard (*The T'ien-hsia Monthly*, IV, p. 54; Music Chronicle), strange statements like the following: 'Most of them [the Chinese musical instruments] are still quite crude*

[VII] CONCLUSIONS

The atmosphere that in former days surrounded the lute player will soon belong definitely to the past—together with so much that was charming in the old Chinese life. But lute music in itself has a bright future.

The present writer is one of those who—naive and overconfident, maybe—believe in the existence of eternal values. He believes that what is really good or beautiful will last for ever; that such things can be ignored, neglected or suppressed, but that they shall never vanish entirely.

It is for this reason that he ventures to publish the preceding pages on the lore of the Chinese lute, desultory and incomplete as they are. For the intrinsic beauty of the lute and its music are such as to justify his confidence that others will continue where he left off.

*and simple: they do not admit of the development of highly finished techniques Moreover, the tone qualities of the musical instruments are none too pleasing. The seven-chord ch'in (七絃琴) has hardly any sound at all.' Then the author of the article in question goes on to say that all Chinese instruments must be 'corrected', so as to make them reproduce the Western tempered scale. Such a proposal, involving as it does the perversion or wanton destruction of precious musical data, could only be made in a time like the present, where every day there is more music but less musicality, and where various sound-producing instruments throw the greatest masterpieces of Western music to the crowd to be scrambled for.

APPENDIX I

Occidental Literature on the Lute

1 J. J. M. Amiot, *Mémoires sur la musique des Chinois tant anciens que modernes* (Mémoires concernant les Chinois, vol. VI), Paris 1780.

This comprehensive work is the first detailed description of Chinese music published in Europe. Its learned author discusses Chinese musical theory in general, the twelve sonorous tubes, and some of the more important instruments used in the ceremonial orchestra. His sources are personal observation and such authoritative Chinese works as the *Lü-lü-ching-i*[1] by the Ming prince Chu Tsai-yü,[2] and the *Lü-lü-chêng-i*,[3] an official publication dated 1713. This book shows the same merits and the same defects as other works by 18th-century missionaries on China. These learned priests made an excellent use of their daily contact with the flower of the Chinese literati; they carefully noted down the information supplied by the latter, and followed their advice regarding the books to be selected for further reference. On the other hand, the missionaries believed implicitly what their informants told them, and thought that their opinions on Chinese antiquity were unquestionable truth. Thus, for instance, with regard to music, the Chinese informants of our author gave him nothing but the traditional Chinese views on music, as explained in some officially sanctioned standard works of later date. Yet this book by Father Amiot is a remarkable effort; when read critically, it will supply even the present-day student of Chinese music with much useful material.

The author gives considerable attention to both *ch'in* and *sê*. In the first chapter of this essay I already quoted one of his remarks on the importance of the lute in Chinese cultural life (cf. above, Chapter I, page 3). Interesting is a list of books relating to the lute, which the author gives on p. 24. Unfortunately the titles are given in transcription only, without author or date; therefore some of the items I could not identify. As the list shows

1 律呂精義   2 朱載堉   3 律呂正義

which books on the lute were studied by Court circles in the 18th century, I reproduce it here, with my identifications added between brackets.

(49) *Kou tchouen kin pou.*

(50) *Chen ki mi pou* (*Shên-chi-pi-pu*,[4] by the Ming prince Chu Ch'üan; cf. Appendix II, no. 11).

(51) *Tay kou y yn* (*T'ai-ku-i-yin*,[5] same author).

(52) *Kin jouan ki mong* (*Ch'in-juan-ch'i-meng*,[6] same author).

(53) *Sien ko yao tché* (*Hsien-ko-yao-chih*.[7] The *Lü-lü-ching-i* mentions a *Hsien-ko-yao-lu*[8] by an unknown author).

(54) *Tchoung ho fa jen* (*Chung-ho-fa-jên*,[9] a Ming treatise by an unknown author, mentioned in the *Lü-lü-ching-i*).

(55) *Y fa kin pou* (*I-fa-ch'in-pu*).[10]

(56) *Tchan tchou kin pou* (*Chang-chu-ch'in-pu*,[11] a Ming handbook mentioned in the *Lü-lü-ching-i*).

(57) *Hoang sien kin pou* (*Huang-hsien-ch'in-pu*,[12] a Ming handbook mentioned in the *Lü-lü-ching-i*, better known as the *Wu-kang-ch'in-pu*,[13] pub. 1546; Huang Hsien occupied an official position during 1488–1505).

(58) *Siao loan kin pou* (*Hsiao-luan-ch'in-pu*,[14] a Ming handbook mentioned in the *Lü-lü-ching-i*).

2 J. A. van Aalst, *Chinese music* (Imperial Maritime Customs, special series, No. 6), Shanghai 1884 (re-issued at Peking in 1933).

For many years this book was for occidental students the standard work for information regarding Chinese music. Though it contains not a few misstatements, and although most of its general observations are antiquated, it still is a usable book. It has a wider scope than Amiot's work, as here popular Chinese music is also included. There are many illustrations, but they are very poorly done.

The *ch'in* is treated on pages 59–62. The description found there is generally correct; only it should be remembered that the author's observations on lute music are based on the lute of the ceremonial orchestra, and that therefore the tuning, for

---

4 神奇秘譜
5 太古遺音
6 琴阮啓蒙
7 絃歌要指
8 絃歌要錄
9 中和發軔
10 遺法琴譜
11 張助琴譜
12 黃獻琴譜
13 梧岡琴譜
14 蕭鸞琴譜

[*Appendix 1*] OCCIDENTAL LITERATURE ON THE LUTE 173

instance, does not apply to the lute as solo instrument. On p. 60, the explanation of the finger technique of the right hand, the last sign (abbreviation of *ch'uan-fu*)¹⁵ is wrongly explained; cf. the same sign in the list given by me above, p. 127, no. 10.

3 G. Soulié, *La Musique en Chine* (Extrait du Bulletin de l'Association franco-chinoise), Paris 1911.

When compared with the preceding item, this book shows considerable progress. It is far more scientific than van Aalst's, and the illustrations are more accurate and better executed. On the basis of its quality this work should long ago have superseded van Aalst's in sinological circles. For some reason or other, however, it has remained comparatively unknown, and until recent years van Aalst's book continued to appear in catalogues at a prohibitive price; that in 1933 it was reprinted, unrevised, tends to show how few are the serious students of music among present-day orientalists.

On p. 30 the author gives a fairly detailed description of the *ch'in*. He gives a list of 44 abbreviated signs used in *ch'in* notation, which means an improvement on the meagre list given by van Aalst, though it contains many inaccuracies; these will appear on comparing this list with the one given by me above, p. 124. On p. 36 a page from a *ch'in* handbook is reproduced, and explained in detail. On p. 115 a short lute composition (*Ku-ch'in-yin*)¹⁶ is given in Western notation.

4 A. C. Moule, *A list of musical and other sound-producing instruments of the Chinese* (Royal Asiatic Society), Shanghai 1908.

This paper contains accurate descriptions of a great variety of Chinese musical instruments. The author adopted the method followed by V. C. Mahillon in his excellent *Catalogue descriptif et analytique du musée instrumental du Conservatoire Royal de Bruxelles* (1893); he tries to be as detailed as possible with regard to measurements and transcription of the scales. Next to the instruments used in ceremonial music, we also find descriptions of very popular instruments, used in the streets of Chinese towns. These data are important, for street music undergoes many changes, and generally leaves no written records.

Pages 106–9 treat of the *ch'in*; the material is taken from Amiot, van Aalst, etc., and no new data are added.

¹⁵ 全扶   ¹⁶ 古琴吟

5 L. LALOY, *La Musique chinoise* (part of the series: Les Musiciens célèbres), Paris, no date.

This small book, although of necessity rather popular, still is a very sound and useful survey of Chinese music, with the cultural and ideological aspects especially stressed. The illustrations are well chosen and of excellent execution. Contents:

1 Les sources.
2 La doctrine.
3 Les destins.
4 Le système.
5 La gamme.
6 Les gammes nouvelles.
7 Les instruments.
8 La notation.
9 Musique religieuse.
10 Musique de chambre.
11 Musique populaire.
12 Musique de théatre.
13 Espoir.
14 Mélodies notées.

Pages 68–76 and 91–5 treat of the *ch'in*. The author duly stresses the importance of lute ideology, the deep significance of this instrument and its music. Historical and cultural background are briefly, but very aptly, sketched. This book I recommend as the best introduction to the subject of Chinese music in general.

6 M. COURANT, *Essai historique sur la musique classique des Chinois, avec un appendice relatif à la musique coréenne* (in: Encyclopédie de la musique et dictionnaire du Conservatoire, part I, pp. 77–241), Paris 1924.

M. Courant, the well-known French sinologue, to whom the orientalistic world is already heavily indebted for his magnificent Korean bibliography (*Bibliographie coréenne*, Paris 1894), has put us under a further obligation by this most detailed study on Chinese classical music. This essay is the most scientific and accurate account of Chinese music I know. Here for the first time the subject in its entirety has been investigated and reviewed by a competent scholar, who could consult all sources in the original, and in addition to that was—if my information is correct—himself a musician of no mean ability. Chinese musical theory is analyzed in detail, and its often obscure expressions are translated into Western terminology. Historical problems are discussed in detail, and in groping for their solution the author shows much discretion. First reading through the preceding item by Laloy, and then working through this essay by Courant, will in my opinion be the best preparation for anyone who proposes to do some research in Chinese music. Courant's essay is divided into four parts:

1 Théorie musicale.
2 Instruments.
3 Orchestres et choeurs.
4 Les Idées cosmologiques et philosophiques.

The *ch'in* is treated on pp. 163–75. After a careful description of the instrument itself, the author goes on to an investigation of its theoretical side, and discusses its tunings in detail. Then he gives about a dozen *ch'in* melodies in Western transcription, all taken from the *T'ien-wên-ko-ch'in-pu-chi-ch'êng* (cf. App. II, no. 18). He admits that these versions are arbitrary, as they must be because of the fundamental differences existing between the Chinese scale and ours; or, as the author puts it: 'Ce serait sans doute fausser l'essence des systèmes harmoniques chinois que de les vouloir réduire à nos formules' (p. 169). Yet his transcriptions are useful to give the student at least a general idea of what *ch'in* music looks like. I may add that execution on the cello comes nearest to the tone of the Chinese original. The essay ends with an extensive bibliography of Western and Chinese sources consulted, and a useful index where the reader finds the Chinese characters for every name and term occurring in the essay.

I may add in passing that the few pages treating of Korean music (pp. 211–20) are less satisfactory. To supplement what is given here, one should consult A. Eckardt, *Koreanische Musik*, Tokyo 1930. Sinologues I would refer to the *Ak-hak-kwe-pôm*.[17] This is the great Korean standard work on Chinese and Korean music, written in Chinese, and profusely illustrated. It was written in 1493 by the scholar Syông Kyôn 成俔. The Korean original is now extremely rare; fortunately in 1933 a good photographic reprint was published at Keijō, by the Koten-kankō-kai.[18]

[17] 樂學軌範   [18] 古典刊行會

APPENDIX II

Chinese Literature on the Lute

A GENERAL

1 *Ch'in-tsao*,[1] a collection of about fifty motifs of ancient melodies. This book contains no musical notation; only the title of each tune is given, with a few words about its composer, the circumstances that inspired him, the significance of the music, etc. As the oldest list of lute melodies extant, this book has great documentary value. Opinions differ as to whether its authorship must be ascribed to the famous literatus and musician Ts'ai Yung,[2] (133–92), or to the equally famous man of letters K'ung Yen.[3] The text is to be found in the *Tu-hua-chai-ts'ung-shu*,[4] a collection of reprints of classical works published in 1799 by Ku Hsiu[5] and the *P'ing-ts'in-kuan-ts'ung-shu*,[6] a collection of texts published by the great authority on the classics Sun Hsing-yen.[7] I have used the excellent Japanese official edition (*kampan*),[8] pub. in 1832 in one vol., where the text as established by Sun Hsing-yen is reprinted, together with the preface by the scholar Ma Jui-chên,[9] dated 1805.

2 *Ch'in-shih*,[10] 'History of the Lute', in 6 chs.; cf. *Imperial Catalogue*, ch. 113, leaf 8 verso. The author of this treatise is the great scholar of the Sung period, Chu Ch'ang-wên[11] (style: Po-yüan,[12] 1041–1100). Chs. 1–5 contain biographies of more than 150 famous lute players, chronologically arranged; the 6th ch. treats of the lute itself, and is divided into eleven parts. These discuss:

    1 Sonorous tubes.[13]
    2 Strings.[14]

1 琴操
2 蔡邕
3 孔衍
4 讀畫齋叢書
5 顧修
6 平津館叢書
7 孫星衍
8 官板
9 馬瑞辰
10 琴史
11 朱長文
12 伯原
13 瑩律
14 釋絃

  3 Dimensions.[15]
  4 Form.[16]
  5 Tones.[17]
  6 Modes.[18]
  7 Songs.[19]
  8 Manufacture.[20]
  9 Beauty.[21]
  10 Significance.[22]
  11 History.[23]

  The preface to this book is dated 1084. The author, prevented through illness from taking part in the literary examinations, devoted the greater part of his life to literary pursuits. He was especially interested in those objects that are dear to the literatus; his researches in this field are collected in his *Mo-ch'ih-p'ien*,[24] preface dated 1066. The author's grandfather, Chu I,[25] was an expert on the lute, and Chu Ch'ang-wên continued his tradition. The *Ch'in-shih* is written in excellent, highly polished prose. Unfortunately, historical details and precise information are sacrificed to the style; it is further to be regretted that the author never mentions his sources. Still the book contains much useful material. I used the edition as published in the *Lien-t'ing-shih-êrh-chung*,[26] a collection of reprints pub. at Shanghai in 1921; the originals were collected by Ts'ao Yin[27] (1658–1712).

3 *K'ao-p'an-yü-shih*,[28] 'Desultory Remarks on Furnishing the Abode of the Retired Scholar', in 4 chs.; cf. *Imperial Catalogue*, ch. 130, leaf 2 recto. The title of this book refers to an ode of the *Shih-ching* (Decade of Wei, 2),[29] which opens with the line: 'He built his hut near the stream in the vale.'[30] This book contains very detailed descriptions of all the objects belonging to the traditional outfit of a scholar of refined and cultured taste, e.g. old books and scrolls, incense, utensils for making tea, etc. To each of these objects a *chien*,[31] 'memorandum', is devoted; the *Ch'in-chien*[32] is to be found at the end of ch. 2. The compiler is the

15	明度	24	墨池篇
16	擬象	25	朱億
17	論音	26	楝亭十二種
18	審調	27	曹寅
19	聲歌	28	考盤餘事
20	廣制	29	箇
21	盡美	30	考盤在澗
22	志言	31	箋
23	叙史	32	琴箋

well-known Ming scholar T'u Lung.³³ In China this book was extremely popular; it was published in various editions, and may be found in several *ts'ung-shu*.³⁴ A nicely edited Japanese reprint appeared in 1803, with a preface by the Japanese sinologue Hayashi Jussai³⁵ (1768–1841).

4 *Tsun-shêng-pa-chien*,³⁶ 'Eight Treatises on Living in Accordance with Nature' (the title page of the original Ming edition, dated 1591, reads *tsun* 尊 instead of *tsun* 遵, which could be rendered as: 'venerating, valuing' life), 8 chs.; cf. *Imperial Catalogue*, ch. 123, leaf 2 recto. Compiled by Kao Lien,³⁷ a poet and playwright of the later part of the Ming dynasty. About his life and career little is known; a short biographical note may be found in the *Ming-tz'û-tsung*,³⁸ ch. 4. His *Tsun-shêng-pa-chien* is an extensive encyclopedical collection, chiefly bearing a medical character; it indicates how, by following Taoist rules, one may live in good health and attain to a high age. But besides these, a great variety of other subjects are treated, special attention being given to dress, food etc. Thus this book is an important document for our knowledge of daily life and customs during the Ming period. As the title indicates, the work is divided into 8 sections. For our present subject the 6th section is the most important. It bears the title *Yen-hsien-ch'ing-shang*:³⁹ 'Refined enjoyment of elegant leisure'. This section discusses all subjects dear to the scholar: paintings and how to collect and preserve them; inkstones and ink, paper, brushes, brush stands, ornamental rocks, seals, etc. It is in this section that we also find a discussion of the lute, entitled *Lun-ch'in*⁴⁰ (pp. 70 ff.). Here the author gives a concise, but fairly accurate survey of the study of the lute. Thereafter we find some pages on cranes and how to rear them.

5 *Ch'in-ching*,⁴¹ 'Classical Book of the Lute', in 14 chs., by the lute master Chang Ta-ming,⁴² called Yu-kun. First preface by the Ming scholar Yeh Hsiang-kao⁴³ (cf. *Ming-shih*, ch. 240), dated 1609; second preface by Liu Ta-jên;⁴⁴ author's preface dated 1609. Undated colophon by Ch'ên Wu-ch'ang.⁴⁵ The original, finely executed Ming edition of this valuable book is extremely

---

33 屠隆, style: Ch'ang-ching 長卿, *Chin-shih* in 1577.
34 叢書
35 林述齋
36 遵生八牋
37 高濂
38 明詞綜
39 燕閒清賞
40 論琴
41 琴經
42 張大命, 右袞
43 葉向高
44 劉大任
45 陳五昌

rare; but occasionally Chinese or Japanese manuscript copies may be found. About Chang Ta-ming, who later also published a collection of tunes in notation, the *Yang-ch'un-t'ang-ch'in-pu*,[46] little is known except that he was a man from Fukien. The *Ch'in-ching* is remarkable in that it does not contain a single lute tune in notation. The work is concerned with musical theory, rules for the lute player, how to read the *ch'in-pu*, notes on famous old tunes and instruments, hints for appraising antique lutes, how to build lutes, how to select the correct surroundings for playing the lute, and finally an extensive collection of quotations from older literature.

6 *Ch'ing-lien-fang-ch'in-ya*,[47] 'Elegance of the Lute, from the Blue-Lotus Boat', in 4 chs.; cf. *Imperial Catalogue*, ch. 114, leaf 7 verso. A comprehensive collection of literary data concerning the lute, compiled by Lin Yu-lin[48]; author's preface dated 1641. Also, there are two prefaces by Ming painters, the first by Li Shao-chi,[49] the second by Chou Yü-tu[50] (for biographical notes cf. *Ming-hua-lu*,[51] chs. 6 and 4). The author says that he wrote this book while traveling by boat through Kiangsu Province, hence the title. The book contains valuable material though collected without much discrimination; many of the original sources quoted from are either lost now or difficult to obtain.

7 *Ch'in-hsüeh-ts'ung-shu*[52] (Collected Writings on the Study of the Lute); first edition (1911) in 32 chs., second enlarged edition in 43 chs. (1925). The collected writings of the contemporary lute expert Yang Tsung-chi.[53] In my essay I have repeatedly quoted from this work. It is, as far as I know, the only really original and thorough study by a modern Chinese on the lute and all questions relating to it. The author was a teacher of music in a school at Peking. This book is the result of the study of a lifetime, by a man who not only was a well-known lute player himself, but also had excellent opportunities for consulting literary and actual materials. Though one may not always agree with the author's conclusions, still it is a work that no serious student of the lute can afford to ignore. It is especially important to scholars not

46 陽春堂琴譜
47 青蓮舫琴雅
48 林有麟, style: Jên-fu 仁甫.
49 李紹箕
50 周裕度
51 明畫錄
52 琴學叢書
53 楊宗稷, style: Shih-po 時百 lit. name Chiu-i-shan-jên 九疑山人.

living in China or Japan, for here they will find data that are unobtainable outside the Orient: the author relates his discussions with great living lute masters, his experiences with curio dealers when buying antique lutes, his own attempts at constructing lutes, etc. A list of the various items this collection contains will show its rich contents.

- A *Ch'in-ts'ui*,[54] various studies on lute music, especially on the tunes; the fourth section deals with old instruments.
- B *Ch'in-hua*,[55] miscellaneous notes on the lute.
- C *Ch'in-pu*,[56] a special study on the oldest *ch'in* tune preserved, the Yu-lan[56] manuscript; further, a study on the tune *Liu-shui*.[57]
- D *Ch'in-hsüeh-sui-pi*,[58] stray notes of the author on various subjects connected with the lute.
- E *Ch'in-yü-man-lu*,[59] same as the preceding.
- F *Ch'in-ching*,[60] 'Mirror of the Lute', a collection of well-known tunes, transcribed in the special notation invented by the author: the *chien-tzû* are given both in their original and their unabbreviated forms; pitch and measure are accurately indicated. These notations should be a great help to everyone who tries to learn how to play the lute without a teacher.
- G *Ch'in-sê-ho-pu*,[61] tunes for lute and *sê* together, with special discussion of the tuning of the *sê*.
- H *Ch'in-hsüeh-wên-ta*,[62] all kinds of problems regarding the lute, discussed in dialogue form.
- I *Ts'ang-ch'in-lu*,[63] a most detailed description of the lutes in the author's collection.
- J *Ch'in-sê-hsin-pu*,[64] tunes for lute and *sê* together.
- K *Ch'in-ching-hsü*,[65] sequence to item F.
- L *Yu-lan-ho-shêng*,[66] a reaction upon the author's discussion of the *Yu-lan* tune, by Li Chi,[67] another contemporary scholar. Besides the items enumerated above, the collection contains several minor essays on musical theory, the sonorous tubes, etc.

54 琴粹
55 琴話
56 琴譜, 幽蘭
57 流水
58 琴學隨筆
59 琴餘漫錄
60 琴鏡

61 琴瑟合譜
62 琴學問答
63 藏琴錄
64 琴瑟新譜
65 琴鏡續
66 幽蘭和聲
67 李濟

8 *Ch'in-shu-ts'un-mu*,⁶⁸ a *catalogue raisonné* of practically all books on the lute that have been preserved, either in their entirety, or in title only, in 6 chs. Published by Chou Ch'ing-yün,⁶⁹ a great collector of books and manuscripts, and a friend of Yang Tsung-chi, the author of the preceding item. First preface by the famous bibliophile Miao Ch'üan-sun,⁷⁰ dated 1915,⁷¹ second preface by the author, dated 1914. Two additional chs., entitled *Pieh-lu*,⁷² list books about music in general. The items are arranged chronologically, and details about the authors and the editions are added; often the prefaces are reprinted in their entirety. See my remarks above, Ch. III, section 1.

9 *Ch'in-shih*,⁷³ biographies of famous lute players, in 8 chapters, compiled by Chou Ch'ing-yün. First preface by Yang Tsung-chi, undated. Author's preface dated 1919. The author intended this book as a supplement to the *Ch'in-shih* of Chu Ch'ang-wên (see above, no. 2). It is a useful source book, containing a tremendous number of biographical notes on people who in some way or other were connected with lute music: we find famous lute masters, well-known lute makers, editors of lute handbooks, etc. All items are arranged chronologically, and the sources indicated. The last chapter (*kuei-hsiu*)⁷⁴ is devoted specially to lady lute players.

10 *Chin-yü*,⁷⁵ subtitle: 'Special Publication on the Study of the Lute'.⁷⁶ Published by the 'Chin-yü Lute Association',⁷⁷ Shanghai 1940; one vol., 338 pages text, 16 pages photographs, one in colour.

This is a collection of 10 special articles on the lute, written by members of the Chin-yü Lute Association, all of them prominent experts on this instrument and its lore. The association was founded in 1939, sponsored by such well-known lute players as Messrs Ch'a Chên-hu,⁷⁸ Hsü Yuan-po,⁷⁹ P'êng Ch'ing-shou⁸⁰ and Wu Ching-lüeh.⁸¹ Most of the members belong to the Yü-shan branch of the Kiangsu School. This branch was established by the Ming musician Yen Chêng.⁸² In 1614 this master published his handbook, *Sung-hsüan-kuan-ch'in-pu* (see below, page

---

68 琴書存目
69 周慶雲
70 繆荃孫, 1844–1919.
71 旃蒙單閼 i.e., 乙卯.
72 別錄
73 琴史
74 閨秀
75 今虞
76 研究古琴之專刊
77 今虞琴社
78 查鎮湖
79 徐元白
80 彭慶壽
81 吳景略
82 嚴澂, style, Tao-chêng 道澂, literary name T'ien-ch'ih 天池, 1547–1625.

226). Next to a wealth of information on Yen Chêng and his school, this publication contains authoritative essays on all the more important aspects of the study of the lute, and gives several lute melodies, both in the traditional and the modern Chinese notation.

Also, this book contains four lists that will be of interest to the student of the present condition of lute studies in China. The first is a list of 223 present-day lute players, giving their full name, age, native place, occupation and address. The second lists 95 of the more prominent lute players; each item gives name, style and literary name of the person concerned, the school of lute playing to which he belongs, the lutes and lute handbooks in his collection, his favourite melodies, his publications and his hobbies. The third is a list of 75 antique lutes that are well known to connoisseurs. Each item is headed by the particular name of the instrument (examples above, pp. 104–5), and its model. Then follow its material (i.e. the kind of wood used for upper and lower board of the sound box), the colour and crack-marks of the lacquer, the quality of its tones, the material used for the tuning pegs, its date and the inscriptions inside the sound box and on the outside, the name of its builder, and the name of the present owner of the instrument. Finally, the fourth list gives particulars about 40 new lutes, built by present-day lute experts.

B SPECIAL

11 *Shên-chi-pi-pu*,[83] handbook for the lute, in 3 chs., by the Prince of Ning.[84] The author's literary name was Ch'ü-hsien[85] ('Emaciated Immortal'), therefore this handbook is also referred to as *Ch'ü-hsien-ch'in-pu*. Author's preface dated 1425. For details about the author, see below, pp. 214–15, where a list is also given of the books published by him. This is the oldest printed *ch'in-pu* preserved, but unfortunately extremely rare. The only Chinese catalogue in which it is mentioned is that of the famous Ming library, T'ien-i-ko; but various kinds of disasters have ravaged this library, and a recent study on the books that are left does not mention this valuable item (see *T'ien-i-ko-ts'ang-shu-k'ao*,[86] by the modern bibliographer Ch'ên Têng-yûan,[87]

[83] 神奇秘譜 [84] 寧王, personal name Chü Ch'üan (朱權, died 1448).
[85] 臞仙   [86] 天一閣藏書考   [87] 陳登原

Shanghai 1932). The Library of the Cabinet (Naikaku-bunko)[88] in Tokyo has a fine first edition, and I possess a beautifully executed manuscript copy. This handbook is a magnificent example of Ming printing: three large-sized volumes, printed in big characters on good paper. It was already famous during the Ming period. Kao Lien (*op. cit.*, *Yen-hsien-ch'ing-shang*, p. 78) says: 'The people of our day think the handbook *Shên-chi-pi-pu* by the Prince of Ning the best. But one should try to obtain the first, large-sized edition. The author had the text carefully collated and revised, so that every dot and every stroke is correct. This is a good handbook, which should be treasured. The later editions are not worth being looked at.'[89] The only objection to this handbook is that the author has not been consistent in his system of notation, and that the *chien-tzû* therefore have become unnecessarily complicated. One gets the impression that the compiler purposely made the notation obscure, so that only expert players could use it. He was very particular about a strict observation of the rules for the lute player: in his preface he says that, properly, only high officials should be allowed to occupy themselves with the lute.

12 *Pu-hsü-t'ang-ch'in-pu*,[90] another early Ming handbook, in 9 chs.; compiled by Ku I-chiang.[91] First preface by Sun Ch'êng-ên (cf. *Ming-shih-tsung*,[92] ch. 74), dated 1551; second preface by Wang T'ing,[93] undated; third preface by Ch'ên Chung-chou[94], dated 1559. Ch'ên Chung-chou did not sign his preface; he only added the imprint of a seal with his literary name Kang-i-tzû.[95] There is a colophon by Wang Ying-chên[96] (cf. *Ming-shih-tsung*, ch. 51), dated 1559. This handbook, too, is a fine specimen of Ming printing. Though rare, it is sometimes found in Chinese catalogues. Its contents are remarkable because of their originality: a great number of well-known tunes are given, but all were revised by the compiler, who considerably improved their musical value. The book bears an outspoken Taoist character.

---

88 內閣文庫
89 近世以寧藩神奇秘譜為最，然須得初刻大本，臞仙命工校訂點畫不訛，是為善譜可寶，若翻刻本不足觀.
90 步虛堂琴譜
91 顧挹江

92 孫承恩, 明詩綜
93 王挺
94 陳中州
95 亢惕子
96 王應辰

13 *Ch'in-pu-ho-pi-ta-ch'üan*,[97] not divided into chs., compiler Yang Piao-chêng;[98] first preface anonymous, and undated; second preface by Liu Yü,[99] dated 1503. *Imperial Catalogue*, ch. 114, leaf 7 verso. The two preceding items were examples of handbooks edited by scholars of high culture; this one was published by a literatus of very low scholarly standing. The tunes are given in a kind of simplified version, and all—as indicated by *ho-pi* in the title—are accompanied by words. This text of the songs must be of the editor's own making, for it is written in a queer mixture of literary language and colloquial. The text is interspersed with refrains like *ya-ya*, *ai-ya*, such as are used only in Chinese popular music. Yet this handbook seems to have been very popular; it was printed in an extraordinarily great number of copies, so that even now it can easily be bought. It saw a second edition, which can be distinguished from the first by the fact that in the second one the picture after the prefaces (representing the author playing the lute) is missing.

14 *T'ai-ku-i-yin*,[100] in chs., compiled by Yang Lun,[101] lit. name Tung-an;[102] cf. *Imperial Catalogue*, ch. 114, leaf 8 recto. Preface by Li Wên-fang,[103] colophon by Lü Lan-ku,[104] both undated. A good Ming handbook, much better edited than the preceding item. The *Imperial Catalogue* is much incensed at the fact that on the picture in the first volume the author is shown together with Chung Tzû-ch'i,[105] the famous lute player of antiquity.[106] The arrogance of this picture seems to have been recognized even at an early date, for most copies which I have seen were printed from a revised block, where the image of Chung Tzû-ch'i has been deleted from the unorthodox picture. To this handbook there is usually added a supplement by the same author, entitled *Po-ya-hsin-fa*;[107] to this Yü Yen[108] added a preface, dated 1609.

15 *Wu-chih-chai-ch'in-pu*,[109] in 8 chs., by the famous lute master Hsü Ch'i.[110] First preface dated 1724, second, by Huang Chên,[111] dated 1722; third, by Hsü Chün,[112] undated; fourth, by Chou

97 琴譜合璧大全
98 楊表正
99 劉御
100 太古遺音
101 楊倫
102 桐庵
103 李文芳
104 呂蘭谷
105 鍾子期
106 繪鍾子期像而以已像厠其後尤爲妄誕
107 伯牙心法
108 兪彥
109 五知齋琴譜
110 徐祺
111 黃鎮
112 徐俊

Lu-fêng,[113] dated 1721. This may be said to be the most popular handbook in existence. Printed in a large number of copies, it is nowadays easily obtainable at bookshops in China and Japan. The introductory chapters are very rich in contents, giving general information on the lute and its history, and an outline of *ch'in* ideology. It contains no new tunes, but all have been revised by Master Hsü Ch'i, and the tunes are recorded by his son (Hsü Chün, the writer of the third preface) and two of his pupils (the writers of the second and fourth prefaces), in the way the master used to play them. The tunes are recorded very carefully, with many additional indications regarding tempo, expression, etc. The scholarly standard of the book is not high: the style of the introductory parts is not very polished, and shows many misprints. But this does not detract form the musical value of the tunes. From a musical point of view, this handbook is the best of those published during the Ch'ing period.

16 *Tzû-yüan-t'ang-ch'in-pu*,[114] in 12 chs., by Wu Hung.[115] First preface by Li T'ing-ching,[116] second by Chang Tun-jên,[117] third by Ch'iao Chung-wu,[118] all dated 1802. Wu Hung continued the tradition of Hsü Ch'i (see the preceding item). The three people who wrote the prefaces were his pupils, who published the tunes as played by Master Wu Hung. This handbook is typical for the *ch'in-pu* of the Ch'ing period: in the introductory chapters not a word is said about the ideology of the lute. Instead we find lengthy discussions on musical theory; for these, as the preface says, Chang Tun-jên, who was a great mathematician, was responsible. Ch. 12 gives a number of tunes with the words added to the notation; this part was edited by Li T'ing-ching. A curious feature is that the title page bears the date 1801, while the prefaces are dated one year later.

17 *Ch'un-ts'ao-t'ang-ch'in-pu*,[119] in 6 chs., by Ts'ao Shang-chiung.[120] First preface by Yen P'ei-nien,[121] undated; author's preface dated 1744. Co-editors were Su Ching[122] and Tai Yüan.[123] This book gives various well-known tunes in comparatively

---

113　周魯封
114　自遠堂琴譜
115　吳灯, style: Shih-po 仕柏.
116　李廷敬
117　張敦仁
118　喬鍾吳
119　春草堂琴譜
120　曹尙綱, style: Ping-wên 炳文.
121　閻沛年
122　蘇璟
123　戴源

simple versions. The editing is very carefully done. With the *Wu-chih-chai* handbook, this *ch'in-pu* is much recommended by present-day lute masters. In 1864 it was republished by the lute master Chu T'ung-chün.[124]

18 *T'ien-wên-ko-ch'in-pu-chi-ch'êng*,[125] in 16 chs., published by T'ang I-ming,[126] in 1876. Author's preface, with the same date. This handbook, as indicated by the title, is a collection of reprints from other handbooks. Well-known tunes are often given in as many as five or six different versions. Many of the good *ch'in-pu* being very rare, it was the compiler's intention to put their contents at the disposal of lute students in a convenient form. The introductory chapters (which fill 4 volumes) are also compiled from other handbooks. This collection is very handy for quick reference. It is to be regretted, however, that the publisher confined himself to simply reprinting the various tunes, in exactly the same form as he found them (the sources being indicated in the lower part of the outer margin); thus there is no unity in the notation of the tunes. This inconsistency in the use of various *chien-tzû* will confuse the beginner. It would have been much better, if the publisher had transcribed all tunes in a uniform system. Some of his own compositions are inserted among the others; these are distinguished by the literary name of the compiler, *Sung-hsien*,[127] being printed in the lower outer margin. Still it is a useful book because of its varied contents. It is particularly recommended to such students as do not have a large collection of handbooks at their disposal.

19 *Ch'in-hsüeh-ju-mên*,[128] in 2 chs., by the lute master Chang Ho;[129] author's preface dated 1864. Reprinted several times, in various forms. This is the most elementary handbook for the lute player, recommended by present-day lute masters as the best introduction to the subject. The finger technique is explained clearly, the tunes are few, but each is fully annotated, and accompanied by a simpler score (*kung-ch'ih*[130] system). Anyone desiring to study the lute would do well to start by working through this handbook.

124 祝桐君
125 天聞閣琴譜集成
126 唐彝銘
127 松仙
128 琴學入門
129 張鶴
130 工尺

APPENDIX III

The Lute as an Antique

THE greater part of the articles which surround the Chinese scholar in his library not only serve as decorations, but are also at the same time objects of appreciative study.

A bronze sacrificial vessel of the Han dynasty placed on a carved ebony stand, enhances by its delicate outlines and intriguing patina the antique atmosphere of the library, while the archaic inscriptions inside its cover also furnish the happy owner with material for writing a learned treatise discussing its date and provenance; a coiled dragon of transparent jade lying on the desk serves the double purpose of holding a wet writing brush, and of providing the scholar and his friends with a topic for discussion on the use jade was put to by the ancients.

It is this tendency to appreciate antiques not only as works of art, but at the same time as objects for discussion and investigation, that confers upon the old-fashioned Chinese scholar a distinctly humanistic touch. The type of the Chinese literatus curiously resembles that of the classical scholar of medieval Europe. Just as the old humanist of Europe loved to surround himself with marble busts and bronze statues, caressing their exquisite shapes while at the same time attempting to decide their date and determine their style; or, of a quiet evening, enjoyed unrolling on his heavy desk old palimpsests, while appreciating the powerful writing penned on the greenish parchment, simultaneously trying to detect errors made by the copyists and looking for variant readings: so a Chinese scholar, while lovingly handling his treasures, will ponder over the correct interpretation of their inscriptions, and, dwelling in thought on bygone times, grope for an understanding of the significance the object had at the time when it was made.

To appreciate beauty in a scholarly way is termed in Chinese *wan*.[1] This verb pressupposes as its subject a man of scholarly tastes. 'Enjoying the moon' (*wan-yüeh*),[2] is but a very unsatisfactory transla-

---

1 玩　　2 玩月

tion. Any ordinary person with an innate feeling for beauty may derive enjoyment from gazing at the full autumn moon. But it is only the cultured scholar who is able, when seeing this same moon, to remember some lines by a celebrated poet, to revisualize a painting by some famous artist, and by thus testing his own sensations by those of kindred spirits, experience that exalted joy that comes only from a full intellectual realization of the emotions of the heart. Nothing less than this, and probably more, is implied in the term *wan*.

This somewhat lengthy digression was necessary; without this preliminary understanding it would be difficult to interpret correctly one of the many aspects of that most accomplished of all Chinese musical instruments: the lute. For the lute, next to being a musical instrument, is also a favourite object for antiquarian appreciation.

As I have already pointed out above, the lute, though it is one of the regular paraphernalia of the Chinese scholar, is rarely played. Not because its music is irrelevant; on the contrary, it represents in the opinion of many the apex of Chinese music, quite unsurpassed in China's long history. But to play the lute expertly presupposes a study of years, and a competent master; but few scholars have the leisure and inclination to devote so much time to this art, and good teachers are comparatively rare. Therefore, while the enjoyment of playing the lute is reserved for a small circle of the happy few, appreciation of the lute as an antique lies within the reach of every scholar. It is this aspect of the lute that I propose to treat here.

* * *

When a scholar is lucky enough to obtain an ancient lute bearing inscriptions by the hand of some famous literatus of old, it is an event in his life, and often he will change the name of his library to commemorate the auspicious day. Thus Hsiang Yüan-pien,[3] one of the greatest connoisseurs and bibliophiles of the end of the Ming period, changed the name of his studio into T'ien-lai Hall[4] after he had acquired a lute called *T'ien-lai* ('Harmony of the Sphere').[5] This instrument had belonged to Sun Têng,[6] a famous lute master of the third century A.D. (Cf. the rubbing of the bottom board of this lute, reproduced in fig. 18.)

The predilection of the Chinese scholar for the romantic and the fanciful also found expression in the lute. From time to time iron,[7]

---

[3] 項元汴
[4] 天籟閣
[5] 天籟

[6] 孫登, style Kung-ho 公和.
[7] See fig. 19.

#18: Rubbing of the lute *T'ien-lai*, that belonged to the Ming scholar Hsiang Yüan-pien. On top the name of the lute, then the name Sun Têng, and his style Kung-ho in a square seal. Under the Dragon Pond the inscription: 明項元汴珍藏 'Treasured and preserved by Hsiang Yüan-pien, of the Ming dynasty'. Underneath two square seals, reading Mo-lin 墨林, a literary name of Hsiang. Finally another square seal, reading 子京甫印, Tzŭ-ching being Hsiang's style. (Author's collection)

#19: (right) Rubbing of an iron lute of the Chin period. (Author's collection)

earthenware,[8] and jade[9] lutes make their appearance. Such lutes are useless as musical instruments, but they are highly valued as antiques. Scholars covered them with appreciative essays, lauding the inner significance of the lute and expanding themselves upon the principles of lute ideology. Figure 19 shows a rubbing taken from an iron lute said to have been made by Sun Têng.[10] It came originally from the collection of Hsiang Yüan-pien, but during the Ch'ing period eminent scholars like Juan Yüan,[11] Liang Chang-chü[12] and Chang Ting-chi[13] added appreciative inscriptions.

Such lutes, however, are exceptions. As a rule the antique lutes are made of wood; if they are still in fit condition to be played, this enhances their value. An antique lute should not be a mere curiosity; its strings should be sounded, to revive the forgotten melodies of olden times.

*   *   *

For judging an ancient lute there exist two main criteria: first, the condition of its lacquer, second, the inscriptions it bears.

Before discussing these points in more detail, a few words about the building of lutes are necessary.

The body of the lute, which functions as a sounding-box, consists of two wooden boards, superimposed one upon the other. The upper board, made of *t'ung* wood,[14] is concave, while the lower one, made of *tzŭ* wood,[15] is flat. On the inner side these boards are chiseled out, so that when fitted together they form a sort of oblong box. This box may have various models. Most common is the so-called *Chung-ni* model,[16] shown in figure 30; but many other models exist, varying from a simple straight box (*chêng-ho-shih*)[17] to models showing milled edges (*lo-hsia-shih*)[18] or the shape of a banana leaf (*chiao-yeh-shih*).[19] In the lower board two openings are cut out, which serve to transmit the sound; they may be compared with the two S-shaped sound holes of a violin, which also serve to increase the acoustic power of the instrument. It would seem that apart from minor differences the construction of the lute has remained the same since the Han period.

---

[8] See *China Journal*, XI, 5: J. C. Ferguson, 'A Ceramic Lute of the Sung Dynasty'.

[9] See numerous references in Chinese literature to *yü-ch'in* 玉琴.

[10] See n. 6.

[11] 阮元, 1764–1849.

[12] 梁章鉅, 1775–1849.

[13] 張延濟, 1768–1848.

[14] 桐

[15] 梓

[16] 仲尼式

[17] 正合式

[18] 落霞式

[19] 蕉葉式

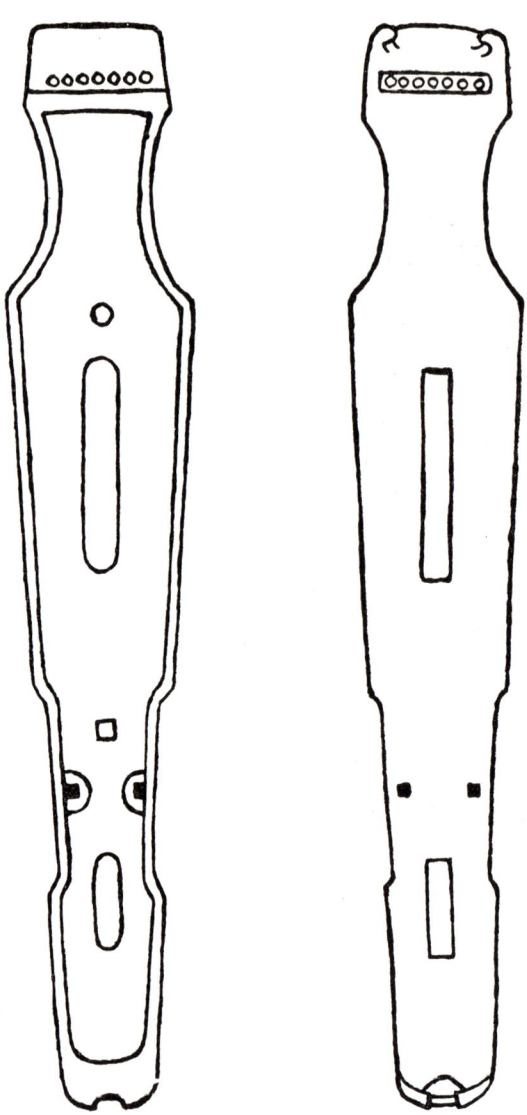

#20: Upper board.   #21: Bottom board.

There are special handbooks for the lute player, the so-called *ch'in-pu*,[20] which generally give more or less detailed instructions as to how lutes should be built. The most extensive of them is the *Yü-ku-chai-ch'in-pu*,[21] published in 1855 by a well-known lute master from Chekiang province, Chu Fêng-chieh.[22] This book does not contain any lute tunes, but is concerned solely with elaborate directions regarding the lute in general. The author not only gives his own opinions, but also often quotes from reliable older sources; for the

20 琴譜   21 與古齋琴譜   22 祝鳳喈, literary name T'ung-chün 桐君.

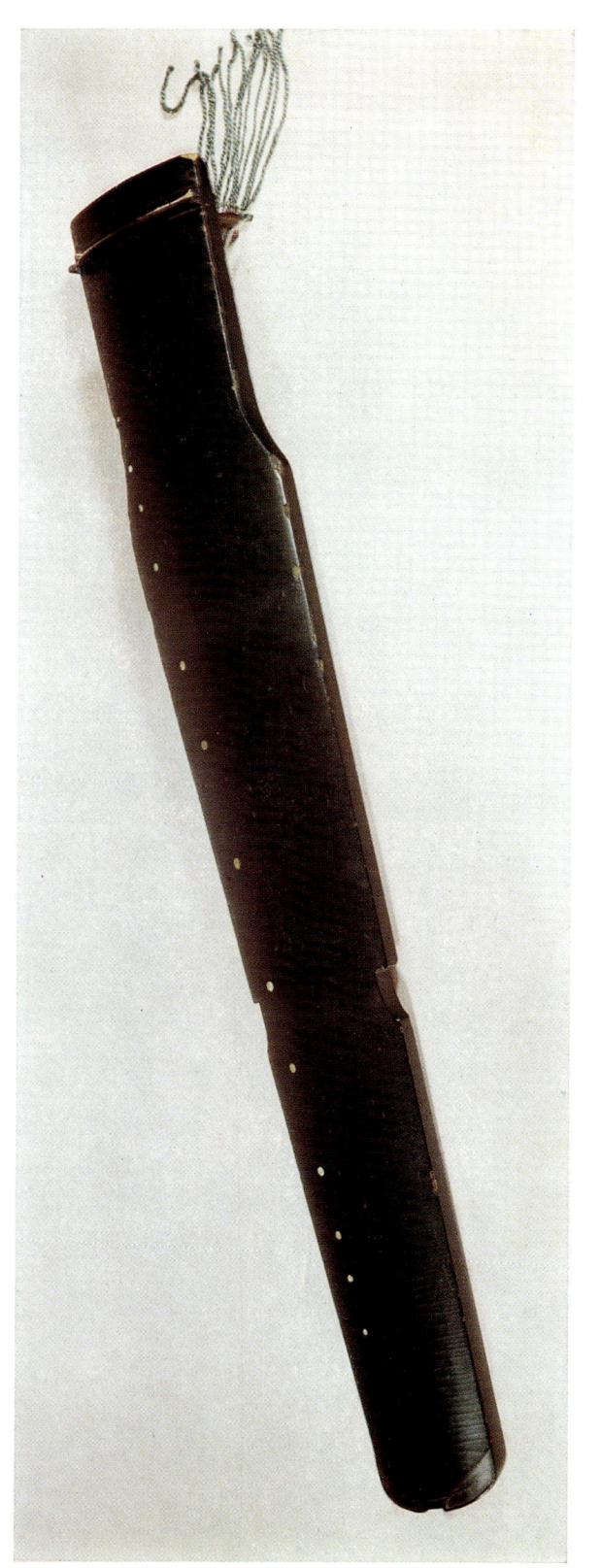

COLOR PLATE: T'ang period lute preserved in the Hōryūji Hōmotsukan in Ueno. Courtesy of Tokyo National Museum and Kōdansha Ltd., Tokyo

following observations I have therefore, unless stated otherwise, relied upon this source.

Just as with the masterpieces of Antonio Stradivari, so also with ancient lutes the sonorousness depends upon the quality of the wood used, and especially on that of the varnish with which it is covered. As regards the wood, *t'ung* and *tzŭ* are preferably chosen, but even other kinds of wood may be used; the most important thing is to see that the material used be old and entirely dry. Dry, decaying pillars from ruined temples, and even boards from excavated coffins are highly recommended. Fanciful associations also play a role; one should try to find a mouldering pine tree overhanging a bubbling mountain stream, or a weather-beaten cedar in a secluded vale.

The two boards having been hewn and chiseled into the proper shape (see figures 20 and 21), they are luted together with a special kind of glue, the main material of which is isinglass. The boards touch each other round the whole circumference, and they are further held together by two studs, one called the Heaven Pillar, *t'ien-chu*,[23] located right above the Dragon Pond, and the other called Earth Pillar, *ti-chu*,[24] to be found under the Dragon Pond. The former is round, the latter square, in accordance with the ancient Chinese belief that Heaven is round and Earth square.

Thereafter follows the most important phase of the building process: covering this sounding-box with a coat of varnish. As the word varnish suggests a rather thin coat, it is a misnomer in this connection; cement would be a more suitable term, as the thickness of this coat varies from 3 to 5 mm.[25] Its constitution resembles that of old Chinese lacquer in general; cf. the directions for making lacquer as given by T'ao Tsung-i[26] in his *Cho-kêng-lu*[27] (original preface dated 1366;[28] 汲古閣 edition, ch. 30, section Hsiu-ch'i),[29] and for a more detailed description, the Ming treatise *Hsiu-ch'ih-lu*,[30] by Huang

---

[23] 天柱
[24] 地柱
[25] A curious parallel is found in the varnish used for covering old Arabian and Persian lutes, especially the *rubāb*; see H. G. Farmer, 'The Structure of the Arabian and Persian Lute in the Middle Ages', *Journal of the Royal Asiatic Society of Great Britain and Ireland*, Jan. 1939, p. 49. There the work *Kanz-al-tuhaf* is quoted: 'Some people powder glass and mix it with glue, which is then poured on the sound-chest in order that the tone of the instrument may be increased.' Farmer points out that in England in 1837 a similar device was discovered by J. F. Grosjean, a harp-maker of London; he said about his discovery: 'My improvement consists in applying vitrified or crystallized matters to sounding boards... Powdered glass ground very fine is sifted evenly over the sounding board, which has previously been warmed and coated with cement.'

[26] 陶宗儀
[27] 輟耕錄
[28] 汲古閣
[29] 髹器
[30] 髹飾錄

Ch'êng[31] (an old manuscript preserved in Japan, published in 1928 in Tokyo by the Tokyo-bijutsu-gakkō-kōyūkai;[32] original preface dated 1625, preface by the modern Chinese editor of the text, Chu Ch'i-ch'ien,[33] dated 1927. There also exists a Chinese reprint in folio of this edition by Chu Ch'i-ch'ien; the texts are exactly the same, except for the omission of the Japanese reading-marks, and a few marginal notes). There are, however, some important differences, as for instance that while applying the lute cement no layer of cloth is added. The *Ch'in-ching*,[34] a handbook for the study of the lute written by a famous lute connoisseur of the Ming period (cf. Appendix II, no. 5), and published in 1609, gives the following directions as to how this cement should be made: 'Ashes from deer horns are the best material, but ashes from cow horns may also be used. One obtains the best results when these ashes are mixed with copper filings [other sources recommend gold or silver filings, and also powdered earthenware shards. Trans.]. When applied for the first time [it is implied that the mixture is diluted with thin glue. Trans.], the mixture is thin, and shows a rough surface. When it has dried, it should be polished with a rough stone. Applied as second coating, the mixture is thicker and more even; after it has become dry, it is polished with water. Polish two times with water, and three times with oil. When applied for the third coating, the mixture should be of fine consistency.'[35] This process is repeated until a perfectly smooth and even surface is obtained. When this is well dried, one proceeds to apply the last coat of lacquer, called, just as in the ordinary lacquer process, *tsao-ch'i*,[36] consisting of several layers of varnish. The colour of this varnish differs considerably: a deep black is most common, but red, greenish, spotted or marbled varieties are also used.

In course of time this coat develops tiny cracks, the so-called *tuan-wên*,[37] 'burst patterns'. It is by observing the shape of these cracks that connoisseurs determine the age of a lute.

On this the *Ch'in-ching* quoted above has the following to say: 'The age of a lute is proved by the *tuan-wên*. If a lute is less than 500 years old, it will not show cracks; the older it is, the more cracks it shows. There are many varieties of *tuan-wên*; the so-called serpent-

---

31 黃成
32 東京美術學校校友會
33 朱啓鈐
34 琴經
35 鹿角灰為上，牛角灰次之，或雜以銅鑢屑

尤妙，第一次灰粗而薄，候乾用粗石略磨，第二次中灰勻而厚，候乾用水磨，二次水磨，三次油磨，次用細灰.

36 糙漆
37 斷文

belly cracks [*shê-fu*],³⁸ run transversely over the upper board of the lute, one or two inches apart from each other, in even segments, giving the lute the appearance of the belly of a serpent. There are also very fine cracks, called "cow hairs" [*niu-mao*],³⁹ resembling hundreds and thousands of hairs; they generally appear on both sides of the lute, but they do not show near the *yo-shan* [i.e. the high bridge on right]; sometimes they may also be found on the upper side of the instrument and on the bottom board. Further, there are plum-blossom cracks [*mei-hua*];⁴⁰ these show a pattern resembling the petals of a plum blossom. Cracks of this shape will not appear if the lute is not over a thousand years old. Of all lacquered implements, only the lute shows *tuan-wên*.⁴¹ The reason is that in most cases of lacquer work as a rule cloth is first applied, while with the lute this is omitted. Another reason is that other lacquer implements are left standing or lying about freely, while the lute day and night bears the strain of the strings. Further, after many years the wood of a lute shrinks, and becomes loosened from the coat of cement, which then cracks. When one tries to polish away these cracks, or even when one tries to cover them with a new coat of shining varnish, this only serves to make them appear more clearly. The genuine *tuan-wên* are clear-cut, like the edge of a sword, and can be distinguished thereby from the false ones.' (ch. 6)⁴² Next to the three kinds of *tuan-wên* mentioned above, some

---

38 蛇腹 also written 蛇蚹
39 牛毛
40 梅花
41 This statement is found in most Chinese books, old and new, on the study of the lute, although a Ming treatise on lacquer in general (the *Hsiu-ch'ih-lu;* see n. 30) states specifically that all lacquered objects are liable in the course of time to develop *tuan-wên* (*op. cit.*, page 20). I have come to the conclusion that the lute experts are wrong and that the *Hsiu-ch'ih-lu* is right. I found *tuan-wên* of various types on the following dated lacquered objects of the Ming period: table tops (in the four corners and along the edges, in one case parallel cracks over the entire surface), boxes of various size and shape (along the edges, and all over the bottom), the undecorated bottoms of plates and trays of carved red lacquer (*t'i-hung* 剔紅), and folding screens (mostly in the four corners of a panel, but often also covering the entire surface in irregular pattern). It is worth noting that I did *not* find *tuan-wên* on lacquered baskets.

The conclusion is that all Chinese lacquer, if applied on a ground of cement, will develop *tuan-wên*, probably because the cement and the lacquer itself have a different shrinking coefficient. I do not feel competent to analyze the physical properties in question, but would suggest this as an interesting subject of research for the technical experts connected with musea of Far Eastern art.

42 古琴以斷紋爲證，琴不歷五百歲不斷，愈久則斷愈多，斷有數等，有蛇腹斷，其紋橫截琴面相去或寸或二寸，節相似，如蛇腹下紋，又有細斷紋，即牛毛斷，如髮千百條，亦停勻，多在琴之兩旁而進岳處則無之，又有面與底皆斷者，又有梅花斷，其紋如梅花片，此非千餘載不能有也，一應漆器無斷紋而琴獨有之者，盖器多用布漆，琴則不用，皆器安閑而琴日夜爲絃所激，又歲久桐腐而漆相離破斷紋隱處，雖經磨礪，至再重加光漆，其紋愈見，然眞斷紋，如劍峰，僞則否.

The *Ch'in-ching* quotes this passage verbatim from a Sung source, the *Tung-t'ien-ch'ing-lu-chi* 洞天清祿集, a small book on various antiques, compiled by Chao Hsi-ku 趙希鵠, member of the Imperial Clan who flourished about 1230. This book, which devotes a special section to antique lutes,*

sources mention also 'cracked-ice bursts' (*ping-lieh-wên*),⁴³ which seem to appear about at the same time as the plum-blossom cracks.

Observations in other handbooks are identical with the above. It should be noted, however, that opinions differ as to the exact number of years necessary to produce the various kinds of *tuan-wên*. The *Yü-ku-chai-ch'in-pu* quoted above gives considerably lower figures than the *Ch'in-chin*: 70 to 80 years for the 'cow hairs', 100 for the 'serpent belly', and 200 to 3000 for the 'plum blossoms'. The truth appears to be nearer to the first of these two estimates.

The handbooks warn especially against false *tuan-wên*: they may be made artificially by alternately exposing the instrument to cold and heat, and by other tricks. But their genuineness or lack of the same can be immediately detected: genuine *tuan-wên* do not break the smoothness of the surface of the lute. If so they would interfere with the music, for while playing the lute the fingers of the left hand often press a string down on the board, and rub it softly to produce

---

*escaped my notice while I was working on this monograph. Although it gives many interesting details about antique lutes, its contents do not, however, affect the main arguments brought forward by me in my work.

The *Tung-t'ien-ch'ing-lu-chi* proves that, during the Sung dynasty, various types of *tuan-wên* were already recognized, and their ages computed. Generally *mei-hua tuan-wên* 梅花斷文, cracks resembling the shape of a plum blossom, are taken to be the oldest; they are said to appear only if an implement is from 800 to 1000 years old. Next come the *p'ing-lieh tuan-wên* 冰裂斷文, cracks resembling burst ice, and thereafter the *shê-fu tuan-wên* 蛇腹斷文, which resemble the even segments on the belly of a serpent; the age of these two varieties is given as from 600 to 800 years. *Niu-mao tuan-wên* 牛毛斷文, cracks resembling fine, evenly distributed cow hair, and *liu-shui tuan-wên* 流水斷文, fine cracks unevenly distributed in a pattern that resembles the conventional Chinese way of representing waves, are generally considered as the 'youngest'; some sources contend that these two types of crack-marks will make their appearance after 70 or 80 years.

Before analyzing these data one must first discard the theory developed by some Ming writers that all these various types of *tuan-wên* will, in course of time, appear in succession on one and the same lacquered object. In other words, that for instance a certain lute that was made in the tenth century, will in the eleventh century have developed cow-hair cracks, which after four or five centuries changed into serpent-belly cracks, which in their turn changed to the plum-blossom type. This, of course, is physically impossible. One could imagine that the serpent-belly type, for instance, if the process of bursting continues, develops into the burst-ice type; but it seems quite impossible that cow-hair cracks would change into burst-ice *tuan-wên*. It seems far more probable that once a lacquered surface has developed bursts, it remains that way; and that the pattern shown by the cracks is determined not by the age of the object in question, but by various other factors such as the nature of the surface on which the lacquer was applied, the constitution of the lacquer, climatic influences, etc. I know of no antique lute preserved to the present day which shows a type of *tuan-wên* different from that recorded by collectors who saw that instrument in the fifteenth or sixteenth century.

Therefore my conclusion is that *tuan-wên* are not to be considered as a criterion for dating a lacquered object; the presence of *tuan-wên* of any kind only proves that an object is at least not newly made. Thus the theories of Chinese lute experts on the value of *tuan-wên* constitutes one of those rare exceptions where a Chinese statement on a peculiarly Chinese object is definitely wrong.

⁴³ 冰裂文

#22: Impression of a seal, engraved in the bottom board: Han-chang-t'ang-chi 含章堂記 (from a lute in the author's collection)

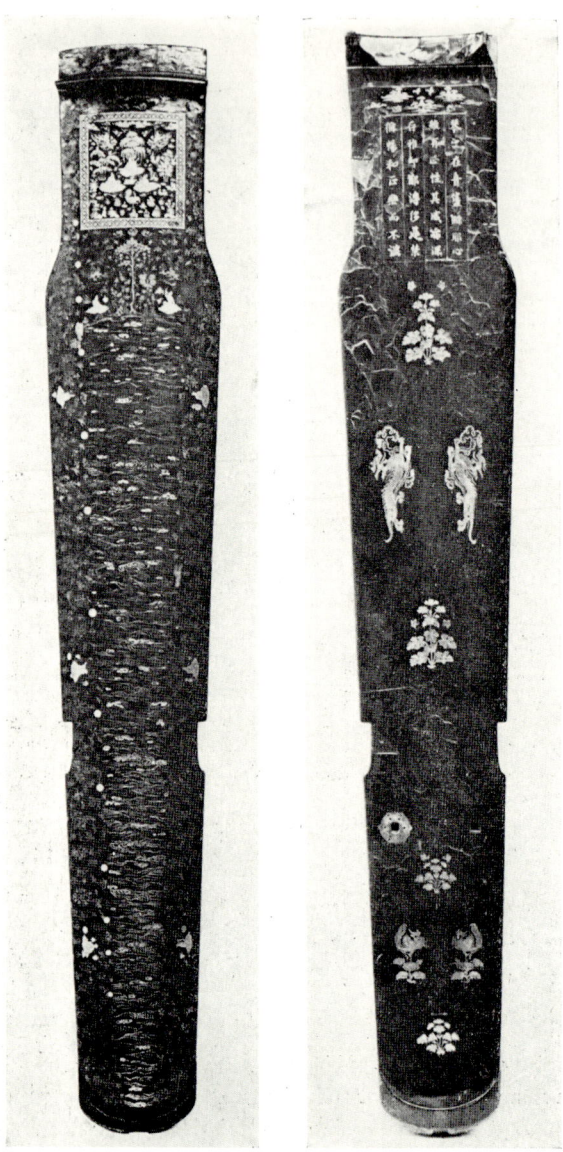

#23: Shōsōin lute: the upper board. After the photo in Harada's Catalogue.

#24: Shōsōin lute: the bottom board. After the photo in Harada's Catalogue.

#25: Shōsōin lute: the enclosure on the upper board. After the photo in Harada's Catalogue.

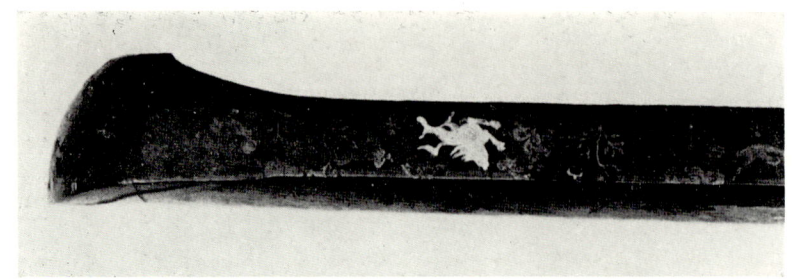

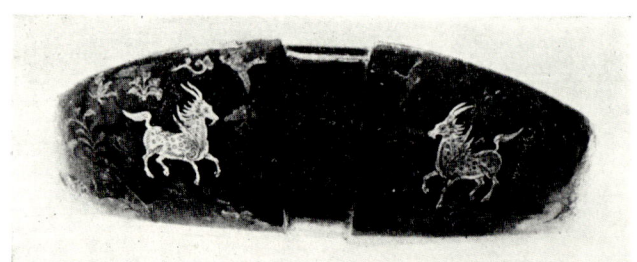

#26: Shōsōin lute: side aspects. After the photo in Harada's Catalogue.

[Appendix 3] THE LUTE AS AN ANTIQUE

various kinds of vibrato. If the surface is not perfectly smooth, the string will rattle. Or, in the words of the Ming connoisseur Kao Lien:[44] 'If one runs one's fingers over artificial *tuan-wên*, they will be felt; but genuine cracks, although they are clearly seen, can never be felt.' (*Tsun-shêng-pa-chien*, chapter xv, p. 75)[45]

As regards the inscriptions of a lute, these may be divided into two categories: those inside the sounding-box (*ch'ih-nei*), and those on the bottom board (*ti-ming*).[46]

Those inside the lute are written or engraved on the inner side of the upper board, at a time when the two boards have not yet been fitted together. The characters are written in two columns, opposite the Dragon Pond, but well to the right and left, so that when the lute is finished, they are barely visible when looking obliquely through the Dragon Pond. Thus these inscriptions can only be written either when the lute is made, or when it has been taken apart for a second time, and entirely rebuilt. They therefore furnish the observer with dependable material for fixing the date of the instrument. These inscriptions mostly state the date, and the name of the builder or rebuilder. A well-known lute preserved at Peking bears, for instance, the following inscriptions: opposite the Dragon Pond, on the right, 'Rebuilt in 1636, by Chang Jung-hsiu from Kiangsu'; and on the left, 'Rehewn by the recluse of the Chiu-i mountain'.[47] According to connoisseurs this instrument dates from the Sung period (960–1279). In the Ming period (1368–1644) its cement was so damaged, that Chang Jung-hsiu found it necessary to take it apart and rebuild it. Then, in recent times ('Recluse of the Chiu-i mountain' is one of the literary names of a contemporary lute master, Yang Tsung-chi) it was again rebuilt, and this fact duly recorded.

While inscriptions inside a lute are usually written in ordinary characters, for the outside elegant and tasteful effects are aimed at. Here the scholar has every opportunity for displaying his refined taste and cultured penmanship. As a rule only the bottom board of a lute is used for inscriptions, it being considered bad taste for the inscriptions to show when the lute is lying on the table while being played.

First the inscriptions are written on the board with an ordinary writing brush, with very thick ink, usually red. When dried, the

---

[44] 高濂
[45] 僞者以手摩之裂紋有痕，眞者有紋可而拂之則無.
[46] 池內, 底銘
[47] 明崇禎丙子古吳張睿修重修，九疑山人再斵.

characters are cut out in the lacquer with a set of fine chisels, the same as used for engraving seals. The depth of the characters is left to individual taste: some like to engrave them deeply, going right through the coat till the wood is reached (*shên-k'o*),⁴⁸ others prefer to cut away only the uppermost layers of the coat (*ch'ien-k'o*).⁴⁹ The carving should be done with considerable care, as the varnish easily chips off, and the cement underneath is very brittle and has a tendency to come off in irregular lumps. Clever engravers, however, often utilize these peculiarities of the material for obtaining original effects; they choose archaic styles of writing, in which rough and irregular outlines are inherent. When the varnish crumbles off, the irregular contours obtained will lend the inscription an appearance of 'antique rusticity' (*ku-cho*),⁵⁰ an effect much appreciated by connoisseurs (cf. fig. 22).

When the characters have been cut out, they are filled up with

⁴⁸ 深刻   ⁴⁹ 淺刻   ⁵⁰ 古拙

white, red, or green paint, sometimes also with gold lacquer. But the latter process is considered too ostentatious to be in good taste.

The simplest type of lute inscription is merely the name of the instrument, usually engraved above the Dragon Pond. Handbooks of the lute give lists of various special names of lutes, mostly borrowed from lute ideology; I refer to pp. 104–5 above.

Further, the whole bottom board of the lute is at the disposition of the amateur for engraving further inscriptions: lines of poetry, appreciative essays, classical quotations, impressions of seals, etc. Even the bottom of the two knobs for fastening the strings may be engraved with a seal or a few characters.

It goes without saying that these inscriptions furnish the connoisseur with abundant materials for exercising his discriminative powers; he must decide whether the dates tally, whether the contents of an inscription conform to the scholarly standards of the alleged writer, whether the style of the writing corresponds with that of other calligraphic specimens of the man who is asserted to have written the inscription, etc. But the appreciation of old lutes necessitates much discretion and experience; numerous snares and pitfalls await the unwary outsider. If the cement of an antique lute has been damaged badly, its owner will peel off the old coat, except those patches where the inscriptions are engraved; thereafter he covers the lute with a new coating, of the same colour as the old one. Then the bewildered observer sees a lute with all the marks of a genuine antique specimen, but with a brand new coat of lacquer. Again, a lute amateur, having obtained a fine old specimen bearing no inscriptions, will decide that it resembles a lute celebrated by some famous old writer. To enhance its beauty he composes an inscription for this lute; then, glancing through rubbings of autographs of the said famous man of old till he has collected from various passages all the characters he needs for his inscription, he copies them out on the lute. This method, known as *chi-tzŭ*,[51] though admittedly running counter to artistic principles, when expertly applied often produces remarkable results. Yang Tsung-chi in his *T'sang-ch'in-lu* openly states several times that he added in this way inscriptions to some lutes in his collection. The owner only means to make in this way an instrument more interesting for himself, but if the lute changes hands, the danger exists that some unscrupulous dealer will try to pass off such an instrument as genuine.

51 集字

A scholar without any real lutes at his disposal may still make studies in this field, for there exist numerous rubbings (*t'a-pên*)[52] taken from ancient instruments, which clearly show their shapes and inscriptions. Generally these rubbings show only the bottom board, but sometimes also copies of the other sides are added. Such rubbings may be traced again, and then a so-called *shuang-kou-pên*[53] is obtained.

After these preliminary remarks I shall discuss three antique lutes; the first and the last on the basis of photos of the originals, the second on the basis of a traced copy of the bottom board.

Those interested in further discussions of antique lutes I may refer to the *Ts'ang-ch'in-lu*,[54] where Yang Tsung-chi,[55] a lute master of Peking, gives detailed descriptions of 53 lutes in his collection. The book is to be found in the *Ch'in-hsüeh-ts'ung-shu*, which are Yang Tsung-chi's complete works; cf. Appendix II, no. 7.

* * *

The first lute to be discussed here, which is probably the oldest in the world, is preserved in Japan, in the Imperial Repository at Nara. This repository, the Shōsōin[56] was built in 752, as the chief treasure house of the Tōdaiji, the famous old temple. A great number of objects used in the Imperial Family were in 756 deposited here, as votive gifts to the chief deity of the temple, the Buddha Vairocana. A propitious fate has spared this repository from the calamities of nature and other vicissitudes, so that up to this day the collection may be seen in practically the same condition as it was more than 1200 years ago. Among these treasures this lute is to be found.

Notwithstanding its considerable age, this instrument has been preserved in excellent condition. Although the strings are gone, its body is still intact, and when newly strung it can doubtless still be played. It was placed in the collection in 817 (the 8th year of Kōnin;[57] cf. *Shōsōin-gyobutsu tanabetsu-mokuroku*,[58] No. 99). Having been left undisturbed for such a long period, this lute constitutes a unique object for the study of the lute in general. Japanese scholars have carefully described the Shōsōin collection, and this lute has received due attention.[59] But as the investigators were not sufficiently con-

---

52 拓本
53 雙鉤本. See T. F. Carter, *The Invention of Printing in China*, New York 1931, p. 12, and my book: *Mi Fu on Inkstones*, Peking 1938, pp. 6 ff.
54 藏琴錄
55 楊宗稗
56 正倉院

57 弘仁
58 正倉院御物棚別目錄
59 See the magnificent *Cataloque of the Imperial Treasures in the Shōsōin*, edited by J. Harada, vol. II; also, *A Glimpse of Japanese Ideals*, Tokyo 1937, by the same author, pp. 120 ff.

[*Appendix 3*] THE LUTE AS AN ANTIQUE 201

versant with the study of the lute to be in a position to recognize all the remarkable features of this instrument, and to settle satisfactorily the various problems it calls forth, I may be allowed here to discuss this lute at some length.

This lute is in the first place remarkable because of its decoration, which is entirely different from all antique lutes which I had occasion to examine.

While antique lutes, as a rule, show no other decoration than their inscriptions, this instrument is covered on all sides with intricate designs in inlaid gold and silver.

The upper board (see figure 23) shows at the top a picture, enclosed by a lozenge-pattern border, all of inlaid gold (see figure 25). In its center a man is sitting beneath a blossoming tree; leisurely reclining against an elbow-rest, he is playing a mandolin-like instrument, which by its round body with the broad band over it, may be identified as a *ch'in-p'i-p'a*,[60] a forerunner of the Japanese *biwa*. Before this figure a repast is laid out on a mat, while on his right an ewer is standing. In front of this central figure one sees two others, sitting on panther hides; the left plays the lute on his knees, while on his left side a low table with some book-rolls on it may be discerned. The figure on the right leans with his left arm on a wine jar, while with his right hand he lifts a horn-shaped wine cup to his lips. In front of these three figures a peacock is dancing, the remaining space being filled with trees, plants, rocks and birds. On the right and left upper corner there is depicted an immortal, riding on a phoenix and bearing a standard, surrounded with a stylized cloud. Two similar genii are to be seen above the enclosure.

Under this enclosure a similar scene appears; here the center is again occupied by a blossoming tree, round which a creeper twines; a bird is perched on its top. To the left one sees a man playing the lute on his knees, a wine jar with a spoon in it standing on his left. The figure on the right is lifting a cup to his lips, and a wine jar of different shape is standing by his side. In front of these two figures a pond is seen, with crabs, snakes and other water animals appearing in its waves. The waters of this pond cover the whole surface of the lute, running downwards right to the end. Its banks run along the two sides of the lute, and show six human figures similar to those described above, three on either side; they are sitting among flowering bushes and flying and resting birds. The two figures, the wave

60 秦琵琶

designs and the thirteen studs are of inlaid gold, the other designs are of silver.

Turning now to the bottom board (see figure 24) again we find at the top an enclosure, containing a poem of eight lines, four characters each, and arranged in four columns. This inscription, like the rest of the decoration of the bottom board, is in inlaid silver. It runs: 'The significance of the lute is to purify evil thoughts by its tones. Even if one's nature is good, it shall still be deeply influenced [by the music of the lute]. It preserves the accomplished music, and drives away the lewd songs of Chêng,[61] restraining flightiness and extravagance. Its music is elevating, harmonious and correct. It brings enjoyment without being licentious.'[62] This is a poem composed to be engraved on a lute (a *ch'in-ming*)[63] by Li Yu,[64] a noted poet of the second century A.D. The inscription is quoted in full in a handbook for the lute of the Ming period (*Ch'ing-lien-fang-ch'in-ya*),[65] and in part in the huge collection of poetic reference, the *P'ei-wên-yün-fu*.[66]

As further decoration the Dragon Pond is flanked on each side by a running dragon, which is intended as a reference to the name of this aperture. Similarly the Phoenix Pool is flanked by two phoenixes, sitting on a flowering plant. Above and below the two holes there appears a flower motif, and above the inscription on top stylized rocks are seen. I would especially draw attention to the *tuan-wên* of the type called in lute terminology *ping-lieh*, 'cracked ice' (see p. 196), which appear round the inscription, and round the Phoenix Pool.

The sides of the lute are decorated with motifs of fabulous animals and flowers (see figure 26).

Inside the Dragon Pond there is an inscription, unfortunately only partly legible, which runs: 清琴作兮□日月，幽人間兮□□□. The missing character in the first line is easily supplemented; it could hardly be anything else than 光, giving the meaning: 'The lute of clear tones has been made, oh!, brilliant like sun and moon.' As for the second part of the other line, however, I would not venture to reconstruct it. Inside the Phoenix Pool is written: 'Made in the third month of the year *i-hai*.'[67] As no definite period is indicated, it is

---

61 The odes of Chêng and Wei 衞, bks. VIII and IX of the *Shih-ching* 詩經, were ancient love songs, and in Chinese literature are constantly used to denote lewd and vulgar music.

62 琴之在音，盪滌耶 (i.e. 邪) 心，雖有正性，其感亦深，存雅却鄭，浮侈是禁，條暢和正，樂而不淫 (i.e. 淫).

63 琴銘

64 李尤

65 青蓮舫琴雅, preface dated 1614, ch. 4.

66 佩文韻府, under *chêng-hsing* 正性.

67 乙亥之年季春造

impossible to say with absolute certainty for which year these two characters of the sexagenary cycle stand. J. Harada[68] proposes 795 A.D., this being the nearest year *i-hai* preceding that in which the instrument is recorded as having been put in the collection (817). Thus this date is quite arbitrarily chosen. Below I shall try to establish the probable date of this lute on sounder evidence.

For appreciating this lute the first question which must be considered—a question which has been passed over in silence by Harada and other students—is whether this instrument was made in China or in Japan. I have come to the conclusion that it was made in China, for the following reasons. In the first place the study of the Chinese lute was introduced into Japan at a fairly late date, i.e. in the middle of the 17th century, with the coming of the Chinese priest Hsin-yüeh.[69] This lute in the Shōsōin, and some other old specimens dating from the T'ang period preserved in Japan, were doubtless brought over from China not to be actually played, but as curiosities, carefully preserved because the Japanese envoys noticed that in China this instrument was a revered symbol of culture.[70] That there lived at the Japanese Court someone who was so deeply initiated in the study of the lute that he could build an instrument like this is highly improbable.

Secondly, I would point out that the lacquer of Japanese-made lutes —such as those which were built later by the Japanese disciples of Hsin-yüeh—is of an entirely different constitution from that of Chinese lutes; doubtless with a view to different climatic conditions, other substances were used in making this lacquer, which produces no *tuan-wên*. None of the many old Japanese-made lutes which I had occasion to examine show these typical cracks. Now the lute under discussion does show *tuan-wên*, and, as observed above, *tuan-wên* of a clearly pronounced Chinese type.

Thirdly, the technique of inlaid work used in the decoration is in the eighth-century inventory of the Shōsōin called *hyōmon*,[71] 'flat pattern'. According to Harada this instrument is the sole example of this peculiar technique.[72] In China however, this technique was applied for decorating lutes as early as the Han period, when it was

---

68 *Catalogue*, English notes on plates in vol. II.

69 心越, Jap. Shin'etsu; for more details about his personality and the role he played in Japanese cultural life, see pp. 225–8 below.

70 For a more detailed argument regarding this question, see pp. 217–24.

71 平文

72 *A Glimpse of Japanese Ideals*, p. 120.

called *yin-chi*,⁷³ so that this fact also tends to show that this lute was made in China, for else we could hardly expect that for the lacquer a technique would have been used which was unknown in Japan.

Having shown that this lute was made in China, I shall next try to arrive at an opinion regarding its age.

In the first part of this article I said that since the beginning of our era the lute has undergone practically no changes. But allowance must be made for the fact that literary evidence points to lutes prior to the T'ang period having been adorned with various kinds of inlaid work; later they were left severely undecorated, their charm consisting in the tone of the lacquer, the *tuan-wên*, and the inscriptions engraved on it. This change must in my opinion be ascribed to two reasons, first, the technique of playing, and second, artistic considerations. The finger technique of the lute in course of time grew more and more involved. To execute the delicate movements of the left hand, a perfectly smooth and even surface is necessary. Richly inlaid lutes, no matter of how good the workmanship, are liable in the course of time to show slight depressions and protuberances, which entirely spoil the tone of a string pressed down on those spots. As to artistic considerations, I may observe that during the T'ang dynasty, when the gorgeous art of India and Central Asia was flourishing in China, there is noticeable a tendency to return to more austere styles, an inclination to return to purely Chinese classical models. This tendency implies a preference for simple and natural beauty rather than artificial effects, for the invisible rather than the obvious. Later, during the Sung period (960–1279), this artistic current reached its summit in the paintings of the so-called Southern School.

Thus all lutes of the T'ang dynasty that have been preserved show no decorations. And when a scholar of the Sung dynasty, Ho Yüan,⁷⁴ embodied in his *Ch'un-chu-chi-wên*⁷⁵ a discussion of old lutes, he found it necessary to draw attention to old texts referring to decorated lutes, implying that in his time such lutes were no longer to be seen.

During the Han dynasty, however, it appears the lutes were occasionally lavishly decorated. The *Hsi-ching-tsa-chi*⁷⁶ written by Liu Hsin⁷⁷ says: 'The Empress Chao possessed a valuable lute, which bore the name *Fêng-huang*; it was entirely covered with figures of

---

⁷³ 隱起; see below, the quotation from the *Hsi-ching-tsa-chi*.
⁷⁴ 何薳, 11th century.
⁷⁵ 春渚紀聞, paragraph *Ku-ch'in-p'in-shih* 古琴品飾, 汲古閣 edition ch. 8, p. 2.
⁷⁶ 西京雜記
⁷⁷ 劉歆, died A.D. 23.

dragons and phoenixes, sages of antiquity and famous women, in a flat relief of inlaid gold and jade.'[78] Further we read in the famous poetical essay on the lute, Ch'in-fu,[79] written by Hsi K'ang:[80] '[The lute] is painted with the five colours, decorated with chased work, covered with designs and various patterns, inlaid with rhinoceros horn and ivory, marked with blue and green; its strings are made of Yüan K'o silk, its studs of jade of the Chung mountain, it shows figures of dragons and phoenixes, and of famous men of antiquity.'[81]

Now the Shōsōin lute serves as an illustration of such descriptions: it is decorated with flat inlaid work, showing dragons and phoenixes, and the figures of ancient worthies. Therefore I am inclined to consider this lute as being anterior to the T'ang period, and ascribe it to, perhaps, the latter part of the Six Dynasties (220-588 A.D.). In China even in former dynasties old lutes were preferred to new ones; therefore it is unlikely that the Japanese envoys brought from China a brand-new specimen, and far more reasonable that they procured a specimen that was already antique in the T'ang period. A study of the design of the upper board, however, enables us to narrow down the date further.

This design has not been sufficiently analyzed by Japanese scholars. J. Harada confined himself to a summary description.[82] A. Matsuoka[83] tries to identify the figures in the enclosure, and claims that they represent the old story of the great lute player Po Tzû-ya.[84] Po Tzû-ya found in his friend Chung Tzû-ch'i[85] the only kindred soul that could understand his music; when the latter died, Po Tzû-ya broke his lute, and never touched the strings again, because no one else in the world could understand his playing.[86] Of course this identification is entirely mistaken: firstly, three persons are seen and not two,

---

[78] Ch. v. 3rd heading: 趙后有寶琴曰鳳凰, 皆以金玉隱起爲龍鳳古賢列女之象.

[79] 琴賦; see Wên-hsüan 文選, ch. 18.

[80] 嵇康, 223-62.

[81] 華繪彫琢, 布藻垂文, 錯以犀象, 籍以翠綠, 絃以園客之絲, 徽以鍾山之玉, 爰有龍鳳之象, 古人之形

[82] See Catalogue, English notes to the plates of vol. II.

[83] Sacred Treasures of Nara, Tokyo 1935, p. 17.

[84] The authoress refers to them as Hakuga and Shōshiki, the Japanese pronunciation of the Chinese names. In this connection I would protest against this distressing habit that many Japanese and also foreign authors have of giving purely Chinese names only in the Japanese pronunciation, when writing in a Western language. (See the very pertinent remarks by L. Giles, in: Sun Tzu on the Art of War, London 1910, p. VIII.) This method is highly objectionable, because it confuses the unwary reader by giving him the impression that Japanese persons or objects are meant. It is to be hoped that this indiscriminate use of Japanese readings will be abandoned.

[85] 鍾子期

[86] See above, p. 73; also, Lieh-tzû 列子, ch. T'ang-wên 湯問, and various other Chinese sources mentioned above.

and moreover the third, who occupies the place of honour, plays the *p'i-p'a*, an instrument definitely belonging to popular music, and incompatible with one of the most revered lute masters of antiquity. And secondly we can hardly imagine Po Tzû-ya playing his beloved instrument while one of his hearers thrums a sort of guitar, and the other drinks deeply from a capacious goblet.

None of the previous students of this matter has realized that the upper board must be viewed as one single picture, lengthened to suit the shape of the lute. There is a pond, or maybe a rivulet, located in a beautiful scene of nature, on the banks of which are assembled a literary company, engaged in cultural pastimes: playing various musical instruments, wine games, composing poetry or appreciating calligraphies (see the book-rolls mentioned above), etc. Such representations of literary gatherings by the waterside abound in Chinese art. Especially famous are pictures representing the literary gathering at the Lan Pavilion. This occasion was immortalized by the *Lan-t'ing-hsü*,[87] an essay by Wang Hsi-chih,[87] the paragon of Chinese calligraphers. In the spring of the year 353 several men of letters met at the Lan Pavilion in order to celebrate the performance of the Vernal Purification ceremony (*hsiu-hsi.*)[88] They seated themselves along the water's edge, and played the literary game of the 'floating cups' (*liu-shang*):[89] cups were placed on lotus leaves floating on the water, and when such a drifting leaf touched the bank on the spot where one of the guests was sitting, he had to empty the cup and to compose a poem. Wang Hsi-chih collected the compositions made by his friends on this occasion, and added a prefatory essay, the *Lan-t'ing-hsü*. It is this essay that became a celebrated model both for literary composition and for calligraphy. Though some scholars doubt its authenticity, it has been copied and carved in stone numerous times, together with a picture of the gathering. This essay and its accompanying picture became so famous indeed, that already in early times it was a much-used motif for the decoration of objects connected with literary life: one finds it carved on the top of an antique writing desk, engraved on the reverse of an inkstone. So wide was its use, that in the 19th century it was even used to form the background of a receipt blank of a bank in Peking![90] Reproductions of

---

[87] 蘭亭序, to be found in nearly all *ku-wên* 古文 collections; translated in various languages, lately by Lin Yu-t'ang, in: *The Importance of Living*, New York 1937, p. 156. 王羲之.

[88] 修禊
[89] 流觴
[90] See Britton, on a horn stamp for receipt blanks, in: *Harvard Journal of Asiatic Studies*. III, No. 2.

[*Appendix 3*] THE LUTE AS AN ANTIQUE

good rubbings representing the text and the picture are to be found in the special Lan-t'ing number of the Japanese periodical *Shoen*.[91] Though greatly varying in detail, in their main lines these pictorial representations are always the same: one sees the pavilion by the waterside, surrounded by an ideal scenery. A brook is winding itself among gnarled trees, quaintly shaped rocks, and flowering shrubbery. Under rustling bamboos the guests are seated on mats and panther hides alongside the water, while attendants are running to and fro with wine jars and writing implements.

The resemblance with the scene depicted on the lute is obvious. There can be no doubt that the designer had in mind a representation of the Lan-t'ing Gathering when he made this decoration. Some details, as the floating wine cups, were left out, but others, like the panther hides on which the guests are sitting, scrolls, wine jars etc., are faithfully reproduced. The Lan-t'ing motif being a favourite decoration for all things connected with literary life, it is only natural that it was chosen also for the decoration of a lute. The musical element was stressed by adding the lutes and the *p'i-p'a*; at a literary gathering old tunes are played on the lute, while the *p'i-p'a* is used for lighter music.

But this motif of the literary gathering does not explain why three figures are set apart in the enclosure, nor does it explain the dominant position of the tree, and the genii floating in the air. These elements, and especially the arrangement of the picture, suggest an entirely different, un-Chinese subject, viz. a Buddhist representation of the Enlightened One, or of one of the deities of the Mahayanic Pantheon. As in such Buddhist representations, here also we find in the foreground a pond, only the lotus flowers are missing to make the resemblance complete. Then on a second plane some minor figures, and finally on the highest plane the chief figure, set apart on a throne —here indicated by the enclosure—the whole placed in paradisaical surroundings. Viewed in this light, all seeming incongruities fall automatically in their right places. The blossoming tree which figures so prominently is the Wish-granting Tree, the Kalpadruma of Indian mythology, which constitutes a regular feature of Buddhist representations, it being identified with the Bodhi tree, under which Buddha received enlightenment. The phoenix perched on top is the fabulous bird Garuḍa, closely connected with the Kalpadruma. The two genii in the upper corner are the indispensable attendants of

---

[91] 書苑, II, no. 4, Tokyo 1938.

#27: Inscription on Shōsōin lute.

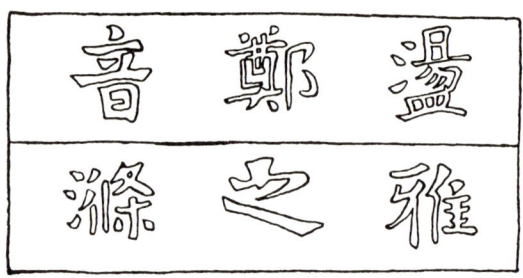

#28: Characters from Wei inscriptions.

every Mahayanic deity. The dancing peacock (Chinese lute ideology presupposes a dancing crane, *wu-ho*,[92] constantly mentioned in connection with the lute player) concludes the Indian element of this representation.

Thus it appears that the artist wavered between two different concepts, a purely Chinese one, that of the Literary Gathering, and

---

[92] 舞鶴. See above, pp. 145–6.

a foreign one, that of a Buddhist picture. Setting to work, he resolved to combine both.

When we now ask ourselves which period in Chinese history could be expected to produce such a dual representation, we immediately think of the Northern Wei period.[93] Under the rulers of this outlandish dynasty, who were fervent Buddhists, Buddhist art reigned supreme, and talented artists, combining Greco-Indian elements with Chinese styles, created works of art the magnificence of which is attested by such archeological sites as Yün-kang and Lung-men.

The style of the calligraphy, as shown in the inscription on the bottom board (see figure 27) confirms this date; when compared with the style of writing as seen on monuments of the Wei period (see figure 28)[94] the similarity is obvious.

On the basis of the above considerations I think we may assume with some confidence that the cyclic characters *i-hai* stand for a year of the Wei period, say 435 or 495. Thus this lute was in the T'ang period already a rare treasure, a suitable object to be offered to the Japanese Imperial Court.

To all appearances this rare instrument is the oldest lute still extant, a unique document both for the study of Chinese art, and for the study of the lute.

* * *

K'un-shan-yü, the second lute to be discussed here, is, according to authoritative Chinese opinion, one of the finest old instruments in existence. Notwithstanding its early date (T'ang period), it has been preserved in perfect condition, and has a remarkably fine tone.

I regret that I can only show here a traced copy of a rubbing of the bottom of this lute (see figures 29 and 30). As it is doubtful, however, whether at the time when I am writing this essay this rare lute is still extant, and as moreover it is connected with one of the most remarkable lute masters of present-day China, I may be allowed to include it in this essay.

This lute was the favourite instrument of Yeh Ho-fu, since the beginning of this century the greatest lute-master in Peking.

Yeh Ho-fu[95] was born in 1863 as the third son of a high Manchu

---

93 Pei-wei 北魏, 386–535.
94 The characters are traced after reproductions in *Shodō zenshū* 書道全集, vol. VII.
95 葉鶴伏, named Ch'ien 潛.

O

official, Grand Secretary Jui Lin.⁹⁶ Jui Lin is well known in history because in 1860 he was the commander of the Manchu forces that fought the British and the French in the battle of Pa-li-chiao. Yeh Ho-fu's elder brother Huai Ta-pu was an ultra-reactionary, and he played an important role during the Boxer troubles.⁹⁷ It would seem, however, that Yeh Ho-fu did not sympathize with the political attitude of his near relatives, and sided more with the reform party; he was keenly interested in Western science, and would talk with animation of the time when he was in charge of installing an electric plant in the Palace grounds. Up to the establishment of the Chinese Republic he occupied several administrative functions, and was well known for his scholarly tastes. His mansion in Peking, where he had collected many choice antiques and a fine library, was frequented by prominent literati and statesmen of the time, as for instance the two leaders of the progressive southern party at the Court, Wêng T'ung-ho⁹⁸ and P'an Tsu-yin.⁹⁹ Up to the end of the 19th century his house flourished; it was only with the Boxer uprising of 1900 that the decline started: during the troubles the greater part of his property was destroyed, and his political position weakened. In 1910 he lost his official position, and was reduced to utter poverty. It was then that he could convert a hobby into a means of support. Since his early youth he had been a lover of music; already as a boy, when his father was an official in South China, Yeh Ho-fu commenced studying the lute under the well-known master Liu Jung-chai¹⁰⁰ from Chekiang. He assiduously kept up this study, and in later years was taught by other lute masters of established fame, as for instance Chu Fêng-chieh (author of *Yü-ku-chai-ch'in-pu* described on p. 192), the Taoist Chang Ho,¹⁰¹ author of the standard introductory handbook for the lute player, the *Ch'in-hsüeh-ju-mên*,¹⁰² the Ch'an priest K'ung Ch'ên,¹⁰³ author of the lute handbook *K'u-mu-ch'an-ch'in-pu*,¹⁰⁴ Li Hsiang-shih¹⁰⁵ from Chekiang, and others. When the political changes had deprived him of his official income and his private means had dwindled to nothing, he moved to a small house near Lung-fu-szû, and earned his living by teaching the lute.

In the autumn of 1936, one year before his death, I had the privilege

---

96 瑞麟; see his biography in *Ch'ing-shih-lieh-chuan* 清史列傳, ch. 46.
97 See Bland & Backhouse, *China under the Empress Dowager*, pp. 130, 137, 141.
98 翁同龢, 1830–1904.
99 潘祖蔭, 1830–90.
100 劉容齋
101 張鶴, style Ching-hsing 靜薌.
102 App. II, 18.
103 空塵
104 枯木禪琴譜, published in 1893.
105 李湘石

of studying the lute under his guidance. Yeh Ho-fu was a personification of the noblest traditions of the old-fashioned Chinese literatus; never rebelling against the fate which had deprived him of nearly everything, he lived quietly on in an enviable equanimity, enjoying playing the lute and composing poetry. His personality may be characterized by a quotation from Mencius: '... not extravagant when rich and honoured, not forsaking his principles when poor and in a mean condition ... that constitutes the great man.'[106]

Often I heard Yeh Ho-fu play on the *K'un-shan-yü*, his favourite lute, and on more than one occasion I heard him praise its superior qualities. At that time, however, I had no opportunity to copy its inscriptions. And when in 1937 I again visited Peking, the master had died—just one month before my arrival. As he left no sons, his scanty belongings were scattered, and among them also his lutes. No one could inform me as to the whereabouts of the *K'un-shan-yü*. So I gave up all hope for studying this unique instrument more closely, and only retained the memory of its exquisite tones, its interesting *tuan-wên* (of the type 'serpent belly'),[107] and its beautiful greenish patina. But a lucky accident came to my aid; when I got back to Tokyo, I found in the collection of R. Taki,[108] a Japanese musicologist who had visited Peking some years previously, a rubbing of the bottom board of this lute. The rubbing being badly done, the inscriptions were hardly legible (see figure 29); having studied it carefully during many evenings, I finally succeeded in deciphering all of it except the legend of one seal. Then I made a tracing after this rubbing, which is reproduced here (see figures 30 and 31).

The name *K'un-shan-yü*[109] appears at the top, three characters in chancery script (*li-shu*)[110]: 'Jade from the K'un-lun mountains'. The best jade coming reputedly from the K'un-lun slopes, long associated with Taoist lore, this name indicates value and rarity.

Underneath, on either side of the Dragon Pond, two lines of poetry are engraved. They extol the rare qualities of this lute: 'Its accomplished tones of clear profundity sing like tinkling girdle ornaments of jade; excellent material of high purity comes from the K'un-lun mountains.'[111]

These lines of poetry, together with the three characters at the top, formed the original inscription of this lute, as attested by the lowest

---

[106] Book III, part II, 2: 富貴不能淫，貧賤不能移 .... 此之謂大丈夫.
[107] See p. 138.
[108] 瀧遼一
[109] 崑山玉
[110] 隸書
[111] 雅韻清幽鳴玉珮，良材高潔發崑岡.

inscription. They were perhaps written by the great literatus Li Yung.[112] I have compared their style with specimens of Li Yung's handwriting as reproduced in vol. x of the Japanese collection *Shodō zenshū*, and find them indeed very similar.

The inscription in cursive script (*ts'ao-shu*)[113] was written by one of the most famous lute players of the early Ch'ing period, Chou Lu-fêng,[114] co-editor of one of the standard Chinese handbooks of the lute, the *Wu-chih-chai-ch'in-pu*.[115] It does not say where Chou Lu-fêng obtained this lute, but only praises its high qualities. The inscription might be translated: 'The material of this lute was reared on the southern slopes of I Mountain; it obtained its fragrance by the side of the Hsien Pond. Vague and vagrant, its tones are remote like high mountains and flowing streams.'[116]

This text consists entirely of allusions to the tenets of *ch'in* ideology. As regards the I-shan (a mountain in Shantung province), according to tradition the mythical Emperor Fu Hsi gathered there the wood for building the first lute. *Hsien-ch'ih* (lit. Hsien Pond), is the name of the music attributed to the mythical Emperor Yao. *Kao-shan-liu-shui* (high mountains and flowing streams), is the name of a famous lute tune, ascribed to the ancient lute player Po Tzŭ-ya.[117]

At the end of this inscription there is engraved an impression of a seal with the style of Chou Lu-fêng: *Tzŭ-an-fu*.[118] In the middle there is a fine large seal, reading: *Chou-lu-fêng-chia-ts'ang*[119] (Preserved in the family of Chou Lu-fêng).

The smaller seal to the left of this large seal is unfortunately illegible: apparently it is the seal of another owner of this lute, for I have succeeded in deciphering the penultimate character *chên*;[120] presumably the last two characters read *chên-ts'ang*,[121] 'treasured and stored away by...' The small square seal to the right reads: *Hsi-shih-chih-pao*,[122] 'A treasure rarely found in this world.'

The two white spots under these three seals indicate the holes for the two knobs to which the strings are fastened.

The lowest inscription (see figure 31), which is engraved in small regular style (*hsiao-kai*)[123] on either side of the Phoenix Pool,

---

[112] 李邕, style T'ai-ho 泰和, literary name Pei-hai 北海, 678–747.
[113] 草書
[114] 周魯封, style: Tzŭ-an 子安.
[115] 五知齋琴譜, preface dated 1721.
[116] 毓質于嶧山之陽, 尋芳于咸池之側, 蓬然與高山流水俱兮.
[117] See p. 205.
[118] 子安父; *fu* 父 in this case is the same as *fu* 甫, meaning 'styled'.
[119] 周魯封家藏
[120] 珍
[121] 珍藏
[122] 希世之寶
[123] 小楷

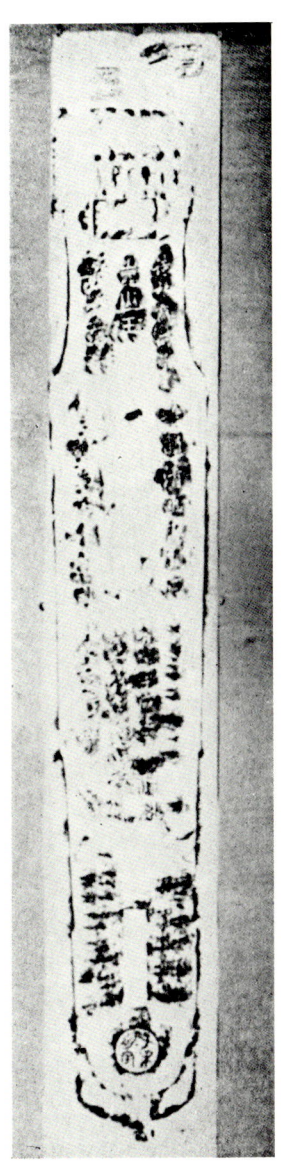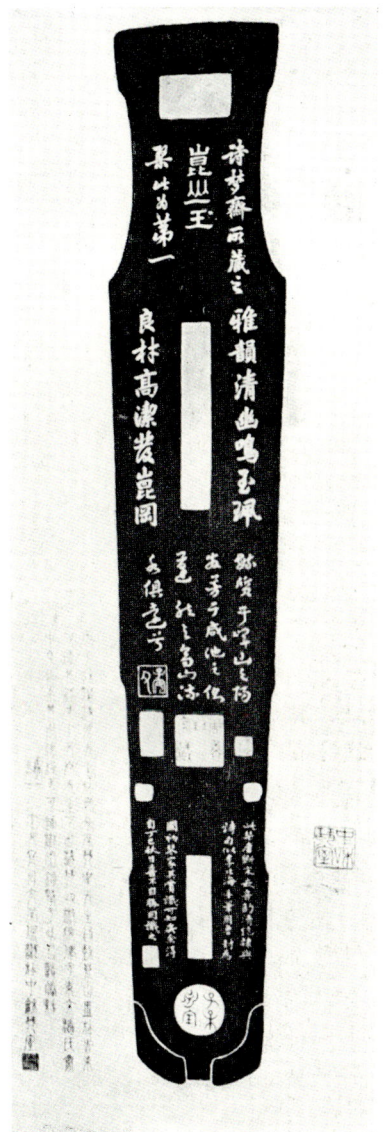

#29: Rubbing of the bottom board of the lute of Yeh Ho-fu.

#30: Tracing after the rubbing reproduced in #29.

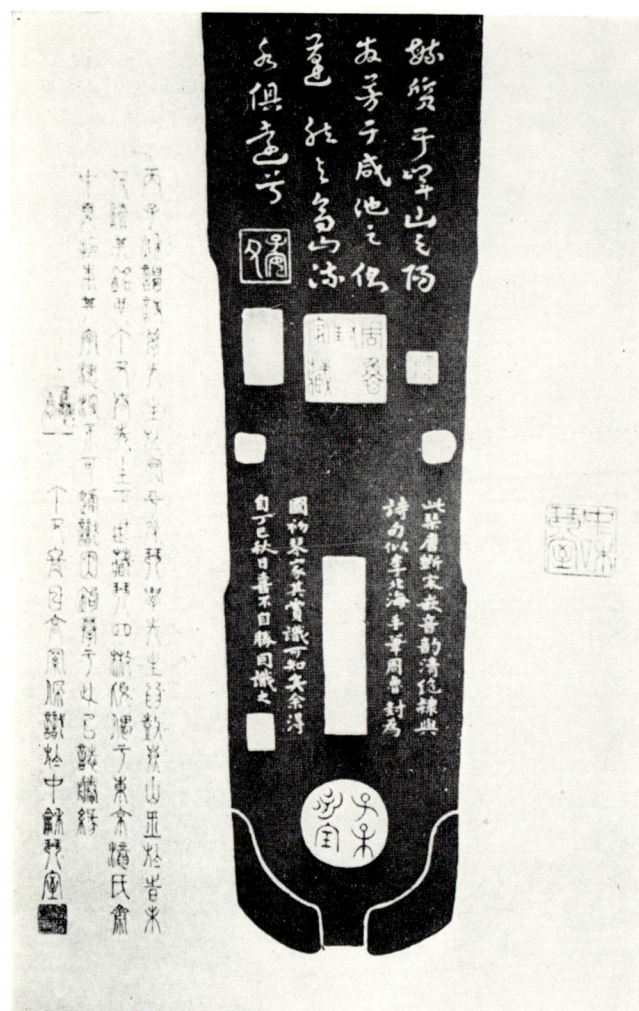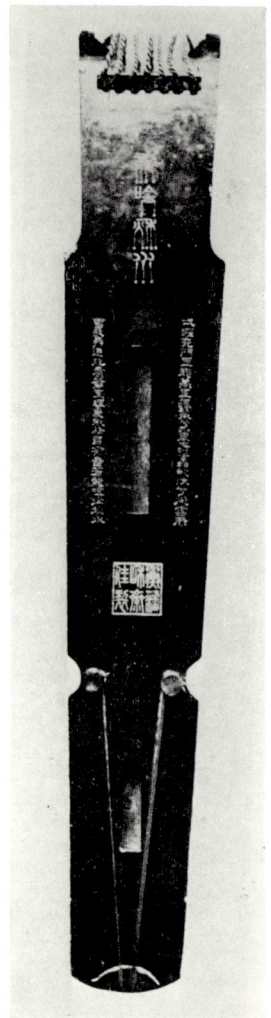

#31: Lower part of the tracing.

#32: Bottom board of the lute made by the Prince of Hêng. (Collection of *Cheng Ying-sun*, Peking)

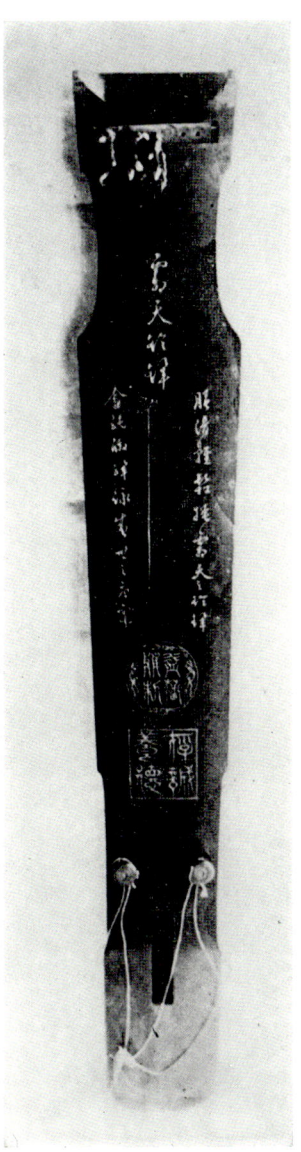

#33: Bottom board of a lute made by the Prince of I, preserved in Japan. Name: *Shuang-tʻien-ling-to* 霜天鈴鐸 'Bells on a frosty day'. The round seal reads: *I-fan-ya-chih* 益藩雅制 'Elegant product of the I fief'; the large square seal has the legend *yu-chʻêng-yang-tê* 游誠養德 'rejoicing in sincerity, nurturing virtue'. The grass-characters on either side of the Dragon Pond read 脆滑輕鬆搖霜天之鈴鐸, 翕純淑繹詠盛世之唐虞 'Crisp, gliding, light and loose, its tones tinkle like bells on a frosty day; harmonious and pure, it sings the golden age of Yao and Shun.' This lute was brought to Japan by the Ming refugee Chu Shun-shui, and later presented by him to his faithful Japanese disciple, the Sinologue Andō Seian (page 247). This instrument is still preserved in the Andō family, and in 1949 I had an opportunity to examine the inscriptions inside the sound box, facing the upper aperture in the bottom board.

On right:

'Upper and lower board joined together on an auspicious day of the 8th moon of the year 1579. Elegant product made by the Taoist Huang-nan, Prince of I, having obtained an old block of *tʻung* wood.'

萬曆己卯歲仲秋月吉旦合
益國潢南道人獲古桐雅製

On left:

'Tʻu Kuei, literary name Ssŭ-tʻung, a lute player of Nan-chʻang, supervised the building of this instrument in ancient style, on the high command (of the Prince of I).'

南昌琴士思桐涂桂
奉命按古式監劚

I-wang, the Prince of I, named Hou-hsüan 厚炫, was a famous lute player; he succeeded to the fief in 1557. The *Chʻin-shih* states in ch. II, page 3 *verso* that most of his lutes were built by Tʻu Kuei.

It must be noted that although this lute was brought to Japan by so eminent a scholar as Chu Shun-shui, there are some doubts regarding its authenticity. The famous lute expert Yang Tsung-chi (see page 180, under no. 7) had an instrument with the same inscriptions, which he considered as genuine (cf. his treatise *Chʻin-hua* 琴話, page 15 *recto*).

[*Appendix 3*] THE LUTE AS AN ANTIQUE 213

is signed with the seal of the Ch'ing literatus Ching Chi-chün;[124] it says: 'This lute was hewn during the T'ang dynasty, and in the Sung period its left and right bridges [*lung-yin* and *yo-shan*, see p. 101] were renewed. Its tones are extremely clear. The *li* inscription, and the two lines of poetry thereunder, resemble the handwriting of Li Yung. The appreciative commentary to be seen above was written by Chou Lu-fêng, a lute player of the beginning of our dynasty. When in the autumn of the year 1857 I obtained this lute, I could hardly control myself for joy, and wrote the foregoing to commemorate the occasion.'[125] The word *ch'ien*[126] in the first line of this inscription generally means 'to inlay, to inchase'; but in handbooks of the lute it is used as a technical term, and indicates the process of adding the two bridges to either end of the body of the lute. For these bridges a specially hard kind of wood, like ebony or red sandalwood, is used.[127]

The round seal in archaic script underneath imitates the well-worn legend on ancient sacrificial vessels: *tzû-sun-yung-pao*,[128] 'May my children and grandchildren treasure it for ever.'

When Yeh Ho-fu obtained this lute, he added on either side of the three characters *K'un-shan-yü* an inscription of his own, saying: 'This is the best of all the lutes preserved in the Shih-mêng Library.'[129] *Shih-mêng-chai* was the name of Yeh Ho-fu's studio.

On my tracing, reproduced here, I added in the upper right corner an impression of Yeh Ho-fu's library seal, reading: *Shih-mêng-chai*.[130] The seal in the lower right corner is that of my own library, reading *Chung-ho-ch'in-shih*,[131] cut in imitation of the seal of the Ming Prince Chu Ch'üan (Ning). I also added on the left a colophon, relating the history of this tracing.

* * *

The third lute brings us to the Ming dynasty.

After China had been dominated for the greater part of a century by foreign rulers, with the coming of the House of Ming the country again enjoyed a Chinese dynasty. During this period (1368–1644) the fine arts flourished, protected and encouraged by Imperial favour. Next to the Emperors themselves, there were also several Imperial Princes who were ardent patrons of art and learning. Not less than fifteen Princes are enumerated as having patronized book printing,

---

124 景其濬
125 此琴唐斲宋嵌，音韻清絕，隸與詩句似李北海手筆，周魯封爲國朝初琴家，其賞識可知矣，余得自丁巳秋日喜不自勝，因識之.
126 嵌
127 See *Yü-ku-chai-ch'in-pu*, ch. II, p. 37.
128 子孫永寶
129 詩夢齋所藏之琴此爲第一
130 詩夢齋
131 中和琴室

and some of the superior editions which they had made are still preserved.[132] There was a great activity in artistic studies also. Endeavours were made to bring about a renaissance of the old classical music: here also the most outstanding name is that of a member of the Imperial Family, Prince Chu Tsai-yü,[133] whose works on music, as for example the *Yüeh-lü-ch'üan-shu*,[134] are still considered authoritative. And it was also Court circles that gave the impetus to the florescence of lute studies and lute music which was witnessed in the Ming period.

Four Princes are known as having been especially interested in the lute: the Princes of Ning,[135] of Lu,[136] of I,[137] and of Hêng.[138] Cf. the *Ts'ang-ch'in-lu*.

Prince Ning[139] was typical for his class and his time: deeply interested in artistic and abstruse subjects, not caring much for worldly things, he preferred to pass his days in cultivated leisure. He published books on history,[140] on Taoism,[141] agriculture,[142] geography,[143] medicine,[144] the calendar,[145] on literary games, etc.

Under his literary name Ch'ü-hsien,[146] 'Emaciated Immortal' i.e. crane), he was famous as a lute master; he is credited with having composed two well-known tunes, 'Autumn Geese' (*Ch'iu-hung*),[147] and 'Geese on the Sandbank' (*P'ing-sha-lo-yen*),[148] which are still played to this day. A collection of lute tunes compiled by him, the *Shên-chi-pi-pu*,[149] is still preserved. Other works on the lute written by the Prince, like the *T'ai-ku-i-yin*[150] and the *Ch'in-yüan-ch'i-mêng*,[151] seem to have been lost; some fragments are to be found in the *Tsun-shêng-pa-chien*.[152] Besides being an expert performer, the Prince was also well known as a builder of lutes; unfortunately specimens of his work are extremely rare. When accused of practising black

---

132 See *Shu-lin-ch'ing-hua* 書林清話, ed. 1920, ch. 5.
133 朱載堉
134 樂律全書; see *Imperial Catalogue*, ch. 38, p. 5.
135 Ning-wang 寧王
136 Lu-wang 潞王
137 I-wang 益王
138 Hêng-wang 衡王. See *Ts'ung-ch'in-lu*, quoted above.
139 Personal name, Chu Ch'üan 朱權 (died 1448).
140 *Han-t'ang-pi-shih* 漢唐秘史; see *Imperial Catalogue*, ch. 52, p. 9.
141 *Kêng-shin-yü-ts'e* 庚辛玉册; see bibliographical section of the *Ming-shih* 明史.
142 *Shên-yin-shu* 神隱書; *ibid*.

143 *I-yü-chih* 異域志; *ibid*., ch. 11.
144 *P'ing-chi-ch'i-i-pao-ming-chi* 病機氣宜保命集; see the catalogue *T'ieh-ch'in-t'ung-chien-lou-ts'ang-shu-mu-lu* 鐵琴銅劍樓藏書目錄, pub. 1897, ch. 14, p. 24.
145 *Chou-hou-shên-ching* 肘後神經; see *Imperial Catalogue*, ch. 111, p. 11; the *Ming-shih* gives *shu* 樞 instead of *ching* 經.
146 臞仙
147 秋鴻
148 平沙落雁
149 App. II, 10.
150 太古遺音
151 琴阮啓蒙; see bibliographical section, ch. III.
152 App. II, 4.

magic (*wu-ku*),[153] the Prince retired to a mountain top, and passed his remaining days composing poetry and playing the lute.[154]

I could find less details about the other three princes who are constantly quoted in connection with the study of the lute; but we shall not be far amiss when we assume that they were personalities not unlike the Prince of Ning.

The Prince of Lu is especially known as a builder of lutes. Specimens of instruments built at Hangchow by him or under his direct supervision are often met with in Chinese collections; most bear dates of the Ch'ung-chên period.[155]

Further, lutes made by the Prince of I still exist in a fair number; one dated 1564 is recorded,[156] and one good specimen has been preserved in Japan, brought over from China by the Chinese refugee Chu Shun-shui;[157] the bottom board is reproduced in fig. 33.

The Prince of Hêng, next to being a great bibliophile,[158] was a famous lute amateur. As far as I know, he did not compose new melodies, but instruments built by him are counted among the finest specimens produced during the Ming period. While instruments built by the Princes of Lu and I may occasionally be seen, lutes built by the Princes of Ning and Hêng are very rare, and highly valued by connoisseurs. It is an instrument made by the Prince of Hêng that is reproduced here (see fig. 32).

The name of this lute is *Lung-yin-ch'iu-shui*,[159] 'Dragon Crying in the Autumnal Water'; the four characters in archaic style are to be seen at the top.

On the right and left of the Dragon Pond there appears a poetical essay in chancery script, praising the qualities of the instrument, and explaining its name: 'With one leap the dragon reaches the gates of Heaven; as a stormwind he compasses ten thousand miles in his flight. When he shakes his bristles, thunder and lightning roll and rattle; when he spurts his foam, a rainstorm gathers. Trying to express in an image the tones produced by the supreme Reason of the movement of the atmosphere, and by music and dance in their various manifestations, I at last lit upon a dragon crying in the autumnal waters.'[160] The first part of these lines is descriptive:

---

153 巫蠱
154 See *Ming-shih*, ch. 117; *Ming-shih-tsung* 明詩綜, ch. 1.
155 崇禎, 1628–44.
156 See *T'ien-wên-ko-ch'in-pu-chi-ch'êng*, App. II, no. 18, vol. I, sub *Shou-lu* 手錄.
157 See p. 247.
158 See *Ts'ang-shu-chi-shih-shih* 藏書紀事詩, pub. 1891, ch. 2, p. 18.
159 龍吟秋水
160 一躍天門，罡飆萬里，振鬣兮雷電鑑 (better: 鏗) 轟，噀沫兮風雲際會，鼓舞造化，橐籥至理，爰取物以喻音，若龍吟於秋水.

since ancient times the dragon has been connected with storms and rain.[161] The second part explains why such a seemingly incongruous image as a dragon was chosen in connection with the tones of this lute: the maker meant to express in this name the impressive, superhuman harmony of the universe. The term *t'o-yüeh*,[162] which I have translated as movement of the atmosphere, literally means a bellows: it is a quotation from the *Tao-tê-ching*, ch. v:[163] '[The space] between heaven and earth is like a bellows.' The term *tsao-hua*[164] is also difficult to translate: it means natural evolution, as produced by the agency of the eternal cosmic forces.

Directly under the Dragon Pond one sees the beautiful square seal that marks all instruments of the Prince. It reads: *Hêng-fan-ho-chai-chia-chih*[165] ('Superior product of the Ho Studio, in the Hêng fief').

* * *

The above may suffice to give an idea of what antique lutes mean to the Chinese connoisseur, and what methods are followed for appreciating them.

It must be stressed again, however, that the lute should not be considered as a mere relic of bygone times. It does not primarily belong to the scholar's library, but to the pavilion in his garden, to the rivulets in secluded valleys, to the gnarled pines on the rocks. The lute is one of the many bonds that keep the literatus, notwithstanding his book learning, united with the cosmic forces of living nature.

---

[161] See M. W. de Visser, *The Dragon in China and Japan,* Amsterdam 1913, ch. v.
[162] 槖籥
[163] 道德經, ch. v.
[164] 造化
[165] 衡藩和齋佳製

APPENDIX IV

The Chinese Lute in Japan

ACCORDING to most Japanese sources the flourishing of the study of the Chinese lute in Japan (*kingaku*)[1] in the 17th, 18th and 19th centuries is due to the arrival in Japan, in 1677, of the Chinese Zen priest Hsin-yüeh (Jap. Shin'etsu).[2] This Chinese priest, who came to Japan as a refugee fleeing the troubles that marked the later years of the Ming dynasty, was a great lover of the lute; when he came to Japan he brought several Chinese lutes with him, and propagated the study of the lute in that country.

The problem is whether or not the Chinese lute was played in Japan even before the arrival of Shin'etsu. Both old and new Japanese authors disagree in their attitude to this question.

Music since olden times occupied an important place in Japanese cultural life. Old Japanese literature abounds in references to several kinds of musical instruments that were played in Court circles, and by all those who claimed to have elegant and refined interests. Among these several stringed instruments are mentioned; some of them are Japanese, others are of foreign origin. One reads about the *wagon* or *yamatogoto*[3] (a six-stringed cither, each string supported by a strut, *ji*),[4] the *sō*[5] (a 13-stringed cither, a Japanese adaptation of the Chinese *chêng*),[6] the *Shiragigoto*[7] (a cither, as the name implies, of Korean origin), etc. On the other hand most often we find simply the character 琴, read in Sino-Japanese: *kin*, and in Japanese: *koto*, without further indication of what instrument is meant. The pronunciation added in Japanese *kana*[8] to this character in the texts is *kin* or *koto*; sometimes the Chinese character is not used, and we find *kin* or *koto* in *kana* only; and sometimes we find expressions like *kin no koto*, etc. The problem is whether there are passages where the context shows that with one of these terms the seven-stringed Chinese lute is meant.

1 琴學
2 心越
3 和琴
4 柱
5 箏
6 箏
7 新羅琴
8 假名

I may start with giving a few examples, taken at random from the vast field of Japanese literature.

The *Montoku jitsuroku*, historical notes written in Chinese and covering the period 850–8,[9] mentions under the year 853 that a courtier called Sekio excelled in playing the *kin*: 'Sekio especially loved to play the *kin*, and the Emperor presented him with a secret handbook [for this instrument].'[10] Similar references are to be found in the *Shoku Nihon kōki*[11] (chronicle written in Chinese, covering the period 833–50), the *Gyoyūshō*,[12] etc. But especially old novels, written entirely in Japanese, like the *Utsubo monogatari*[13] (10th century), and the famous *Genji monogatari*[14] (11th century) abound in references to instruments called *kin* or *koto*.

Now some older Japanese writers maintain that in the passages referred to above *kin* is the only correct reading, and that the seven-stringed Chinese lute is meant. This is stated, for instance, by the learned physician and musicologist Suzuki Ryū.[15] In his book *Kingaku keimō*[16] (a handbook for the Chinese lute, written in Japanese), he devotes the 39th chapter, entitled, *Hompō kinkōhai*,[17] to the history of the Chinese lute in Japan. There he claims that wherever in ancient Japanese texts we find the character 琴 (he refers to the sources mentioned above), it means the Chinese lute. His argument is that although the Chinese lute was very popular in old Japan, it gradually fell into abeyance, till Shin'etsu's arrival in the 17th century brought about a renaissance. This argument he reiterates in the preface to his edition of the *Tōkō kimpu*.[18] He says: 'In ancient times in our country rites and music flourished; of the eight kinds of musical instruments (i.e. those made of wood, silk, bamboo, clay, metal, stone, leather, and gourd) none was missing. Most popular was the Chinese lute; it was an instrument constantly used by the nobility and high-minded people. This is proved by passages in historical works and other chronicles. But in medieval times, the study of the lute gradually fell into abeyance, and coming to the present time, its tradition was lost, and there was no one who understood this study. In the Kambun period, however, there came the naturalized priest Tōkō Zenji, named Shin'etsu.... Then gradually every-

---

9 文德實錄, completed in 878.
10 關雄尤好鼓琴，天皇賜其秘譜.
11 續日本後記
12 御遊抄
13 宇津保物語
14 源氏物語

15 鈴木龍, 1741–90; for details, see below, p. 235.
16 琴學啓蒙
17 本邦琴興廢
18 東皋琴譜; details below.

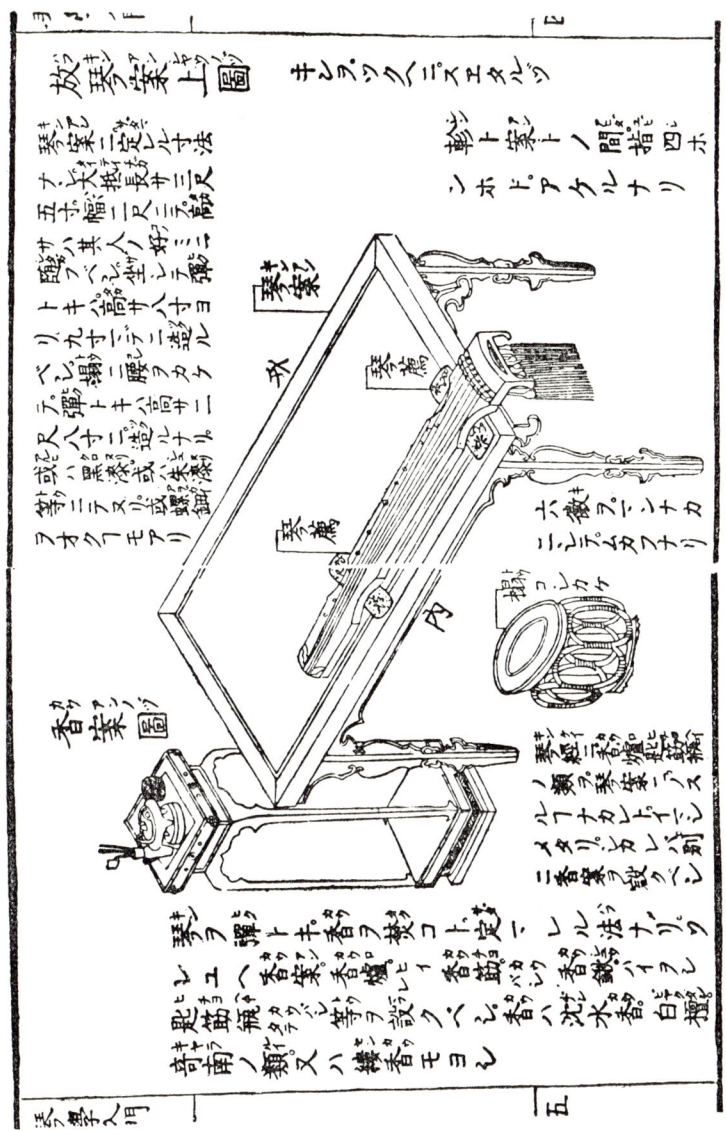

#34: Japanese picture, representing the Chinese lute and accessories, with explanations in Japanese. From the *Kingaku nyūmon zukai* 琴學入門圖解, a simplified handbook for the lute player, written in Japanese; published in one volume at Kyoto, in 1828.

where in our country people started again to study the lute. That now in this late age the tones of the lute that had been silent for several centuries resound again, is due to the merit of Tōkō Zenji. Is this not a great achievement?'[19]

A closer inspection of the passages referred to, however, clearly shows that it is not the Chinese lute that is meant by the character 琴 in old Japanese literature. For we find it mentioned that the instrument in question has struts, that its sounds are heard at a considerable distance, that it is used for accompanying purely Japanese songs, that it is played when lying on the floor, etc. Now we know that the Chinese lute, unlike the *sê* and several varieties of the *chêng*, never has struts; that its tones are so weak as hardly to be audible outside the room where it is played, that its scale cannot well be adapted to the Japanese ones, and that it is made to be played on one's lap or on a special stand—its very structure precluding that it be played when lying on the floor. There can be no doubt that in the passages referred to, the *wagon*, *sō*, or some other Japanese or Chinese cither-like instrument is meant. That yet the word *kin* 琴 was used must be explained by the fact that this term had an elegant, literary flavour. Even at present in Japan the character 琴 is often used to write *koto*, although the character 箏 is the correct one. Further, the *ch'in* 琴, being the Chinese musical instrument *par excellence*, also in China was used in the meaning of 'musical instrument' in general; notice that a piano is called in Chinese *yang-ch'in*,[20] a violin *t'i-ch'in*,[21] etc. When we find in ancient Japanese literature expressions like *kokin*,[22] *dankin*,[23] these must be taken to be literary idioms, taken over from the Chinese. The character *kin* in these expressions does not indicate the Chinese seven-stringed lute, no more than *ken*[24] in Japanese texts indicates the Chinese straight sword.

These facts were realized by other older Japanese writers, for instance the well-known Japanese expert on the Chinese lute, Kodama Kūkū.[25] In a colophon to a manuscript copy of the Chinese lute handbook *Li-hsing-yüan-ya*,[26] he quotes some Japanese writers who aver that the *kin* mentioned, e.g. in the *Genji monogatari*, is the Chinese

---

[19] 蓋我古昔，禮樂之隆，八音之器，諸般皆備，而琴最盛行，爲士君子常御之器，乃諸史傳所載，可以徵矣，中世已後，漸廢不行，及至近代，竟失其傳，無復有道之者矣，寬文中，有歸化僧東皐禪師名心越…於是乎,四方稍復有道琴事者矣，嗚呼，使數百年己絕之徽音再振其響晚世者,東皐師之功，豈不亦偉哉.

[20] 洋琴

[21] 提琴

[22] 鼓琴

[23] 彈琴

[24] 劍

[25] 兒玉空空, 1734–1811; details below.

[26] 理性元雅, by the Ming author Chang Ting-yü 張廷玉; see *Imperial Catalogue*, ch. 114, p. 7 verso.

lute. Then he goes on to say: 'I do not agree with this. Why? The *Genji monogatari* was written about 700 years ago. If the above statement were true, then in old families and famous monasteries there would certainly have been preserved many of these ancient Chinese lutes. Why is it that on the contrary only very occasionally one hears about such a thing? ... In my opinion, our Empire Japan knew the Chinese lute for the first time after the day that Master Shin'etsu came from the west.'[27]

The modern Japanese musicologist Sanjō Shōtarō[28] comes to about the same conclusion.[29]

Some other modern Japanese scholars, however, still keep to Suzuki Ryū's argument, and maintain that it was the Chinese seven-stringed lute that was played on a great scale in ancient Japan. Prof. Tanabe Hisao[30] (well-known Japanese musicologist), for instance, sets forth this view in his *Nihon ongaku kōwa*[31] (Tokyo 1921), on pages 364 ff. To bear out this statement he quotes the following passage from the *Gempei seisuiki*[32] (historical notes covering the period 1161–81): 'She also is a sensitive lady, a great expert on the *kin* [or *koto*]. In former days Po Chü-i of China, calling lute, poetry, and wine his three friends,[33] nurtured his feelings by playing the lute ... This lady, continually singing Po Chü-i's poems and playing the *kin* [or *koto*], purified her heart.'[34] After quoting this passage Prof. Tanabe remarks that it is clear that here the Chinese lute is meant, because of the reference to Po Chü-i and his lute. Now this argument of course does not hold; for the mere fact that Po Chü-i is mentioned does not constitute any proof. Po Chü-i and his lute are often referred to in Japanese novels when *Japanese* music is discussed. I mention, for instance, a passage in the *Genji monogatari*, in the chapter *Suetsumu hana*. The Princess after which this chapter is named is a famous performer on the Japanese *koto*; that here *koto* is meant is evident

---

[27] 予未以爲然，何則，源語之作，距今纔七百餘年，果如其言，則古家名刹，尚可存其器，而何其寥寥聞耶...以予臆見，則皇和之有琴也，擬于越公西來之日.

[28] 三條商太郎

[29] See his *Nihon jōko ongakushi* 日本上古音樂史, Tokyo 1935, p. 137.

[30] 田邊尚雄

[31] 日本音樂講和, Tokyo 1921, on pp. 364 ff.

[32] 源平盛衰記

[33] The quotation is from a poem by Po Chü-i, entitled *Pei-ch'uang-san-yu* 北窗三友; see the excellent study *Hakurakuten to Nihon bungaku* 白樂天と日本文學, Tokyo 1930, by Mizuno Heiji 水野平次, p. 378. For other references to cither-like instruments in the *Genji monogatari*, see *Genji monogatari no ongaku* 源氏物語の音樂, by Yamada Takao 山田孝雄, Tokyo 1934, pp. 80–108.

[34] *Kore mata nasake aru nyōbō nite kin (koto) no jōzu to zo kikoetamaishi. Mukashi Kara no Hakkyoi wa kinshishu (koto, shi, sake) no mitsu wo tomo toshite tsune ni kin (koto) wo hiite kokoro wo yashinai tamaikeri ... shi wo kono kita no kata tsune ni eijite kokoro wo sumashi koto wo danji tamaerikeri.*

from the context. Now a lady called Myōbu says of this eccentric Princess to Prince Genji[35]: 'Her only lover is her *kin*.' Prince Genji answers: 'Then of the "Three Friends" she at least has one ... Let me hear her play.'[36] Thus here also Po Chü-i is mentioned, and here definitely a Japanese *koto* is meant.

This fact is not at all astonishing. The Japanese of olden times, though fairly well versed in Chinese literature, were often amazingly ignorant of what we would call 'things Chinese'. Thus it is very doubtful whether they realized that the *kin* mentioned in their favourite T'ang poetry was entirely different from cither-like instruments in use in Japan. Their knowledge of Chinese ways of living was as limited as that of our European medieval poets concerning daily life in ancient Greece and Italy. During the Heian period several Japanese missions were sent to China; the writings by the members of these missions, who knew daily Chinese life from their own observation, contain excellent accounts of religious and political conditions prevalent in China. But they write little about things Chinese; in this respect they conformed to Chinese literary tradition, which condemned the things of daily life as unworthy to write about. Thus we find in Japanese history that with regular intervals the Japanese deemed it necessary to work up arrears in their knowledge of Chinese reality. They found that they had been associating with terms in daily use in China, things quite different in shape and style from those really used by contemporary Chinese. Therefore, especially during the Tokugawa period, when the seclusion policy of the *bakufu* had limited the intercourse with China to the port of Nagasaki, the Chinese there were eagerly questioned by Japanese scholars: what dresses they wear, what utensils they use, and what Chinese houses and temples look like.[37] Such knowledge was especially important to

---

35 Kaneko ed., Tokyo 1938, p. 207.

36 *kin wo zo natsukashiki kataraibito to omoeru to kikoyureba, mitsu no tomo nite ima hitokusa ya utate aran. Ware ni kikase yo.*

37 The most remarkable example of the results of such an inquiry is the book *Shinzoku kibun* 清俗紀聞, 13 chs. in 6 vols., published in 1799 by Nakagawa Chūei 中川忠英, who served as a *bakufu* official (*bugyō* 奉行) at Nagasaki; this book contains the results of minute inquiries, patiently made with the Chinese at Nagasaki, especially Chinese and Japanese interpreters attached to the government office there. The book gives a detailed account of Chinese customs and Chinese daily life, profusely illustrated with finely executed drawings. The famous Director of the Academy at Edo (the Seidō 聖堂), Hayashi Jussai (林述齋, 1768–1841) added the first preface. Even Chinese refugees were questioned. An interesting example is the *Shunsui shushi danki* 舜水朱氏譚綺, printed in 1708 in 4 vols., and compiled by the Japanese sinologue Hitomi Bōsai (人見懋齋, 1638–96); preface by the scholar Asaka Kaku (安積覺, 1656–1737), dated 1707. This book contains the material regarding 'things Chinese' obtained by Hitomi from the famous Chinese refugee at the Court of Mito, Chu Shun-shui (朱舜水 1600–82). Here we find*

those Japanese who wanted to read Chinese novels: in such texts there occur many terms not to be found in Chinese dictionaries and other ordinary works of reference. Thus in the Tokugawa period we find special Japanese vocabularies of the Chinese vulgar language, where common household words, like spoon, table, comb, etc. are explained by drawings of the Chinese objects.[38]

The pre-Tokugawa Japanese missions to China had as their primary object the study of Chinese religious and political questions, and of Court and ceremonial music. It is quite understandable that the members of those missions were not in a position to study lute music, an art that was confined to intimate literary gatherings and the library of the scholar. Moreover, as we have seen above,[39] in China strict rules prohibited the teaching of the lute to unqualified persons, and, among them, foreigners are especially mentioned. While during the T'ang dynasty it was comparatively easy to obtain lutes, on the other hand teachers were few, and may be supposed to have kept to the rules limiting the transmission of the study of the lute to members of the privileged and highly exclusive class of the literati.

Yet Chinese lutes occasionally ended up in Japan. In Appendix III above I described the remarkable old Chinese lute preserved in the Nara Repository; the famous old temple, the Hōryūji,[40] also has in its collection a Chinese lute, dating from the T'ang period. But these lutes were not actually played. They were regarded merely as curiosities, relics from the 'Land beyond the Seas'.

Finally we must remember that in olden times Japanese knowledge of Chinese music was mainly secondhand, being chiefly obtained through the intermediary of Korea. Now in that country the Chinese lute as a solo instrument never became popular.[41] Although the Chinese lute was taken over together with the ceremonial orchestra, as a solo instrument its place was taken by a special Korean instru-

---

*drawings of Chinese clothing, furniture, temples, envelopes and letters, bills of fare, etc., with the dimensions added, and colour and material recorded with painstaking care.

Paul Carus based his publication *Chinese Life and Customs* (Chicago, Open Court Publ. Co., 1907) on this book, and reproduced a selection from its fine illustrations; see the author's statement on page 1.

38 For instance the *Shōsetsu jii* 小說字彙, published in one volume in 1791. First undated preface by the Japanese sinologue Takayasu Rooku 高安蘆屋, author's preface dated, 1784. The author gives only his literary name, Shūsuien shujin 秋水園主人.

39 pp. 61 ff.

40 法隆寺

41 It should be mentioned, however, that during the Ch'ing period, when many Korean scholars used to visit Peking, a few of them made a study of the Chinese lute. During a visit to Seoul in 1949 I learned that the Korean poet and statesman Shin Ui (申緯, style Han-so 漢叟, literary name Cha-ha 紫霞, 1769-1847) was a great lute player, while in recent years Yun Hae-kwan 尹海觀, is also said to have been quite a creditable performer.

ment, the so-called *hyôn-kêm*.[42] This instrument is still very popular in Korea. It has six strings, of which the three middle ones are strung over sixteen bridges of varying height. It is played with a short rattan stick that serves as a plectrum. According to the *Ryang-kêm-sin-po*,[43] the Chinese lute was introduced into Korea about A.D. 600; the Minister Wang San-ak[44] recommended to use in its place the *hyôn-kêm*, invented by him. This instrument has its own notation, and its music is quite different from that of the Chinese lute.

Therefore we must assume that the character *kin*[45] in old Japanese texts stands for cither-like instruments, either of Japanese, Korean or Chinese origin. Both in China and Korea a great many varieties of the cither called *chêng*[46] were used. Since these instruments were widely used in both countries in both sacrificial and popular music, it is only natural that at an early date they found their way to Japan. And many Japanese thought these cither-like instruments were the Chinese lute so often mentioned in Chinese literature.

It is on the basis of the above considerations that I think we are justified in assuming that it was only with the arrival of Shin'etsu that the Chinese seven-stringed lute became really known in Japan. A few exceptions do not invalidate this argument; they were isolated cases that had no real influence on Japanese cultural life.[47] It was only with the arrival of Shin'etsu that the Chinese lute was really played in Japan, and found enthusiasts in broader circles of artists and scholars.

*   *   *

42 玄琴.

43 梁琴新譜. (See M. Courant, *Bibliographie coréenne*, Paris 1896, part III, p. 133.)

44 王山岳; passed official examination in 552.

45 琴.

46 箏.

47 I mention, for instance, Fujiwara Sadatoshi (藤原貞敏, 807–67), the father of Japanese *biwa* music. He was a member of a Japanese mission to China that arrived there in 838, and made great efforts to study Chinese music. He married the daughter of his Chinese *biwa* teacher, and this girl is said to have been able to play both the *chêng* and the Chinese seven-stringed lute.

Much later the great Japanese sinologue Ogyū Sorai (荻生徂徠, 1666–1728) made a study of the Chinese lute, and wrote a book called *Kingaku taiishō* (琴學大意抄, dated 1722; preserved only in manuscript copies).

This, however, is an entirely theoretical essay, the materials for which have been gathered from various Chinese books on the subject. There is no indication that he really became a lute player.

The same may be said of Ishikawa Jōzan (石川丈山, 1583–1672). He was a great lover of Chinese poetry, who for the greater part of his life lived in retirement on a beautiful spot in the outskirts of Kyoto. His retreat was called Shisendō 詩仙堂; on the walls of his study he hung the images of 36 famous Chinese poets, and there he passed his days. He possessed a Chinese lute that had belonged to the famous Chinese scholar Ch'ên Chi-ju (陳繼儒, 1558–1639), which he greatly valued; but there is no indication that he actually played it. At present the Shisendō may still be seen in its original state, and the lute has also been preserved; nowadays the place is a nunnery.

#35: A banquet at the house of a Chinese merchant in Nagasaki. The diners on the right are playing *morra* with geisha girls. On the left a Chinese is playing the lute, accompanied on the *samisen* (three-stringed Japanese guitar) by a geisha. The picture of the lute is not very clear; it might also be a small *chêng*. From *Nagasakishi-shi* 長崎市史, *Fūzoku-hen* 風俗編, pub. 1925 by the Municipal Office of Nagasaki.

#36: A musical seance in the Chinese Factory at Nagasaki. One Chinese is playing the lute, while his friends accompany him on guitar, mouth-organ and flute. Part of a Japanese picture scroll, now in the library of the Imperial University at Kyoto.

[*Appendix 4*] THE CHINESE LUTE IN JAPAN 225

The priest Shin'etsu was a highly interesting personality. In China he is practically unknown; but in Japan abundant materials[48] about him and his work have been preserved. For in Japan he became famous, and had considerable influence on the cultural life of the time.

Shin'etsu's lay-name was Chiang Hsing-t'ao,[49] and he was born in 1639. Having entered priesthood, he was enrolled in the Yung-fu monastery[50] at Hangchow. When the Manchus invaded China, in 1676 he left Hangchow and set out for Japan. In the first month of the year 1677 he arrived at Nagasaki in a Chinese ship, and there settled down in the Kōfukuji,[51] one of the famous local Chinese monasteries. Shin'etsu then was 38 years old. It appears from his writings that he was a priest of high culture, being at the same time a clever painter, poet, seal-engraver and player on the lute. At that time the great Tokugawa Maecenas, Mitsukuni, Lord of Mito,[52] had established in his fief in Eastern Japan near Edo, a center of learning where he had assembled the flower of Japanese scholarship. Mitsukuni was also greatly interested in Chinese studies, and had, in 1665, summoned to his court another learned Chinese refugee, Chu Shun-shui,[53] and made him his Chinese adviser. When Mitsukuni heard about the arrival of Shin'etsu at Nagasaki, he sent in 1678 a messenger, Imai Koshirō,[54] to invite Shin'etsu to come to Mito. At the time, however, the Tokugawa government did not allow Chinese to travel freely in Japan; they were allowed to stay only at Nagasaki, and for a limited time. Therefore a special permission had to be obtained. This took several years, and only in 1683 could Shin'etsu set out for Eastern Japan. It seems, however, that during the intervening years he could do some traveling in West Japan; for we read that he visited several centers of Buddhist learning, especially monasteries of the Obaku sect,[55] which were traditionally headed by a naturalized Chinese priest. Thus he came into contact with some of the famous Chinese abbots of this sect, notably the priest Mokuan.[56]

Arrived at Mito, Shin'etsu, encouraged by Mitsukuni, started manifold religious and artistic activities. He made a thorough study

[48] Most informative are Shin'etsu's complete works, the *Tōkō zenshū* 東皐全集 in two volumes, compiled by Asano Fuzan 淺野斧山, and published in 1911. This edition also contains a complete biography, and reproductions of Shin'etsu's paintings, his calligraphy, and imprints of some of the seals carved by him. His grave is still to be seen near Mito. Also see E. W. Clement, 'The Tokugawa Princes of Mito', in *Transactions of the Asiatic Society of Japan*, XVIII (1890).
[49] 蔣興儔
[50] 永福寺
[51] 興福寺
[52] 德川光圀, 1628–1700.
[53] See note 37 above, and p. 247 below.
[54] 今井小四郎
[55] 黃蘗宗
[56] 木菴, 1611–84.

of the Japanese language, and was in regular intercourse with well-known Japanese scholars of the time. He founded the Gion temple[57] at Mito, and greatly influenced religious life. At his death in 1695 he was buried with great honour. It lies outside the scope of this essay to give a more detailed survey of Shin'etsu's cultural activities; here we shall concern ourselves only with his teaching of the Chinese lute.

If we were to believe the notes made by older Japanese lute enthusiasts, Shin'etsu had more than a hundred pupils who under his guidance studied the Chinese lute. Although this is an exaggeration, still the number of his lute disciples seems to have been considerable. Only a few of these, however, became really proficient on this instrument, and transmitted Shin'etsu's teachings along to their own pupils. Best known are the doctor of Chinese medicine, Hitomi Chikudō, and the Japanese sinologue Sugiura Kinsen.[58] Shin'etsu taught his pupils the finger technique and made them practise on simple lute melodies, for the greater part musical versions of famous Chinese poems. These tunes were eagerly noted down by his pupils, and it is on the basis of such manuscripts that afterwards the *Tōkō kimpu*[59] was published.

It is difficult to ascertain whether Shin'etsu as a lute player, judging by Chinese standards, ranked as an expert. At one time, basing my opinion upon the tunes preserved in the *Tōkō kimpu*, I was inclined to think that he was but a mediocre performer. For in this handbook only very simple and much abbreviated lute melodies are given; they lack all the grandeur of real lute music. On the other hand we have a letter of Hitomi Chikudō to Shin'etsu,[60] from which it appears that Shin'etsu advised him to use the well-known Ming handbook *Sung-hsüan-kuan-ch'in-pu*;[61] this would imply that Shin'etsu taught his advanced students on the basis of this handbook—which is by no means an easy one. Therefore it would seem that the handbook that bears Shin'etsu's name, the *Tōkō kimpu*, represents only the tunes that Shin'etsu taught to beginners. For advanced students did not need a special handbook; they could use the great Chinese *ch'in-pu*. Taking into consideration the meager evidence available, I now think we had better leave the question of Shin'etsu's abilities as a lute expert undecided. That he was not one of the great Chinese musicians,

---

57 祇園寺
58 See p. 232 below.
59 See p. 232 below.

60 *Tōkō zenshū*, II, leaf 44.
61 松絃舘琴譜, preface dated 1614; see *Imperial Catalogue*, 113, leaf 8 verso.

however, appears from the fact that he left no important compositions of his own.

When he came to Japan, Shin'etsu brought three Chinese lutes with him. Best known is the instrument called *Yü-shun*[62] (Jap. Gushun), a fine Ming specimen, covered with red cement. This instrument was long preserved in the treasury of the Tokugawas of Mito. In 1834 the celebrated Mito scholar Fujita Tōkō[63] was ordered to compose a Chinese essay, to be written inside the cover of the box this lute was kept in. This essay, entitled *Gushun kinki*,[64] is to be found reprinted in Fujita's complete works, the *Tōko ikō*,[65] and the original may still be seen on the box, now, together with the instrument itself, in the Imperial Museum, in Ueno Park, Tokyo. Secondly Shin'etsu had a lute called *Su-wang*,[66] (Jap. *So-ō*); this lute he presented to his pupil Hitomi Chikudō, and for some generations it was preserved in Hitomi's family. At present it seems to have been lost. Thirdly a lute called *Wan-ho-sung*,[67] (Jap. *Mankakushō*), preserved in the Gion temple in Mito.

In addition Shin'etsu taught his pupils how to make lutes themselves. These Japanese-made lutes are built from *kiri* wood, the same material as the Japanese *koto* is made of. Instead of the coat of cement of the Chinese lutes, the Japanese ones are covered with ordinary lacquer. This has the advantage of not being affected by the humidity of the Japanese climate; but on the other hand such a coat does not develop those tiny cracks (*tuan-wên*)[68] which give the sound-box of an antique Chinese lute its peculiar beauty. Of these Japanese-made Chinese lutes many are still preserved. I have in my collection seven specimens, which are in good condition and show interesting inscriptions. They are easily distinguishable from genuine Chinese specimens by the lacquer coating, and by the fact that the tuning pegs (*chên*),[69] are much shorter than those of the Chinese lutes. This is because the Japanese lute players rarely had a real lute table (which has a special cavity for the pegs), and usually played the lute either on an ordinary low table (see fig. 34), or on the floor.

Later Japanese lute players often could obtain real Chinese lutes from the Chinese in Nagasaki. Occasionally among the Chinese living there, or passing through, there were some who could play the

62 虞舜
63 藤田東湖, 1806–55.
64 虞舜琴記
65 東湖遺稿, edition of 1877, vol. 2, leaf 25.
66 素王
67 萬壑松
68 See above, pp. 194–7.
69 軫

lute. But probably they were not great virtuosi. Nagasaki pictures often show Chinese playing the lute, usually accompanied by other stringed instruments, and serving to enliven a dinner party (figs. 35 and 36). This fact alone already shows that those Chinese lute players were not real experts, for such would certainly not thus offend against the rules for the lute player.

Through Shin'etsu's teachings, and by studying Chinese books on the lute, Japanese players also became acquainted with lute ideology. It is not without interest to observe how in Japan there arose with regard to lute ideology controversies similar to those found in China.

In Chapter III, section 3 above, we have seen that lute players of the Confucianist school denied Buddhist priests the right to play the lute. Now in Japan about half of the lute players were Buddhist priests, and Japanese lute tradition is founded upon the teachings of Shin'etsu, a Zen priest. The famous doctor of Chinese medicine, Murai Kinzan,[70] took exception to this. He learned the lute from a Chinese scholar who passed through Nagasaki, and claims to have the only real lute tradition. In the colophon to his *Kinzan kinroku*[71] he says: 'The lute is the great instrument of the Holy Sages, it includes all music. Of those things that the Superior Man has always with him, the lute is dearest to him, he does not suffer to be separated from it.[72] The Way of the Lute which in the Middle Age flourished in our country has now become lost. The methods of the lute as now practised in our country are all based upon the teachings of the two priests Shin'etsu and Mansō;[73] their methods for the greater part are those used by vulgar people of the Ming and Ch'ing periods. How could these two priests know the difference between elegant and vulgar? Therefore I did not relish the way these two priests play the lute, and for myself I have sighed over this for a long time. But traveling to Nagasaki, I met a Chinese called P'an Wei-ch'uan, and he taught me how to play the lute, and the finger technique.'[74]

Shin'etsu's pupils spread the study of the lute over the entire country. First the *kingaku* flourished among people of taste in Edo, roughly from 1770 till 1780. Its heyday falls in the subsequent

---

70 See below, p. 248.
71 *Ibid.*
72 Quoted from *Fêng-su-t'ung-i*; see above, p. 72.
73 See below, pp. 232-5, 247.
74 琴者聖人大器,而爲樂之統矣,君子所常御者,琴最親密,不離於身,我東方中古琴法已亡,今海內琴法,皆出于心越萬宗二僧氏之手,多是明清俗間之法也,二僧氏安知雅俗之分乎,余故不喜二僧氏之琴,竊歎嗟久矣,嘗游長崎,邂逅于清人潘渭川者,偶受琴法手勢.

Kansei and Bunka periods (1789-1817). During this period, playing the Chinese lute developed into a veritable craze: everyone who wanted to show his interest in elegant literary pursuits studied this instrument and wrote essays and odes in praise of its music. It was especially favoured by those in direct contact with Chinese studies, such as the *jukan*,[75] the Japanese sinologues in the service of the shogun, and by the so-called *tai-i*,[76] the doctors of Chinese medicine attached to the government. In addition, by all who were attracted by exciting novelties. Therefore we need not be astonished to find among these lute enthusiasts even some *rangakusha*,[77] students of Dutch learning. Many Japanese lute students soon dropped this subject, but there were also not a few more serious musicians, who carried their study through with great enthusiasm. Some even devoted their whole life to this music.

This sudden flourishing of the Chinese lute in Japan becomes quite understandable when one thinks of the fact that the Japanese scholars realized that now at last they had obtained the real Chinese lute, the name of which had been familiar to them for so long through their studies of Chinese literature. For as has been pointed out above, there can be no doubt that even as late as the Tokugawa period the greater part of Japanese lovers of Chinese studies fondly believed that the character *kin*[78] in Chinese texts stood for an instrument very much like the Japanese *koto*. This is proved by an inspection of Japanese illustrated editions of old Chinese books: there one regularly sees old Chinese poets playing upon the Japanese *koto*!

The seven-stringed lute however was too typically Chinese ever to become really a part of Japanese life. The music of the Chinese lute is based upon principles fundamentally different from those underlying Japanese music, and moreover its study presupposed a solid knowledge of the Chinese language, both written and spoken. As is well known, the Japanese have evolved a special way of reading Chinese texts, consisting of paraphrasing the Chinese in the Japanese vernacular; in this process the order of the words is drastically changed. As the text of the lute melodies could of course only be sung in the Chinese way, the Japanese lute player, when wishing to accompany his play by singing, had to learn how to read the text in the Chinese pronunciation. In Japanese handbooks for the Chinese lute, the Chinese pronunciation is added to the characters of the text

[75] 儒官 [76] 待醫
[77] 蘭學者 [78] 琴

in *kana*.⁷⁹ It goes without saying that thus the text became meaningless to the average Japanese hearer. As a reaction to this, the Japanese lute player Uragami Gyokudō⁸⁰ composed purely Japanese texts for the lute melodies. It seems that shortly after the introduction of the Chinese lute into Japan by Shin'etsu, efforts were made to adapt the lute to Japanese music. The *Gyokudō zōsho kimpu*⁸¹ says: 'Then it was asked: "Onoda Tōsen⁸² used to play Japanese songs on the Chinese lute; but fearing that this was contrary to the principles of lute ideology, he did not show these attempts to others. Have you heard about this?" I answered: "In the Kambun period [1661–73], the naturalized priest Shin'etsu stayed at Mito; he excelled in playing the lute. Onoda Tōsen continued his teachings. The shogun ordered the official musician Tsuji Buzen-no-kami together with Onoda Tōsen to work out Chinese lute versions of Japanese songs. When these versions were ready, they were played in the palace of the shogun."'⁸³ These attempts, however, seem to have had but scant success. The majority of Japanese lute players aimed at singing the lute melodies in as purely Chinese a way as possible. Some even especially went to Nagasaki, there to learn from the resident Chinese the real Chinese pronunciation.

With the Tempō period (1830–44),⁸⁴ it seems that the interest in the Chinese lute decreased, and that its music ceased to be a subject of social importance. Henceforward experts on the lute must be sought for in some isolated monasteries, and in some exclusive circles of retired scholars. With the Meiji Restoration in 1868 a crave for Western things flooded the country, and later, in 1894, the Sino-Japanese war further decreased the interest in the Chinese lute. In the beginning of this century the Chinese lute had become a curiosity in Japan, and only very few people still knew how to play it. A final blow was the Great Earthquake in 1923, when numerous lutes in private collections and curio shops were destroyed. It is only in recent years that Japanese musicologists again are taking an interest in this charming instrument, which for two centuries was so intimately connected with the cultural life of the later Tokugawa period.

---

⁷⁹ Thus the study of the Chinese lute stimulated, just as the Chinese reading of Buddhist texts introduced by the Obaku sect 黃檗宗 did, the study of the Chinese spoken language in Japan.

⁸⁰ See pp. 237–9.

⁸¹ See p. 237.

⁸² See p. 236.

⁸³ 又問,東川野廷賓,嘗被國歌於七絃恐失琴意,不示之人,子聞其說乎,曰,寬文中,歸化僧心越留錫水府,善鼓琴,廷賓傳心越彈法,德廟命伶宮辻豐前守與廷賓,謀被本邦之樂于七絃,曲成也,進奏於殿中.

⁸⁴ 天保

[Appendix 4] THE CHINESE LUTE IN JAPAN

* * *

The materials regarding the transmission of the Chinese lute in Japan have never been assembled. Japanese sources occasionally give short lists of well-known teachers and their pupils, but none of these can make any claim at completeness. For more than four years I have been trying to supplement these lists. Some facts I discovered in prefaces or colophons to Japanese books and manuscripts on the Chinese lute, some on tombstones of lute players, some in the works of Tokugawa sinologues, and some in inscriptions on Japanese-made Chinese lutes. Finally I collected some minor data during a stay at Nagasaki. I have tried to assemble these scattered materials, and at last succeeded in piecing together a historical table to the transmission of the study of the Chinese lute in Japan, which is presented here. It is still far from complete, but yet it contains more materials than any of the Japanese tables I know of. Each of the persons tabulated is briefly discussed, and their activities with regard to the study of the Chinese lute are given in outline. A perusal of this list may give the reader a fairly correct idea of how, and by whom, the Chinese lute was studied in Japan, and what its cultural significance was.

The most important sources were the following:

a A manuscript entitled *Kingaku denju ryakkei*,[85] 'An outline of the tradition of *kingaku*', written by the Japanese lute expert Shinraku Kansō,[86] and dated 1813. The text of this manuscript, which was appended to a Japanese manuscript-extract from the well-known Chinese *ch'in-pu*, *Ch'in-hsüeh-hsin-shêng*,[87] by Chuang Chên-fêng,[88] I have published in my article 'Chinese Literary Music and its Introduction into Japan'.[89]

b An essay by the Japanese sinologue Nakane Shuku,[90] entitled *Shichigenkin no denrai*.[91] This essay is to be found in his posthumously edited works, the *Kōtei ibun*.[92]

c A list entitled *Kinkyoku sōden keifu*,[93] to be found in the *Tōkō zenshū*.[94]

d Two manuscript albums, now in the collection of the Japanese scholar Nakayama Kyūshirō.[95] In these albums several members of a Japanese association of lute lovers that in the eighties

---

85 琴學傳授略系
86 See pp. 240–2.
87 琴學心聲
88 莊臻鳳, author's preface dated 1664.
89 Commemoration volume for Professor Mutō, Nagasaki 1937.
90 中根淑, lit. name Kōtei 香亭, 1839–1913.
91 七絃琴の傳來
92 香亭遺文, edited by Shimbo Iwaji 新保磐次, Tokyo 1916, pp. 442–56.
93 琴曲相傳系譜
94 東皐全集, II, leaf 61.
95 中山久四郎

gathered in a temple at Edo under guidance of the lute master Kodama Kūkū,⁹⁶ wrote down essays and poems on the lute, stray notes on the study of the lute, tunes in notation, etc. Each member wrote and attached his seals. Thus these two albums, though small and badly worm-eaten, contain valuable materials.

I have divided my list into two parts. The first I call *naiden*⁹⁷ ('inner tradition'); this is the line of Japanese lute players headed by the priest Shin'etsu. The second, which I call *geden*⁹⁸ ('outer tradition'), contains those Japanese lute players who learned the lute from Chinese laymen.

NAIDEN, THE INNER TRADITION

1 *Sugiura Kinsen*, named Masamoto,⁹⁹ a Confucianist scholar attached to the *bakufu*. He seems not to have published any literary works, and is chiefly known as an expert on the Chinese lute. He was first taught the lute by Hitomi Chikudō, then continued his studies under Shin'etsu himself. He carefully collected the various tunes taught by the master, and after ten years of study, published in the Hōei¹⁰⁰ period (1704–11) a handbook for the lute, called after the master *Tōkō kimpu*.¹⁰¹ The first preface to this book is written by the famous Director of the Tokugawa Academy (the Seidō),¹⁰² the sinologue Hayashi Hōkō (1644–1732);¹⁰³ further there is a preface by the Japanese lute player Hitomi Tōgen¹⁰⁴ and by the scholar Kō Gentai¹⁰⁵ (1649–1723). Kō Gentai was of Chinese descent, his grandfather being a Chinese from Fukien Province and interpreter at the Chinese office in Nagasaki; Gentai was known as an excellent calligrapher. The *Tōkō kimpu* gives a number of minor lute melodies in simple setting. As shall be seen below, this handbook was reprinted several times. I may mention here already, that the edition of 1827 is the easiest to obtain. This edition, in three volumes, contains about twenty tunes; all have the word added to the notation, and the Chinese pronuncia-

---

96 See p. 240.
97 內傳
98 外傳
99 杉浦琴川, 正職
100 寶永
101 東皐琴譜
102 聖堂 For details about this Academy, known as the *Shōheizaka gakumonjo* 昌平坂學問所, see my article 'Kakkaron, a Japanese echo of the Opium War', in: *Monumenta Serica*, IV (1939), no. 2.
103 林鳳岡
104 See p. 235 below.
105 高玄岱

Historical table of the tradition of the Chinese lute in Japan

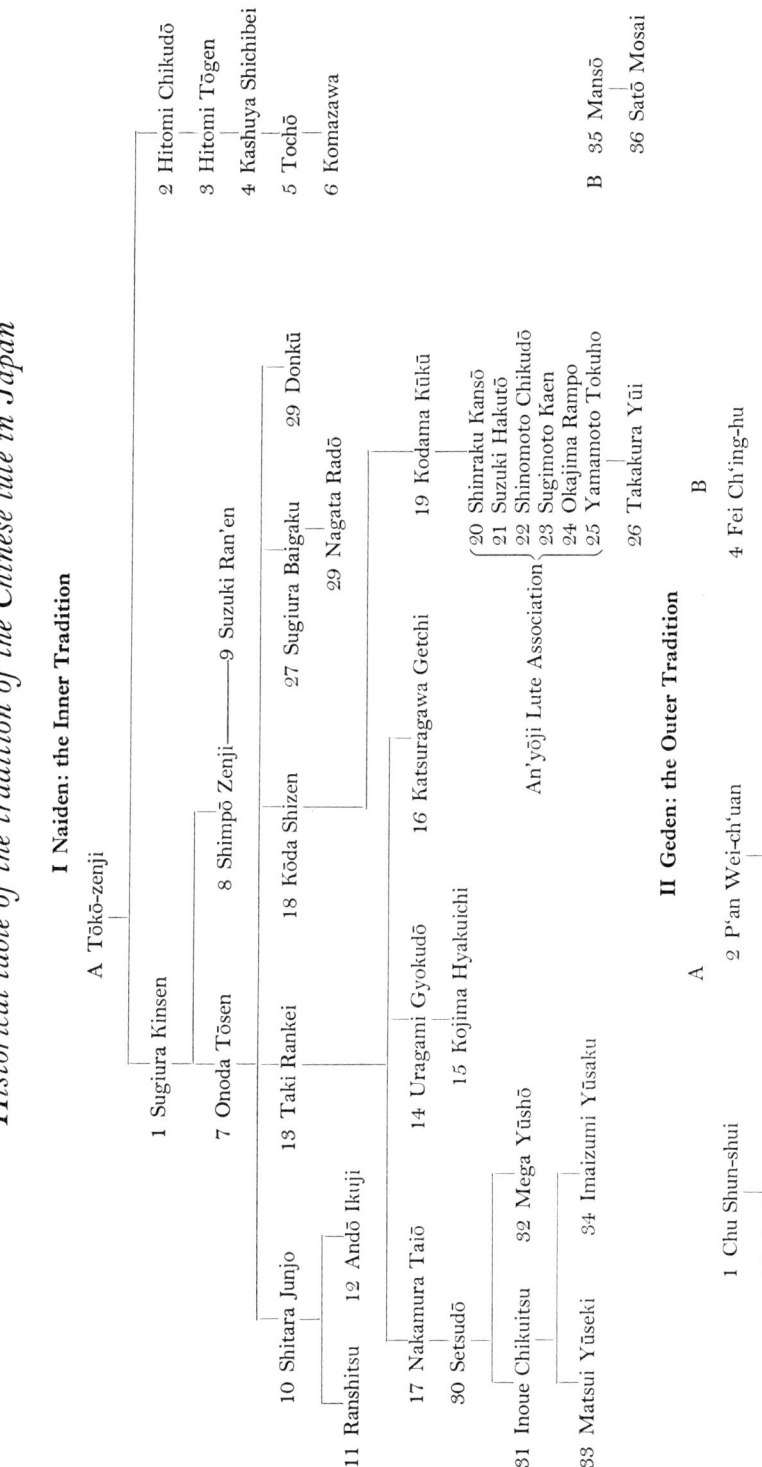

tion is indicated in the Japanese *katakana* syllabary. The famous calligrapher Nukina Kaioku[106] (1778–1863) added a preface, and the lute player Kojima Hyakuichi (see below no. 15) wrote a colophon. The latter says that this edition goes back directly to manuscripts collected by Shin'etsu's pupils.

2 *Hitomi Chikudō*,[107] 1628–96; named Setsu,[108] styled Gikei;[109] other name: Yūgen;[110] lit. names Chikudō and Kakuzan.[111] Originally he was a doctor of Chinese medicine. Afterwards he concentrated upon Chinese literary studies, and was appointed a *jukan*,[112] Confucianist scholar in the service of the shogunate. As such he was ordered by the shogun to assist Hayashi Shunsai[113] (also known as Gahō,[114] 1618–80), head of the Seidō (see above), in compiling the *Zoku honchō tsūgan*,[115] a historical work.

Chikudō is considered the greatest of Shin'etsu's lute disciples. He must have started the study of the lute very soon after Shin'etsu's arrival in Eastern Japan, for in 1685 his relations with the master were so intimate, that Shin'etsu presented him with a Ming lute. On this occasion Chikudō wrote the following note: 'Tōkō Zenji presented me with an antique lute, saying: "I wished to wait till I would meet someone with a true understanding of music, and then [give him this lute and] at the same time transmit its Way. Now, having met a man of elegant tastes, I feel I must give him this lute." I was deeply moved by these kind words and felt it was more than I deserved. Now this lute has inside the upper hole an inscription of some tens of characters, saying that it was made in the year 1564, that is, 121 years hence. That this object has lived through such a tumultuous period in Chinese history, and, escaping the vicissitudes of war, landed in this country, means that a propitious fate watched over it. I wished to engrave an elegant name on its bottom board, and asked the master for one. He named this lute *Yün-ho-t'ien-lai*, and below I engraved a seal reading *Hêng-hua*.[116] This lute I regard as a treasure of

---

106 貫名海屋
107 人見竹洞
108 節
109 宜卿
110 友元
111 鶴山
112 儒官

113 林春齋
114 鵞峰
115 續本朝通鑑
116 *Hêng-hua* 'Flower of the Hêng-fief'; apparently this lute was made by the Prince of Hêng, famous as a lute builder. See p. 215 above.

my house.'[117] In Chikudō's family the lute tradition was continued, his first pupil being his son, Hitomi Tōgen.

3 *Hitomi Tōgen*,[118] named Gin,[119] style Ronan.[120] He was taught the lute by his father, and inherited from him Shin'etsu's lute *So-ō*, and instruments for building lutes. He also was a Chinese scholar, but little is known about his writings.

4 *Kashuya Shichibei*,[121] studied the lute under Hitomi Chikudō. Little is known about him, except that he was a merchant of Edo, a dealer in antiques, with a great interest in music. Some sources say that he also studied the lute under Onoda Tōsen (see below, no. 7).

5 *Tochō*,[122] styled Chōkō,[123] also Shishuku;[124] lit. names Shōka Dōjin,[125] Goteki Sannin,[126] and Katei Dōjin.[127] Well-known painter, poet and engraver of seals. During the Temmei period[128] (1781–9) he published a book with imprints of seals carved by him. He was a great lover of the Chinese lute, having been taught by Kashuya, and also by Kodama Kūkū (see below, no. 19). There is preserved an interesting manuscript by his hand, an essay written in Japanese and entitled *Kinden setsu*;[129] its date is 1782.[130] Here he first gives an outline of *ch'in* ideology, and then goes on to discuss the transmission of the lute in Japan. He says that during a stay at Nagasaki, he was taught the Chinese way of reading poetry by a Chinese there, Kung Yün-jang,[131] lit. name Hsüan-chai.[132] Thus he could accompany his playing on the lute with singing the Chinese poems. It is of interest to note that he explains his lit. name *Goteki*,[133] 'The Five Inclinations', as referring to his love for the lute, poetry, calligraphy, painting, and cutting seals.[134]

6 A certain *Komazawa*.[135] Of him we know only that he was a

---

117 東皋禪師賜僕以一古琴, 諭曰, 欲待知音者並傳其道, 今欣遇雅尚, 不得不己爲贈, 僕深感懇篤之言, 且自愧之, 其爲琴也, 龍池之中有數十字之題者, 所謂嘉靖甲子製, 及今百二十一年也, 經中朝亂離之際能免兵燹而到此, 可謂物之幸也, 僕謂題佳名於琴腹, 而請之師, 即題曰雲和天籟, 而其下以衡華二字爲印, 以爲家寶.
118 人見桃源
119 沂
120 魯南
121 甲州屋七兵衞
122 杜澂
123 澂公
124 師叔
125 松窠道人
126 五適散人
127 華亭道人
128 天明
129 琴傳說
130 This essay was published by the contemporary scholar Mimura Seisaburō 三村清三郎 in the Japanese monthly *Shoen* 書苑, vol. II, no. 1 (1938), under the title '*Goteki Sensei kinden setsu*' 五適先生琴傳說.
131 龔允讓
132 遜齋
133 五適
134 琴詩書畫印
135 駒澤某

man from Susaka in Shinshu,[136] and that he studied the lute under Chikudō. Yet he must have played some role among players on the Chinese lute, for several sources mention his name.

7 *Onoda Tōsen*,[137] 1684–1763. Named Empō[138] (other sources give Teihin),[139] also Kunimitsu;[140] lit. name Tōsen. Chiefly famous as an expert on the Chinese lute. He studied the lute under Sugiura Kinsen, of whose family he was a hereditary follower. He is said to have had hundreds of pupils, who under his guidance made a study of the Chinese lute. Once the Tokugawa shogun Yoshimune[141] (1684–1751) summoned him to his court, and made him play for him the Chinese lute.

8 *Shimpō Zenji*,[142] no details known.

9 *Suzuki Ran'en*,[143] 1741–90; named Ryū;[144] style, Shiun.[145] Originally a doctor of Chinese medicine, a disciple of the famous doctor Asai Tonan[146] (1706–82). He was an eager student of Chinese literature, and made a special study of Chinese music. In 1816 there appeared at Osaka a book by him on musical theory, entitled *Ritsuryo bensetsu*.[147] He studied the Chinese lute under Shimpō Zenji (above, no. 8), and published in 1772 a small edition of the *Tōkō kimpu* in one volume. An advertisement on the last page of this book says that another study by him on the Chinese lute, entitled *Kingaku keimō*,[148] was also going to be published. I have, however, never come across printed editions of this book; but I obtained a finely calligraphed manuscript copy. Ran'en himself also built lutes. The *Kinzan kinroku* (see below, *geden*, no. 3) on leaf 8 mentions a lute called *Hsüan-hsiang*,[149] built by Ran'en after the model of the T'ang lute preserved in the Hōryūji. The inscription in the upper hole runs: 'Copy of a lute of the K'ai-yüan period [713–41], preserved in the Hōryūji in Yamato. Made by Minamoto (the original name of Ran'en) Ryū from Kyōto in the autumn of the year 1784.'[150]

136 須坂, 信州
137 小野田東川
138 延寶
139 廷賓
140 國光
141 吉宗
142 新豐禪師
143 鈴木蘭園
144 龍
145 子雲
146 淺井圖南
147 律呂辨說
148 琴學啓蒙
149 玄響
150 大和國法隆寺所藏開元琴之製天明四年甲辰之秋平安源龍造之

10 *Shitara Junjo*,[151] a man from Edo. With the four lute players described hereafter (nos. 13, 18, 27 and 29), he belonged to the most famous lute disciples of Onoda Tōsen. Unfortunately I could find no further details about him.

11 *Ranshitsu*,[152] the best-known lute pupil of Shitara Junjo. He was abbot of the Shinryūji,[153] a temple in Asakusa,[154] at Edo. In his later years he fell ill, and became blind; but this did not prevent him from continuing to teach the lute. This he only stopped when his end drew near and he lost the power of speech.

12 *Andō Ikuji*,[155] of whom nothing is known, except that Shitara Junjo considered him one of his best pupils.

13 *Taki Rankei*,[156] 1732–1801, named Motonori,[157] also Yasumoto,[158] styled Chūmei;[159] lit. name Rankei, also Eijuin.[160] Famous doctor of Chinese medicine, attached to the shogunate. Well known as a student of Chinese literature, and especially well read in old Chinese books on medicine. He studied the lute under Onoda Tōsen, and himself had many pupils who became well known as experts on the Chinese lute.

14 *Uragami Gyokudō*,[161] 1745–1820, style Kumpo,[162] lit. names Gyokudō and Bokusai.[163] A famous painter in the Chinese style from Kyoto. He was an enthusiastic performer on the Chinese lute, and was taught by a direct disciple of Taki Rankei. He published a handbook for the lute, entitled *Gyokudō zōsho kimpu*,[164] in one vol., published at Kyoto in 1791. This contains fifteen tunes, with the Japanese text of the melodies written out in *manyōgana*,[165] a more elaborae style of the Japanese syllabary *hiragana*. From these tunes it appears that Gyokudō made conscious efforts to give the Chinese lute a more Japanese character, for all of the tunes are purely Japanese; I cite titles such as *Aoyagi*,[166] *Sakurabito*,[167] *Ise-no-umi*,[168] *Umegae*,[169] etc. Some of these tunes are meant to be played by a duo of the Chinese lute and the Japanese *koto*.[170] After the prefaces this

151 設樂純如
152 蘭室
153 眞龍寺
154 淺草
155 安藤幾次
156 多紀藍溪
157 元德
158 安元
159 仲明
160 永壽院

161 浦上玉堂
162 君輔
163 穆齋
164 玉堂藏書琴譜
165 萬葉假名
166 青柳
167 櫻人
168 伊勢海
169 梅枝
170 與箏合奏

book gives some stray notes on the history of the Chinese lute in Japan; they are in dialogue form, and bear the title *Tōmon hassoku*.[171] On leaf 7 of this section Gyokudō explains why he tried to adapt the Chinese lute to Japanese music. He says: 'Master Rankei [see no. 13 above] studied the lute under Teihin [i.e. Onoda Tōsen, no. 7]. Visiting Edo on an official mission, I met Master Rankei and asked him to teach me the lute. Later, however, I thought to myself: the words of the tunes taught by him are all pronounced in the Chinese way, so that people who hear these songs cannot understand them. Not understanding them they are not influenced by them. Not influencing the hearers, this music cannot be used for teaching them.'[172] From an introductory note to this book, *Gyokudō kinki*,[173] it appears that the author obtained an old Chinese lute that was made by the Ming scholar Ku T'ien-su[174] in the Kambun[175] period (1661–73); this lute was brought to Nagasaki, where it came into the hands of the Chinese interpreter Liu I-hsien.[176] When Uragami finally obtained this instrument, which was called *Reiwa*[177] and further bore the seal Gyokudō-seiun,[178] he called his study after this lute, i.e. Gyokudō. Gyokudō was buried in the Honnōji[179] at Kyoto. When this temple burned down, his grave was replaced by a simple stone monument that is still to be seen today. On the two pillars the characters *reiwa* are engraved. Further, there still exists a stone tablet, erected in his honour on the place where he used to live, now the grounds of the Hōrinji,[180] in the outskirts of Kyoto. I visited this place in 1937, and made a rubbing of this inscription, written out by the famous Japanese scholar Rai San'yō (1780–1832).[181] The contemporary painter Hashimoto Kansetsu[182] published in 1924 a magnificent volume with reproductions of Gyokudō's paintings, entitled *Gyokudō kinshi iboku shū*.[183] It opens with a painting by Gyokudō's son, which represents the master with his beloved lute on his knees. To this book there is added a treatise called *Uragami Gyokudō*

---

171 答問八則
172 藍溪先生者，學琴於廷賓，余往祇役東都時見先生，請彈法，退而竊謂，其歌曲華音，而人聞之不解，不解則不感，不感則不足爲教.
173 玉堂琴記
174 顧天宿, style: Yüan-chao 元昭.
175 寬文
176 劉益賢
177 靈和
178 玉堂清韵
179 本能寺
180 法輪寺
181 賴山陽
182 橋本關雪
183 玉堂琴士遺墨集

jikō,¹⁸⁴ where one will find full details about his life and his lute.

Cf. also the publication *Uragami Gyokudō*, by Yano Kyōson,¹⁸⁵ one vol., Tokyo 1926. Among the illustrations there occurs a photograph of a lute made by Gyokudō himself in 1786, in imitation of a Chinese lute of the T'ang dynasty made by a member of the Lei¹⁸⁶ family, famous as lute builders. The brocade cover of this lute bears a lengthy inscription written by the well-known Japanese painter and sinologue Tomioka Tessai (1836-1924).¹⁸⁷

15 *Kojima Hyakuichi*,¹⁸⁸ 1778-1835; named Ki;¹⁸⁹ lit. names, Hōrin¹⁹⁰ and Teiseki.¹⁹¹ He is the best known of Uragami Gyokudō's pupils of the Chinese lute. He is described as a man of elegant tastes, learned in Chinese literature and a great calligrapher. His colophon to the *Tōkō kimpu*¹⁹² is written in excellent *li-shu*, the so-called chancery script.

16 *Katsuragawa Getchi*,¹⁹³ 1751-1809; named Hoshū.¹⁹⁴ A doctor of Chinese medicine, physician to the shogunate. Getchi was a *rangakusha*,¹⁹⁵ a student of Dutch learning, and one of the great pioneers of the introduction of Western medical science into Japan. As a lute player he belonged to the school of the other famous doctor, Taki Rankei.

17 *Nakamura Taiō*,¹⁹⁶ named Teiko,¹⁹⁷ style Shiken.¹⁹⁸ He also belonged to the lute school of Taki Rankei, and seemed to have enjoyed considerable fame as a lute expert. Unfortunately little is known about him.

18 *Kōda Shisen*,¹⁹⁹ died 1758; named Chikamitsu.²⁰⁰ A famous mathematician in the service of the shogunate. He studied mathematics under the famous Nakane Hakuzan²⁰¹ (1662-1733), and was an excellent performer both on the Chinese lute, which he learned from Onoda Tōsen, and on the Japanese *koto*. He is said to have published a book on the Chinese lute in 8 chapters, containing 48 tunes; this, however, I have never been able to discover. In his family there were preserved all

---

184 浦上玉堂事考
185 矢野橋村
186 雷
187 富岡鐵齋
188 兒島百一
189 祺
190 鳳林
191 貞石
192 See p. 232 above.
193 桂川月池
194 甫周
195 蘭學者
196 中村太翁
197 貞固
198 子軒
199 幸田子泉
200 親盈
201 中根白山

the instruments for building lutes and for making the silk lute strings, copied after originals that had belonged to Shin'etsu.

19 *Kodama Kūkū*,[202] 1734–1811; named Shin,[203] style Mokuho.[204] (Not to be confused with the Chinese scholar Kodama Kizan,[205] who was also called Shin, but whose dates are 1801–35). A scholar known for his refined tastes, he published many books between 1750–70. He studied the Chinese lute under Kōda Shisen. He lived in Ushigome-ku,[206] a quarter in Edo. There he organized in a temple called An'yōji,[207] in Teramachi,[208] regular meetings of Japanese lovers of the lute. These meetings were attended by a great number of people, over a hundred in all. Most famous among these was Shinraku Kansō (see below, no. 20), who drew up a document regulating these meetings. Later Kūkū changed his family name from Kodama to Shukutani.[209] Kūkū also diligently studied Chinese *ch'in-pu*. I possess a manuscript, copied after the original manuscript by Kodama, which contains extracts from the *Ch'in-ching*,[210] by Chang Ta-ming.[211] In Kodama's preface he says that he compiled this manuscript because he found many discrepancies in the explanations of the finger technique in various Chinese *ch'in-pu*.

20 *Shinraku Kansō*,[212] called Tei,[213] style Shiko,[214] lit. name Aikendō.[215] Originally he was a samurai in the service of the *bakufu*, but later turned to literary and musical studies. He learned the lute from Kodama Kūkū, and seems to have been one of the prominent persons in the lute meetings at the An'yōji. It was he who drew up the rules for these meetings. This document is reproduced in the *Shichigenkin no denrai* by Nakane Kōtei (see p. 231); I translate it below, as it gives a good impression of the atmosphere surrounding the Chinese lute in Japan.

'In former days Ssû-ma Kuang[216] [the great Sung scholar, 1019–86] and his friends organized the *Chên-shuo-hui*,[217]

---

202 兒玉空空
203 愼
204 默甫
205 兒玉旗山
206 牛籠區; nowadays written 牛込.
207 安養寺
208 寺町
209 宿谷
210 See p. 179, n. 41.
211 *Ibid.*, n. 42.

212 新樂閒叟
213 定
114 士固
215 愛閑堂
216 司馬光

217 *Chên-shuo-hui*, originally the name of an official banquet during the Eastern Chin period. Ssû-ma Kuang thus referred to his literary gatherings, where elegant taste was preferred to lavish entertainment.

"True Simplicity Gathering": those attending were served only a couple of times coarse rice and unstrained wine. From this may be gathered the mental attitude of the former sages: although they were honoured and wealthy, they were frugal and restrained themselves; they did not indulge in common habits and prodigality. Now we have concluded a pact among ourselves, following this example. We are poor, and we cannot afford luxury, and by nature we are averse to affectation and pomposity. So by necessity we conform ourselves to the spirit of true simplicity. Accordingly we have drawn up the following articles:

A *Members*: These are the regular members of our community. But also casual members are welcome, provided they are not vulgar. However, those who presume upon their dignity and boast of their wealth and those without learning shall not be admitted.

B *Time*: Every month there shall be one or two meetings, but only on holidays. Wind or rain shall make no difference. We shall gather between 9 and 11 in the forenoon, and separate between 5 and 7 in the afternoon; the meetings shall not be protracted into the night. Those who are late or fail to attend shall not be punished.

C *Place*: The An'yō temple in Ushigome. If necessary this place may be changed, but only for a Buddhist temple or a country retreat, far from the noise of the multitude.

D *Implements*: Tea and cakes, two lutes and two lute tables. If on a certain day there is present someone with much money, wine, fruit and some light dishes shall be allowed in addition.

E *Business*: Besides playing the lute: compose poetry and read books, write characters or paint, sing songs or play on other stringed instruments and flutes, according to each member's individual taste. But when many people meet, the conversation is liable to become noisy. When the talk is about the Chinese Classics, or when literary compositions are discussed, this of course is always elegant. Also it will be allowed to talk about abstruse things, and to criticize vulgar customs. However, talk about official matters and on commercial affairs, shall be strictly prohibited.

When this pact had been drawn up, I reported it to the master, and the master approved of it. But we consisted only of guests, and there was no host; thus, although we aspire at great simplicity, yet there must be someone who sees to the tea and cakes. A member said: "What about each time two members serving in turn?" The master said this was all right. Then I drew up the following list[218] of members regularly attending our meetings.

Drawn up by Shinraku Tei, in 1789.'[219]

This pact is evidently made after the model of Chinese 'Covenants for the Spiritual Community of the Lute' (see p. 69).

The meetings in the An'yōji lasted for about twenty years. About 1825 most of its members had died or were dispersed, and only a few remained.[220]

It was also Shinraku Kansō who, in 1813, wrote the *Kingaku denju ryakkei*, mentioned on p. 231).

He traveled about widely in Japan in search for old lutes, and he saw the relics of Shin'etsu in the Gion temple at Mito. In 1797 he visited the old Chinese school, the Ashikaga Gakkō,[221] and there copied out a manuscript on the lute by Hitomi Chikudō. Later he traveled to Hokkaidō, the extreme north of Japan. At Hakodate he obtained an old beam from a government building; from this he made the upper board of a lute. Then, at Matsumae,[222] he obtained a beam of wood called in the Matsumae dialect *ramani*,[223] said to mean *onkoto*,[224] 'honourable lute'. Using this wood for the

---

[218] Nakane Kōtei, when he copied out this pact, unfortunately left out the list, which must have contained valuable materials for our knowledge of the Japanese lute players of that time.

[219] 琴會約
昔日司馬溫公輩爲眞率會, 脫粟飯濁酒數行而己, 可見先賢用心, 雖在貴富節儉自守, 不趨習俗奢侈也, 今同社相約, 倣而行之, 蓋我輩貧而不能豐盛, 又性質不能矯飾也, 然則出于不得己而暗合眞率意者也, 仍設條例如左.
一會之人, 同社人也, 若不速客不甚俗者弗妨, 但挾貴誇富不解字等人俱不許.
一會之期, 一月一擧或二擧, 惟以暇日, 風雨不更期, 己集酉散, 不卜其夜, 失期者不到者並不罰.
一會之地, 牛門外安養精舍也, 若有故則換之必以佛院若別業, 蓋避人家雜沓也.
一會之具, 一茶一菓, 琴二張几二坐, 若當日頗有力者別供酒核點心等不復妨.
一會之事, 彈琴之餘, 賦詩誦書, 作字描畫, 或唱詞曲弄絲竹, 從各所好, 但衆人相會, 語言易譁, 或談經史論文章, 固自佳, 說鬼毀俗, 又無不可, 特不許說雲路談市井耳.
約成以告先生, 先生曰善, 而帷有賓無主, 雖眞率誰能辨茶菓, 同者曰, 每會二人輪次以執其事, 可乎, 先生曰善, 於是擧常會者名. 別列左.
　　　己酉花期　　　新樂定誌

[220] See the charming essay by Sugimoto Kaen, translated below on pp. 243-4.

[221] 足利學校
[222] 松前
[223] 蘭馬尼
[224] 御琴

bottom board, he built a lute, which he took with him to the island Etoro.²²⁵ That was in 1807, just when the Russian commander Khvostov made raids on Sakhalin, Naiho and Shana;²²⁶ in the general confusion this lute got lost. In 1811, however, Shinraku again found it in the house of a Japanese gentleman in West Japan; a Japanese ship that was in the north during the Russian raids had brought the instrument back! On this occasion Shinraku wrote an enthusiastic note, stressing that the instrument of the Holy Sages is protected by Heaven against barbarian invasions and the vicissitudes of the ocean.²²⁷

21 *Suzuki Hakutō*,²²⁸ another prominent member of the lute association of the An'yō temple.

22 *Shinomoto Chikudō*,²²⁹ also a pupil of Kodama Kūkū. His name was Ren,²³⁰ his style Shion.²³¹ He was known as a sinologue, and flourished in the beginning of the Meiwa period²³² (1764–72). Shinomoto was no mean Chinese stylist: Prof. Nakayama's manuscript album²³³ contains an essay by him, entitled *Hanshu yayūki*,²³⁴ which is written in excellent Chinese.

23 *Sugimoto Kaen*,²³⁵ named Chūon,²³⁶ style Ryōzai,²³⁷ a physician attached to the shogunate. He was a prominent figure in the lute association of the An'yōji. In 1828 he wrote a preface to a manuscript lute handbook compiled by Yamamoto Tokuho. There he refers to the meetings in the An'yōji, which by then had well nigh come to naught. As this preface gives a good insight into the spirit in which those meetings of lute lovers were held, I translate it below.

'In my younger years I studied the lute under Kodama Kūkū and the priest Ranshitsu.²³⁸ Among the pupils of Kodama there

---

225 擇捉島

226 See Sakamaki, 'Japan and the United States, 1790–1853', in: *Transactions of the Asiatic Society of Japan*, XVII (1939), page 178.

227 In 1949 I purchased in Tokyo a Japanese manuscript entitled *Kanso kinwa* 間叟琴話, which gives detailed information on the study of the Chinese lute in Japan in the later part of the Tokugawa period. In my Chinese publication *Tung-kao-chan-shih-chi-k'an* (東皋禪師集刊, The Commercial Press, Ltd., Chungking 1944, page 119) I gave a more elaborate version of the 'Historical Table of the Tradition of the Chinese Lute in Japan' above, (facing page 212);

when I have had time to work out the data contained in the *Kanso kinwa* I hope to publish a new historical table, incorporating this additional material.

228 鈴木白藤
229 篠本竹堂
230 廉
231 子溫
232 明和
233 See above, pp. 231–2.
234 泛舟夜遊記
235 杉本枓園
236 忠溫
237 良齋
238 See no. 11 above.

were Shinomoto Chikudō,[239] Shinraku Kansō,[240] Okajima Rampo,[241] and Yamamoto Tokuho,[242] all members of our lute association. But Tokuho since his youth was most keen, and excelled all others in playing the lute. Tokuho is named Rin, his literary name is Kakoku; he is a man from Ushigome, in Musashi [i.e. Edo].

Now I am a physician, I have to run hither and thither, and I cannot follow my inclinations. Tokuho however has clearly written out the transmitted lute tunes, and having made them into a handbook, asked me to add a few words by way of a preface.

The lute stands for the music bequeathed by high antiquity. One must have hills and mountains in one's breast, and one's belly must be full of ink [i.e. one must be a cultured literatus], before one may touch the lute. For its elegant tones cannot enter the ears of a vulgar person. Now Tokuho's work is violent, his occupation is vulgar in the extreme, he being a so-called unmounted police officer.[243] In the presence of others his conversation is tasteless, and his features are unattractive. But when Tokuho has one moment of spare time, he reads books and plays the lute, happily giving himself over to this music. He would not exchange his lot for that of the greatest men in the realm. How could it be otherwise? His refined disposition and his aloofness from earthly things can be judged hereby.

Now I for one am old and stupid; thirty years I have toiled in official life. Going back in my thoughts to past times, I realize that the trees on the graves of Kūkū and Ranshitsu have grown, while all the members of our lute association, one after the other, have passed away. Only I and Tokuho are still hale and hearty. Alas, human life is transitory, like a dream or like an illusion. Union and separation follow no fixed rules, sadness and mirth alternate with each other. Therefore I am glad that I and Tokuho are still in full health. This by way of a preface. Written by Sugimoto Ryō, called Chūon, in the autumn of 1828.'[244]

239 See no. 22.
240 See no. 20.
241 See no. 24.
242 See no. 25.
243 徒監察 *kachi-yoriki*. The *yoriki* were police officers in the service of the *bakufu*. Constantly mixed up in brawls of unruly samurai, and implacable persecutors of all partisans of the opposition to the Tokugawa government, they formed a much feared but greatly despised class.

244 余少時學琴兒玉空空及釋蘭室，其從空空學也，篠本竹堂，新樂閑叟，岡島蘭甫，山本德甫，皆同社，而德甫少年銳往最善鼓云，德甫*

24 *Okajima Rampo*,²⁴⁵ another prominent member of the An'yōji lute association.
25 *Yamamoto Tokuho*,²⁴⁶ one of the leaders of the An'yōji gatherings. The character of this police officer with elegant tastes has already been described. The manuscript albums of Prof. Nakayama give many examples of his literary activities. I quote one of his poems:

ALONE ON A DAY IN WINTER

'My humble door is securely fastened, seldom visitors come near it. I tend the dwarf plum tree that keeps me company in the twilight; the wind shakes its fragrant petals, and scatters them over the stone table.

And I see with astonishment that the blossoms form brilliant studs on my lute.'²⁴⁷

26 *Takakura Yūi*,²⁴⁸ a pupil of Yamamoto Tokuho, who collected the tunes taught by him.
27 *Sugiura Baigaku*,²⁴⁹ 1734–92; named Kai,²⁵⁰ style Shiyō;²⁵¹ lit. names Baigaku and Gengai.²⁵² A man of scholarly interests from West Japan. Having come to Edo, he learnt the lute from Onoda Tōsen.²⁵³ After he returned to West Japan, he there continued the tradition of the lute.
28 *Nagata Radō*,²⁵⁴ named Ikei,²⁵⁵ style Shiran.²⁵⁶ Originally a merchant, he later devoted himself entirely to the study of the Chinese lute. He traveled extensively in Japan, everywhere searching for old lutes, and teaching the art of playing it to a great number of scholars and noblemen. He started his studies of the lute under Sugiura Baigaku, and continued them until his death, at the venerable age of 70.

名鄰，號蝸殼，武州牛門人也，既而余爲刀圭，東西奔走，不能遂其好也，一日德甫，淨寫所傳琴曲，以爲譜，乞余言，夫琴者太古遺音也，其人胷有丘嶽，腹貯墨汁，然後始可彈，何者，雅音不入俗耳也，德甫之職劇矣，其爲務也俗極矣，所謂徒監察者也，在他人，言語無味，面目可憎，而德甫乃得片時半日之閑，讀書彈琴，陶陶乎樂，即南面百城，不能以代焉，此豈無得而然爲哉，其胸襟之洒落不汙塵土，亦以是可知耳，余也暮鈍，勞々宦海三十年矣，追思往事空空蘭室墓木己拱，同社諸子亦相繼而下世矣，獨余與德甫安健耳，嗚呼，人生茫々，如夢如幻，聚散無常，悲觀頓異，而喜余之與德甫無恙也，於是乎言。
文政戊子仲秋杉本良忠溫撰

245 岡島蘭甫
246 山本德甫
247 冬日獨坐
柴門深鎖展踪稀，培養盆梅伴落暉，
風散香葩零石案，詡看琴面點清徽。
248 髙倉雄偉
249 杉浦梅岳
250 恢
251 士容
252 元愷
253 See no. 7.
254 永田蘿堂
255 維馨
256 子蘭

29 *Donkū*,[257] abbot of the Shōrinji,[258] in Fukagawa,[259] at Edo. Another pupil of Onoda Tōsen.
30 *Setsudō*,[260] 1783-1852; named Chizan,[261] lit. name Chōkai.[262] Chief priest of the Gansenji,[263] a temple in Dewa,[264] north of Tokyo. He started his studies of the Chinese lute in Nagasaki, and afterwards was taught by Radō[265] and by Nakamura Taiō.[266] Round 1828 he settled down in Osaka, and assembled many pupils, teaching them the Chinese lute and calligraphy.
31 *Inoue Chikuitsu*,[267] 1814-86; called Genzō,[268] foremost pupil of Setsudō. He must have been a musician of importance, for he is mentioned in many sources. Unfortunately I could discover no further details about him.
32 *Mega Yūshō*,[269] 1826-96; lit. names Teizai[270] and San'yū-zōro.[271] A doctor of Chinese medicine, born at Osaka in a wealthy family, in which many old Chinese books and manuscripts had been preserved. He himself being a voracious reader, he greatly augmented this collection, which he left to the Sumiyoshi Shrine at Osaka (later this shrine presented the books to the Osaka Library). He studied the Chinese lute under Setsudō, and collected seven antique lutes. He is further known as a painter and poet.
33 *Matsui Yūseki*,[272] named Ren.[273] A distinguished lute player of Edo, pupil of Inoue Chikuitsu. He possessed a dress of a Ming official, and used to play the lute clad in this garb.
34 *Imaizumi Yūsaku*,[274] 1848-1931; lit. name Mugai.[275] The last great Japanese performer on the Chinese lute, a well-known scholar and connoisseur. In 1877 he went to France, and worked in Paris under the great art-historian Guimet, in the Museum for Far Eastern Arts. After a stay of six years, he returned to Japan, and was employed in the Ministry of Education at Tokyo. He occupied various posts in the Japanese museum world, e.g. Director of the Fine Arts Department of the Im-

257 曇空
258 象林寺
259 深川
260 雪堂, Real name: Tōzaka Bun'yō
261 痴山
262 鳥海
263 願專寺
264 出羽
265 See no. 28 above.
266 See no. 17 above.
267 井上竹逸
268 玄藏
269 妻鹿友樵
270 貞齋
271 三友草廬
272 松井友石
273 廉
274 今泉雄作
275 無礙

[*Appendix 4*] THE CHINESE LUTE IN JAPAN 247

perial Museum at Tokyo, thereafter Director of the Ookura Museum (Ookura-shūko-kan).²⁷⁶ He learned the lute from Inoue Chikuitsu, and eagerly collected materials for the history of the Chinese lute in Japan. I have several manuscripts about the Chinese lute by him in my collection, and most of the books and manuscripts in Prof. Nakayama's collection bear his seal.

35 *Mansō*,²⁷⁷ other name Chikuan,²⁷⁸ a Chinese priest who played the lute; no further details known.

36 *Satō Mosai*,²⁷⁹ named Itchō,²⁸⁰ a sinologue who learned the lute from the priest Mansō. No source gives his name, but there is preserved a book on the Chinese lute published by him, the *Kokin seigi*.²⁸¹ To this book Mansō added a preface, which is printed in facsimile. This book gives a survey of the study of the lute, illustrated with finely executed pictures. The greater part of these pictures are copied after those in the *Yang-ch'un-t'ang-ch'in-pu*.²⁸²

GEDEN, THE OUTER TRADITION

1 *Chu Shun-shui*,²⁸³ Jap. Shu-shunsui, 1600–82; name Tzû-yü,²⁸⁴ style Lu-hsü,²⁸⁵ lit. name Shun-shui. Famous Chinese refugee at the Court of Mito; he died just before Shin'etsu arrived there.²⁸⁶ When he came to Japan, he brought some Chinese lutes with him. He himself apparently was not a lute player, but, as all Chinese scholars (and especially those of the Ming period), he had made a study of the lute, and knew how it was played. Chu Shun-shui gave one of his lutes, a Ming specimen made by the Prince of I,²⁸⁷ to his Japanese pupil Andō Seian²⁸⁸ (1620–

276 大倉集古館
277 萬宗
278 竺菴
279 佐藤茂齋
280 一張
281 古琴精義, in 2 vols., published in Kyoto.
282 See above, p. 121.
283 朱舜水
284 之瑜
285 魯嶼
286 For Chu Shun-shui, see E.W. Clement, 'Chinese Refugees of the Seventeenth Century in Mito', in: *Transactions of the Asiatic Society of Japan*, XXIII. His complete works, under the title of *Shu-shunsui sensei bunshū* 朱舜水先生文集 were published between 1711–15, at Edo, by the Mito clan. This beautiful block print, in 28 chs. and 1 appendix, now is scarce. Further, there has been preserved a manuscript in 10 chs., entitled *Min-shuchōkun-shū* 明朱徵君集, compiled on the command of the Lord of Kaga 加賀. 1912, Inaba Iwakichi 稻葉岩吉, on the basis of these two collections, published the *Shu-shunsui zenshū* 朱舜水全集 in one stout volume. This is the most complete collection of materials regarding this interesting personality. In 1913 the Chinese scholar T'ang Shou-ch'ien 湯壽潛 published a Chinese edition of Chu Shun-shui's works, under the title of *Shun-shui-i-shu* 舜水遺書; this book is based upon Inaba's edition.
287 I-wang 益王; see picture of this lute, fig. 33.
288 安東省庵, 1620–1701.

1701), and he also presented him with some Chinese handbooks. These materials were preserved in Andō's family, and later they were studied by Murai Kinzan (see below).

2 *P'an Wei-ch'uan*,[289] a Chinese scholar who passed through Nagasaki, and taught the lute to Murai Kinzan.

3 *Murai Kinzan*,[290] 1733–1815; named Shun,[291] style Tanen;[292] lit. names Rokusei Dōjin[293] and Seifuku Dōjin.[294] A doctor attached to the shogunate, notorious for his ugly face. He was a great Chinese scholar, and an eager book-collector. Author of numerous books on medical subjects. Full materials about his activities as a student of the Chinese lute are to be found in his book *Kinzan kinroku*,[295] in one vol., published in 1806 by the Kenkakuzam-bō.[296] This nicely edited book opens with an autograph preface by the well-known Japanese scholar of Korean descent, Rijun,[297] Japanese name Takamoto[298] (1738–1813). Then follows a section called *Kindenki*,[299] where the author relates how he studied the Chinese lute. He was not satisfied with the tradition established by Shin'etsu, whom, being a priest, Kinzan deemed unworthy to touch the lute. In 1785 in Nagasaki he met the Chinese scholar P'an Wei-ch'uan, and from him learned the lute. Therefore Kinzan considers himself the only Japanese who possesses the real Chinese lute tradition. Then the author goes on to relate in great detail the history of the six Chinese lutes in his collection; they were called *Hsü-wei*,[300] *Chiao-hsüeh*,[301] *Lan-ssû*,[302] *Hsüan-hsiang*,[303] *Ku-yen*[304] and *Hsiao-ssû*.[305] He says that later he continued his studies of the Chinese lute on the basis of the materials of Chu Shun-shui, preserved in the family of Andō Seian. In addition, the book contains a number of lute melodies in notation. It closes with a colophon by the author, and an autograph colophon by the doctor of Chinese medicine, Ooki Kojō[306] (1741–1811).

4 *Fei Ch'ing-hu*,[307] a Chinese at Nagasaki.

289 潘渭川
290 村井琴山
291 枕
292 大年
293 六清道人
294 清福道人
295 琴山琴錄
296 劍閣山房
297 李順
298 高本
299 琴傳記
300 續尾
201 蕉雪
302 蘭思
303 玄響
304 古雁
305 孝思
306 大城壺城
307 費晴湖

5 *Kikusha-ni*,[308] the Nun Kikusha, 1753–1826; lay name Tagami Michi.[309] Her husband having died young, she became a nun and devoted her whole life to writing poetry and practising the tea ceremony. She left a collection of Japanese and Chinese poetry, entitled *Taori-giku*,[310] to be found in the *Keishū haika zenshū*,[311] pub. in 1922 by Katsumine Shimpū.[312] This nun was famous as a musician, and played the Chinese lute. It is not clear where she first learned to play this instrument. But during a stay at Nagasaki, in 1796, she was taught by the Chinese Fei Ch'ing-hu, who also taught her how to read Chinese poetry in the Chinese way. The *Taori-giku* contains a poem presented to her by Fei Ch'ing-hu, together with a note in which Fei Ch'ing-hu praises her talents (*Keishū haika zenshū*, page 360).

308 菊舎(車)尼
309 田上ミチ
310 手折菊

311 閨秀俳家全集
312 勝峰晉風

INDEX

Aalst, J.A. van, 172, 173
Adṛçyā, 50
Ai, emperor, 39
Ak-hak-kwe-pôm, 103, 175
Alchemy and Other Chemical Achievements of the Ancient Orient, 47 n.
Amiot, J. J. M., 3, 16, 171
Analytic Dictionary of Chinese and Sino-Japanese, 11 n.
Anāthapiṇḍada, garden of, 52
Andō Ikuji, lute player, 237
Andō Seian, 247, 248
Annotated Bibliography of Selected Chinese Reference Works, An, 121 n.
An'yōji, 240-2
Arlington, L. C., 53 n.
Artificial finger nails, 119 n.
Asai Tonan, 236
Asaka Kaku, 222 n.
Asano Fuzan, 225 n.
Aṣṭasiddhi, eight magical powers, 50

Backhouse, E., 210 n.
Bakufu, 222, 232, 244 n.
Beal, S., 52 n.
Bibliographie coréenne, 174, 224 n.
Biggerstaff, K., 121 n.
Birds associated with the lute. *See* Crane, Geese, Pheasant, Phoenix
Biwa, Jap. four-stringed guitar, 201
Bland, J. O. P., 210 n.
Bodde, D., 11 n.
Boodberg, P., 16 n.
Buddha, 51, 63 n., 207
Buddhist lute players. *See* Donkū, I-hai, K'ung-ch'ên, Liang-yü, Mansō, Ranshitsu, Setsudō, Shimpō Zenji, Shin'etsu, Ying-shih
Buddhists excluded from playing the lute, in China: 44, 63, 64
    in Japan: 228

Charactères chinois, 13
Carter, T. F., 200 n.
Catalogue descriptif et analytique du musée instrumental du Conservatoire Royal de Bruxelles, 173
Catalogue of the Imperial Treasures in the Shōsōin, 200, 203 n., 205 n.
Cement for covering the body of a lute, 193
Chan-jan-chü-shih-wên-chih, 78 n.

Chan-t'an-ssû, temple in Peking, 53
Chang Ch'ao, Ch'ing scholar, 69
Chang Chi, famous physician of the Later Han period, 154
Chang Chih-ho (8th century), 142
Chang Ho, 19th-century lute master, 187, 210
Chang Hung-ching, 154
Chang I-ch'ang, 83
Chang Jung-hsiu, Ming scholar, 197
Chang K'ung-shan, Ch'ing musician, 99
Chang Liang, 95
Chang-ngo, Moon Goddess, 90
Chang Ta-ming, Ming musician, 121–2, 179, 240
Chang Ting-chi (1768–1848), 191
Chang Ting-yü, Ming scholar, 220 n.
Chang Tun-jên, Ch'ing mathematician, 186
Chang Yu, Sung scholar, 16
Chang Yu-ho, contemporary lute master, 21 n.
Ch'a Chên-hu, 83, 182
Ch'ang-ch'ing, lute melody, 96
Ch'ang-ti, ode of the *Shih-ching*, 7
Changes, Book of. See *Yih-ching*
Chao, empress, 204
Chao Hsi-ku, 195 n.
Chao Wên, ancient music master, 8 n.
Ch'ao Pi, T'ang scholar, 153
Chavannes, E., 143 n., 145 n.
Ch'ên Chi-ju (1558–1639), 224 n.
Ch'ên Chih (Yüan period), 157
Ch'ên Chung-chou, Ming scholar, 184
Ch'ên Fu-yao, Ch'ing scholar, 147
Ch'ên Hao-tzu, 147 n.
Ch'ên Têng-yüan, modern scholar, 184
Ch'ên Wu-ch'ang, Ming scholar, 179
Ch'ên Yang (11th century), 2 n., 15 n.
Chêng, odes of the *Shih-ching*, traditionally denoting lewd and vulgar music, 38–40, 80, 202
Chêng, Chinese cither, ix, 9, 217, 220, 224
Chêng-ho-shih, lute model, 191
Chêng Hung (Han period), 92 n.
Chêng-wên, part of lute notation, 125
Chêng Ying-sun, contemporary lute master, 130
Ch'êng Hsiung, 17th-century lute master, 96
Ch'êng-i-t'ang-ch'in-pu, 71
Ch'êng-lien, famous old lute master, 84
Ch'êng Yün-chi (18th century), 71, 82
Che-p'ai, 83
Chess playing, contrasted to playing the lute, 47–8
Ch'i, ancient state, 39 *and* n.
Ch'i-fu-jên, concubine of Han Kao-tsu, 8
Ch'i-yin-yün-chien, 52 n.

Chia-ku-wên-pien, 6
Chiang Chih-lan, Ch'ing scholar, 69
Chiang Hsing-t'ao, lay name of Shin'etsu, 225
Chiang K'uei, Sung scholar, 9
Chiao-an-ch'in-pu, 34 n.
Chiao-ch'uang-chiu-lu, 107
Chiao-ssû, sacrifice, 39 n.
Chiao-wei, part of a lute, also name of a lute, 101
Chiao-yeh-shih, lute model, 191
Ch'iao Chung-wu, 186
Ch'iao-jên, Fuel Gatherer, 91
Ch'iao-ko, lute melody, 92
Chia-yü, 8 n. See also *K'ung-tzŭ-chia-yü*
Chieh-tzŭ-yüan-hua-ch'uan, xix, 147 n.
Chien-chi, 151
Chien-tzŭ, 5, 29 n., 33, 34, 66, 117, 124–6, 128, 132, 139, 184, 187
Ch'ien, to inlay; special meaning in lute terminology, 213
Ch'ien-ch'üeh-chü-lei-shu, 68
Ch'ien-kung, 120 n.
Ch'ien-lung (1736–95), emperor, 3
Chih, agaric symbol of longevity, 21
Chih-fa, finger technique, 32, 117
Chih-shêng-shih-tien-li-yüeh-chi, xix
Chikashige, M., modern scholar, 47 n.
China Journal, 191 n.
China's First Unifier, 11 n.
China Under the Empress Dowager, 210 n.
'Chinese Refugees of the Seventeenth Century in Mito', 247 n.
Chinese Music, 172
Chin-hsing, lit. 'golden stars', poetical name for the thirteen studs of a lute, 59
Chin-ku-chi-kuan, 98 n.
Chin-p'ing-mei, 152
Chin-yü, lute association, 182
Ch'i-yen, 78 n.
Ch'ih-nei, inscriptions inside a lute, 197
Ch'in, ancient state, 39
  the cither of, 56
Ch'in-chia, 120 n.
Ch'in-ching, 62 n., 63 n., 64 n., 69, 121, 179, 194, 196, 240
Ch'in-ch'ing-ying, 30, 54
Ch'in-ch'ü-ko-tz'û, popular songs set to the lute, 44
Ch'in-ch'ü-pu-lu, 81 n.
Ch'in-fu, 55, 205
Ch'in-hsüeh-hsin-shêng, 231
Ch'in-hsüeh-ju-mên, 5, 187, 210
Ch'in-hsüeh-ts'ung-shu, 9 n., 18 n., 29 n., 34, 47 n., 94 n., 99, 139, 180, 200
Ch'in-huang, 107
Ch'in-juan-ch'i-mêng. See *Ch'in-yüan-ch'i-mêng*
Ch'in-pu, 30–5, 53, 62–6. See also Lute handbooks
Ch'in-pu-ho-pi-ta-ch'üan, 185

Ch'in-sê-ho-pu, by Ch'ing Jui, 9 n., 19, 32 n., 57 n.
Ch'in-sê-ho-pu, by Yang Tsung-chi, 9 n., 181
Ch'in-shê, spiritual community of lute lovers, 68–9
Ch'in-shêng-ching-wei, 15 n.
Ch'in-shêng-shih-liu-fa, 107–16
Ch'in-shih, by Chu Ch'ang-wên, 30 n., 55, 67 n., 177–8
   by Chou Ch'ing-yün, 35, 51 n., 182
Ch'in-shih, lute chamber, 67
Ch'in-shih-huang-ti, First Emperor (r. 246–210 B.C.), 11
Ch'in-shu, 80
Ch'in-shuo, 120 n.
Ch'in-shu-ts'un-mu, 34, 182
Ch'in-tan, lute altar, 50
Ch'in-tao, 35, 54
Ch'in-tsao, 6 n., 42, 54, 79 n., 81 n., 93, 98, 103, 177
Ch'in-tung, lute page, 64
Ch'in Wei-han, lute player of the 19th century, 34 n.
Ch'in-yo, 69
Ch'in-yü-man-lu, 18 n., 181
Ch'in-yüan-ch'i-mêng, 172, 214
Ching, emperor (r. 156–140 B.C.), 40, 56 n.
Ching, ancient music master, 155
Ch'ing-hui-tien-t'u, 13 n.
Ch'ing Jui, Ch'ing scholar, 9 n.
Ch'ing-lien-fang-ch'in-ya, xi n., 59 n., 68 n., 142, 145, 149, 153, 180, 202
Ch'ing-shang-yüeh, class of semi-Chinese music, 40 n.
Ch'ing-shih-lieh-chuan, 210 n.
Ch'iu Chih-lu, Ch'ing scholar, 9 n.
Ch'iu-hung, lute melody, 214
Cho-kêng-lu, 193
Chou Ch'ing-yün, contemporary scholar, 34, 182
Chou-hou-shên-ching, 214 n.
Chou-li, 6 n.
Chou Lu-fêng, lute master of the 18th century, 185–6, 212
Chou Yü-tu, Ming painter, 180
Chu Ch'ang-fang. *See* Lu-wang
Chu Ch'ang-wên (1041–1100), 55, 177–8, 182
Chu Ch'i-ch'ien, contemporary scholar, 194
Chu-chia-shêng, old musical term, 94 n.
Chu Ch'üan. *See* Ning-wang
Chu Fêng-chieh, lute master of the 19th century, 31 n., 192, 210. *See also* Chu Tung-chün
Chu Hou-hsiao. *See* Hêng-wang
Chu Hou-hsüan. *See* I-wang
Chu Hsi (1130–1200), 18, 85
Chu Hsiang-hsien (Liang period), 94 n.
Chu Shun-shui (1600–82), 215, 222 n., 225, 247, 248
Chu Tsai-yü, Ming prince, 171, 214. *See also* Tsai-yü
Chu T'ung-chün, 187
Ch'u-ming-kuang, lute melody, 160

INDEX

Chuang An-hsiang, lady lute expert of the Sung period, 158
Chuang Chên-fêng, Ming musician, 231
Chuang-tzû, the old philosopher and the work connected with his name, 8 n., 46, 47, 64, 91, 110 n., 114 n., 161 n.
Chuang-tzû-mêng-tieh, lute melody, 47
Ch'un-chu-chi-wên, 204
Ch'un-ch'iu, 8 n. See also *Lü-shih-ch'un-ch'iu*
Ch'un-ts'ao-t'ang-ch'in-pu, 98, 186
Chung-ch'i. See Chung Tzû-ch'i
Chung-ho-ch'in-shih, name of author's library, adopted when he obtained a lute bearing the name *Chung-ho*, made by the Ming prince of Lu, 213
Chung-ni-shih, lute model, 191
Chung-shan, mountain famous for jade, 205
Chung Tzû-ch'i, famous ancient connoisseur of music, 73, 97 *and* n., 98, 185, 205
Chung-yung, 84 n., 114 n.
Chü-shê-yo, 69 n.
Ch'ü Yüan (4th century B.C.), 95
Ch'ü-yüan-wên-tu, lute melody, 95
Chüan, ancient music master, 143–5
Chün-tzû, 26, 43
Clement, E. W., 225 n., 247 n.
Coda, 87
Coffin boards used for building lutes, 193
Confucius, 8, 38, 84, 91, 93–4
Courant, M., 22, 94 n., 95, 143 n., 174–5, 224 n.
Cow-hair cracks, 195, 196 n.
Cracked-ice bursts, 196, 202
Crane, associated with the lute, 52, 58, 77, 90, 105, 126, 141–7, 208

Dhāraṇī, 51
Donkū, Jap. lute player, 246
Doré, H., 152 n.
Dragon, associated with the lute, 81, 103, 104, 119, 128, 215
Dragon in China and Japan, The, 216
Dragon Pond, aperture in bottom board of lute, 80, 103, 193, 197, 199, 202, 211, 215, 216
Dragon's Gums, part of lute, 101

Eckardt, A., 175
Edo, 222 n., 225, 228, 232, 235, 238, 245, 246
Eight sorts of musical instruments (sounds), 72, 218
Êrh-hu, two-stringed violin, 1, 2, 95
Essai historique sur la musique classique des Chinois, 22, 174
Essays in Zen Buddhism, 134 n.

Fa-ch'ü, 53 n.
Fa-hsien, famous priest of the 4th to 5th century, 52 n.
Fan-i-ch'in-pu-chih-yen-chiu, 21 n., 139 n.
Fan Li, 62
Fan-li, introductory notes to Chinese books, 32

Fan-yin (fan-shêng), 'floating sounds' or harmonies, 60, 86, 130, 135, 137
Farmer, H. G., 193 n.
Fei Ch'ing-hu, 248
Fêng-chao. See Phoenix Pool
Fêng-huang, name of a lute, 204
Fêng-huang-hsiao, flute, 103
Fêng-su-t'ung-i, 6 n., 42, 70, 228 n.
Ferguson, J. C., 88 n., 191 n.
Forke, A., 47 n., 136 n.
Fox Strangeways, A. H., 133 n.
Franke O., 11 n.
Frozen condition of the mind, 45, 58 n., 111
Frühling und Herbst des Lü Bu-we, 24 n.
Fu-ch'in, cither, 9 n.
Fu Hsi, mythical emperor, 6 n., 42, 79, 80, 113, 212
Fujita Tōko, 227
Fujiwara Sadatoshi, 224 n.
Fu-ku-pien, 15
Fu-wên, part of lute notation, 125

Garuḍa, 207
Geese, associated with lute, 8, 93, 103
Gempei seisuiki, 221
Gems of Chinese Literature, Prose, 91 n.
Genji monogatari, 218, 220, 221
Genji monogatari no ongaku, 221 n.
Geschichte des Chinesischen Reiches, 11 n.
Giles, H., 91 n.
Giles, L., 205 n.
Gion, temple, 226, 242
Glimpse of Japanese Ideals, A, 200 n., 203 n.
Glissando, 51, 115
'*Goteki Sensei kinden setsu*', 235 n.
Granet, M., 38
Grosjean, J. F., 193 n.
Gushun kinki, 227
Gyokudō kinshi iboku shu, 238
Gyokudō zōsho kimpu, 230, 237
Gyoyūshō, 218

Hakurakuten to Nihon bungaku, 221 n.
Han Chiang, Ch'ing scholar, 53, 54
Han-shih-wai-ch'uan, 42 n., 50
Han-shu, 62 n., 103 n.
Han-shu-li-yüeh-chih, 39 and n. 37
Han-t'ang-pi-shih, 214 n.
Hashimoto Kansetsu, modern painter, 238
Harada, J., modern scholar, 200 n., 203, 205
Harp (*k'ung-hou*), 56
Harvard Journal of Asiatic Studies, 16 n., 206 n.

Hayagriva, the Mantrayanic Aspect of Horse-Cult in China and Japan, 52 n.
Hayashi Hōkō, 232
Hayashi Jussai, 179, 222 n.
Hayashi, K., modern musicologist, 40 n., 63 n.
Hayashi Shunsai, 233
Hei-ho ('Black Crane'), name of lute, 158
Hêng-hua, name of lute, 234
Hêng-wang, named Hou-hsiao, prince of Hêng (Ming period), 214–16, 234 n.
Hitomi Bōsai, 222 n.
Hitomi Chikudō, lute player, 226, 232, 234–5, 235, 236, 242
Hitomi Tōgen, lute player, 232, 235
Hōbōgirin, 51 n., 134 n.
Ho-chien Hsien-wang, Han prince, 40, 56
Ho Liang-chün (16th century), 59 n.
Ho-ling-lu, 142 n.
Honnōji, 238
Ho-pai, Indian priest-musician, 51
Hōrinji, 238
Ho-shih-yü-lin, 59 n.
Ho Yüan (11th century), 204
Hōryūji, 223, 236
Hou-han-shu, 92 n.
Hsi-ching-tsa-chi, 204 and n.
Hsi-hsiang-chi, 20 n.
Hsi K'ang (223–62), 55, 56, 157, 160, 205
Hsiang, prince (571–540 B.C.), 8
Hsiang, river, 92, 93, 97
Hsiang-ho-ching, 146
Hsiang-ling, lute melody, 81
Hsiang Yüan-pien (1525–90), 107, 190, 191
Hsiao, river, 92, 97
Hsiao-chuan, 11. *See also* Small-seal script
Hsiao-hsiang-shui-yün, lute melody, 97
Hsiao-kai, small regular script, 212
Hsiao-tzû, 33 n.
Hsieh-ch'in-shih-wên-ch'ao, 19
Hsieh Chuang (421–66), 104
Hsieh Fang-tê (1226–89), 19
Hsien-ch'ih, music attributed to Yao, 212
Hsien-jên-chien, part of lute, 101
Hsin-yüeh. *See* Shin'etsu
Hsiu-ch'ih-lu, 193, 195 n.
Hsiu-ling-yao-chih, 107
Hsiung P'êng-lai, Yüan scholar, 9 n.
Hsü Ch'ang-yü (Wu-shan-lao-jên), 83
Hsü Chên (Han period), 11–12
Hsü Ch'i, famous lute master of the Ch'ing period, 185
Hsü Ching, Ch'ing scholar, 12
Hsü Chün, Ch'ing scholar, 185
Hsü Hung, lute master of the Ming period, 107

R

Hsü-sou-shên-chi, 142
Hsü Yuan-po, 182
Hsüan, emperor (73–49 B.C.), 30 n., 56
Hsüan, ancient ocarina, xix, 100, 163
Hsüan-ho, 142–7
Hsüeh-ch'in-ch'ien-shuo, 21 n.
Hsün-tien, lute melody, 81
Hsün-tzû, old philosopher, 81 n., 84 n.
Hu-chia-shih-pa-p'o, lute melody, 94, 159
Hu Wên-huan, Ming scholar, 120 *and* n.
Hu-yüeh, Central-Asiatic music, 40
Hua-ching, 147 n.
Huai-nan-tzû, old philosopher, 24 n., 30, 42
Huai Ta-pu, son of Jui Lin, 210
Huan I (Chin period), 95
Huan T'an, Han scholar, 35, 54, 56
Huang Chên, Ch'ing scholar, 185
Huang Ch'êng, Ming scholar, 193–4
Huang Hsien (15th century), 172
Huang-hsien-ch'in-pu, 172
Huang-mên-ku-ch'ui-yüeh, class of palace music, 40
Huang-ti, mythical emperor, 80, 143, 144
Hui, emperor (r. 194–188 B.C.), 39
Hui, thirteen studs of a lute, 123
Hui-ch'in-shih-chi, 21 n.
Hui-tsung, emperor (1101–25), 47
Hyôn-kêm, Korean lute, 224

I-chiao-chin-li, lute melody, 95
I-ching. See Yih-ching
I-hai, priest-musician of the Sung period, 51
I-hsin, name of a lute, 102
I-lan, lute melody, 93
I-li (Book of Ceremonies), 9 n.
Imai Koshirō, 225
Imaizumi Yūsaku, 246
I Mountain, 70 n. 79, 212
Imperial Catalogue (Ssû-k'u-ch'üan-shu-tsung-mu), 107, 178, 179, 180, 214 n., 220 n.
Importance of Living, The, 106 n., 206
Inaba Iwakichi, modern scholar, 247 n.
I-nien-lu, 107 n.
Inoue Chikuitsu, lute player, 246
In Search of Old Peking, 53 n.
Invention of Printing in China, The, 200
Ishikawa Jōzan, 224 n.
I-wang, named Hou-hsüan, prince of I (Ming Dynasty), 214–15, 247
I-yü-chih, 214 n.

Japan and the United States, 243 n.
Japanese physicians who were Chinese lute experts. *See* Hitomi Chikudō, Katsura-

gawa Getchi, Mega Yūshō, Murai Kinzan, Sugimoto Kaen, Suzuki Ran'en, Taki Rankei

Japanese songs played on the Chinese lute, 230, 237
Jetavana, Buddha's favorite abode, 52 n.
Johnson, O. S., 47 n.
Journal Asiatique, 47 n., 142 n.
Journal of the R.A.S. of Great Britain and Ireland, 193 n.
Juan Yüan (1764–1849), 191
Jui Lin (1810–74), 210
Jui-ying-t'u-chi, 143
Jukan, sinologues in the service of the *bakufu*, 229, 234

Kachi-yoriki, unmounted police officer of the *bakufu*, 244 n.
Kalpadruma, 207
K'ang-hsi-tzŭ-tien, 13, 14
Kanso kinwa, 243 n.
Kanz-al-tuhaf, 193 n.
Kao Lien (Ming period), 179, 184, 197
Kao-shan-liu-shui, lute melody, 66, 97, 98, 212
Kao-tsu, emperor (206–195 B.C.), 8
K'ao-p'an-yü-shih, 59 n., 60 n., 63 n., 67 n., 147 n., 178
Karlgren, B., 11
Kashuya Shichibei, lute player, 235
Katsumine Shimpū, modern scholar, 249
Katsuragawa Getchi, 239
Keishū haika zenshū, 249
Kêng-shin-yü-ts'e, 214 n.
Kibat, O., 153 n.
Kikusha, nun, 249
Kinden setsu, 235
Kingaku, Jap. reading of *ch'in hsüeh*, 217, 228, 231
Kingaku denju ryakkei, 231, 242
Kingaku keimō, 218, 236
Kingaku nyūmon zukai, 219
Kingaku taiishō, 224 n.
Kinkyoku sōden keifu, 231
Kinzan kinroku, 228, 236, 248
Kiri wood, 227
Kishibe Shigeo, ix n., 11 n.
Ko-chih-ts'ung-shu, 120 n.
Kō Gentai, 232
K'o-ch'uang-yeh-hua, lute melody, 99
Kochūhen, 13
Kōda Shisen, 239–40
Kodama Kizan, 240
Kodama Kūkū, 220, 232, 235, 240, 244
Kōfukuji, 225
Kojima Hyakuichi, lute player, 234, 239
Kokin seigi, 123, 247
Koreanische Musik, 175

Komazawa, lute player, 235
Kōtei ibun, 231
Koten-kankō-kai, 175
Koto, Jap. cither, 9 n., 217, 227, 229, 237, 239
Kuhn, F., 153 n.
Ku-chin-chu, lute melody, 142
Ku-ch'in-shu, 158
Ku-ch'in-yin, lute melody, 160 n., 173
Ku-cho, antique simplicity, 198
Ku Hsiu, Ch'ing scholar, 177
Ku-huan-shê-yo, 69 n.
Ku I-chiang, Ming musician, 184
Ku-i-ts'ung-shu, 29 n.
Ku Pa, ancient music master, 8 n., 81 n.
Ku T'ien-su, Ming scholar, 238
Ku-wên, ancient writing, 13–14
K'u-mu-ch'an-ch'in-pu, xix, 53, 210
Kuan-chü, ode of the *Shih-ching*, 7
   lute melody, 96
Kuan-chüeh, part of a lute, 102
Kuan-tzû, ancient philosopher, 47
Kuang-han-yu, lute melody, 89
Kuang-ling-p'ai, 83
K'uang, ancient music master, 143
Kuei-ch'ü-lai-tz'û, famous essay by T'ao Ch'ien; lute melody, 96
K'uei, ancient music master, 7 n.
K'un-lun mountains, 143, 211
K'un-shan-yü, name of a lute, 209
Kung-ch'ih, simple Chinese notation, 139, 187
Kung Yün-jang, 235
K'ung-ch'ên, priest-musician of the Ch'ing period, 53, 210
K'ung-hou, harp, 56
K'ung-ku-ch'uan-sheng, 'Echo in an empty vale', 136
K'ung-tzû-chia-yü, 161 n.
K'ung Yen (268–320), 56, 177
Kuo-ch'ao-ch'i-hsien-lei-chêng, 9 n.
Kuo Mao-ch'ien, Sung scholar, 44 n.
Kuo Mien, Sung musician, 97
Kuo Tzû-chang (16th century), 151 n.
Kuo Yü-chai, Ch'ing scholar, 66

Laghimā, 50
Laloy, L., 22, 24 n., 107 n., 174
La Musique chinoise, 22 n., 107 n., 174
La Musique en Chine, 22 n., 173
Lan-t'ing Gathering, 206, 207
Lan-t'ing-hsü, 206
Lao-tzû, the ancient philosopher, 64
Legge, James, 7 n., 39 n., 43 n., 91 n., 114 n., 115 n.
Lei family, famous lute builders during the T'ang period, 55

INDEX

Lêng Ch'ien, 15th-century musician and painter, 107
Lêng-hsien. *Same as* Lêng Ch'ien
Lewisohn, W., 53 n.
Li-chi, Book of Rites, 6 n., 8, 18 n., 23, 42, 69 n.
Li Chi, contemporary scholar, 29 n., 181
Li Chia-yin (6th century), 158
Li Chih-hsien, wife of Ch'ing Jui, 9 n.
Li Ch'ing, Ming author, 142 n.
Li Hsiang-shih, 19th-century lute master, 210
Li-hsing-yüan-ya, 220
Li Mien, 120 n.
Li-sao, poem by Ch'ü Yüan; lute melody, 96
Li Shao-chi, Ming painter, 180
Li-shu, chancery script, 13, 211, 213, 239
Li Ssû (died 208 B.C.), 11, 13
Li-tai-cho-lu-hua-mu, 88 n.
Li T'ai-po (701–62), 113 n.
Li T'ing-ching, Ch'ing scholar, 186
Li Wên-fang, Ming scholar, 185
Li Yen-nien (179–117 B.C.), 39
Li Yu (2nd century), 202
Li Yung (678–747), 212, 213
Liang Chang-chü (1775–1849), 191
Liang-yü, priest-musician of the Sung period, 51
Liao-shih-yüeh-chih, Account of Music of the Liao History, 40 and n.
Lieh-hsien-chuan, 142
Lieh-tzû, the old philosopher and the work connected with his name, 8 n., 45, 46, 47, 58 n., 79 n., 81 n., 97, 112 n., 205 n.
Lieh-tzû-yü-fêng, lute melody, 47, 90
Lien-ch'i, regulation of breathing, 47
Lien-t'ing-shih-êrh-chung, 178
Li K'uang-i, 120 n.
Lin Pu (967–1028), 48, 145
Lin Yu-lin, Ming scholar, xi, 180
Lin Yu-t'ang, 106 n., 113 n., 206 n.
Ling, duke (534–493 B.C.), 143–4
Ling-ho, lute name *(Reiwa)*, 238
Ling-hsü-yin, lute melody, 90
List of Musical and Other Sound-producing Instruments of the Chinese, A, 173
Liu Ch'êng-fu, modern scholar, 94 n.
Liu Chi (1311–75), 99
Liu Chih-fang, Sung musician, 47 n.
Liu Hsiang (77–6 B.C.), 72 n.
Liu Hsin (died A.D. 23), 204
Liu I-hsien, interpreter at Nagasaki, 238
Liu Jung-chai (19th century), 210
Liu-shu-ching-yün, 12
Liu-shui ('Flowing Streams'), 20, 98, 130
Liu Ta-jên, Ming scholar, 179
Liu Tsung-yüan (773–819), 68 n., 92, 149 n.

Liu Yü, Ming scholar, 49 n., 185
Lo-hsia, lute model, 191
Lu, ancient state, 39, 93
Lu Chün (died A.D. 172), 14
Lu-ming, ode of the *Shih-ching*, 7
  lute melody, 66, 96
Lu-wang, named Ch'ang-fang, prince of Lu (Ming dynasty), 214, 215
Lü-ch'i-hsin-shêng, xix
Lü Lan-ku, Ming scholar, 185
Lü-lü-chêng-i, 171
Lü Pu-wei, 24 n., 30
Lü-shih-ch'un-ch'iu, 98
Lü-yin-wei-k'ao, 9 n.
Lun-yü, 8 n., 32 n., 38 n., 115 n.
Lung-ch'êng-lu, 68 n., 149
Lung-ch'ih. *See* Dragon Pond
Lung-ti, flute, 103
Lung-yin, part of lute, 101, 213
Lung-yin-ch'iu-shui, lute name, 215
Lute altar, 50
Lute builders. *See* Hêng-wang, I-wang, Lei family, Lu-wang, Ning-wang
Lute chamber, 67
Lute handbooks. *See* Ch'êng-i-t'ang-ch'in-pu, Chiao-an-ch'in-pu, Ch'in-ching, Ch'in-hsüeh-hsin-shêng, Ch'in-hsüeh-ju-mên, Ch'in-pu-ho-pi-ta-ch'üan, Ch'in-sê-ho-pu, Ch'in-yüan-ch'i-mêng, Ch'un-ts'ao-t'ang-ch'in-pu, K'u-mu-ch'an-ch'in-pu, Li-hsing-yüan-ya, Lü-ch'i-hsin-shêng, Po-ya-hsin-fa, Py-hsü-t'ang-ch'in-pu, Shên-chi-pi-pu, Shu-huai-tsao, Sung-fêng-ko-ch'in-pu, Sung-hsüan-kuan-ch'in-pu, Ta-huan-ko-ch'in-pu, T'ai-ku-i-yin, Tê-yin-t'ang-ch'in-pu, T'ien-wên-ko-ch'in-pu-chi-ch'êng, Tzû-yüan-t'ang-ch'in-pu, Wên-hui-t'ang-ch'in-pu, Wu-chih-chai-ch'in-pu, Yang-ch'un-t'ang-ch'in-pu. Japanese handbooks for the Chinese lute, see *Gyokudō zōsho kimpu*, *Kingaku keimō*, *Kingaku nyūmon zukai*, *Kingaku taiisho*, *Kinzan kinroku*, *Kokin seigi*, *Tōkō kimpu*
Lute, lady experts. *See* Chuang An-hsiang, Li Chih-hsien, Kikusha
Lute melodies. *See* Ch'ang-ch'ing, Ch'iao-ko, Ch'iu-hung, Ch'u-ming-kuang, Chuang-tzû-mêng-tieh, Ch'ü-yüan-wên-tu, Hsiang-ling, Hsiao-hsiang-shui-yün, Hsün-tien, Hu-chia-shih-pa-p'o, I-chiao-chin-li, I-lan, Kao-shan-liu-shui, K'o-ch'uang-yeh-hua, Ku-ch'in-yin, Kuan-chü, Kuang-han-yu, Kuei-ch'ü-lai-tz'û, Li-sao, Lieh-tzû-yü-fêng, Ling-hsü-yin, Liu-shui, Lu-ming, Mei-hua-san-nung, Mo-tzû-pei-ssû, Na-lo-fa-ch'ü, Nan-fêng, Ou-lu-wang-chi, P'ing-sha-lo-yen, Shên-jên, Shih-t'an, Ssû-ch'in, T'êng-wang-ko, Yang-ch'un, Yen-kuo-hêng-yang, Yu-lan
Lute names. *See* those enumerated on pp. 104 and 248. Also see fig. 33 and Chiao-wei, Fêng-huang, Hei-ho, Hêng-hua, I-hsin, K'un-shan-yü, Ling-ho, Lung-yin-ch'iu-shui, Shuang-t'ien-ling-to, Su-wang, T'ien-lai, Wan-ho-sung, Wu-ming, Yü-shun
Lute lovers, spiritual community of, 68–9
Lute page, special servant for carrying the lute, 64

Mahāvairocana Sūtra, 50
Mahillon, V. C., 173
Maṇḍala, magic circle, 50
Mankakushō, lute name, 227

INDEX

Mansō, Chinese priest in Japan, 228, 247
Mantrayana, 50, 51, 52 n., 134
Manuel des superstitions chinoises, 152 n.
Ma Yung (79–166), 23, 56
Mao Chin (1599–1659), 121 n.
Mao Chung-wêng, Sung musician, 47, 90
Mao Min-chung, Yüan musician, 47, 92
Maspéro, H., 47 n.
Matsui Yūseki, lute player, 246
Matsuoka, A., modern scholar, 205
Mega Yūshō, 246
Mei-hua. See Tuan-wên
Mei-hua-san-nung, lute melody, 95
Mémoires concernant l'Asie Orientale, 7 n.
Mémoires concernant les Chinois, 3 n., 171
Mencius, 43 n., 84 n., 211
Mêng Tʻien (died 210 B.C.), 9
Mê Ti, des Sozialethikers und seiner Schüler philosophische Werke, 136 n.
Mi Fu on Inkstones, xii n., 200 n.
Miao Chʻüan-sun (1844–1919), 35, 182
Mien-chʻin-hsieh-hsüeh-yüeh-lu, 20 n.
Mimura Seisaburō, modern scholar, 235 n.
Ming-hua-lu, 180
Ming-shih, 121 n., 179, 215 n.
Ming-shih-tsung, 184, 215 n.
Ming-tzʻû-tsung, 121 n., 179
Min-pʻai, 83
Min-shuchōkun-shū, 247 n.
Mi-ta, 83
Mitsukuni, 21, 225
Mizuno Heiji, modern scholar, 221 n.
Mo-chʻih-pʻien, 178
Mokuan, 225
Mononobe Mokei. *See* Ogyū Sorai
Montoku jitsuroku, 218
Monumenta Serica, 232 n.
Mo-tzû, the old philosopher, 136
Mo-tzû-pei-ssû, lute melody, 136
Moule, A. C., 173
Murai Kinzan, lute player, 228, 248
Music of Hindostân, The, 133 n.
My Country and my People, 113 n.

Nagata Radō, lute player, 245
Naikaku-bunko, 184
Nakagawa Chuei, Nagasaki official, 222 n.
Nakamura Taiō, lute player, 239, 246
Nakane Hakuzan, 239
Nakane Shuku (Kōtei), 231, 240, 242 n.
Nakayama, K., modern scholar, 231, 243, 245, 247

Na-lo-fa-ch'ü, lute melody, 53
Nan-fêng, lute melody, 42, 80
Nārada, 53 n.
Nārāyana, 53 n.
Naropa, 53 n.
Nihon jōko ongakushi, 221 n.
Nihon ongaku kōwa, 87, 221
Ni-ku, archaizing, 40 n.
Ning-wang, named Ch'üan, prince of Ning (Ming dynasty), 172, 183, 214 n., 215
Ni Tsan (1301–74), 58, 59 *and* n.
Niu-mao. See Tuan-wên
No, ode from the *Shih-ching*, 6
Notes de bibliographie chinoise, 29 n.
Nukina Kaioku, 234

Obaku sect, 225, 230 n.
Ocarina, 163
Odes, Book of. See Shih-ching
Ogyū Sorai, 29 n., 224 n.
Okajima Rampo, lute player, 244, 245
Ooki Kojō, 248
Ongaku shiryō no chōsa, 21 n.
Onoda Tōsen, 230, 235, 236, 237, 238, 239, 245, 246
Ou-lu-wang-chi, lute melody, 47
Ou-yang Hsiu (1007–72), vii n., 19–20, 51, 153

P'ai-shiao, Pandean pipes, xix, 27
Pan Ku (32–92), 30 n.
P'an Tsu-yin (1830–90), 210
P'an Wei-ch'uan, Chinese at Nagasaki, 228, 248
Pao-kung, ancient music master, 156
Pa-ta-la, percussion instrument, 13
P'ei-wên-yün-fu, 202
Pelliot, P., 7 n., 29 n.
P'êng Ch'ing-shou, 182
Pheasant, associated with lute, 52, 131, 136
Phoenix, associated with lute, 81, 89, 103, 104, 105, 111, 129, 134, 207
Phoenix Forehead, part of a lute, 101
Phoenix Pool, 80, 103, 202, 212
Phoenix Tongue, part of a lute, 103
Phoenix Wings, part of a lute, 103
Pillars used for making lutes, 193
Ping-ching, name of a lute, 18
Ping-lieh. See Tuan-wên
P'ing, Duke (557–532 B.C.), 143, 144
P'ing-chi-ch'i-i-pao-ming-chi, 214 n.
P'ing-ts'in-kuan-ts'ung-shu, 177
P'ing-sha-lo-yen, lute melody, 214
P'i-p'a, ix n., 1, 2, 20 n., 40, 51 n., 56, 83 95, 129, 201, 206, 207
Plum-blossom cracks, 151, 195, 196 n.
Po Chü-i, T'ang poet, 221

Po Tzû-ya, ancient lute master, 8 n., 73, 81, 84, 97, 98, 205, 206, 212
Po Ya. *Same as* Po Tzû-ya
Po-ya-hsin-fa, 52, 185
Pu-an (1115–69), 52
Pu-an-yin-su-ch'an-shih-yü-lu, 52
Pu-hsü-t'ang-ch'in-pu, 89, 146, 184
Pu-tzû. See Chien-tzû
Pu-wang-shih, 54

Rai San'yō, 238
Rangakusha, 229, 239
Ranshitsu, lute player, 237, 244
Reiwa, lute name, 238
Rijun, 248
Rites, Book of. See Li-chi
Ritsuryo bensetsu, 236
Rubbings, of lutes, 190, 191, 200, 209, 211
Ryang-kêm-sin-po, 224

Sachs, Dr C., ix n.
Sacred Treasures of Nara, 205 n.
Sakamaki, S., modern scholar, 243 n.
Sanjō Shōtarō, modern scholar, 221
San-ts'ai-t'u-hui, 121–2
Satō Itchō (Mosai), lute player, 123, 247
Sê, Chinese cither, viii, 7–9, 11 *and* n., 12, 16, 20 n., 27, 72, 163, 171, 220
Sê-pu, 9
Serpent-belly cracks, 195, 196 n., 211
Setsudō, lute player, 246
Shang-yang, bird, 127
Shao Yung (1011–77), 92
Shê-fu. See Tuan-wên
Shên-chi-pi-pu, 87, 90, 92, 94–6, 98, 146, 172, 183–4, 214
Shên-chia-shêng, old musical term, 94 n.
Shên Chou (1427–1509), 67
Shên-i-ching, 142
Shên-jên, lute melody, 81
Shên-nung, mythical emperor, 6, 72
Shên Wên-ying, Ch'ing scholar, 20 n.
Shên-yin-shu, 214 n.
Shên Yo (441–513), 94
Shêng, ancient mouth organ, 20 n., 163
Shêng Hsün, 157–8
Shichigenkin no denrai, 231, 240
Shih-chi, 62 n., 143, 164
Shih-ching (Book of Odes), 6, 38 n., 43, 54 n., 66, 72, 96, 145 n., 146 n., 202 n.
Shih-hsiang, ancient music master, 8, 81, 84
Shih-pên, 72
Shih Shêng-tsu (13th century), 20 n.
Shih-t'an, lute melody, 51, 53, 54
Shih-wên, ancient music master, 8 n.

Shimpō Zenji, lute player, 236
Shin'etsu, 21, 203, 217–18, 221, 225–8, 230, 232–5, 242, 247
Shinomoto Chikudō, lute player, 243, 244
Shinraku Kansō, lute player, 231, 240–2, 244
Shinryūji, temple at Edo, 237
Shinzoku kibun, 222 n.
Shiragigoto, Japanese cither, 217
Shisendō, retreat of Ishikawa Jōzan, 224
Shitara Junjo, lute player, 237
Shodō zenshū, 209 n., 212
Shoen, 207, 235 n.
Shoku Nihon kōki, 218
Shōsetsu jii, 223 n.
Shōsōin, 200, 203, 205, 223
Shōsōin-gyobutsu tanabetsu-mokuroku, 200
Shou-shih, postures of the hands, 118–19
Shou-yin, coda, 87
Shu-ching (Book of History), 7 n., 42, 79, 81 n.
Shu Hsi (3rd century), 54
Shu-huai-tsao, 96
Shu-i-chi, 142 n.
Shu-lin-ch'ing-hua, 214 n.
Shu-p'ai, 83
Shuang-t'ien-ling-to, name of lute, fig. 33
Shun, mythical emperor, 6, 42, 56, 72, 80, 81, 155
Shun-shui-i-shu, 247 n.
Shunsui shushi danki, 222 n.
Shu-shunsui sensei bunshū, 247 n.
Shu-shunsui zenshū, 247 n.
Shuo-fu, 104 n., 158 n.
Shou-wên, 11–12
Shuo-wên-hsieh-tzŭ-chien, 12
Shuo-wên-hsieh-tzŭ-ku-lin, 12 n.
Shuo-wên-shih-li, 12
Siddhi, magic power, 50
Singing girls, 20, 41, 48
   forbidden to touch the lute, 63
Small-seal script, 13, 14
Sō, Japanese cither, 217, 220
Soulié, G., 21, 126, 127, 128, 130, 131, 135, 139 n., 160 n., 173
'Southern Wind', 72. *See also Nan-fêng*
Ssŭ-ch'in, lute melody, 81
Ssŭ-ma Ch'ien (born 145 B.C.), 38, 143
Ssŭ-ma Hsiang-ju (179–117 B.C.), 39, 68
Ssŭ-ma Kuang (1019–86), 240
Ssŭ-shih-êrh-chang-ching, 63 n.
Stradivari, A., 193
Study of Chinese Alchemy, A, 47 n.
Su Ching, Ch'ing scholar, 186
Su Shih (Tung-p'o), xi, 92, 159

Su-wang (So-ō), lute name, 227, 235
Su Wu (died 60 B.C.), 95
Su-yüan-shih-pu, xi n.
Sugimoto Kaen, lute player, 243–4
Sugiura Baigaku, 244
Sugiura Kinsen, lute player, 226, 232–4, 236
Sui-shih-yin-yüeh-chih, 40 (n. 44)
Sui-tʻang-yen-yüeh-tiao-yen-chiu, 40 n.
Sun Chʻêng-ên, Ming scholar, 184
Sun Fêng, 156
Sun Hai-po, modern scholar, 6
Sun Hsing-yen (1753–1808), 177
Sun Jou-chih, Liang scholar, 143 n.
Sun Têng (3rd century), lute master, 190, 191
Sun Tzu on the Art of War, 205 n.
Sung-fêng-ko-chʻin-pu, 83, 96
Sung-hsüan-kuan-chʻin-pu, 182, 226
Sung-yü-chi, 114 n.
Suzuki, D. T., 134 n.
Suzuki Hakutō, lute player, 243
Suzuki (Ranʼen) Ryū, 218, 221, 236
Syông Kyôn (15th century), 175

Ta-chʻing-chi-fu-hsien-chê-chuan, 53 n.
Tagami Michi, 249
Ta-hsüeh, 82 n.
Ta-huan-ko-chʻin-pu, 107
Tʻa-pen, lute rubbings, 190, 191, 200, 209, 211
Tai-i, doctor of Chinese medicine, 229
Tai Kʻuei (died 396), 158
Tai Yüan, Chʻing scholar, 186
Tʻai-ku-i-yin, qualification of lute music, viii
Tʻai-ku-i-yin, by Chu Chʻüan, 172
  by Yang Lun, 62 n., 86, 185
Tʻai-pʻing, music of Emp. Shun, 80
Tʻai-shan, mountain in Shantung, 73, 97, 101
Tʻai-tsung, Sung emperor, 156
Taishō-issaikyō, 51 n., 63 n.
Takakura Yūi, lute player, 245
Takata Tadachika, 13
Takayasu Rooku, 223 n.
Taki Rankei, 237, 239
Taki Ryōichi, modern musicologist, 21 n., 211
Tanabe Hisao, modern musicologist, 87 n., 221
Tʻan-chi-tsʻung-shu, 69 n., 107
Tʻang I-ming, Chʻing scholar, 187
Tʻang-shan-fu-jên, concubine of Han Kao-tsu, 8
Tʻang-shang-yüeh, court music, 3
Tʻang-shih-hua-pu, 148 (fig. 16)
Tʻang Shou-chʻien, modern scholar, 247 n.

Tao-chien-lu, 151
Tao-tê-ching, 17, 45, 111 n., 134, 216
Tʻao Chʻien (372–427), 19, 91, 142 n.
Tʻao Hung-ching (452–536), 151 n.
Tʻao Tsung-i (14th century), 193
Taori-giku, 249
Tê-yin-tʻang-chʻin-pu, 66
Teng, S. Y., 121 n.
Tʻêng-wang-ko, lute melody, 96
Ti-chu, stud inside lute, 193
Ti-ming, inscriptions on the bottom board of lute, 197
Ti I, Chʻing scholar, 69 n.
Tʻi-mu, superscription, 88
Tiao, modes, 86
Tiao-i, musical patterns, 86, 87
Tʻieh-chʻin-tʻung-chien-lou-tsʻang-shu-mu-lu, 214 n.
Tʻien-chu, stud inside lute, 193
Tʻien-hsia Monthly, The, 168 n.
Tʻien-i-ko, Ming library, 183
Tʻien-i-ko-tsʻang-shu-kʻao, 183
Tʻien-lai, lute name, 190
Tʻien-lai-ko, name of library, 190
Tʻien-tzʻû, adding words to a melody, 96
Tʻien-wên-ko-chʻin-pu-chi-chʻêng, 31 n., 99, 146, 153, 175, 187, 215 n.
Ting Fu-pao, contemporary scholar, 12 n.
Ting Hsiung-fei, Chʻing scholar, 69 n.
Ting Ling-wei, 142
Tochō, lute player, 235
Tōdaiji, 200
Tōhō gakuhō, 21 n.
Tōko ikō, 227
Tōkō kimpu, ed. by Suzuki, 218, 226, 236
   ed. by Sugiura, 232, 239
Tōkō Zenji. *See* Shinʼetsu
Tōkō zenshū, 225 n., 226 n., 231
Tokugawa Academy, 222 n., 232, 234
'Tokugawa Princes of Mito, The', 225 n.
Tomioka Tessai, 239
Tʻoung-pao, 24 n., 147 n.
Tōyō ongaku kenkyū, 63 n.
Transactions of the Asiatic Society of Japan, ix, 225 n., 243 n., 245 n.
Tsʻai Yen, daughter of Tsʻai Yung, 94, 155
Tsʻai Yung (133–92), 54, 56, 94, 96, 101, 102, 155, 157, 159, 177
Tsʻai-yü, 65
Tsʻang-chʻin-lu, 199, 200, 214
Tsao-chʻi, lute varnish, 194
Tsʻao-shu, cursive script, 212
Tsʻao-tʻang-chi, 155 n.
Tsʻao Yin (1658–1712), 178
Tsêng Tien, disciple of Confucius, 8

Ts'ui Hui, 159
Ts'ui Piao, Chin scholar, 142 n.
Tsuji Buzen-no-kami, musician, 230
Tsun-shêng-pa-chien, 33 n., 47 n., 60 n., 147, 152, 179, 197, 214
Ts'ung-shu-shu-mu-wei-pien, 120 n.
Tu-hua-chai-ts'ung-shu, 177
T'u Lung, Ming scholar, 63, 179
Tuan, part of a lute melody, 88, 98
Tuan-wên, cracks in lacquer of old lutes, 18, 194–7, 202–4, 211, 227
    mei-hua type, 151, 195, 196 n.
    niu-mao type, 195, 196 n.
    ping-lieh type, 196, 202
    shê-fu type, 195, 196 n., 211
    false or faked varieties, 196
    on Japanese lutes, 203
Tuan Yü-tsai (1735–1815), 12
Tung Ch'i-ch'ang (1555–1636), 121
Tung-chuang-lun-hua, 58 n.
Tung-kao-chan-shih-chi-k'an, 243 n.
Tung-t'ien-ch'ing-lu-chi, 195 n.–196 n.
Tung-t'ing, lake, 92, 97
Tung T'ing-lan, T'ang musician, 94
T'ung, wood for making lutes, 4, 102, 191, 193
Twelve sonorous tubes (*lü*), 79 and n., 103
Tzû, wood for making lutes, 4, 191, 193
Tzû-hsia-lu, 120 n.
Tzû-kung, disciple of Confucius, 62, 160
Tzû-lu, disciple of Confucius, 8
Tzû-t'an, red sandalwood, 4
Tzû-yüan-t'ang-ch'in-pu, 168, 186
Tz'û-yüan, 53 n.

Umehara, Sueji, 11 n.
Uragami Gyokudō, 230, 237–9
Utsubo monogatari, 218

Vairocana, 200
Vibrato, 2, 51, 78, 108, 115, 119, 125, 129, 132–4, 137
Vibrato ritardando, 78, 108, 115, 132
Vīṇā, Indian stringed instrument, 51
Visser, M. W. de, 216 n.

Wagon, Japanese cither, 217, 220
Wai-tiao, minor modes, 86
Wan, 189–90
Wan-ho-sung, name of lute, 227
Wan-yüeh, moon-viewing, 189
Wan-yüeh-yo, 69
Wang Cho, Ch'ing scholar, 69 n.
Wang Chün, Ch'ing scholar, 12

Wang Hui-chih, son of Wang Hsi-chih, 95
Wang Hsi-chih (321–79), 95 n., 206
Wang Kuang-ch'i, modern musicologist, 21 n., 139
Wang San-ak, 6th-century Korean minister, 224
Wang T'ing, Ming scholar, 184
Wang Yen-po, 160
Wang Ying-chen, Ming scholar, 184
Wang Yü, Ch'ing painter, 58 n.
Wan-sung, 83
Wei, coda, 87
Wei, ancient state, 68, 93
Wei, odes of the *Shih-ching*, 38–40, 202 n.
Wei Hsiang, Han scholar, 30 n.
Wei Yeh (960–1019), 155
Wên, king, 81, 96
Wên, prince (426–387 B.C.), 38, 56, 155
Wên-fang-yo, 69
Wên-hsüan, 54 n., 55, 205 n.
Wên-hui-t'ang-ch'in-pu, 120 and n., 121–3
Wêng T'ung-ho (1830–1904), 210
Wieger, L., 13
Wilhelm, R., 24 n.
Wu, emperor (140–87 B.C.), 39
Wu [Wang], king, 81 and n., 143
Wu-chang, music composed by Confucius, 39
Wu Ch'ên (1249–1331), 70, 73
Wu-chih-chai-ch'in-pu, 34 n., 71, 79, 109, 120 n., 136, 185–7, 212
Wu Ching-ch'ao, Ch'ing scholar, 19
Wu Ching-lüeh, 182
Wu Hung, Ch'ing scholar, 186
Wu-kang-ch'in-pu, 172
Wu-ming, lute name, figs. 1a, 1b
Wu-p'ai, 83

Ya-ch'in-chao-shih-ch'i-p'ien, 30 n.
Ya-ch'in-ming-lu, 104
Yamada Takao, modern scholar, 221 n.
Yamamoto Tokuho, lute player, 243, 244, 245
Yamatogoto, 217
Yang, emperor (r. 605–17), 40 n.
Yang-ch'un, lute melody, 116 n.
Yang-ch'un-t'ang-ch'in-pu, 64 n., 65, 121–3, 180, 247
Yang-hsin, 43, 46
Yang Hsiung (53 B.C.–A.D. 18), 30, 54
Yang Lun, Ming musician, 52 *and* n., 62 n., 86, 185
Yang Piao-chêng, Ming musician, 49 n., 66, 71, 76, 90 n., 92, 99
Yang-shêng, nurturing life, 46
Yang Shou-ching (1835–1915), 29 n.
Yang Tsung-chi, modern musicologist, 29 n., 34, 35, 94 n., 99, 139, 182, 197, 199, 200

Yano Kyōson, 239
Yao, mythical emperor, 55, 81, 155, 212
Yao, part of lute, 101
Yeh Chang-po, Ch'ing scholar, 21 n.
Yeh Hsiang-kao, Ming scholar, 179
Yeh Ho-fu (died 1937), 209
Yeh-lü-ch'u-ts'ai (1190–1244), 78 n., 83
Yeh Mêng-tê (1077–1148), 145
Yen, ancient music master, 143
Yen-kuo-hêng-yang, lute melody, 95
Yen Chêng, 83, 182, 183
Yen P'ei-nien, Ch'ing scholar, 186
Yen-tsu, knobs on the bottom board of lute, 103
Yih-ching (Book of Changes), 79 n., 87
Yin-ch'i, special kind of inlaid work, 202, 205
Yin-yüeh-tsa-chih, 21 n., 51 n.
Yin-yüeh-tz'ŭ-tien, 94 n.
Ying, the people of, 114 n.
Ying-jên-kua-ho, 114 n.
Ying Shao (2nd century), 70, 72, 98
Ying-shih, priest-musician of T'ang period, 51
Yo-shan, part of lute, 101, 213
Yoshimune, Tokugawa shogun, 236
Yu-lan, lute melody, 29 n., 181
Yung-fu, monastery at Hangchow, 225
Yü, mythical emperor, 81
Yü-ch'iao-hsien-hua, 92
Yü-ch'iao-tui-wên, 92 n.
Yü-fu, the Old Fisherman, 91
Yü-hai, 35
Yü-ko, lute melody, 92–3
Yü-ku-chai-ch'in-pu, 31 n., 192, 196, 210, 213 n.
Yü-shan-p'ai, 83
Yü-shun, lute name, 227
Yü Yen, Ming scholar, 185
Yüan Chan, Chin scholar, 158
Yüan Chi (210–63), 56
Yüan Hsien, disciple of Confucius, 160
Yüeh-chi, 6 n., 23–6, 36–8, 41, 42, 80 n.
Yüeh-ch'in, moon-shaped guitar, 1, 20 n.
Yüeh-fu, Bureau of Music, 39
Yüeh-fu, a genre of songs, 39–40, 44
Yüeh-fu-shih-chi, 44 n.
Yüeh-hsüeh-kuei-fan (Ak-hak-kwe-pôm), 103, 175
Yüeh-lü-ch'üan-shu, 65, 214
Yüeh-pu, Board of Music, 107
Yüeh-shu, 2 n.

Zuhon-sōkankai, xi